The Thin Green Line

Outwitting Poachers, Smugglers, and Market Hunters

Terry Grosz

Johnson Books
BOULDER

Published by Johnson Books, a division of Johnson Publishing Company, 1880 South 57th Court, Boulder, Colorado 80301. Visit our website at www.JohnsonBooks.com. E-mail: books@jpcolorado.com.

9 8 7 6 5 4 3 2 1

Cover design: Debra B. Topping
Cover photo: Supplied by Wyoming Fish and Game Department

A note on the photo section: These pictures were supplied over the years to the author for teaching purposes. In all cases where the provenance of the photographs are known, we have contacted the photographers and the pictures are used with their permission. In those cases where the source of the photos could not be traced, we are unable to acknowledge the photographers by name, but nevertheless we thank them anonymously for their contribution to conservation law enforcement.

Library of Congress Cataloging-in-Publication Data
Grosz, Terry.
   The thin green line: outwitting poachers, smugglers, and market hunters / Terry Grosz.
      p. cm.
   ISBN 1-55566-348-6
   1. Grosz, Terry. 2. Undercover wildlife agents—United States—Biography. 3. Wildlife crimes—United States—Anecdotes. I. Title.
   SK354.G76A3 2004
   363.28—dc22   2004010439

Printed in the United States by
Johnson Printing
1880 South 57th Court
Boulder, Colorado 80301

Printed on ECF paper with soy ink

Contents

Preface

The Thin Green Line, the last book in my series, tells of a time when the reality of future wildlife survival, mentally kept at bay during my professional youth, finally "met the road." Based on thirty-two very active years in the wildlife law enforcement arena, I feel that the world of wildlife is in its autumn. Some of you may question the accuracy of this reasoning, and some knowledgeable folks familiar with the great outdoors may even go so far as to point out recent successes in the world of wildlife. Such success stories include the white-tailed deer, numerous turkey subspecies, lesser snow goose, Canada goose (most subspecies), striped bass, moose (to a degree), and a few other species. Truth be known, because of a lot of hard work by wildlife agencies, luck, and many species' innate adaptability, these populations have in fact partially recovered or exploded. However, I challenge those readers to examine the overall health and future of the world of wildlife. For example, show me healthy populations of sardines, Atlantic and Pacific salmon, cod off the Grand Banks, tuna, marlin, swordfish, abalone, sturgeon (national and international), paddlefish, oceanic reefs (25 percent gone as we speak), and sharks (declining worldwide). Since I opened up Pandora's box to prove a point, let's keep this top spinning just for grins. How about those great pods of whales, sea otter species (northern, southern, and giant), Labrador ducks, harp seals, Steller's eiders, great auks, Pacific black brant, manatee, many species of crocodiles, spotted cats, the Hawaiian goose, sea turtles, golden plovers, Laysan teal, many neotropical bird species, and spectacled eiders? They have all diminished greatly, are classified as threatened or endangered, or have moved across that great divide into extinction!

And let us not forget the grizzly bear (one hundred thousand originally in North America and Mexico—now about one thousand remain in four Western states and maybe a few in Mexico), sixty-five million bison (that makes one hell of a story all by itself when all the smoke from the black-powder guns has cleared), two to four *billion* passenger pigeons (believed to be the largest flock of birds in the world at that time—the last one died in 1917 in the Cincinnati Zoo), seventy million pronghorn (that's right, more numerous than the bison), Carolina parakeet, heath hen (collected into extinction in 1934 by colleges adding to their museum collections), ivory-billed woodpeckers, thirty-plus million beaver (we know about the early trappers and their exploits from 1810 to 1840 to feed the beaver hat craze), gray wolves originally distributed from coast to coast, red wolves, mule deer (declining rangewide), band-tailed pigeons, Florida panther, trumpeter swans, whooping cranes, hordes of waterfowl (especially northern pintail, Pacific white-fronted geese, canvasbacks, redheads, black ducks, and Aleutian Canada geese), desert tortoise, desert bighorn sheep, black-footed ferrets, many subspecies of peregrine falcon, California condors, and bald and golden eagles, just to mention a *very* few.

Now that I am on this tear, let's not stop there! This routine of national resource destruction isn't germane just to the world of wildlife. How about those great expanses of our precious public lands?

Let's take those known for their grazing resources, which are currently home to many cattle ranchers and sheepherders. "Home" because the government provides exclusive grazing rights at less than the going domestic price per animal unit per month (AUM) for those millions of acres. In other words, it subsidizes an inefficient way of life that should have gone the way of the gray wolf and the bison. Truth be known, the seventeen Western states holding the major portions of public lands in the continental United States produce *only* about 6 percent of all beef raised in this nation! The majority of beef production comes from feed lots in Florida, Texas, and Louisiana. Our public lands, in almost every venue, are showing major wear and tear from historically out-of-control grazing, hoof pounding, and erosion as a direct result of those abhorrent grazing practices. Along with those overgrazing abuses are the declines of quality range plants and fish and wildlife populations. Bottom line, it is hard to make a living on lands that resemble the top of a pool table. Aware of those destructive land-use practices, one recent idiotic secretary of the Interior titled those users currently destroying the public lands with their livestock,

"Good Stewards of the Land." Now you can see one reason why the Department of the Interior has historically been classified as a dumping ground for political hacks!

Let's not stop there. Take a look at your national forests and how they are managed. Most virgin timber of value on public lands is gone (98 percent harvested by the 1980s). That which remains is basically commercially and geographically inaccessible. In many of the national forests, especially in the Pacific Northwest, much of the remaining standing timber is third and fourth generation. In some of those forests, folks supporting logging interests see fit to kill the gentle, endangered spotted owl. Then, stupidly, they nail the owls' bodies to trees with spikes in protest of the federal Endangered Species Act of 1973 because the act restricts logging in some areas in order to protect those remaining few owl populations. With that bit of brave handiwork accomplished, the killers drive off on roads built by the U.S. Forest Service at public expense to subsidize the logging industry!

Now we face the knee-jerk specter of wildfires in the West. The oft-proposed solution is to let the logging industry have at the remaining stands of timber to remove fuel for anticipated wildfires. What hogwash! Having come from a logging background, I can't see any timber company taking just the trash wood from our forests in order to reduce available fuels. They make their *big* money on the largest, best, and most sought-after commercial grades and species of timber (Douglas fir, sugar pine, redwood, incense cedar, etc.). And if one doesn't think that is what they are going after, just look at who the White House put on the council to make those forest harvest management decisions. It isn't commercial fishermen.

If that doesn't sink your bobber, take the *last* remaining extensive virgin temperate rain forests in the world, located in southeastern Alaska, where National Forest timber was recently sold out from under the American people by crooked, scheming Alaskan and federal politicians to the Japanese lumber industry in the name of a few hundred jobs. Raw logs are taken to Japan, processed, and then brought back to the United States to be sold at a profit! Sitka spruce trees that are four and five hundred years old, lost forever from one of the last and most unique coniferous forest ecosystems in the world! All for a few hundred jobs. Come "autumn," many of those giants will be gone.

Let's move on to our commercial fishing industry. Therein resides another fine example of the time-worn story of politics, excess, greed, and ego. Politics for sanctioning unwise fishing activity during all seasons and allowing excessive harvest levels. Add greed and ego to that chemistry and you just put the finishing touches on another sad chapter involving humankind and the world's pelagic natural resources. Overharvesting the fisheries stocks in the waters off North America is the norm. Hell, for that matter, it's the norm in the world's oceans! Species of Pacific salmon, sardines, halibut, crab, cod, lobster, abalone, and redfish are just a few among many populations of concern. Upon discovering declining fisheries stocks and profitability, many commercial-fishing folks clamor for greater latitude to destroy that which remains on the grounds that it won't hurt the resource. Take a look worldwide at the commercial fishing fleets and canneries today. They are severely diminished in size and number. Why? I wonder if the extensive use of drift nets and long lines had anything to do with drastic reductions in oceanic populations? Or flooding the zone with ultramodern foreign fishing fleets, removing and processing every species caught—many times just for dog, cat, or mink food! Or illegal fishing practices by U.S. fleets in their own waters taking short salmon, short crabs, or female crabs; fishing in closed zones or during closed seasons; illegally using fish pews (like a one-tined pitchfork used to stab unwanted fish lying on the deck after a dragnet haul, which fish are then tossed over the side to die); and overfishing.

I went ocean fishing off Sitka, Alaska, in 2000. The *season* limit, for sport fishermen like me, was *two* salmon! Imagine that! Alaska, the last great frontier at one time awash in salmon. But only two salmon per season for the sport fisherman (which I support if it helps the salmon populations) because of reduced numbers. Yet, the commercial fishermen in Alaska continued hauling in salmon by the ton alongside the sport fishermen as if there were no tomorrow. Again, another classic example of Alaskan politics run amuck, with a healthy dose of greed, stupidity, and ego. Actually, this mindset speaks volumes to the basic thinking of many Alaskans: "Hurrah for me and to hell with tomorrow!" Taking it that last step, look once again at the number of canneries closed down in Alaska, British Columbia, Washington, Oregon, and California. *Then* ask yourself if autumn is not upon the world of wildlife in the commercial fishing arena.

Oil exploration and drilling on public lands is another unique arena needing closer examination. Filth, contamination, pollution, access roads across fragile environments, and open oil pits (migratory bird deathtraps) are among the end products of producing fossil fuels to meet our nation's needs. The little-known fact is that the government often hardly knows what it is truly owed by the oil companies for the privilege of fossil fuel reclamation on public lands. Who is owed what is predicated on production numbers and figures supplied of course by the oil interests. As a gut check, examine the identical situation with the Native Americans and the sordid oil and gas production picture on tribal lands. It is anyone's guess what is removed from their lands, but according to the Indians, it is one hell of a lot more than the amount for which they are being compensated. Again, keep in mind that production figures are supplied by the oil and gas interests. These concerns are supported by the Office of the Inspector General for the Department of the Interior, which manages to stay *very* busy investigating oil companies for thefts of crude oil, natural gas, and fraud on tribal and public lands. That office also stays quite busy investigating the Department of the Interior for gross mismanagement of funds received and held in trust for the Native Americans from oil and gas production on tribal lands. Everywhere you look from the regulatory agencies' perspective, you see outstretched hands covered with pieces of silver and smeared with the life blood of the land.

U.S. oil fields produce on the average *only* seventeen barrels of crude oil per day per well! Without a doubt, the United States is on the downside of oil production. Wells in the Middle East produce many thousands (some over ten thousand) of barrels per day per well! Is it not time to look seriously at alternative fuel for our transportation systems? After all, we put a man on the moon in a decade. It stands to reason that *if* we wanted to create an alternative source of fuel and develop land transportation utilizing such fuels, it would be possible.

The next time we have a national issue like the latest war with Iraq, watch the sequence of events. Gas prices inch up slowly and then rapidly, sometimes and in some places rising as much as seventy cents per gallon over previous prices. After a spate of price gouging, they start to decline after the media point out that the price per barrel of crude on the world market has remained constant. *Then* note the profits of the major oil companies the next quarter when they report their earnings to the stock market. I have yet to see less than 273 percent to 600 percent earnings in the previous quarter rung up by those interests! And they say they have not gouged the American consumer when it comes to the prices charged from the refinery. Note how that system hardly creates a ripple with the politicos. It is almost as if it is expected. On it goes without diminution, and when the fossil fuel resource is destroyed through excessive use, those involved in the industry will clamor for more government support because the resources have been severely impacted, along with their lives. "Support" such as drilling in the Arctic National Wildlife Refuge or other protected heritage lands. *If* we are down to just seventeen barrels per day per well on the average in the United States, I would certainly entertain the notion that autumn is upon us in that arena as well.

Greed and ego, the basic tenets of these destructive ways, are present in almost every commercial venue humankind pursues. Pick any industrial activity. Then through closer examination, see if what I'm saying isn't right on the money. For example, let's take the early railroads. The railroads never instituted safety measures during their boom days until the bottom line could be justified. To hell with employees injured or killed on the line due to lack of Westinghouse air brakes or automatic couplers, because broken bodies could be discarded and cheaply replaced. To hell with the passengers riding the rails who were killed or injured by the thousands in numerous train wrecks because of poorly laid track, hastily built wooden trestles, speed-happy engineers, or schedule overlaps between trains causing collisions (the railroads finally set up the nation's time zones currently in use to avoid collisions). Just the bottom line on the earnings statements, please! Shortcuts of such nature continue to dominate the "Iron Horse" type of business thinking to this day. Meanwhile, spilled fuels, hazardous materials, and toxic chemicals continue to negatively impact wildlife on a daily basis along the many thousands of miles of iron rails. I'm not sure there ever was an "autumn" in that industry.

The mining industry is another contributor to this country's overall "good." The mining industry has a history in the West of destroying and polluting the lands, water tables, and river systems; killing every living thing in the waterways; sickening its workers; and then fleeing, letting the government (and the government allows this) pick up the clean-up tab.

Those living in or familiar with mining areas, look around. Hey, you folks in Libby, Montana. What kind of legacy did the W. R. Grace Company leave you when the mining of vermiculite was found to be hazardous to your health? How many major mining operations do you see that have left the area in a hazardous state, only to let the Superfund folks (you and me) pick up the clean-up tab? Hey, Colorado. What about the Summitville Mine disaster? Could the destruction of seventeen miles of trout stream have been avoided *if* the state of Colorado had required reasonable bonds to insure against such toxic spills instead of playing politics as it did? As I said, pick any industry and apply the same questions based on the ethics and principles you know to be right. Just see if greed and ego are not smack-dab in the middle of everything. This and much, much more continues to be the destructive legacy left for those yet to come.

So I say, the world of wildlife in most of its aspects is in the autumn of its time. But truth be known, "summer" is gone for almost everything else we cherish related to the resources of the land. I guess you now understand my feelings based on many years of experience, which led to my thinking in this last book. I wonder how long it will be before humankind is in its own autumn?

This book also describes the culmination of a conservation officer's thirty-two-year vision quest pursuing and putting those in the business of extinction out of business. This conservation officer did not succeed in his endeavors, and the plants and animals, the American people, and those generations yet to come were the ultimate losers! I did not win because I and others like me were overwhelmed by the forces of humankind and its ever-present, often destructive expansion into every niche of the world. We did not win because of insufficient personnel and budgets. We did not win because of thoughtless elected officials feathering their own nests and those of their friends or special interests. We did not win because many courts and prosecutors failed to appreciate the seriousness of the natural resources fight or simply chose not to prosecute to the full extent of the law. We did not win because the American people in general did not understand or appreciate the values of their natural resources, just didn't give a damn, were too involved ripping their share off the face of the earth, or all of the above. We did not win because of thoughtless decisions by Service leaders, even though they were congressionally mandated to protect, preserve, and enhance the resources. We did not win because of sick, lame, shortsighted, or lazy conservation officers shirking their duties. We did not win because our minds were ready to go but the battered body said, "You have got to be kidding." We did not win because of the "system." We did not win because some senior field supervisors failed to anticipate problems, failed to protect their officers from political attack, or lacked the guts or competence to lead. We did not win because our current educational system failed to impress upon young minds the values of their national heritage. We did not win because those elected to Congress saw fit to fritter away the national coffers in many directions other than the natural resources arenas — directions oftentimes strongly smelling of "pork." We did not win because many of those sitting in the White House saw fit to sell the nation's natural resources to the highest bidder, in so doing lining the greedy, outstretched hands of mining, lumbering, commercial fishing, grazing, oil exploration, electrical transmission, windpower, and like interests with pieces of silver. We did not win because the bad guys were hungrier or sharper then the officers in pursuit. We did not win because the American people don't like to be regulated (when is the last time you drove over the speed limit?). We did not win because the American people did not get involved in helping the cause. We did not win because ...

The battle continues to be loyally fought by approximately ten thousand hopelessly outnumbered and underfunded conservation officers across North America. It is a battle that I am now convinced cannot be won. But it is a good and just fight and must be fought for those unborn generations, if for no other reason! There is something to be said for dedicating oneself to putting natural resources back at the top of the system rather than taking them out in body bags at the bottom. As long as we have officers who are dedicated hunters of those savaging this continent's natural resources, the battle will be courageously fought. Not always won, but always fought. Because of that enforcement presence, those walking on the dark side will have to look over their shoulders before illegally pulling a trigger, running an unlawful gill net, spearing spawning fish, scooping falcon nests (removing eggs or young), managing illegal transmission lines electrocuting thousands of birds of prey with a turned head and blind eye, putting out poisoned carcasses to kill anything that might eat their precious range maggots (sheep), scooping waterfowl nests in Alaska to add native stock to their captive propagation flocks, smuggling wildlife across the borders, destroying migratory birds through the cyanide-heap leach-mining process, and running dirty oilfield and oil-pit operations that kill hundreds of thousands of wildlife species annually. Everywhere God turns, He is witness to the destruction of His voiceless critters.

As I have said many times in my books, wildlife dies without making a sound. The only voice it has is yours, and if you are not squalling like a smashed cat, you are part of the problem. Often it takes even more than that. As a citizen of this great country, you must understand that our natural resources, in every aspect, are limited! Unwise use will continue pushing many species downward into the black hole of extinction and further the exhaustion of our remaining resources.

Hopefully, you are not able to identify yourself or your actions from the events described in this six-book series. Don't do what other weaker and less forward-thinking individuals have chosen to do in these stories. Walking on the dark side, breaking conservation laws (or any laws for that matter), will do nothing for the soul of this country—or for you. You must avoid those who walk on the wild side, even to the point of turning them in to the law for their misdeeds. If you don't, then you are allowing those folks to steal from you, your children, and future generations. There is no other way to say it. It is simply stealing our natural resources, with dire consequences for those yet to come. Surely you wouldn't tolerate anyone stealing prized possessions from your home. I hope you harbor the same feelings when it comes to someone stealing your and your children's national heritage.

Teach your children the values of the natural resource world and the important quality it brings to everyone's lives. Make sure those lessons are so well ingrained that your children follow that lead, teaching their children in turn. Take your kids with you into the fields of dreams of our natural resource world so they can enjoy their time not only with you but in and among the natural wonders God has created. Spending time with your loved ones in this manner provides life rewards for you and them, especially long after you are but a memory. Get off your dead last parts over the fence and vote! Let your elected officials know how you feel and keep an eye on them. Many times elected officials will go off on tangents of their own. They are supposed to be our voices, not a voice unto themselves. Congress today is seemingly a voice unto itself, and look where that has gotten us!

Get involved and join organizations that favor wise use, enhancement, and preservation of our natural resources; organizations such as the Nature Conservancy, Trout Unlimited, the Rocky Mountain Elk Foundation, Ducks Unlimited, the Mule Deer Foundation, the National Wildlife Federation, or other just as dedicated but smaller organizations. Strongly support those organizations with your sweat and money. Protecting our natural resources is just like raising children. It is a twenty-four-hour, seven-days-a-week endeavor. Jump in and support your Fish and Game directors, commissioners, and agencies. They have a tough job, but you can make it easier by adding your voice of concern and reason. Even if they don't go the way you expect or believe, they will at least have the counsel and wisdom of your voice to help direct their decisions. So go for it!

I had, and still have, a wonderful life. I have been blessed with a wife not of this world and three children who have made their dad proud, along with a passel of grandkids possessing smiles and hopes for the future. I was blessed with being able to live in a profession seldom known or experienced by the masses, and given a body that more or less held up so I could enjoy my quest in its most profound sense. I lived in a time that carried a taste of times past, all the while projecting a fleeting look into the future. A look into the world of wildlife and humankind, if you will, that in many instances no longer exists due to the passage of time and death of the moment. During those times I met a world of people possessing great vision, dedicated souls, and stout hearts. I also met great numbers of the devil incarnate, and let many know that they had crossed the line. Fortunately for me, I was protected by two guardian angels who ended up worn out and feather thin as they kept me alive and constantly heading into the soft breezes or forceful winds.

I have seen tigers in the jungles of Indonesia (the rarest in the world); salmon in streams so numerous they pushed each other out onto the banks into the waiting jaws of ten-foot-tall brown bears; big bluestem grasses so thick it made your thigh muscles sore to walk through them and so high that they were taller than the cab of my pickup; and band-tailed pigeons in oak forests by the thousands that, when they exploded from the trees, made a tremendous racket reminiscent of the passenger pigeons of old. I have rested within ten feet of hundreds of thousands of night-feeding waterfowl in California rice fields, and when they flew, I could feel the soft breeze of all those flapping wings on my face. I have observed migratory birds pouring out of the Arctic into the Dakotas ahead of the first blizzard of the year in such numbers that they were reminiscent of the days of old. I have looked into the mystical eyes of a surprised gray wolf not twenty feet away, and when I blinked he was gone. I have seen sturgeon of such length break the water's surface beside my speeding sixteen-foot patrol boat in the Sacramento River of California that their bodies exceeded the length of the vessel! And *I never saw the head or the tail.* I have been so close to a grizzly in Alaska that I could smell his fetid, fish-laced breath and hear the rumblings of the "chowder" digesting in his stomach. I have fished in Alaskan waters where *every* cast produced a fish weighing five pounds or more; been so close to Roosevelt elk in northern California that I could hear their ruminations and smell their meals digesting when they belched; survived looking into the fierce eyes of a golden eagle as I removed its talons from a trap; seen grown men, stout as great oaks, crying from the heart and soul over the resource destruction around them; and more ... much more.

Sitting here writing these words, I see the faces of old friends and good people like Charlie Dennis, Joe Oliveros, Jim Bartee, John Finnigan, Herb Christie, Tom Yamamoto, Leo Badger, and Otis, Oliver, and Wallace Barnes, now long gone. With those memories comes the smell of juniper wood in campfires long out; smells from the good earth in Clover Valley after the rains, now vanished in recent droughts; smells of curing mountain grasses borne on the fall winds, now lost in this year's fires and overgrazing; and views of a pool in a stream still holding the swirl of a large trout, telling the story of a hapless grasshopper, now drought dry as they play across my soul like the dying strains of a bull elk's hopeful bugle.

Summer is gone, not only for me but for the world of wildlife I endeavored to protect. With it has gone part of our human essence and soul, along with the hopes of God. Since white Europeans came to this great continent, a lot of trails have been plowed under, one after another, as if there were no end. And in the world of natural resource destruction, there isn't.

Those who have read *Wildlife Wars* and *A Sword for Mother Nature* have enjoyed the light-hearted tales of a young man hell-bent on saving the world of wildlife and possessing few worldly cares. In those adventurous days of my youth, I did not see the darkening clouds gathering on the horizon. Continuing those earthly travels, the tales of a young man growing older and wiser by the moment but still dreaming of an unfinished mission are told in *For Love of Wildness*. The title says it all. This time, I cast a glance at those darkening clouds, observing them but still writing them off as nothing more than another set of winter storms. I venture into the "fall" of my years in the books titled *Defending Our Wildlife Heritage*; *No Safe Refuge: Man as Predator in the World of Wildlife*; and the book you are reading now, *The Thin Green Line*. In these stories, you will experience the massive challenges being faced, accompanied by the weight of mortality brought on by years of bodily abuse in the line of fire. The fact that there just aren't enough hours in the day or enough life left in the old carcass to "catch 'em all" becomes an ever-present concern, a deadly theme made all the more serious with those realizations of the continuing exhaustion of life and time. However, the end being near professionally and physically still didn't add the word "quit" to the vocabulary. I continued pushing on to the very end of my quest until I was finally brought down by mandatory government law enforcement retirement in June 1998.

But the adventures do not end there! As these stories are written, there is a six-foot-seven, 260-pound man stationed in Bismarck, North Dakota, who is bringing my vision quest full circle. Meet Rich Grosz, one strap-steel-tough individual who is still faster than Agent Mark Webb. As you can probably surmise, he is my firstborn and, like his dad, a special agent for the U.S. Fish and Wildlife Service. This meeting of the reader and Rich is made all the more important as I pass the public service torch from my tiring arthritic and numbing diabetic hands to his grip of vision, strength, and steel. The man you have come to know through these books is professionally no more. But there is a very able chap following in his footsteps, carrying on the good fight for you and yours. Rich is on a vision quest like his dad, with the full support of his family as I had of mine. He possesses the eyes of an eagle, like his grandfather, the hearing of an owl, and the energy of a shrew. Nothing is lost on this young man regarding the urgency within the world of wildlife or its challenges. He is keenly aware of the destruction that comes to one's being and family through pursuing a career in conservation. Like his dad, he gives that potential personal destruction a backward glance as he surges forward through the ranks of the unwashed, running them to ground for their illegal indulgence.

Extinction is forever! I hope Rich will not be faced with such a black cloud on his watch, be it critter or himself. I also hope he draws my two guardian angels from God's motor pool. They served the American people and me well for over thirty-two years, a little feather thin from their endeavors but a force to be reckoned with and counted upon. As you read the last word in the last chapter, sit back and think over my thirty-two years of trails. Imagine what they represented, not only for me but for you as well! I hope this six-volume series has told us something about who we were and what we have become. I and others like me gave our all attempting to save a little corner of the earth and its riches for folks like you. In the process, we used up our bodies, and sadly, many times, our families.

When it comes to "plowing under a trail," please don't let pride, greed, ego, absence of thought, excesses, or prejudice allow you to participate. Remember the lessons of history. If you don't, then you will go the way of the passenger pigeon.

Thank you for the hours we spent together running down the various trails in the books. I hope that in those many stories and in your mind's eye, I left you with a legacy. I also hope you came away with the feeling that "God stood by Terry when the fists and bullets were flying, and Terry stood by Him when His voiceless creatures needed help." Remember, we are responsible for the legacy of our ancestors and the future of our children. May the good Lord take a liking to you and yours as I quietly wait for my next "assignment."

Acknowledgments

WALKING INTO MY seventh grade classroom and looking around, I found myself in love. My new teacher was petite, fairy-like, and beautiful in a magical sort of way. Her dark-brown hair, beautiful smile, and challenging eyes made it difficult for anyone to resist her charm. I soon discovered that her skills as a teacher and caring as a human being far exceeded her physical beauty.

In those days I lived in Quincy, a small community in the Sierra Nevada Mountains of Plumas County in California. It was a hardscrabble area, with the lumber industry being king. The people were of tough, self-reliant stock, and their kids, especially the boys, were wilder than March hares. At home, if you stepped out of line, you got a damn good thrashing. If you wanted to "hoot and holler," you had to do it outside your parents' reach. So school became one of those "free-fire zones" where many of us males aired out our limited behavioral skills.

Teachers were always fair game, just so long as you didn't piss them off to the point that they reported your transgressions to your parents. If they did, you got "whanged" at school and again when you got home. Getting caught wasn't cool. Your buddies who scurried under the leaf litter when you were run to ground by a teacher would soon reemerge and would give you a "sandpapering" that would take the hide off a shark. So you had to be skillful and high stepping in order to attack the system through the teacher.

However, in that class, with a teacher who was not only beautiful but extremely gifted, especially when dealing with young hellions, we tried to be gentlemen. To do otherwise in Miss Billiejean McElroy's class was folly. First of all, you lost your place in line in her eyes as a good student. Then your buddies magnified your errors to the world, currying favor at the same time, and you lost even more face. So if you weren't careful, you caught hell coming and going.

"Magical" would be the word for my relationship with Miss McElroy. I was a poor, nearly illiterate kid more interested in finding something to eat and in hunting and fishing than anything else. But I always had curiosity, be it crawling around in old collapsed mineshafts with my .22 killing rats, exploring historical sites for purple bottles from the gold rush days of '49, or digging worms to catch the wily trout. Miss McElroy, seeing that developing innate curiosity in me, especially my interest in anything adventurous, set to work. At first she was unobtrusive so as not to make it look like favoritism or an effort to make a teacher's pet out of a sow's ear. She just quietly encouraged me with her special attention, as only she could do, to look at the world of books. She did it so skillfully that soon she had me hooked and exploring just about every corner of that new world. Those corners included seafaring tales, Civil War adventures, cattle ranching, cowboys, the frontier, the Second World War, wildlife, mountain men, lost treasure, gold mining, and historical exploration. Testing me, she discovered that I could read and comprehend over eight hundred words a minute, and the floodgates were opened. Soon, under her gently guiding hands, I was reading a book a week as she carefully exposed me to the charms of the written word. I found myself constantly challenged as I learned many things. She sparked in me a lifelong interest in books and the special world they represented, a world that even a poor, illiterate kid from a background of hard work and toil could enjoy. That interest still burns brightly in me to this day.

It is for that moment of recognition of a child's potential and subsequent gentle guidance that I wish to acknowledge my teacher Miss Billiejean McElroy (Durst). Thank you, Miss McElroy, for introducing me to the wonders of the world, and then for teaching me how to read its pages.

Dedication

WHEN I FIRST SAW Mr. Thurman Black, he reminded me of the cartoon character Dagwood Bumstead: long legs and a gawky walk, hair tousled, squalling, "By George" or "Won't That Sink Your Bobber" at some event, and leaning into the wind like it was blowing at sixty. However, it didn't take long for me to realize that Mr. Black was a gifted scholar and many-faceted teacher. The man was such a vibrant, dynamic personality that his talents soon permeated the school and we began to realize what a unique human being stood before us.

Mr. Black was brimful of ideas. He initiated the American Field Service program, and soon one of our students was overseas. To help with finances, he began a "fire-starter" program, selling milk cartons filled with sawdust and diesel oil. He dug through barrels of cafeteria trash to get enough milk cartons for the project. Soon money was pouring in to defray the costs of our exchange student. He created a snack bar in the gym where the Student Council made money selling snacks to the crowds during home basketball games. Soon this spirit spread throughout the student body. He was elected "Teacher of the Year" his second year on campus!

In the classroom, his energy and abilities as a teacher were not of this world. He brought such believability and dynamic raw energy to every subject that soon his classes were booked solid. It was obvious that to Mr. Black, the reality of education carried an urgency to impart knowledge and ideals to his students. His contact with a student's mind was as fleeting as his one-hour classes, so his energies went into overdrive. It soon became apparent that a one-hour class under Mr. Black was a magical trip. Many times it seemed I had no more than gotten seated when the bell rang for the next class!

Those classes were loaded with life's experiences and common sense mixed with useful, everyday survival information. Also woven throughout were ethics, courage, and how to look down the road with conviction to take one's place in the world. All of us learned that those stars were reachable!

I came from a dirt-poor, one-parent family and had no future except as a laborer in the lumber industry. Doing the work of a man since nine, I lied about my age and went to work in a box factory at fifteen and as a logger at sixteen. Times were tough, and I went hungry for a lot of things in those days. Then along came Mr. Black, seemingly borne on a mystical wind. He not only spoke my language but swept me into his energy field. The man was a veritable fountain of life, providing an insight into a whole new world.

Mr. Black was aware of my hardscrabble background. He also saw in me more possibilities than as a laborer in the lumber industry. He began redirecting my energy by instilling a drive to be everything I could, plus more. He taught me to set high standards and, if I failed to reach them, to come up with a Plan B and try again. We became great friends.

When I graduated from high school, I eagerly looked forward to the future, not through rose-colored glasses but with reality and vigor honed by a teacher who took time to lead with his mind and soul. In college I earned bachelor and master of science degrees. I spent the next thirty-two years in public service in state and federal law enforcement. Upon retirement, I began writing, authoring six books (one a National Outdoor Book Award winner) and along the way earning an honorary doctorate in environmental stewardship. I married the woman of my dreams and had three children and six grandchildren. They too have felt the teachings of Mr. Black through their dad and "grandpaw."

It is in memory of Mr. Thurman Black, a Man for All Seasons, dear friend, quintessential teacher, and mentor, that I gratefully and humbly dedicate this book.

one

Ephraim in the Office and the Outback

I STEPPED OFF THE PLANE at Stapleton International Airport and walked up the ramp into the passenger waiting area. My new regional office law enforcement staff and Tom Striegler, my new assistant special agent in charge, were there to meet me. After I shook Tom's hand, he introduced me to my all-female staff, who, without being obvious, were examining me closely to discover anything that would reveal the character of their new boss. After greetings done all around, we headed for our vehicle like a gaggle of geese.

"Who is minding the office, Tom?" I asked casually.

"No one," came Tom's reply. "There isn't much doing right now, so I thought I would let the ladies come to the airport and meet their new boss."

There would be plenty of time for getting to know one another, I thought, and I would have preferred to leave someone in the office to at least answer the phones. After all, it was a government office established to provide a public service. That casual attitude was a portent of many off-kilter things I would soon discover within the administration—or lack thereof—of my new assignment.

It was June 1981, and I was the new special agent in charge for the U.S. Fish and Wildlife Service's Division of Law Enforcement in the Denver Regional Office. I was in charge of the Rocky Mountain/Prairie States Region, or the states of Montana, Wyoming, Colorado, Utah, North Dakota, South Dakota, Nebraska, and Kansas, an area roughly 750,000 square miles of resource-rich habitat, with all the associated species of wildlife and wildlife-related law enforcement problems. Those problems were exacerbated by what I considered to be borderline criminally negligent management by senior Service leaders and historically deliberate insufficient funding for the Division of Law Enforcement. Little did I realize that those would be the more manageable problems compared to the administrative and personnel mess that I would face in my office.

I had been the assistant special agent in charge in Minneapolis for two years before my recent selection for the special agent in charge position over a handful of candidates from across the Service, including my current assistant special agent in charge. After being notified of my promotion, I heard nothing more about it for a month, which was unusual because the special agent in charge was a senior management law enforcement position within the Service. These agents directed and oversaw congressionally mandated wildlife investigations by the thousands, and their presence was so critical that the lack of their operational guidance for agents in the field could result in untold liabilities, official embarrassment, or even the worst-case scenario of the death of the investigator or those investigated. These positions were also important as key law enforcement advisers to the non–law enforcement regional directors, those officials in the highest governmental positions within the Department of the Interior, responsible for setting management direction and administrative course for regions covering the entire nation. In short, when these positions were vacated, they were advertised and filled almost immediately.

I began to hear rumors that owing to funding shortfalls (the Denver law enforcement office was supposedly $34,000 in the red), Regional Director Don Minnich was now toying with the idea of leaving the special agent in charge position vacant to save money. His thinking was that he would operate with just Assistant Special Agent in Charge Tom Striegler. *What the hell can he be thinking?* I thought. That is just asking for legal troubles when someone screws up in the field because the investigating officer got bad advice or no advice at all from an overworked second-in-command. There was a good reason for having both a special agent in charge and an assistant. In the complex world of law enforcement, having two supervisors to troubleshoot every major decision provided the best approach to any problems that required a law enforcement response. I also found it strange that the budget issue had not been resolved *before* the advertising and selection of the position. It was almost as if the regional director had "magically" become aware of the funding shortage only after the selection had been made.

At last I received a call from Brian Burns, chief of personnel for the Denver region. He informed me that Regional Director Minnich had now decided to fill the special agent position as a temporary six-month appointment. According to Burns, Assistant Special Agent in Charge Striegler, after not being selected, had begun talking to the regional director about this money-saving arrangement. With that kind of administrative maneuver immediately after my selection, I began to have doubts about the wisdom of my pending transfer to a region that appeared to be as screwed up as Hogan's goat.

Sitting down with my bride that evening, I discussed the possibility of a six-month appointment and its ramifications for my family. There really wasn't any way I could afford to maintain my family in Minnesota while living in Denver. But as we discussed those financial issues over dinner, just as I had decided that such dual residency was out of the question, Donna brought me up short.

"That's what you think, mister!" said my wife and best friend. "You go, and we will manage. It is just that simple. This is the opportunity we planned on for the last seven years, and you are not going to pass it by. I will find a way to make it work financially, even if I have to send the kids down to Prior Lake [which was only about two hundred yards from our home] every night to catch some fish so we have something to eat. Honey, it is almost as if by proposing the six-month temporary position, someone is trying to eliminate you before you have a chance to fulfill your dream." Her eyes were the prettiest deep blue at that moment, and I had to smile at the love of my life and her "sand." She continued, "If you don't go, that will leave the way open for the regional director to select someone else under whatever pretense. After that person gains six months' experience as the agent in charge, he may beat you out if the position is readvertised. No—you are going to Colorado, and that is that!"

The way she spoke and those flashing beautiful eyes told me I was off on another adventure, and the family would catch up when the going got good. Damn, I thought, God blessed me with a real woman, and I was not going to disappoint her.

"OK," I said, "if that's what you want, I will have a go at it. It seems that if I was selected for the full-time position, I'll get selected for the six-month temporary one as well, right?"

She just grinned, knowing all was well now that she had had her say. It usually was with that woman. Many times over the years I thought she must have a direct pipeline to God, and He had learned not to mess with her when she had her dander up. Even my kids thought so, and many times that fear kept them in line when I wasn't around. Hell, that fear *still* works on the kids.

Calling Burns in Denver the following day, I told him to tell the regional director I was going to throw my hat in the ring for the temporary position, and that it only stood to reason, since I had been selected for the full-time position, that I should be selected for the lesser part-time one. The chief of personnel just chuckled. I found out later that he thought the regional director was a klutz and relished the thought of the battle that would likely follow my throwing my hat into the ring once more.

Two days later, Deputy Regional Director Bob Shields (who was a top-notch administrator and later became a good friend) called and told me to report to Denver in ten days. The regional director was going to give me a two-week tryout. I had never heard of such a thing as a "tryout" after being selected for the permanent position, but I answered that I would be there.

"Good," he said, "and when you get here, come up and see me first thing. We have a major administrative and personnel problem in your shop, and I want you to get it squared away."

"Yes, sir," I replied, "just as soon as I get there, we have a date."

Hanging up, I sat back and let my thoughts slowly rattle around in my head. Here I was, the shiny brand-new special agent in charge of the largest geographic region in the nation (even bigger than Alaska). I was only thirty-nine years old, making me the youngest special agent in charge in the nation at the time! In 1974, when I had been selected as senior resident agent for North and South Dakota, I had told Donna that I was going to work my way up the ladder and wanted to be special agent in charge in Denver before I turned forty! In order to achieve that goal, we would have to move several more times, and one of those moves would have be to Washington, D.C., for at least two years as a desk officer. Throughout, I would have to be involved in all aspects of the profession in order to become known and thoroughly learn the ropes. I would also have to be lucky because there were only thirteen such field positions in the nation (since then reduced to seven). My bride voiced her strong support and advised me that I had better get on with it. However, she added that once the children hit high school, my peregrinations would have to cease. She had very strong feelings that once the kids reached a certain age, they should have a strong and stable base for their life experiences. I agreed and set my sails into the winds of adventure. With the grace of God, a lot of hard work, good timing, and tremendous support from my wife, I had just accomplished an almost impossible goal! Damn, the feeling of that accomplishment was almost indescribable!

Then came the realization: supervision of twenty-two independent-as-pigs-skating-on-ice special agents, the largest geographic district in the nation, a zillion miles of Canadian border running along my northern boundary with all the wildlife smugglers to guard against, extremely limited or nonexistent funding, an assistant who was disappointed over the fact that he had not been selected for my position, eight state fish and game agencies that did not consider the Division of Law Enforcement in my region to be much of a partner, Service sister division officials who cared not a whit if my division sank or swam, a questionable regional director (who eventually moved on to Washington)—and did I mention no operating funds? All of a sudden, my shoulders seemed kind of small for the workload I was about to try on for size. I also discovered that the size of my head, after swelling over my success in attaining this position, was rapidly shrinking.

Ten days later found me sitting in my Denver office for the very first time. Leaning back in my chair, I finally had the opportunity to drink in the feeling of becoming a special agent in charge after only ten and a half years in the Service. That was in the days when most other special agents in charge were at least ten years older than I. Damn, it felt good! There went my head expanding again. ... Then I remembered the region's lousy law enforcement fiscal condition and asked my new administrative officer to bring me the budget documents for that year, and the next year's proposal as well. I could hear her stirring around in the office next door, putting together my request, all the while muttering loudly to herself. Why all the grumbling over a simple request? I thought. Then, like a cow moose in heat, she stomped down to my deputy's office and informed him that I wanted to see the budget in a tone indicating that she felt the request was criminal in nature. In a voice loud enough for God to hear, she asked, "Is it all right?"

Damn, I thought, Tom is an ex-military man and understands the chain of command. What is the problem? Certainly when the boss made a request, it didn't have to be cleared through his second-in-command. Maybe after working closely with Tom over time, she had just forgotten who was the new commander! When I finally received the budget documents, I thanked her. That courtesy was met with a head thrown back in disgust and a loud, indignant snort as she took her carcass out of my office under a head of steam. Oh well, I thought, it's good that she has such a strong loyalty to Tom, and I can put up with a bit of an attitude until she gets used to me. Boy, was I to find out where the cow moose crapped in the clover before that particular professional relationship ended!

Reviewing the budget for the current year, the one supposed to be $34,000 in the red (keep in mind that one reason that I supposedly couldn't be transferred from Minneapolis to Denver was because of moving expenses), I was surprised to find that it was actually $54,000 in the black! I telephoned Tom, whose office was at the far end of our complex, and asked him to join me. Tom was the one who should have been most knowledgeable about the division's financial status, and he had been the one advising the regional director regarding the state of our budget. When he arrived, I said, "Tom, I have been going over the books and find we are not in the hole $34,000 but are $54,000 in the black. Am I not reading this document correctly?"

"Oh well, it is just how you figure the budget," he said, then spun on his heel, as in the military, and whisked out the door as if on a mission of greater importance. I thought that behavior was a bit strange since I still had several more questions—unless something was riding his tail that needed hiding. You know, folks, a man my size doesn't get that big by being last in line. I wondered if Tom knew that!

Several days later, after a preliminary study of my office staff's work performance, I realized I had a bear-sized ethics and personnel problem. I discovered that not only were they antagonistic toward me, but most of them had only temporary status and were undergraded and poorly intergraded in the office infrastructure. They also appeared to have a hostile attitude toward other Service employees, the public, and their own officer corps within the region. It quickly became obvious that there would have to be a lot of ass-kicking and name-taking before this mess was squared away. In fact, with one exception, the original office staff, including my deputy, was replaced over the next two years with more talented and dedicated people. By damn, those were two tough years—years that basically took me away from many of the regional resource issues in order to address these profoundly pressing administrative problems.

Remembering my pledge for an early meeting to Assistant Regional Director Bob Shields, I asked my secretary for directions to his office and beat it downstairs to find him. I had met Bob weeks earlier during my interview for the position and had liked him from the outset. He was quiet and unassuming, but I could tell he was the knowledge behind the region's management team and the one most respected by the professional rank and file.

"Good afternoon, Chief; what did you want to talk about?" I asked as I stepped into his office.

"Close the door," was his curt, surprising reply. I did, and sat down in front of his desk to wait until he finished reviewing a piece of congressional correspondence. He put it down slowly, as if methodically switching gears in his head. Then he looked up at me for a long moment with deeply questioning eyes before standing up, extending his hand, and saying only warmly, "Welcome aboard." He sat back down and thought quietly with his head in his hands for a moment before looking up. "After our discussion today, you may want to turn around and go back to your old job in Minneapolis," he said bluntly.

"I'm listening," I said with no emotion in my voice or eyes.

"Terry, your law enforcement district stinks! Many of the officers aren't motivated, and it is almost like they're sitting on their hands, except on payday. They don't seem to have the energy to get out of their own way, much less try new things that need doing. And they don't have an ounce of respect for the law enforcement office or its personnel here in the regional office." Pausing, he gave me a hard look as if seeking a reaction.

"Go ahead, Chief. So far you haven't told me anything I don't already know and realize needs fixing," I replied quietly. He seemed shocked that I had already reached that level of knowledge, and he looked at me for a long second in disbelief. I gave him a hard stare in return, letting him know he wasn't dealing with someone who had just fallen off a turnip wagon.

"Next, that administrative office of yours needs a shake-up from stem to stern, and I do mean a shake-up! That includes firing some or all of them if necessary. The quality of their work is consistently below regional standards, and they seem to need little excuse to screw off most of the time. I see them going home early and arriving late to work. They take hour-long breaks and spend over an hour at lunch instead of the half hour they are allotted. As a result of this poor attitude, your guys in the field are calling me out of frustration, asking for help because their own office doesn't respond to their requests!"

I interrupted, "What kind of help are the field officers requesting?" While still in Minneapolis I had heard about the administrative problems in the Denver office, but I hadn't been aware that the officers had routinely been calling the deputy regional director for assistance that should have been provided by their own law enforcement staff—in essence being forced to bypass the chain of command. If they were doing that, I thought, I had a worse problem than I had imagined.

"They are having trouble getting their expense vouchers and case reports processed, and calls for direction and guidance go unanswered. They also feel that Tom isn't cut out to lead field officers, and in my estimation that feeling is validated in what I have seen of his everyday performance."

"OK," I said, "I'm getting the picture. Anything else?"

"Jesus, man! How much more do you need? You don't have any kind of a field operation, our state counterparts resent us for being so damn lazy, you don't have any kind of administrative staff, and your operating budget is nonexistent! Can't you see the train's headlights coming? Surely you can't be that stupid!"

Ignoring his question and feeling he had pretty much said what needed saying, I stood up to leave. Looking him dead in the eyes, I said, "I do want one commitment out of you before I leave. I will clean up the problem and put the division back on a professional footing. But I will do it at my speed and as I see fit. If you agree, then you have a new special agent in charge for the region. If not, I'm out the door and you can select someone else to clean up the mess left by my predecessor."

He gave me the biggest grin, stood up to shake my hand once more, and said again, this time with enthusiasm, "Welcome aboard, Terry!"

For the next two months, I went through every Office of Personnel Management administrative directive as a refresher. Knowing I was heading for the rocks with Tom and the rest of my staff, I wanted to know exactly where the legal rough spots were going to be and how they should be handled. I read every directive the previous special agent in charge had issued to the field (and ended up revoking most of them), became familiar with our current and proposed budgets, then started learning about the field officers' personalities, abilities, and individual work ethics. I also reviewed the permit issuance, case management, and telephone response systems provided by my staff. I worked with the administrative officer on all fiscal documents passing through her hands, especially those relating to travel vouchers. I discovered that some agents were owed up to $7,000 in back travel expenses and had been using their personal savings to continue the government's law enforcement operations!

That particular chore with the administrative officer took a little doing. I finally initiated a little sit-down with her in which we discussed who was the boss and talked about her clearing my requests for information through my deputy. After that session, it became very apparent that she was not a happy camper. She stormed down to the human resources officer to ascertain whether I could legally talk to her in that manner. This trip to human resources became an almost daily routine after our little discussion sessions—until the day she left my office for another job. One bear down, many more to go!

Her discomfort went off the charts even more when I brought in a lower-graded but brilliant fiscal clerk from another division to go through her files and find out what the hell was going on. I had received numerous calls from the public and field officers regarding administrative issues that should have been routinely processed long before. Dozens of such documents had fallen through the cracks, and something clearly just wasn't right. The problem called for drastic measures, and Tami Bruhn, the little seventy-four-pound fiscal clerk on loan from Marv Duncan in the Budget and Finance Division, seemed to be the remedy. Bringing in a lowly fiscal clerk from another division to examine the books of a lordly administrative officer made for a Fourth of July every day! But damn it, I had no other choice. My administrative officer would tell me everything was all right, but I still kept getting numerous calls from the field and public regarding my office's administrative failures. Tami discovered a major breakdown within the administrative system, including such problems as unpaid bills going back two years, and worse! Deputy Director Shields had been right. I had an administrative nightmare, and a total housecleaning appeared to be in order.

What I saw during that first two-month examination of the operations side of my picture also made me cringe. I had field officers who should never have been accepted into the Service, promoted, or given within-grade pay increases. Many officers were poorly motivated or highly suspicious of the regional office in general and the law enforcement office specifically. Hell, some of them were highly suspicious of work! All had lousy equipment at best, and only one had a four-wheel-drive vehicle in a region where they should have been standard issue! Many officers enforced laws selectively, ignoring others, especially the Lacey Act, and my deputy led that pack. The Lacey Act is a federal conservation law that prohibits taking any wildlife (and now plants) in violation of state, federal, or international (and now tribal) laws and transporting those items across state, federal, or international (and now tribal) lines. It seems that the Service, in its infinite wisdom, did not fiscally support Lacey Act enforcement in a region that was basically "Mr. Lacey Act." Many of my staff didn't enforce it at all, mostly out of pure damn laziness! That was especially hard for me to understand because approximately one-third of the nation's nonresident hunters hunted in my region on any given day during the season, with a fair number of them breaking state hunting regulations at every turn. When they took their ill-gotten game across state lines, they had a Lacey Act violation as well. With that and all the other illegal take, wildlife smuggling, illegal sales of wildlife, and transport across the state and international borders of wildlife parts and products, the magnitude of the problem became hugely apparent. Yet Service leaders continued to sit on their dead hind ends, doing nothing fiscally to alleviate the problem, and in the process, allowed the destruction of thousands of animals in direct violation of federal law! No wonder that, if something that blatant could be ignored, there are $700 toilet seats and $600 screwdrivers being purchased by the military.

That wasn't the only shoe I found ready to drop. For the most part, the states, with their fairly extensive numbers of conservation officers, held the Service's law enforcement division in low regard or utter contempt. There were problems with egos and states' rights attitudes clashing with what little competition my officers provided; conflicts over state versus federal authorities and the personalities of my officers versus theirs; issues related to the lack of work from my guys, who were drawing larger salaries and in most cases better retirement than their state counterparts; clashes over who would protect what species; the states' dislike for the federal Endangered Species Act, which was frequently taken out on my officers; and so on.

Let me see, that was shoe number two, wasn't it? Well, shoe number three was the mess I found in the regional office's permit-issuing function. In those days the law enforcement division issued federal wildlife permits to the public for eagles and migratory birds—eagle feather possession (for Native Americans), import and export, falconry, and other like categories. Close review of the permitting system showed that *thirteen months* was the average time between application and permit issuance, rather than the expected and commonsense period of thirty to forty-five days!

Then there was shoe number four: the deputy regional director's statement regarding my men and their expense accounts was right on the money. It was taking an average of *eleven months* instead of, again, a reasonable thirty to forty-five days between the time of submission of expense accounts submission and receipt of payment! No wonder they were calling Deputy Director Shields out of sheer desperation. Damn, now I was sure I had more than a bear of a problem. It was a nest of bears, all seeming to have extra rows of teeth!

Well, hell. Since I am on a roll, how about shoe number five? Officers can rattle around the country enforcing federal laws to their hearts' content, but it does no one any good, including the U.S. Attorney's Office, unless the men produce case reports detailing their efforts. Examination of that administrative function in my office showed that most case reports were taking an average of *twelve months* from the time of receipt of the draft for typing (no computers in those days—at least none that I could afford—until they were back in the officers' hands. That made for *real good* relations with our U.S. attorneys, and many times the region's congressional offices, needing information *now!* In fact, my officers had closed most cases in the standard course of things before they received their initial case reports back from the regional office.

None of my six field supervisors had a secretary, so all case reports were sent on tape to the regional office for copying into the final reports. The machine responsible for receiving and indexing these tapes cost $10,000, and it was still taking twelve months to get the final documents back into the hands of the submitting agents! Imagine being an underpaid office staffer typing case reports from tape, day in and day out. It was plain to see that each field supervisor needed a secretary, or the case management system could never be fixed.

Then, how about shoe ... oh, hell! I have lost count at this stage. The respect shown by the regional office to the Division of Law Enforcement was also the pits. Other folks had observed many of the law enforcement staff routinely screwing off in various ways and as a result had developed a total disregard for the division and its function within the scheme of the region's wildlife management. I tested how bad the situation was on several occasions when I announced to my staff that I had to leave early for a fictitious meeting. I would leave the building, drive off (knowing they would be looking out the window to make sure I was gone), then quietly return and park off to one side of the lot. Within minutes, *every time,* I would see one or several of my staff coming out of the building and driving off, leaving for the day! If I went to any supervisors from other divisions for assistance, they would find a polite excuse to deny my request because of this type of behavior. I don't care how tough or great a manager you are, or the kind of a program you run—without cooperation from your professional kin, so to speak, you will fail. Custer was a classic case in point. ...

After those first two months, I realized I needed to replace my entire staff (except one young woman named Bernadette who had a lot of potential—and today is a major facility supervisor) and start over if I wanted to manage the region's natural resources through the law enforcement function the way it was meant to be done! That was one hell of a realization: the gathering of personnel data leading up to firing individuals, then all the work associated with rehiring, all the work involved in training the new staffers, and on it went. *I complained because I had no shoes until I saw a man who had no feet. ...*

The next two years were a bear. In fact, they were the toughest two years of my professional life! I tried every known management scheme to get my staff to straighten up and fly right, all to no avail. There were times when I would literally shut down the office and put the entire staff to typing case reports or permits to eliminate the backlog while I answered the telephone. Man, you talk about hostile females who felt that kind of detail work was not in their job descriptions! There wasn't a day with such details on the radar screen during which the human resources officer didn't receive a visit or two from my disgruntled employees. Thank God the deputy regional director and the chief of personnel stood behind me and guided me through those minefields. A few times, in order to show my appreciation, I treated my staff to drinks after work in the bar in the building that housed the regional office. I had to quit the practice after several times in that barrel. It seemed I would always get a phone call as we were leaving the office, and staying to respond would usually take half an hour or more. By the time I arrived in the bar to pick up the tab (I never drank), the bill usually exceeded $100! That was with a staff numbering only five. The last time this happened, I reached the bar to discover that each employee had six full drinks sitting in front of them, in essence, showing the level of unhappiness they felt at having to work.

But I finally got the mess cleaned up with a lot of assistance from many good people in the regional office. New staff hires replaced the ladies rapidly abandoning the ship to get away from the crazy man at the helm; my deputy moved to Washington, D.C., in part to avoid a run-in with me over his failure in my absence to provide funds in a timely manner to an agent in an ongoing covert operation; the deputy regional director stood firm on his original clean-up request; better agents were recruited for vacant field positions; and I had my two guardian angels and the constant support of my bride each night when I came home after another hostile day at the office.

During that two-year rebuilding period, I had a chance to look over my district and figure out its other problems. I was not surprised to find many bears in that soup too. I had eagles electrocuted daily by antiquated transmission lines (in one case ninety dead bald and golden eagles per mile were reported in the Buffalo Basin in Wyoming); cyanide-heap leach-mining operations poisoning migratory birds by the untold thousands; uncovered oil pits by the tens of thousands killing migratory birds and endemic wildlife species by the hundreds of thousands; commercial-market hunters and other organized rings of poachers killing the biggest and best of the big-game species; Native Americans illegally trapping eagles (some on national wildlife refuges), killing them, and selling their parts; Native Americans illegally gill-netting walleye from the major reservoirs along the Missouri River and selling their catches; Native Americans smuggling their eagle-feather craft "artifakes" into Canada and selling them to locals or to European buyers for their collectors' markets; the illegal taking of migratory game birds, especially Canada geese, over baited areas along the Missouri River in South Dakota by so-called hunters; federal employees from the Animal Damage Control Division of my own agency violating the federal Airborne Hunting Act as they illegally took animals from aircraft being used outside their authorities; civilians doing the same with private aircraft (we seized at least ten aircraft that were forfeited to the government during one year alone when fur prices were high); wetlands owned or administrated by the Service in the Dakotas and Montana being drained by maverick dirt farmers; intentional cattle trespass on the national wildlife refuges and subsequent destruction of their ranges; wildlife and fish of all types, including exotics, being illegally imported or exported across the Canadian border; sheep ranchers placing poison by the bucketful on federally leased lands to still any heartbeat other than their range maggots; cattlemen, guides, and outfitters killing grizzly bears protected by the Endangered Species Act; and hardly an extra dime's worth of fiscal support from my parent agency to address many of these issues.

Just to show how bad it was, there were three years in the 1980s when I received a federal budget on October 1 (that was when Congress got off their dead hind ends and passed a budget bill) in which I was already broke for that fiscal year—*before* my officers had worked one day! I didn't even have enough money to pay salaries, much less buy gas for their patrol vehicles, pay per diem, or the like. It was times like that that tried my soul in light of the fact that we law enforcement officers in the Service were paid to protect, preserve, and enhance the natural resources of the United States for the American people, and for those yet to come.

But all that aside, life was pretty damn good! I was starting to get excellent field officers into the squad through a careful selection process. Many older officers, seeing the handwriting on the wall, were retiring. Lazy officers who couldn't get out of their own way were transferring to other regions. My ever-changing office staff was getting better as the old guard got the hell out of Dodge and the other regional office divisions were slowly beginning to gain respect for my division. In fact, by the time I retired, my new staff had the reputation of being the best in the regional office! Plus, I was beginning to win over some of the state law enforcement leaders. Not all, mind you, because attitudes and memories of slights die hard. But we were finally starting to work together as a team to put those in the business of extinction *out* of business. The division, through good investigative efforts, was also gaining ground in cases prosecuted through the U.S. attorney's office and the federal courts. Last but not least, I was getting to know the critters in the district and understanding the roles they played in the ecosystem as well as identifying those needing assistance to survive. It was ironic that one of those species needing assistance was a *real* bear.

That bear was the grizzly bear, or Ephraim, as the fur trappers of old came to respectfully call it. When I arrived in 1981, anywhere from seventeen to twenty-five grizzlies out of a population of approximately one thousand were illegally taken by man every year. That doesn't seem like many, but when a population had been reduced from an estimated 100,000 to about 1,000, that level of killing could not continue if the species were to survive—especially because the grizzly has the lowest rate of recruitment of any mammal in the United States! It takes about ten years from the birth of a grizzly until that bear produces a breeding replacement. With such a low reproductive rate, any loss of grizzlies, especially females, became a matter of grave concern. And many of the annual deaths were females, many no doubt defending their cubs.

After taking the time to locate the worst illegal drains on the region's resources, I looked to applying my officers' talents to stop that kind of destruction. The grizzly easily floated to the top of the list of animals for which we could play a valuable role in survival and management. But how to do it? Even though the great bear was protected under the government's Endangered Species Act, there was almost zero protective activity from Service law enforcement in Region 6 because of nonexistent budgets. What efforts there were mostly involved investigations after a bear was dead, and therefore no real possibility of preserving or increasing the population. There was a fair supply of money for the Service's Endangered Species Division for biological management of the bear but nary a nickel for the chaps carrying badges. There we went again! Why did it seem as if I were always going into a fiscal gunfight with just a pocketknife?

One wintry spring day in 1983, a day that ultimately became "the day of the grizzly," I was in Montana trying to settle a pissing contest between two of my agents and several members of the Montana Depart-

ment of Fish, Wildlife, and Parks. It seemed that two state fish and
game captains in key grizzly areas were refusing to cooperate with my
two Montana agents. I also suspected that they had forbidden their
subordinate officers to work with my officers on most bear issues.
Most of the problems stemmed from the question of who had legal
jurisdiction over the bear. Clearly, the Fish and Wildlife Service had
primary jurisdiction over species covered under the Endangered
Species Act of 1973. However for years the state of Montana had
managed and protected the bear because of its endemic status under
their state statutes. Now Montana found itself playing second fiddle,
which did not bode well, especially among their wildlife agency leaders. Unfortunately, that ill feeling was sometimes manifested down
through the ranks.

In that particular pissing contest (yes, there were others), my officers needed to get their acts together and work more closely with the
state officers. In addition, the two state captains in question needed to
get off their high horses and work with the Service. Bottom line, it was
a matter of both sides getting their heads out of their hind ends and
working together for the benefit of the bear and its survival. If they
didn't, the bear's slide toward extinction in the state of Montana
would accelerate, and then none of us would have this magnificent
species as part of our lives.

In order to give an example of the degree of bitterness on both
sides, I'll start with the meeting between the two warring field fac-
tions, the assistant state director for the Montana Department of Fish,
Wildlife, and Parks, and yours truly. What a session that was! I had
met earlier that day with the assistant director for Montana and laid
out the problem as I saw it and a solution. He seemed to be a reasonable man and agreed, with a few stipulations. Then the meeting between all parties concerned took place in the assistant director's
conference room.

Walking in with Agent Rod Hanlon and his senior resident agent
(SRA), Joel Scrafford, I met Captains Lou Kis and Chet Ramsey.
Sticking out my hand in friendship to Captain Kis, a man I had never
met before, I said, "Good morning, Captain, my name is Terry Grosz,"
and shook his hand. But when I extended my hand to Captain Ramsey,
he said, "I ain't got no use for you or any other goddamned stinking
fed, now or ever!" So no handshake there ... With that over, we all sat

down, and suffice it to say, the personal aspect of the meeting went rapidly downhill from there! However, before the meeting was over, I had directed my men to be more cooperative—in fact, I told them that if they couldn't work with their state counterparts, they should find another region to work in! I didn't care if they got along personally, but they were damn sure going to get along professionally *or hit the road.* There was just too much at stake to let personalities get in the way! That wasn't going to happen on my watch if I could do anything about it. The assistant director for Montana was a little less direct, but he made the message clear to his folks as well that we had to work together for the sake of the bear. We did manage handshakes all around after that air-clearing session. No brotherly love, mind you, but handshakes just the same. Things got a little better after that, but only a little.

Part of the historical problem between the agencies was that the Service, with its limited law enforcement program, was only a bit player. I had only two men for the entire state of Montana. Custer had way more than that in 1876 at the Little Greasy Grass, and look what happened to him! We had no effective patrol program for the backcountry, where the majority of the illegal bear killing was taking place. I simply didn't have the resources to even start such a program, much less sustain it. The Service leadership in Washington, D.C., including Clark Bavin, chief of law enforcement, cared little for any kind of grizzly protection program in the backcountry. Bavin could never see any of his officers on the back of a horse. He seriously believed that the FBI was tops in the enforcement world and that all federal agencies should be modeled after it. Since the FBI didn't routinely ride horses, neither would Service officers.

Without being able to carry our share of the load, I could not expect the Montana officers working their hind ends off in the backcountry to respect us, and that was a big part of my problem. The issue of the conflict of personalities between my officers and their Montana counterparts could be overcome in part if we could just find a way to pull our weight in the field. When it came to investigations, we held a candle to no one, but our backcountry prevention effort just wasn't enough. I would have to find the money to fund such a program because without it, the great bear would continue its slide toward extinction. It was that simple.

After that meeting, I hooked up with Joel Scrafford to meet some key Yellowstone National Park Service personnel. Those individuals, chief among them Joe Fowler, had been giving Joel a terrific supporting hand even though they had serious funding problems of their own partly because Joel was an ex–Park Service employee and partly because if they needed a top criminal investigator for a bear or big-game critter that had been illegally taken in the park and transported, Joel or his Great Falls agent, Rod Hanlon, supplied that expertise.

I had known Joel since my days as an SRA in Bismarck in the mid-'70s. Joel had been sent to North Dakota as a result of my constant growling at Chuck Hayes, then special agent in charge in Kansas City, about the need for more North Dakota officers. All of a sudden, here came Joel along with a grouchy phone call from Hayes. "Fire the son of a bitch," were his words! "You got your man, now get rid of the son of a bitch because all he does is trap muskrats and sit on his ass." So much for getting a new man, I thought as I tried to calm my supervisor down. "I want him gone in thirty days," was his last sputter.

"Yes sir, Chief," I halfheartedly replied. Damn, I thought. I really needed some help if I was to settle the wetland easement wars in the Dakotas. But I sure as hell couldn't do it if I fired anyone who came to help! No matter how one looked at it, North Dakota sure came with its share of problems.

Several weeks later, my new man and his family arrived. He was tall and lean as a stick and had a set of eyes that spoke of good things if I could just reach his soul. He had a lovely and multitalented wife named Patti and two fine, well-mannered boys, one of whom went on to become an attorney in Montana and the other to play pro football with several NFL teams. As far as first impressions went, this officer and his family were winners regardless of what my special agent in charge had said.

Joel and I went right into the wetland easement wars (drainage by dirt farmers of any Department of the Interior administered wetlands in their way so they could plant more $1.58-a-bushel wheat), and I watched for the traits that would allow me to fire the man in accordance with my supervisor's instructions. I saw nothing but a very fine law enforcement officer and warrior. Joel was great with people, especially angry ones (which was just about every farmer in the eastern half of the Dakotas), got along well with state and refuge officers, was quickly accepted by the U.S. attorneys for his legal expertise, was one hell of a law dog when it came to apprehending poachers in general or smugglers from Canada, and taught me quite a few things about the workings of the profession as well! There was no way I was going to fire this guy. Plain and simply, he was as smooth as a "schoolmarm's thigh" and of outstanding value to the Service, the critters, and the people of the United States. Bringing my German thickheadedess into play, I decided *Joel was staying if I had my say!* Needless to say, Chuck Hayes and I had lots of let's say lively discussions over the next few months, but Scrafford stayed! Several years later, after replacing me as the SRA in the Dakotas, Joel was transferred to Billings as Montana's Service law enforcement supervisor.

After I met and thanked the park folks for their outstanding support of my limited program, it was getting late. Joel and I retired to a house trailer I had gotten free from the federal Emergency Management Authority, which I kept in Yellowstone to reduce travel expenses because staying in any motel or lodge in the Yellowstone area cost an arm, a leg, and one's firstborn! Joel and I cooked up a nice supper of elk steak, fried spuds, fresh green salad, and some of his world-class biscuits. After the repast, we washed the dishes and got out a bottle of his favorite Canadian whiskey. Sitting back in the afterglow of a great meal, we poured four fingers each and began to unwind and discuss Ephraim. Joel was also my SRA for Wyoming, and most grizzlies in the lower forty-eight states called that chunk of real estate made up of Montana and Wyoming home. If I was to have a successful back-country grizzly patrol, Joel would have to be my right hand. He was in charge of the region's grizzly bear states and had good horse sense and a real love for the outdoors and the bear. I decided that evening, surrounded by the sense of history permeating Yellowstone, that I would place my trust in him for management of the new program. The great bears needed help, and I was determined to see that they got it regardless of Washington. With a strap-steel-tough man like Joel in charge, I foresaw only success if I could just realize the resources.

By our second four-finger pour of the smooth whiskey, Joel was starting to loosen up. We talked about everything from our mutual love of wildness to the history of the park as snowflakes the size of silver dollars fell silently from the dark gray winter skies. It wasn't quite as momentous a meeting as the Yellowstone founding fathers

had had around their campfire in the early 1870s when they decided
to make that area into a national shrine, but in its way just as important to Ephraim and, in a sense, the American people.

Joel poured out the entire litany of problems with the state of Montana and the grizzly as he saw it. I just listened because the man was
on a roll, a side I had seldom seen in Joel, and a lot of what he was saying was valuable new information for me. Joel talked about the major
enforcement problems in the backcountry with the guides and outfitters, with their dirty hunting camps and collateral attractive smells for
the hungry bears. He talked about the killing of elk by the hunters
who left them overnight in the forest because they were too far from
camp to bring back, then came back the next day to recover the meat
only to discover Ephraim feeding on the carcass. Then Ephraim
would be illegally killed as he defended his meal. He talked about how
the U.S. Forest Service was interested mostly in getting the tree off the
stump and not in the welfare of wildlife, the bear, or folks using the
backcountry. He talked about how many of the foresters ignored the
conservation laws or had no use for them because those concepts just
weren't in their makeup or management philosophy. There were
many nonbelievers on the law enforcement side of the Forest Service,
according to Joel and the whiskey. He spoke at great length regarding
the Forest Service's responsibility for creating and enforcing backcountry regulations since it was the managing agency for so much of
the bear's habitat. Such backcountry regulations should require bear-
proof food and feed containers and clean camps. No matter how important these things were to the bear's survival, nothing was being
done. Then he discussed bright spots in the Forest Service such as John
Mumma, a leader among the forest supervisors in grizzly bear country,
who believed a healthy ecosystem was the direct responsibility of the
Forest Service.

And so it went, the green supervisor listening to a sage subordinate
who, with a hatful of history and a snootful of good whiskey, had a
grasp of the problems but no solutions. When the whiskey gave out,
we went to bed, snuggling deep in our sleeping bags as the trailer, now
without heat, took on the cold of its wintry surroundings. Joel soon
began to snore heavily, but I lay there for hours digesting not only a
fine meal but the many ideas now whirling around in my head. They
were only ideas at that stage, but with a little money and the right kind

of officers ... Sleep finally came as the snow continued to pile up silently, clothing Yellowstone Park in her winter dress.

Daylight the next morning in a driving snowstorm found Joel and me parting company in the stillness of Yellowstone National Park at 22 degrees below zero. It was great to be alive, I thought as my truck picked its way through the many elk and bison herds on and alongside the snow-covered highway leading out of the park. Damn, it was mighty easy to imagine myself back in the early days of the mountain men, who might have seen exactly the same scene on a snowy morning 160 years before. I only needed to see Hugh Glass trudging along on a set of "bearpaws" with a .54-caliber Hawken rifle over his shoulder to make my day complete. ...

My head was still full of excitement from my dreaming the night before. In a short time I had picked up a lot of vital information on the people involved with the great bear, other government agencies' philosophies, problems, and personalities, and the life history of the grizzly from Joel. Much of what he had told me was long on problems and short on solutions. But I had listened carefully, and now my fertile, some may say foolish, mind was racing, as was my truck through the white "wilderness" before me.

I don't remember much more of that trip home as I fought my way south through the blizzard blowing across Montana, Wyoming, and Colorado. In fact, that was the first time in my life that I traveled that far all in four-wheel drive! I do remember formulating a plan on how to get at the bear problem in the backcountry, knowing it would work if given half a chance and a little funding. Damn, there was that funding thing again! I felt like the Indian hanging on to the tail of a wounded bull bison with an arrow sunk deep behind its shoulder. I continued south with a mind full of wild and wonderful ideas as the snow swirled in behind my truck, quickly erasing my tracks on the deserted roadway near Split Rock, Wyoming. Not so deserted that I didn't notice the old wagon trails paralleling the road that in the mid-1800s led hopeful souls to the lands of their dreams.

The next day in my office was a classic example proving the existence of guardian angels. I was sitting at my desk composing a letter to an irate congressman regarding a questionable seizure of totally protected redhead ducks from one of his friends and constituents. As life would have it, the ducks turned out to be ring-necks, a legal species, which had been seized by one of my too-damn-dumb-and-arrogant-to-know-the-difference officers. My secretary broke into my train of thought to announce that there was a person waiting to see me. I told her to send the chap in, but I was so engrossed in my letter that I let him just stand there as I finished putting my thoughts on paper.

Finishing my sentence, I looked up to see a little ol' half-pint son of a bitch in a rumpled suit standing there quietly examining me. "Hi, I am Amos Eno from the National Audubon Society, and I need to talk to you," he squeaked out.

Great, I thought. Now the Audubon folks have a bone to pick with me over some bird issue. Impatiently sitting back in my chair, I said, "It's your nickel. I suggest you have at it, Mr. Eno."

Ignoring my flippant attitude, he said, "You are having grizzly bear problems, and I think I can help. The Audubon Society is interested in helping you get the money to work through the grizzly problem, but *only* if you have a viable solution to the illegal killing."

Man, all of a sudden I wasn't so tired and the letter to the congressman could wait. "What kind of money are we talking?" I asked, thinking the Audubon group couldn't possibly have the amount I needed to set my plan into motion.

"Well," Amos said, "it's not like Audubon has the kind of money you probably need, but I know how to get it if you have a viable plan."

"I do have a plan, and if I can implement it, I figure law enforcement can reduce the illegal mortalities by at least 85 percent, if not more," I stated flatly, amazing even myself with my level of confidence.

"Don't shit me, Mr. Grosz; I am serious," he replied rather testily.

I took a better look at him. He wasn't much bigger than a small duck, but there was an energy about him that told of a much larger person than he appeared. Even when he was standing still, that energy told me he was a real man and should be treated accordingly! Who the hell is this guy? I thought. Well, Terry, there is only one way to find out, so let's see if this dog can hunt.

"Mr. Eno, as you can see, I'm a very busy man. I do in fact have a plan to save the grizzly, but it is expensive and will take a couple of years' hard work by a lot of folks before it will be successful. But it *will* be successful. And, I am not shitting you, as you put it. I can reduce the illegal deaths of the grizzly bear by at least 85 percent, *if not more!*" I looked at the man's dark, intense eyes for any sign that I had run him back into his hole.

"Tell me your plan," he replied impatiently, as if he had a right to know. He drew a chair up in front of my desk and just sat there eyeballing me. Well, I thought, this little shit is not a runner. In fact, he was looking more and more like a fighter. My kind of a man! I was really beginning to like this little fellow.

Without a moment's hesitation and for some reason trusting him as I would a close friend, I laid out my grizzly bear backcountry patrol plan. I hadn't worked out the details to perfection, but what I had developed was good, and I knew it would work if given a chance. I had not yet tried out my idea on any of my trusted officers, as I was wont to do, to look for holes, but for now that didn't seem to matter. I was on a roll and just kept pouring on the steam. Amos hardly even blinked, just listened intently. When I was finished, he stood up quickly.

"I have to run. I have a plane to catch, but you had better count on putting your plan into action just as soon as I get back to D.C." For some reason I had no doubt that this little chap was going to move the Service mountain, and in short order. "How much will you need to get the job done—and I do mean get the job done?" he asked.

"I will need a quarter of a million dollars put into my base and one more special agent position created in Montana. With that, I will be able to reduce the illegal killing by at least the figure I gave you."

"You'd better be able to because not only is your ass on the line but mine as well," he said coldly.

"Well, Mr. Eno, welcome to the firing line. I hope you have cast-iron shorts," I said with a grin, extending a friendly hand. He shook it pretty damn firmly for such a little guy and was gone just as fast as he had come.

Within moments I was having second thoughts about this conversation. What the hell did you just do? I asked myself. A perfect stranger with a disarming manner has penetrated your defenses, discovered your grizzly bear plan, and headed out the door like a mink hot on the trail of a trout dinner. That was my first meeting with Amos and, fortunately for the critters, not my last. I discovered he was a unique man, driven like a dynamo. You could go to the bank on his handshake, and he was fearless when it came to protecting the natural resources. Kind of like a sow grizzly protecting her cubs ...

Two days later, my secretary told me Chief Clark Bavin was on the phone. What the hell did I do now? I thought as I picked up the phone and greeted the chief warmly. "What the hell are you doing out there, Terry?" was his not-so-nice greeting in return.

"Damned if I know, Chief; suppose you tell me," I responded, now somewhat on the defensive.

"Who the hell have you been talking to?" he asked brusquely.

"Anyone who will listen to what I have to say," I answered.

"Don't get smart with me, mister," he barked. "I am serious—who did you talk to?"

"Clark, I have no idea since you haven't given me a subject of conversation to work with." I was getting a little hot under the collar. I didn't mind a damn good ass-chewing but if I weren't let in on the reason why, my German stubbornness would quickly roll out the big guns like those on a Panther tank.

Clark bellowed. "Goddamnit, Ray Arnett called me this morning and told me to get my ass in gear and get a grizzly bear backcountry patrol program up and going in your region." Ray Arnett was assistant secretary for Fish, Wildlife, and Parks, Department of the Interior.

"Makes sense," I responded, "since this region has more live grizzly bears than the others and more being killed illegally as well. I can see why the assistant secretary would want some action." I couldn't quite believe what I was hearing. That little mouse of a fellow Amos Eno, who had been in my office not more than a couple days earlier, must have the heart of a lion with a collateral bite because some of the biggest chiefs were falling in with my way of thinking. That was a historical first!

"That bastard Arnett wants me to come up with $250,000 for your grizzly bear program, and I don't have the money, nor do I know what the hell he is talking about," Clark continued.

"Well, Clark," I said through a large grin, "tell Arnett no, you don't have the money." I knew very well that no one tells an assistant secretary, especially one like Arnett, "where to get off." At least not more than once! I added, "It is understandable why you don't know about the grizzly bear backcountry patrol program because I just came up with the idea several days ago in a blinding snowstorm."

"Terry, you dumb shit, *no one* tells the assistant secretary to go piss up a rope," he tensely fired back. "As for your grizzly bear program, get a copy of it in here so I can take a look at it before I authorize anything."

"Clark," I said, "I think this cat is out of the bag, and it is too late for you to do anything about it, plan or no plan."

"That's what you think, mister," he said. "I won't have my special agents doing any kind of backcountry patrol work. Agents are god-damned criminal investigators, not backcountry cowboys. As far as I am concerned, that goddamned bear can go to hell in a handbasket be-fore I let my Division do that kind of work."

"Clark, this job is growing and becoming a whole lot more compli-cated than wearing a suit and tie like someone in the FBI trying to look important. Sometimes you have to take the battle to the bad guys, and in this instance, that battle is in the backcountry with the mud, lousy food, and danger from wrecks with horses as well as the bear. Tell you what," I continued, "I'll call my source and have him tell the Service to pony up the money from somewhere else. Would that strike your fancy?"

"Well, that sounds better than me having to come up with the money," he said. I just grinned. Clark always had money for his pet projects. He sometimes forgot that I had studied under him for two-and-a-half years in the Washington office and knew exactly what kind of a manager and schemer he really was! "Get that bastard Arnett off my neck, will you," he growled, "and fast. I have to run over to the main Interior for a meeting now, but try to have that done before I get back." With that, he hung up, leaving me to ponder just how power-ful this Eno fellow really was.

A call to Amos's office quickly got him on the phone. "Morning, Amos," I said.

"Got the bastards stirred up, didn't I?" he responded happily.

"You sure did," I exclaimed. "But we need to get Arnett off Bavin's ass before he kills me and any chance of the program."

"Don't worry," he said, "I already have the funding worked out, and it won't come out of law enforcement's underfunded hide. It will come out of all the other bloated program bastards' carcasses in Interior."

"Good," I said. " That ought to piss off all the rest of the program chiefs if they aren't already pissed at law enforcement." Amos just snickered. I continued, "How the hell did you get to Arnett to start things rolling so fast?"

"Terry, are your bears still dying?" he asked testily.

"You know better than to ask that question. You damn well know they are."

"Therein lies your answer," he coldly replied. "We must get moving, and I am doing my share. When that money gets there, you need to get trucking; otherwise, crooked elements within the Service will steal it away, and then your ass will be a grape as far as I am concerned."

"You just get the money here, Amos, and I will put it to good use," I said.

"Good. Then let's hear no more about the details on my end. I'll do my share and protect the division of law enforcement as well as your miserable carcass. You in turn, my friend, need to give me some political ammunition by saving some bears *fast* so I can keep up the pressure on Interior. Without that, I am screwed, and there are a number of people standing in line to apply the pressure, if you get my meaning," he said laughingly.

"When will I see this phantom money?"

"My guess is you will be given the green light within two days."

Damn, I was floored! Nothing moves in two days within government except a declaration of war, and then only if the enemy blindsided us as they did at Pearl Harbor. That goes double for the Fish and Wildlife Service. God, these developments were unreal, and I was still finding them hard to believe. Then I heard the whirring of several sets of wings and fired off a quick thank-you to the old boy upstairs as I began to make mental plans for moving the Service rock off dead center into a mainstream of motion.

Two days later, my new regional director informed me that Assistant Secretary Arnett had authorized me to spend $250,000 and added one more law enforcement position in the state of Montana to address the rampant illegal grizzly killing. I could still hardly believe my good luck. Good ol' small-as-a-duck Amos! Clark never said any more about my agents working in the backcountry except that every time we got photograph publicity, he let me know he thought we were poorly dressed and setting a bad example for the officer corps. What the hell did he expect us to be wearing sitting in a saddle thirty-five miles in the outback at 20 below—a suit and tie?

Taking my lead like a catfish with an Eagle Claw number 6 hook and a gob of worms, I got the show on the road. I called Joel and told him to contact a reputable seller of horseflesh and purchase enough horses for four riders (one for Wyoming, three for Montana) and the appropriate number of pack animals. All he could say was, "I don't know how you did it, but keep it coming!" Then I got on the telephone to Dick Branzell Sr., an SRA stationed in Reno. After exchanging pleasantries, I inquired about the professional merits of his son, who was also a Service special agent. Dick said he was green as a gourd, being so new to the Division of Law Enforcement, but he had been raised with a good work ethic, was developing fast, and could do any job placed before him. I had known Dick a long time and knew that when he said something, I could go to the bank with it. After thanking him, I wrote up a justification and contacted my personnel office to establish a new law enforcement position in Missoula, Montana.

I finished that chore in near record time, then called Special Agent Rick Branzell Jr. I knew Rick from my earlier teaching assignments at the Federal Law Enforcement Training Center and liked what I had seen from the very first time I had met him. Even though I had a hell of a load to carry with the rebuilding of my office staff, working without a deputy because mine had recently transferred to Washington, and all the other activity, I had still found time to teach at the Service's national academy. The teaching was a lot of hard work, but it gave me a chance to look over the crop of new officers, keeping the good ones in mind so that when I needed to fill a regional position, I had a real-time reference to draw from. Hence my association with young Mr. Branzell. He was about six feet tall and built like a block of granite. He was smart and, like his dad, had a good work ethic. He had a bit of a temper and impatience, which I liked as well. He would need a little of that temper as well as strong fiber in order to work in a new program with some pretty hard-headed Montana state officers. Finally, he was fearless, loyal, and strong as a bull and understood the field of law enforcement. I had found my man, a little grizzly, if you will. Now, if he would just accept my job offer.

Rick's familiar voice came over the line. "Afternoon, Rick, got a minute?" I asked.

"Terry, you old son of a gun, how you doing?"

"Very well, Rick, and you?"

"Fine as frog's hair," he responded in his comical way. "What's up?"

"I won't beat around the bush. I need you to come and work for me in Missoula, Montana."

The line went silent for a moment. Then Rick said, "When do you want me there?"

"I need you there in thirty days, or just as soon after that as possible."

"You got your man," he replied. "I'm on my way and will be there shortly."

"Great!" I exclaimed. "I will have the paperwork overnight-mailed to you, and you need to get in touch with my new administrative officer, Tami Bruhn, so she can steer you through the moving minefield."

"Not much to move," he replied. "I'm single, so I can move pretty fast."

"Welcome aboard, Rick. Bring your work boots, riding gear, and hog-leg because I have a tough one for you."

"We working Ephraim?" he asked.

"You got that right," I said, "and hard."

"See you when I get there," he replied, and with that, we hung up. Another thing I liked about the man. No fanfare, just the facts and move on. And moving on we were!

I got hold of my other two officers who would also be working the backcountry, afoot and on horseback: Jim Klett, a young officer stationed in Lander, Wyoming, and Rod Hanlon from Great Falls, Montana. They both barely knew what a horse was, much less how to ride one. However, they were excellent officers and "soldiers" and accepted their new assignment with aplomb. I advised the two of them to check with their backcountry state counterparts to find out the best kind of equipment to use on this kind of detail, then get that information to Joel for ordering purposes. I also let them know we were on a short leash, and I wanted my folks in the backcountry by late summer of 1983. They were in the backcountry protecting Ephraim by the end of that summer. At that time in their careers, Jim was one of the best investigators in the Service, and if Rod ever got on your trail, the only way to get him off would be to shoot him. Two very good men for one hell of a tough, dangerous assignment.

With logistical preparations under way, the real work began. As the information rolled in from the men in the field regarding equipment needs outside Joel's purchasing authority, I went to work with my new administrative officer. Tami was the same young fiscal clerk I had used early on to identify and solve the problems created by my previous administrative officer. She had been newly promoted to that position after her predecessor had lumbered on. You talk about a tough little half-pint! She was not much bigger than a small bug, but she was a Service brat possessing a detailed knowledge of the agency and its history. She was quick as a whip, understood the Service's administrative system, and was totally loyal to her boss and her agents. I only had to tell her anything once, and she would be off. Many times when I was without a second-in-command, I had to lean on her to assume some of those duties as well. She took on that responsibility without a complaint, and her work was always outstanding. In this case, she soon had three-quarter-ton, four-wheel-drive vehicles heading for the men in grizzly country to pull their horse trailers. State-of-the-art horse trailers, tents, saddles, heavy-caliber firearms for self-defense, optics that weren't forty years old, heavy-duty clothing, custom-made White Packer boots (to avoid turned ankles when dismounting), backcountry portable radios with some range for a change, bridles, cotton rope by the drum, and more followed at a whirlwind pace.

One day my little pistol of an administrative officer came into the office hotter than a firecracker. "What's up?" I said, looking up from a rather complex undercover case report.

"Those bastards!" she said.

"*Tami,*" I said, "you can't talk like that. If Dave heard you, you would get a swat right across your last part of the fence." Dave was her well-respected dad, who was in charge of a Service fish hatchery— God rest his soul.

That got a grin out of her and lessened the fire, but only just a little. "They took our money!" she exclaimed.

"What are you talking about?" I asked.

"Some bastard in Washington took $50,000 of our grizzly bear money, and I can't get his office to give it back."

"Settle down, young lady," I said. "Who took the money?"

To make a long story short, the Budget and Finance Office in Washington had taken the $50,000, claiming it was to pay for the administrative work to process the original $250,000 sent to the region. That is odd, I thought. My little Miss Tami is doing all the administrative work. Why does Washington have to steal one-fifth of the funding just for the few minutes' worth of work they had to do? I never saw that money again, and Amos couldn't get it back without busting a lot of chops. So we had to write it off as a damn good lesson for a still-learning special agent in charge on how to guard money in the future. Never again did I have any of my hard-won money siphoned off for such a miserable thieving excuse. It was a lesson Amos never forgot either! We had met the enemy, and he was one of us. Another sterling example of how little the senior Service leadership at that time cared about saving the grizzly bear ...

Administrative problems aside, grizzlies are at the top of the food chain, fearing nothing. They are at home in some of the wildest country in North America. Unfortunately, so are the Rocky Mountain elk, bighorn sheep, mule deer, and moose. These are some of the most sought-after big-game trophy animals in North America, not to mention some of the finest eating going. Let me tell you, there's nothing like moose steak heavily spiced with Greek seasoning, cooking slowly over coals from an open campfire in a cast-iron skillet, with sliced potatoes, onions, green pepper, and fresh garlic cooking away in another large skillet, biscuits browning in a Dutch oven, and a peach cobbler going in another Dutch oven. (Let me assure you, there were many such cooks in the high country, and my region held the best in the United States! In fact my previous regional director, Ralph Morgenweck, used to tease me by telling others in the Service directorate that I wouldn't hire agents who couldn't cook.) Throw in the high-mountain coolness, the clean air, and a hard but successful day afoot or on horseback, and being met with the smell of that kind of cooking as you enter camp, and you know for sure you are experiencing a bit of heaven on earth.

Every fall thousands of hunters, along with their guides and outfitters, invaded the homes of the grizzly. Many of these invaders kept dirty camps with horse feed or human food (or both) scattered about where a hungry grizzly needing to load up with winter grits could find it and eat to his hearts content. That is, until a 250-grain .338 slug ripped through his towering frame and put an end to the feast! It is only natural for the great bear to try to put every ounce of food into his boiler so he can make it through winter hibernation, so it was no wonder those camps were considered prime habitat for an Ephraim habituated to such culinary experiences. That made them prime illegal killing fields for outfitters too damn lazy to run a clean camp!

Additionally, many bears over the years had become habituated to move toward the sound of shooting with so many hunters in the backcountry. Many times this pursuit provided the hungry bruin with a warm gut pile or a cooling carcass of a large elk, deer, bighorn sheep, mountain goat, or moose. Last but not least, with that many people roaming around in the backcountry, it was not uncommon to roust a bear from its daybed or from a fresh kill, or to surprise mama with her cubs. When that happened, a recipe for disaster was likely to be whipped up immediately. This was bear country, pure and simple. A man couldn't forget that fact for a New York minute if he wanted to avoid a scarred, shattered life or even death.

Realizing I needed lots of manpower to put my play into production, I called my state and federal law enforcement counterparts in Idaho, Montana, and Wyoming to an important meeting. This must have surprised them because the Service's Division of Law Enforcement had heretofore been a nonentity in grizzly backcountry enforcement. I invited all the National Park Service chiefs of law enforcement whose areas held the great bear to the same meeting. I discovered this gesture had raised the hair on the hind ends of some of the state folks, who considered Park agents to be just as bad as Service agents. I also invited all the folks from the National Forests who had their Level IV law enforcement officers working backcountry where grizzly bears lived.

Slowly the contents of the grizzly bear pot were beginning to simmer and thicken like a good gumbo. I had just about everyone popping their lips like a grizzly in a daybed and looking at each other like a bunch of African meerkats. It was downright amazing how armed, badge-carrying adult males could "woof" at each other when one stepped into another's piss puddle! What right did the Forest Service have at such a meeting? They didn't have any authority to enforce state or federal bear regulations and were too damned scared of their shadows to do so anyway. Why was the Park Service invited to a grizzly bear meeting? All they did was chase "bumpers" within the park and had no authority outside the park's boundaries. If all the state conservation organizations had done their jobs the right way in the first place, we wouldn't be in this mess with the bear. Truth be told, all they did was drink whiskey, chase skirts, make Dutch-oven biscuits, and sing cowboy songs! And what was the Fish and Wildlife Service doing? They were a collection of airheads with no hair on their asses who had no backcountry experience or presence. They were afraid of the dark, had pea-sized *cojones,* and were broke all the time. ... And so it went. As the day of my "pissing party" got closer, everybody got more and more territorial, digging in to protect their respective pieces of turf and pissing on every stump in the forest. In that part of the West, that was a lot of stumps!

After setting up the meeting at the Irma Hotel in Cody, Wyoming, Buffalo Bill's old establishment, I was ready to let her rip. I figured we might as well meet in the heart of bear country and in a building that was steeped in history. After all, with a little luck, we could be making history ourselves if the good Lord took a liking to us. Also, I mistakenly thought that at that historical location, the lads wouldn't have as many burrs under their saddles, knots in their throwing ropes, or deeper-than-normal creases in their stylish Montana Peak cowboy hats. Again, I was to be proved dead wrong and to learn a valuable lesson in the process. Protecting a species from extinction is never a simple task. It comes from the combination of many parts, hearts, minds, and souls, including some possessing oil-and-water bases, if you get my drift. ...

Come the day, I had a conference room in the Irma Hotel packed with the major actors from all the entities, all wondering what the hell the Fish and Wildlife Service was doing in their world. Walking into that room was a real treat. I didn't know most of these folks, nor they me. I represented a wing of government held in low regard by the states-rights-conscious folks, and certainly not in high regard by the get-the-tree-off-the-stump boys from the Forest Service. Last but not least, there sat the Park Service, an elite bunch in their own thinking. Many of them mistakenly figured that their authority and abilities allowed them to go anywhere and do anything. They didn't think they needed anyone else in the saddle to get the job done. I was sure they were trying to figure out what I had in mind and how they fit in, since they controlled the parks and no one else would be allowed in. You could just feel the electricity in the room as I entered, feeling every eye in the place on my carcass like a bunch of robins eyeing a large worm.

I started the meeting off with an introduction of myself as the new special agent in charge for the Service in the Rocky Mountain region. Swinging right into the history of our mutual enforcement problems, I outlined what I thought were the past and present issues and collective hopes for the future. Woven into that part of the presentation were the latest statistics on the rising grizzly bear mortality rate. I spoke frankly about the Service's extreme shortcomings in the field of grizzly bear enforcement, historically and currently, and then covered the particulars of the Endangered Species Act. I discussed the number of backcountry users and how it was rising every year, with bear-kill figures going up proportionately. By then you could have heard a mallard feather hit the old, well-worn wooden floor. Every set of eyes was on me, and many set jaws were jutting forward as well, especially after the implication in the statistics that what had historically been considered effective in the enforcement arena was suspect in light of the growth pattern of human users and increasing bear deaths.

Switching gears, I outlined my optimistic enforcement philosophy, which emphasized the cooperative work of all entities with an interest in wildlife conservation specifically as it related to Ephraim. Hardly anyone moved except to shovel more Beechnut, Redman, or Copenhagen into their tight-lipped mouths as they maintained their physical distance from each other. However, it was apparent that the chaps were going to respect my time on the floor and reserve judgment until I had had my say.

Then I directly and intentionally stepped into the morass of grizzly bear law enforcement. I pointed out that what we had been doing to date to protect the bear had more or less failed. The kill figures attested to that fact. I stood looking at the tough, leather-skinned, bronzed and sunburned sons of bitches assembled in the room for a few moments for effect. Man, that statement put a lot of backs straight up in their chairs, especially those of the "cowboys" from the various state fish and game agencies. I went on to say that continuing in our losing ways would guarantee the loss of the bear from our current ecosystems, including the national parks. Now there wasn't a sound in the room. It was so quiet that you could have heard a mouse pissing on a ball of cotton. I said, "Gentlemen, I have a far-reaching proposal for your consideration. I have based that proposal on every bit of information I have been able to glean from anyone who would talk to me about the backcountry in the last two years—its problems, its personalities, and the bears. I may not be a cowboy in the true sense of the word, but I am not totally unfamiliar with the ways of the backcountry. And I am a good wildlife law enforcement officer or I wouldn't be standing here in front of the professionals who carried on the backcountry programs to date with a proposal daring to try something else." I could hear my own heartbeat and feel the animosity oozing from a few corners of the room at this indirect criticism of a bunch of hardened veterans. In their eyes, I hadn't experienced a whit of their trials in the saddle. And they were right.

"Part one of my proposal involves using my Service authority to cross-credential every Park Service officer who rides the backcountry on grizzly patrols and successfully qualifies with one year or more of law enforcement service carrying a badge in their agency." There was a discernible ripple of movement across the room and hushed voices discussing the magnitude of what I had said. No one had ever before done this kind of thing in the United States—and I was just getting warmed up. Such an administrative move would give the Park Service officers the same enforcement authority, *off the park,* that my officers carried. Whooo-ee, that turned some heads, not to mention tightened a lot of hind ends! I could practically see the piss puddles increasing in size and number. All the while I was speaking, I was watching my seasoned officers for their reactions. There had been none so far, so I felt I was still in the ball game. I continued, "Next, I would like to make sure all the states represented here today ensure that their officers are currently cross-credentialed under Service authorities." More ripples slipped across many faces in the room like a slight breeze on the prairie moving across the big bluestem grasses. "Then," I continued, "I would like to do the same with the Forest Service officers who qualify for such cross-credentialing." Man, that ripped it! I could see hurried, hushed conversations beginning in every corner of the room. Cross-credentialing those lads in the Forest Service was totally unheard of. I could already picture many high-ranking, anti–law enforcement members in the Forest Service killing that offer. There was no way they were going to stick their necks out that way, bear or no bear.

Now came the tough part, and since I was already in manure over the tops of my boots, I decided to let the remaining shoe drop. "Looking throughout the region, I see many of you on backcountry patrols that, in the overall picture, do little to help the bear population. Individually or in small groups, we are too little too late. Additionally, when you are in the backcountry, some of you see Forest Service violations and do little or nothing about it. Many of you in federal service see state fish and game violations and look the other way because you don't get along with the state or don't want to get involved because you don't carry state credentials. Some of you state officers see violations that should be handled in federal court yet handle them in state court, thereby adding another rock in your box because you miss an opportunity to jerk these killers up by their stacking swivels. Cross-credentialing will help eliminate most of those excuses."

I had stepped on quite a few toes at that point, but I figured we had to hit the bottom in order to start back up, and we were there. "I think we can do better. I would like to propose that subsequent to the cross-credentialing program, we form backcountry patrol teams of mixed agencies. Then, using Forest Service–supplied information about the licensed outfitter locations and the information our biologists have on the location of the bears, insert these teams into our worst problem areas. In essence, we'll be starting a massive contact program with backcountry users. As an educational program, I suggest we contact every hunting camp, because that is where most of the illegal killing is currently occurring, and make sure the hunters understand the laws of the land and life history of the bear. Their responsibility starts with a clean camp, and the users must understand in no uncertain terms that if a grizzly bear is killed, its death will be investigated just like a homicide. In short, if a bear does not have powder burns on its hide, someone is going to court. That system of contacts will also go for all those we run across individually hunting or recreating outside the outfitter's camps."

I went on, "By organizing and collectively putting many teams into a managed and planned operation, we can cover every major hunting camp in grizzly country. Those folks will be hesitant to do any wrong, knowing you lads might be just over the next hill. This kind of saturation in the backcountry need not go on all year but just during the weeks prior to hunting season when the camps are being established, and through the season until the bears go into hibernation. Last but not least, I propose that we all work to support the Forest Service in coming up with backcountry regulations regarding clean camps, and through our joint enforcement efforts support the Forest Service by strongly enforcing any such regulations. If we do that, I can see the bear expanding his range some day and becoming a problem because of his increasing numbers as he moves into the frontcountry. But for now, through our joint efforts, we need to get the bear on the road to recovery. Well, gentlemen, I have said enough. It is open for discussion."

For about a minute there wasn't a question, just a lot of quiet discussion. Then a slightly built young man rose from a trio of Wyoming game wardens at a table toward the front of the room and said, "You don't have any kind of idea what goes on in the backcountry on these horseback patrols, do you? What do you think this is, biscuits and cowboy songs? We aren't interested in joining any mixed teams who will just bumble around in the backcountry wasting our time. Plain and simply, we will continue to work among ourselves in the back-country doing the job as we know it needs doing." The room grew silent in embarrassment over the strong words and frankly expressed feelings. With that, the two other officers got up and the Wyoming trio walked dramatically out of the room.

Damn, I thought. I really needed those three officers from Wyoming because the backcountry area they routinely worked was of extreme importance to the proposed new program and the bear's survival. Those three worked the area hard, but I still could see benefits from the team concept in that microecosystem. Those three officers, whom I had never officially met, were well respected by the law enforcement community. To lose them before the program even got started really hurt, but I wasn't about to give up just because they had defended their ground. Hoping I wouldn't have a mass exodus, I held my breath.

Then, as if someone had thrown open a switch, the room broke into excited conversation with questions on cross-credentialing, when would we start, how would we report our activities, how would we share our equipment, how would we get some of the hard-nosed supervisors in the Forest Service to go along with the idea, could the Service help fund per diem costs if the Park Service joined in without funding, and so on. For the next three hours there was a lot of discussion, getting to know each other, setting up the cross-credentialing process, and working out other details. By the end of the day, I was spent. My brain felt as if it had been fried, there were so many questions and problems without solutions. But throughout the discussions were liberally sprinkled with enthusiasm. Best of all, hope and acceptance from a multitude of damn fine officers was the word of the day. Don't get me wrong—not everyone was on my horse, but many were, and the others were sure as hell looking at it! The young Wyoming game warden who had spoken his piece had been right. This wasn't biscuits and cowboy songs. In fact, it had the makings of a real bitch, almost like keeping a handful of mercury from leaking through your fingers! But it had potential as a start toward working together in saving a very precious piece of heritage that was all but gone in the lower forty-eight.

For the rest of that summer I lived on the road, meeting with other agency supervisors, working out backcountry patrol plans, resolving equipment- and horse-sharing issues, providing per diem for some officers whose agencies would not pay for their travel expenses on grizzly patrols, making friends with those in support of the idea, and leaning on those against it. By that fall, many hurdles had been overcome or were in the process of being worked out. Even at that late date, not everyone had bought in, but by and large the show was on the road.

Several weeks before hunting season, many of the teams ventured forth for the first time, and man, were the backcountry users surprised. A fair number of folks were apprehended breaking various state or federal laws, and sometimes when someone fired a gun at night, the teams camping a short distance away saddled up and shortly thereafter showed up in the camp where the shot had come from. You talk about a surprised camp! Soon the word began to spread. Then came our first really big challenge. Rogue bears habituated to camp food would come marauding. They had learned that there were good grits in such places and were not inclined to be scared off. This behavior of course created a dangerous situation for all involved. Instead of shooting the bear as in times past, because they were fearful of the backcountry riders as never before, outfitters began to say, "All right, you guys don't want us to shoot the bears, come and get your goddamned bear." With help from biologists from the respective agencies and the Service's Animal Damage Control Division, many of the problem bears were quickly moved. The guides couldn't believe the service they were experiencing. The team concept along with a liberal use of common sense among the partners began paying big dividends. The most important dividend was that the bear was slowly beginning its long trek back from the brink of extinction.

Among the new believers in our system of backcountry user contacts were the federal courts and attorneys. By informing everyone about the Endangered Species Act, we educated the backcountry users regarding the law and their personal responsibility. Also, the courts were impressed with the serious efforts being made by our moving the problem bears when we could. The courts' handling of our bear-killing cases took a turn for the better, except in Montana (where the traditional Western thinking that a man can protect his property at any cost still pervades many juries' thinking).

As the teams moved more and more throughout the backcountry, you could almost see a mental change taking place among the outfitters, guides, hunters—and even the riders! The users were now trying to avoid conflicts with the bear by keeping cleaner camps and taking more thoughtful care of their game. In addition, many more folks seemed to better understand what was required of them in order to avoid crossing swords with the bear and its protectors.

Don't get me wrong, we still had bear killers on the prod, and we investigated them to the fullest extent of the law, even to the point of bringing in metal detectors to locate spent bullets and cartridges at the crime scenes. Soon the word was out big time: don't shoot a grizzly unless you have to! We saw the old "shoot, shovel, and shut up" philosophy starting to wane. It didn't disappear, but it became less and less of a byword or normal thought process. It was just too risky to continue with the old outlaw ways. There were still a million bugs in the system of equipment supply and personalities, but, the program seemed to be working better than I had ever imagined, in large part due to the resolve, talent, and professionalism of the backcountry riders, biologists, and folks from the old Animal Damage Control Division.

At the end of each patrol, team leaders would send me a uniform report on where they had ridden, what they had found, number of contacts made, evaluation of attitudes of the users, and the like. They also recorded the hours spent on patrol. When the snow finally flew in sufficient quantities at the end of the first year to send the bears to bed, I gathered up the patrol sheets and began looking through them for any information I might use to strengthen future operations and see how the program was working. In that first year, over 7,600 hours were spent in the saddle in the effort to educate humans and keep the bear from lethal encounters! *I could not believe it!* To have that kind of dedication shown in black and white, not to mention in sweat and hard work, was nothing short of remarkable! We still had lots of holes in the areas covered and many disbelievers in the ranks, but here was proof that many had overcome their personal or professional dislikes to work together for the good of the bear and the American people. Let me tell you, in the face of all the problems, that was a real tribute to those officers, biologists, and Animal Damage Control folks. Against all odds, they were making it work, and the great bear began to step back from the brink of extinction! The bear mortality figures provided by Service biologists showed that the kill figures were reduced after only one season in the new program. The next spring, according to these figures, we had a few more breeding female bears than in the previous years.

The summer of the second year, several people who had adamantly opposed the program either retired or were moved to Washington, D.C., or other places, and with even more teamwork-oriented replacements, the backcountry patrol concept gathered steam. Several of the Forest districts were now looking down the road at the possibility of regulations for bear-proofing camps.

That fall the riders went back and discovered that just about all the backcountry users were aware of the program, and many of those users now grudgingly supported it. They had begun to realize the value of the grizzly as a key component and representative of pristine wilderness. With that mind-set change, many began working to avoid conflicts between their camps, hunters or hunting programs, and the bear. We still had the hard cases, but the riders reported in their patrol documents that an evolution in thinking was taking place. It was now possible to see that people using the backcountry had a different opinion of the bear, its place in history, and the part they and it played in the ecosystem. That fall, due in large part to the obvious attitude change among the users, only—I say *only*— 5,600 hours were spent in the backcountry by the horseback riders, and again, the bear mortality rate continued sliding downward.

Needless to say, Amos Eno was beside himself with joy at the successful grizzly bear program. The next year of the patrols, only 3,400 backcountry hours were needed because of the previous years' educational efforts and if I am not mistaken, that year the illegal kills of the grizzly in the Yellowstone ecosystem reached *zero*! Those guys breaking their backs and hind ends in the saddle, rain, snow, or shine, hour after hour, with little or no sleep and certainly no biscuits and cowboy songs, had done it! I knew we would do well, but reaching zero mortality in such a short time was a tribute to the lads working in the program to use that wildlife management tool called law enforcement.

Then, as I saw it (through an admittedly narrowed and less than circumspect set of eyes), many of the very high bigwigs who had had little or nothing to do with the effort other than occasionally interacting with one another in high-level meetings, began to take credit for parts of the program's successes as their own handiwork. Don't get me wrong—there were a lot of chiefs who had made the program successful through their support of their backcountry riders. And there were others who supported the initiation and implementation of backcountry regulations to clean up the camps. But as is always the case in politics, the bandwagon was soon carrying a load of "pretenders." I noticed none of the men who had quietly and without fanfare done all the fine hard work on the ground and in the saddle getting on *that* bandwagon. They remained apart from this circus in the making, doing their jobs and ignoring the high chiefs clawing all over themselves to get some of the credit their riders had made possible. I just shook my head and walked away from that frogpile and its amplexus.

The next year, as was Service policy, any money generated outside the scheme of the normal law enforcement budget process (such as our $200,000), was absorbed within the entire law enforcement budget and then dispensed equally across the nation on a per-agent funding basis. This meant that I lost my fiscal power to continue the backcountry patrol at the needed levels. It was also one of those years when the Service also failed to give the Division of Law Enforcement much coin of the realm for anything. With that loss of funding, the backcountry efforts began to diminish, as did the number of high chiefs in the frogpile. As a result, I had to reduce our patrol efforts by over 90 percent. Amos got busy with other, more pressing environmental matters, and so did we. When we backed off supporting the program, thereby losing contact with our counterparts, they backed off to a degree as well. I guess they figured it was our bear, and if we were not interested in it, why should they be? Not that they stopped their efforts, but overall, efforts were not at the levels of the program's heyday. Slowly the illegal kill figures started to rise above the zero figure, but the situation wasn't as bad as it been in the past. It seemed that the bear got a breather through the education the officers had spread around to the backcountry users, which helped reduce the killing frenzy. Many users backed off from using a high-speed bullet in exchange for compliance with new Forest Service regulations regarding clean camps. In short, a terrible period of time seemed to have passed as the backcountry user grew up and began accepting the bear as part of the ecosystem, thanks to the tireless efforts of officers working the backcountry afoot and on horseback. Because of their increased numbers, the bears began to migrate into the frontcountry as the Forest Service forged ahead into the twenty-first century with new regulations regarding clean camps and bear-proof food containers. The Forest Service stepped forward, looked down the road, did the right thing, and is to be congratulated for these changes.

Aldo Leopold, long considered the father of modern wildlife management, espoused five main tools to be utilized within the wildlife management arena. One of those tools was law enforcement. It was not considered better or worse than the other tools, but it is one very strong reason that the grizzly bear is as healthy as it can be in light of the presence of humankind and all the ecosystem changes in the lower forty-eight states today. The constant presence of those officers over a three-year period, with law enforcement refreshers still going on today, got the message through to the backcountry users, in effect changing the way that they interacted with the great bear. With the inception of the U.S. Forest Service's timely backcountry regulations mandating clean camps and the use of bear-proof containers, the bear took a further step back from the brink of extinction. The vigorous investigations conducted by the Service and its counterparts into any illegal bear killings had a sobering effect on those inclined to foolishly pull the trigger. The National Wildlife Forensic Laboratory and state forensic laboratories brought to bear-killing investigations forensic tools that were rock solid in any court of law. And last but not least, the courts began taking judicial notice in matters of illegal take, and many of those inclined to run the risk of illegal killing are finding that road to be a rocky one. As a result of these changes and the constant application of the best possible bear biology from the states, Forest Service, National Park Service, tribes, and the Fish and Wildlife Service, it is safe to carefully say that *the bear is back*. In fact, there are now grizzlies in locations where they have not been seen for the past fifty to seventy-five years! Today, as I predicted at that meeting so long ago, we seem to have more bears and bear problems in the front-country mountain towns and fields. It's not like it was in the days of old, but none of us can reclaim our youth either. This too is a tribute to those men of iron who took a chance and made a radical new program work. They can claim credit for bringing the great bear back to where it is today, for those yet to come to see, fear, and yet enjoy. To their credit, those officers and agencies continue today with modified bear programs, working the bear further and further away from that black hole of extinction. Come to think of it, they are doing the same for humankind.

There is another man, tiny in frame but huge in stature and know-how in moving political mountains, who stands tall in saving the bear. Amos Eno has quietly moved on to other things in life, but he has to smile at some of his greatest accomplishments, one of which was saving Ephraim. Without his push, the mountain would never have come to Mohammed.

As a footnote, that young cowboy and Wyoming game warden named Tim Fagan who talked about biscuits and cowboy songs before he walked out of that meeting so long ago has mellowed since then—not a lot, mind you, but some. Recently he sent me a Christmas card, and it seems he is now riding with the Cody special agent, Tim Eicher, in the backcountry, making sure Ephraim is managing to hold his own in their neck of the wilderness. My guess is it is more to keep Tim out of trouble than anything else. Those joint rides include keeping a sharp eye on the gray wolf, a recent problematic introduction into the same ecosystem, as well.

Here again, old habits die hard, and the wolf like the bear is struggling to survive through the natural and unnatural at the hand of humans. However, if the killing gets bad, there is a backcountry patrol plan that may work again if everyone can get together, stop pissing on the stumps, and mash their collective asses into the saddles.

Knowing Tim Eicher and Tim Fagan the way I do, I doubt either of them are singing cowboy songs while they are riding together because neither one could carry a tune in a bucket if he had to. But I know one of them does in fact make good biscuits.

As for the great bear, and now the wolf, only time and changing attitudes will tell. But I would make one suggestion to any backcountry user who may be reading these lines: don't kill a bear or wolf in either Tim Eicher's or Tim Fagan's district unless you want to pay the price.

I too have mellowed over the years, all the while cherishing the relationships I developed during some damn hard times. I pray that Ephraim and his maker have taken notice of those hardships and the men who worked through adversity to protect that unique bit of our nation's heritage. But Lord, next time you give me a double barrel of Ephraim in the office and the outback, please give me a broader set of shoulders to carry the load!

two

Teal Hunting in Colorado—An Excuse for "Open Season"

THERE ARE THREE SPECIES of North American teal (ducks) commonly found in the United States. The blue-winged teal is the largest of the three and primarily a prairie-nesting species. The uniquely colored, less common northern cinnamon teal is primarily a western species, and the green-winged teal is national in distribution and the smallest of the three, weighing only about ten ounces. Being the smallest "puddle ducks" of the North American waterfowl and the most susceptible to cold weather, they are one of the first to migrate south in the fall. In fact, it is common to find the blue-winged and northern cinnamon teal wintering in Central and South America long before Old Man Winter roars forth from the lands beyond the north wind.

With the exception of a small number of green-winged teal, the greatest numbers of these species have already migrated south before the nation's general waterfowl hunting season commences. Because these early migrations represent a loss of hunting opportunity, the sportsmen and their respective fish and game departments some years ago petitioned the Fish and Wildlife Service for teal seasons that would occur prior to the general waterfowl hunting season. With provisions for special seasons allowed under the controlling statutes of the Migratory Bird Treaty Act and being strongly supported biologically, the Service agreed to the requests and authorized a special season providing for the harvest of these little, fast-flying species of waterfowl, which make for excellent eating.

This is where the "Goodie Two Shoes" portion of this story ends. Historically, almost all of those partaking in the sport of hunting waterfowl in North America have had a very difficult time identifying in the air or in the hand the fifty-plus species of ducks, geese, and swans commonly frequenting the United States. Hell, not only the hunting community but many county, state, tribal, provincial, and federal conservation officers have great difficulty identifying such species, especially when the birds are in their eclipse phases (molting) or juvenile plumage. That problem is even worse in regard to the identification of the females of such species as mallard, northern pintail, wigeon, scaup, gadwall, redhead, and canvasback. Problematic identification is the fundamental flaw in allowing a special early hunting season for a particular species. To be truly candid, the entire sport of hunting waterfowl (whose identification accuracy is mandated by law) is fatally flawed for the same reason. Most American hunters do not take the time to educate themselves about the different waterfowl species they are pursuing—those unique life histories and the traits that would allow them to identify a bird not only in the hand but also in the air. Hunters wait all year for the special waterfowl season to commence. As that hallowed opening day draws near, they find themselves at sporting goods stores purchasing new types of ammunition, perhaps a new shotgun, and the proper licenses and duck stamps; putting the final touches on the training of their dogs; leasing hunting areas; scouting out the hunting prospects; "brushing" up their blinds; purchasing the latest decoys, duck and goose calls from Cabela's, and the latest mechanical decoys that actually move; and in most cases not doing a lick of work to sharpen their skills in waterfowl identification. Yet waterfowl hunting regulations are species specific. To go outside those guidelines is to violate state *and* federal conservation laws.

The birds' speed in flight is a complicating factor. Many times a hunter has but a few seconds to identify birds as they whiz by at dizzying speeds over decoys or overhead. Fog, rain, reduced light, snow, and high winds provide additional identification challenges. Last but certainly not least are the shooting hours. The laws generally allow waterfowl hunters to take such species from a half hour before sunrise to sunset. Now, think about that. You're out in a blind or in a pass-by shooting area, it is still semidark, and the birds are plowing along at speeds of forty-five to fifty-five miles per hour. Add more than fifty species to choose from, many of which are still undergoing plumage changes at that time of the year, which means that many appear to all intents and purposes as indistinguishable gray or brown ducks. Add into that pot of confusion the hunters hurriedly trying to identify the species speeding into view while making the mental calculations and adjustments necessary to bring the critters down with their short-range shotguns. As you can see, the possible makings for a real illegal "hoorah" are now front and center. Now throw into this concoction what I call "zorks"—all those other forms of water and shore birds that under the right conditions can closely resemble the waterfowl species hunters are trying to lawfully harvest. For the most part, such birds have been totally protected by the Migratory Bird Treaty Act since 1918! Even non–waterfowl hunters can understand the problem. And it doesn't end there! Once you have the bird in hand, how do you tell exactly what you have? If the bird is a juvenile or still molting, wet and bedraggled, or recently mauled by your hard-mouthed dog, identification can be difficult, but you had better know what the hell you have in the bag lest the friendly game warden sauntering by discovers an illegal kill and presents you with an unwelcome citation (that is, assuming he or she happens to know the identity of whatever the hell you killed). And the beat goes on. ...

It's truly amazing how many thousands of waterfowl hunters whom I checked over my thirty-two years of wildlife law enforcement across the nation, when asked what kind of ducks they had in their bags, responded with something like, "I have four gray ducks and two brown ducks." To be fair, many hunters know the ubiquitous mallard drake, northern pintail drake, and northern shoveler with its oddball bill. However, for the brown females, birds in various stages of plumage change, or the less common diving ducks, it is almost always a guessing game. Over the years I wrote several thousand citations for taking restricted species to hunters who didn't have a clue to the identification of a critter they had killed. Sadly, most of those citations were for totally restricted species such as canvasbacks, redheads, wood ducks, hooded mergansers, or females of many species (states often restrict the taking of females because they are the waterfowl population's brood stock and future).

Again, not all hunters are of this ilk. Many make an effort to learn at least the local species of ducks and geese and to shoot only those they can positively identify. Many duck clubs make a huge effort to restrict the shooting of females or restricted species by financially penalizing their members who kill them ("twenty-dollar birds" they are called in some circles). And thank Heaven, there are a number of parents and older siblings continuing to teach younger hunters the right way to enjoy their sport through better identification and understanding of the species. However, if my experience working in many of the finest waterfowl shooting areas in the nation is any indicator, the American hunter has a long way to go in the arena of duck identification.

Remember that I was one of only about ten thousand county, state, tribal, provincial, and federal conservation officers in *all* of North America. Think about that! Only ten thousand wildlife officers of every ilk for over 350 million people, of whom a substantial number are outdoor recreationists. Suffice it to say, Custer had better odds than the critters. ... During the course of my career I easily checked more than ten thousand waterfowl sportsmen in all types of conditions, locations, and occasions. Sadly, I encountered *only nine* waterfowl hunters during that period who *really knew their birds through sound and accurate waterfowl identification procedures!* I'm sure some readers are thinking, "Yeah, right! I'm sure Terry remembers that only nine sportsmen really knew their ducks out of all those thousands of hunters he contacted." Well, believe it. I was trained academically in waterfowl identification and wildlife management by some of the finest professors WHO ever instructed at the college level—Drs. Stan "Leather Tie" Harris, Rich "Always Swam Upstream" Ridenhour, Archie "He Who Ran Faster Than His Whippets" Mossman, and Chuck "Easygoing" Yocom, just to mention a few. I attended one of the finest applied wildlife science institutions of its kind, Humboldt State College in Arcata, California. During the years following graduation, I prided myself on my waterfowl identification skills and took time to teach that science in colleges and to state and federal wildlife law enforcement institutions for over twenty-seven years. So believe it or not, I made it a point to remember excellence in the field in waterfowl identification. Three of those nine knowledgeable folks were young boys hunting with their dads, who were teaching them the right way to enjoy their sport. I checked one of those lads in the marshes of Utah, one at a roadblock in Wyoming, and one on the Butte Creek Gun Club in California. Of the adults who really knew their waterfowl identification, I wrote multiple citations to one in a Utah marsh for carrying 59 lead shot in a steel-shot zone and possessing an unplugged shotgun (i.e., a gun capable of firing more than three shots). That occasion was witnessed by Utah Fish and Game Officer Larry Davis. I met the remaining five adults in California. It quickly became obvious in my discussions with those chaps over exceeding their bag limits that they were well versed in waterfowl identification. I ended up writing *all* of those knowing chaps citations for unplugged shotguns and for taking or possessing over-limits of waterfowl. Those five occasions were witnessed by Deputy U.S. Game Management Agent Tim Dennis from Maxwell. Any further doubts?

Don't get me wrong; I fully support the sport of hunting waterfowl. For years it was my own one true love in the hunting arena. If my worn-out knees would let me, I would still be in the marshes enjoying the king of sports. However, doing it right takes dedicated work in waterfowl identification; it also takes great control and a real spirit of conservation. The heart of the sport is the opportunity to go and enjoy nature at its best, and if you get anything, it is a bonus. That's why they call it "hunting," not "killing."

"Stomp the Son-of-a-Bitch"

THE SMELL OF a freshly plowed field rose up to meet me as I trudged my way through the rows of recently tilled earth. Pausing, I glanced eastward but saw only the continuing dark of early morning. I turned back and labored onward, loosening the zipper on my camouflage hunting coat to avoid breaking into a heavy sweat. Another hundred yards of hard walking brought me in sight of a darkened mound in the middle of the field. As I paused again to rest quietly, I became aware of a soft breeze out of the west and the sounds of whistling wings overhead heading toward some ponds a hundred yards away. A smile came to my face at these signs of another good day to come. I moved on and finally arrived at my destination, a large stack of hay bales in the middle of a freshly plowed alfalfa field. I circled it until I found a break in the tight stacking, then climbed to the top, laid down my gear on the edge nearest a farm road to the northeast, and began the work at hand. At first removing the tightly stacked bales was hard, but after the first two, I was off and running. My plan was to build a hiding place in the hay stack from which I could observe several ponds to the north. I stacked the bales I had removed along the front and sides of my "hidey-hole" so I could sit on one bale in the hole and look between those placed along the front and sides without chance of discovery. My hiding place was now complete. From all sides, the stack of hay appeared to be just that. Anyone driving along the farm roads around my position would not notice anything out of the ordinary, yet I had a commanding view of the ponds in question. Reaching into my "possibles" sack, I removed my Leupold Zoom 60 spotting scope and 7 × 50 binoculars, laying them within easy reach. Alongside those tools of the trade I laid my notebook, a bottle of water, and an Italian hard salami that I considered good game warden's breakfast fare. However, if I had been with one of my officers, Agent Leo Suazo, that idea would have changed to the breakfast burritos made by his loving wife, Janell. Boy, let me tell you, that little woman can cook. (For the record, she really *is* tiny — about the size of a teal, now that I think about it.) I would give up my time-proven Italian salami for her burritos in a heartbeat.

I was west of Fort Lupton, Colorado, and it was the first day of the early teal season. For several weeks I had been scouting north of Denver, checking all the likely-looking bodies of water for the presence of teal. Now, Colorado isn't what I would call a really great duck-hunting state compared to Texas, California, Maryland, or Mississippi. But if you know where to look, have an "in" with a land-owner, or purchase hunting rights on some of the major bodies of water, you can do all right. In my wanderings during those last few days before teal season, I had located about half a dozen likely areas containing many small flocks of teal. Most were blue- and green-winged teal, with only the occasional cinnamon, in large enough numbers that if I could find them, others could as well. The area I was now staking out was the best of the lot. It consisted of three small ponds, with a wealth of the type of vegetation, loaded with mature seed heads, preferred by teal. It harbored about a hundred teal at any given moment. In fact, it almost seemed to be a minor staging area where the birds gathered to fatten up before continuing their southward migration. On two of the occasions that I had checked out this area, I had noticed an old, beat-up Ford pickup that had been painted in patches of natural colors as a form of camouflage. There had been a large, heavy-set, bearded fellow behind the wheel and another older fellow with him. They seemed very interested in my teal ponds, and I couldn't help but believe I would see them again once the shooting started. Each time I saw them, I pretended to be just another local and quickly left the area—but not before spying my haystack. I discovered a hiding place for my patrol truck by an abandoned farmhouse not far from the haystack, and my plan was complete.

Headlights announcing the arrival of two vehicles at the locked gate by my ponds quickly brought me back from my daydreaming. Both drivers turned off their headlights, and soon I could hear the chain holding the lock being pulled free. The two vehicles, still without lights, drifted quietly through the gate like a couple of ghosts on a mission. The sound of the chain being pulled back through the gates told me to expect locked access if I wanted to enter the same way. A smile crossed my face as I remembered my "master key," a set of bolt cutters in the patrol truck parked about half a mile away. Federal conservation officers, or state conservation officers cross-credentialed as deputy federal officers, when faced with probable cause that hunting of migratory game birds is occurring behind locked gates, are allowed to use devices such as pick sets or bolt cutters to enter those lands without a warrant. The government is liable for any damages those officers cause, but by careful cutting I could limit that liability to just one link of chain. ... Officers of the law will usually just use "shank's mare," walking in to settle the issue. However when speed is of the essence, to avoid the culprits' escape or destruction of evidence, out come the bolt cutters or other tools of the trade, and bad guys, grab your last part over the fence! Remember that wildlife dies without making a sound. The only voice it has is yours and that of the conservation officer. If those human voices aren't squalling like smashed cats, then they are part of the problem.

Soon, with the light of the oncoming day filling my high-light-gathering binoculars, I observed three dark shapes walking to the one duck blind located on the middle pond. Not a bad position, I thought. That pond held the most ducks, and was the one birds flew back and forth over to get to the other two ponds. Soon the air was full of whistling wings and the high-pitched fluting calls of teal disturbed from their resting place on the ponds. There were also recognizable calls from mallards, northern pintail, and American wigeon as well as the low, croaking calls of the gadwall. Hunting season had yet to open for those species. I could hear the swishing sounds of the flocks passing overhead, punctuated by the occasional slapping of colliding wings. I watched the birds as they flew around for a few moments in confusion before silently and purposefully dipping to drop back into the ponds they had just vacated. *Boom-boom—boom-boom-boom— boom-boom* went seven quick shots announced by flame from the muzzles of three shotguns. A roar of wings announced hundreds of confused, milling duck bodies quickly filling the air. *Boom-boom- boom—boom-boom* went five more quick shots, bringing even more confusion to the fleeing waterfowl. Over the next fifteen minutes, I heard twenty-three more shots as I watched thirteen ducks fold and drop like sinkers into the pond area holding decoys. Thirty-five shots fired, and I had yet to identify *a single bird!* It was still too dark to identify what had fallen, and that was with my master's degree in wildlife management and many years of teaching waterfowl identification at the national academy, not to mention hundreds of hours in the field observing the critters in flight ... Damn, I found myself cursing this half-hour-before-sunrise allowance of shooting through clenched teeth! When I hunted waterfowl, I *never* shot before sunrise! Even with all my training and experience, I didn't want to risk making a mistake.

Since all the fields surrounding the ponds had been plowed and were devoid of cover, there was no way for me to get closer without being seen. I had briefly considered hiding in the bushes around the ponds, but they were small enough to make that strategy an invitation to trouble in the form of a face full of flying shot or premature discovery by a hunter looking for a downed duck. I would just have to wait for a little more light to do what I did best. However, patience was never one of my sterling virtues.

The shooting had tapered off by the time it got light enough for me to identify any ducks killed by my three shooters, so I was out of luck in terms of identifying species; I had seen little other than the number of birds killed. In frustration, I all but crawled into the spotting scope at 25× power to see what my lads were up to. At that moment, a flock of green-winged teal came zipping over the decoys and was killed outright by what appeared to be some damn fine shooting. This type of flock shooting was repeated several times until my shooters had a limit of teal each, not counting any kills that might have happened during moments when I could not identify the birds because of poor light or their low flying over the ponds right in front of the guns. About then, seven northern shovelers whistled over the ponds, surprising the gunners below. Leaving as fast as they came in, the birds zoomed back up out of the ponds, circled out of range, and then, sensing everything was all right, dropped straight into the decoys in front of the blind. A blazing nine shots killed every duck in that small flock! After that an older shooter in hip boots and bib overalls ventured out into the pond, scooped up two handfuls of dead ducks that were floating on the water, and threw them toward the blind. This action was repeated twice, and most of the carcasses appeared to be blue-winged teal (based on the lack of spatulate bills, the cobalt blue coverts, and the secondary wing patches seen through the spotting scope). Then the man walked over to the seven dead northern shovelers floating in a small clump just outside the decoy set. I could see him bend over and pick up one of the ducks as he looked long and hard at the unusual bill. Shovelers aren't called that just for the hell of it. They have large, shovel-shaped bills that are very distinctive. They have elongated intestines so they can easily digest a diet high in microscopic critters and vegetative matter. However, with such a diet, this midsized duck possesses flesh thick with orange fat that is considered less than desirable at the table. Shovelers, with their distinctive bills and manner of flying with their heads slightly down, should not be mistaken for any other bird. I had a blind full of dummies, or those killing just for the hell of it.

"Hey," yelled the man in bib overalls, "what the hell is this?"

The large man with the beard stood up in the blind and yelled, "Hold the damn thing up." The other man did as instructed, and the man in the blind called, "Spoonies" (another name for shovelers).

"Do we want to keep them?" asked the man in bib overalls.

"Hell, no. The season isn't open on those yet, and besides, they taste like shit," yelled the man with the beard. The man in overalls tossed one of the shovelers into the reeds on the far side of the pond. The bearded one stood up again and hollered, "Don't do that. Some goddamned game warden will find them. *Stomp the son of a bitches!*"

"Bibs" began stomping the shovelers into the soft muddy bottom of the pond. That maddened the chap in the haystack looking at the shooters through the "big eye"! I quickly drew a rough sketch in my notebook showing the approximate locations of the stomped ducks. There is always a certain degree of difficulty in locating ducks stomped in the mud somewhere in the bottom of a pond. Don't worry, little ducks, I thought, someone will atone for this act of greed and stupidity. *Big time!* "Bibs" returned to the blind, forgetting the one shoveler he had tossed into the vegetation at the pond's edge, and the three continued their little shoot.

Meantime, my big hunt was now on. Out from my haystack I crawled, making sure there were no farm vehicles running down the nearby roads to observe my exit. Dropping to the ground, off I trotted across the plowed field in a hunched-over position. Arriving at the road's edge, I sprinted across and dove under the fence, did a quick combat roll, and threw myself into the cover at the edge of the marsh. Then I crawled and squirmed my way toward the road leading into the ponds. Once there, I used the cover provided by the two parked vehicles (including the painted-over Ford) and was now in a position to cut off my lads. Crawling under the Ford, I watched my shooters through the binoculars to see what else might develop. It wasn't long in coming. The soft *crump* of shotguns in the distance told of other teal hunters having a go at their sport. That shooting stirred up other ducks, and soon there were small flocks trading back and forth in the skies, looking for that little patch of wet earth they could call a safe haven. Five mallards swung around the upper side of the ponds and started to land in the northernmost one. A few very convincing mallard calls from my teal shooters changed their minds, and within moments all five came slipping and sliding into the middle pond. Six shots from three guns spelled death for every bird. Soon all that was left were a few feathers floating in the air and ripples in the water around the cooling dead bodies. That's it! I thought. I started out from my hiding place, but then caught myself. Wait a minute, Terry—let's see what they do with those birds just killed. Federal judges always liked to hear anything that might demonstrate illegal intent. Soon the third shooter, a lanky fellow, went out to retrieve the dead mallards after carefully looking all around. Picking them up without much ado, he headed for the blind after again carefully looking all around to check for anyone, such as a game warden, who might have observed his lawless acts.

Soon the lanky man and the bearded one left the blind and walked briskly toward their vehicles. Both were carrying heavy handfuls of ducks and looking around them nervously. I slid back under the Ford as far as I dared and waited as they opened the doors to the two vehicles. From my limited vantage point, I could see the lanky one tossing mallards, wigeon (another midsized puddle duck), assorted teal, and a gadwall behind the seat of his truck. I couldn't see what the bearded fellow was doing because I was lying underneath his truck, but I figured that revelation would occur in due time. Back to their blind they went, and shortly after that, all three came back out with limits of teal in their hands as if nothing out of the ordinary had occurred. Sliding backward from under the Ford and using it for cover, I waited until all three shooters were within grabbing distance before stepping into view.

"Morning, fellows; federal agent. Looks like the shooting was good in your neck of the woods. I would like to check your licenses, duck stamps, and shotguns if I might," I cheerfully announced. To say the least, there was surprise aplenty at my salutation. But I had to give them credit—after the initial scare, they exhibited plenty of cool.

"Damn, you scared the hell out of us, boss. Where the hell did you come from?" grunted the bearded one.

"Down the road," I calmly replied. That initial contact with outlaws whose hands were caught in Mother Nature's cookie jar was always the best part of the day. I enjoyed playing the dumb-shit game warden for all it was worth. This situation looked pretty damn good, kind of like having your last part over the fence caught in the jaws of a great bear.

The lads laid their ducks on the hood of the Ford for all to see, as if that was it, and began unloading their shotguns. Checking their ducks like any good government dummy, I found a mixed bag of blue- and green-winged teal. Their plugs, licenses, and duck stamps were all in order and after that little business detail, we began to chat like long-lost friends. We discussed the morning's hunt, how good these little ducks would taste after being baked in the oven, and our favorite duck-cooking methods, and their hunting history at these ponds. It seemed they hunted the ponds the first weekend of every teal season and had been doing so ever since Colorado had instituted a teal season. Between smiles at their stories of past hunting prowess,

I wondered how many illegal ducks they had taken over the years before this day of reckoning.

Then they dropped an unexpected bomb. The bearded one mentioned that he and the lanky man were from Denver and were "high ups" in a local chapter of Ducks Unlimited! As if that would cut any mustard, I grimly thought. I had pinched a lot of shooters from Ducks Unlimited over the years and found them to be like folks from any other walk of life, basically a mixture of the good, bad, and ugly. I just shook my head and clamped my teeth down a little harder. Here they were from an organization established to help the duck, yet these two yahoos, figuring they had helped ducks in the past, believed they were now entitled to help themselves to the ducks of the future. The man in the bibs was the landowner, whose common sense seemed to tell him that he'd best remain unheard. Well, I thought, from the sound of shooting still going on, I had business elsewhere that day and had better get on with the business at hand. Walking to the front of the Ford and leaning on the hood, I began taking revenge for the duck.

"Gentlemen, I have been here all morning. Is there something any of you would like to tell me?"

They all looked at each other in false puzzlement and then innocently asked what I was talking about.

"Well," I said, "I would bet if I were to look behind the seats of these pickups, I would find all kinds of illegal treasures. And I would bet a month's salary that if I were to drag that pond, I would find a mess of spoonies stomped into the mud, not to mention the one tossed into the weeds at the pond's edge. Now, I really hope I don't have to drag all this out any further, but if I do, there will be three chaps going to Denver with me for an appointment with the local federal lockup. Do we have an understanding, gentlemen?"

They all looked at me in complete shock.

"What will it be, gentlemen? Cooperation or a trip to the lockup?"

They were as quiet as those spoonies at the bottom of the pond until "Bibs" quietly asked, "What is going to happen to us?"

"Well, to start with, all the birds are going to be piled at my feet. Next, some or all of you are going out to dig up those spoonies from the mud and retrieve the spoonie at the edge of the pond. With that, we will figure out who shot what, and then the paperwork begins. As I see it, all of you will be cited for taking an over-limit of teal. All of you will be cited for taking migratory waterfowl during the closed season once the mallards, wigeon, spoonies, and gadwall see the light of day from behind the seats and the bottom of the pond. Lastly, citations will be issued for wanton waste. Stomping ducks to the ringing order of, 'Stomp the son of a bitches' is really not the way of a good sportsman. In short, I would say you gentlemen are looking at fines in the neighborhood of one thousand to fifteen hundred dollars each. As far as any jail time, probation, or hunting restrictions, that will be up to the magistrate."

Man, you could have heard a mallard feather hit the dirt one hundred yards away. The bearded one, whose name turned out to be Jerry, opened the door to the Ford, and out came ten teal, two mallards, and a gadwall. Robert, the lanky one, fished out another ten teal, six mallards, one wigeon, and a gadwall from behind the seat of his truck.

"May I see all of your driver's licenses and hunting licenses once again, gentlemen?" I asked. Within moments, I had all the requested items. "Now, gentlemen, the spoonies from the bottom of the pond and the edge of the pond, please," I uttered with scarcely veiled disgust. That took a little doing, but finally all the birds were located by my three sheepish-looking lawbreakers.

While the men looked for the spoonies, I took their driver's licenses and began filling out Field Information Forms on the hood of the Ford. After seizing and tagging the ducks, I gave back the driver's licenses and explained how the federal court system process operated. Boy, talk about mute. These three men were as quiet as mice pissing on a ball of cotton! "Any questions?" I asked. When none were forthcoming, I said I was through with them and they could leave. I saw three whipped pups load up without a word and leave without a backward glance. I found that strange but quickly shoved the thought out of my mind. I had work to do, not to mention some other shooters to check if the shooting continued long enough for me to locate and reach them.

Hiding the ducks, I walked back to my hay pile and retrieved the rest of my gear. While walking back to my patrol truck across the plowed field, I was stopped by a Colorado Division of Wildlife officer on loan from another district who was also working teal hunters in the area. After we exchanged greetings, he asked what had brought out the "mighty feds." After all, the teal hunting was very slow, and the hunters were killing hardly anything. In fact, he said, since the advent of the early teal season in Colorado, he had never made a case anywhere. They were just like fly fishermen (known for not breaking the law), he informed me. It was hardly worth the time to work them.

I waited until he left to avoid embarrassing him before working my truck back to my pile of dead birds to clean them before they spoiled. Fifty-one ducks later, I finished tagging my evidence, washed my hands, and then listened for any other shooting close by. The teal hunting had dropped off to almost zero, if the sounds of shooting were any indication. Bluebird weather and a limited resource to shoot at has a way of doing that to the hunting public and game wardens alike. Realizing my day was probably done as far as catching any other teal hunters outside the law, I headed the nose of my truck for the barn, but not before scouting for another teal cherry patch to work the next day.

I had been pretty close in my estimation of what my lads were facing in court. Each man forfeited $1,350, escaping any further punishment. I later found out from my sources that the two Ducks Unlimited fellows had just received recognition from a national conservation organization. I guess they figured if they stayed quiet, maybe their infractions wouldn't become known to publicly embarrass them. The next year that marsh was drained and planted in alfalfa. I guess the memory of that day was just too much for "Bibs." It surely wasn't done because of the high price of alfalfa! I never said anything about this episode until the writing of this story, and I am sure my Ducks Unlimited chaps kept their mouths shut.

I still speak at Ducks Unlimited gatherings and donate several sets of my books to the organization annually to help it raise funds to assist in its work with the waterfowl. After all, the work it does is valued and needed. There are a world of damn fine Ducks Unlimited members out there doing what is right. However, I have never seen my two Ducks Unlimited shooters from that morning of stupidity at any meeting I have attended. I guess maybe that's for the best. After all, what would we have to talk about?

If It Flies, It Dies

WORKING SOUTH OF GREELEY writing several errant "teal" hunters citations for taking closed-season waterfowl (they had eleven mallards and no teal), I heard a lot of shooting in an area to the east.

The shooting remained static in one location, and I surmised it was coming from an area next to a local dairy. Picking up the pace, I sped through the citation issuance so I could move on to that fast and furious shooting. After finishing the paperwork, I asked my chaps if they had any questions, and hearing none, headed east for my noisy group of shooters before they quit for the day or the birds quit flying. A few miles later, I discovered that to get anywhere close to the shooters, I would have to go through a complex of homes, cattle barns, and locked gates. That would easily give me away, especially if the shooters were from the dairy complex, so I began to circle the area on farm roads, looking for another way in. There weren't any straight shots into the shooting area from the roads, and all entry points appeared to be in full view of anyone involved for at least half a mile. Stymied for the moment, I concluded that the best approach would be to walk into the area in the early morning under cover of darkness another day. Now, some readers may be champing at the bit at that decision. Why not roar in and grab them now? you say. Well, first of all, a lot of shooting may not be illegal. If they shot the way I did when I was younger, they were just making the ammunition manufacturers happy, if you get my drift. Also, if there is gross illegality, the shooters have often done away with the evidence before you get there by "stomping" the illegal ducks into the mud, replacing the plugs in their shotguns, tossing their lead shot into the pond, or running the overages to the nearest house or barn, all in an effort to frustrate the long arm of the law. I wanted to catch all the culprits red-handed. Besides, trying to walk in for half a mile in view of God and everybody during the light of day could allow the chaps a chance to escape out the other side. Bottom line: if you are going to fire a shot, make it a killing one. ...

Locating an out-of-the-way hiding place in order to watch and listen, I began cleaning my evidence ducks from my earlier run-in. While cleaning those ducks, I counted sixteen shots from the middle of the rolling farmlands from what appeared to be two shooters using 12-gauge shotguns. I watched several bunches of ducks moving to and fro over the area but none dropping from the sky after being shot at by my unseen gunners.

About then a farm rig clattered down the road, and the driver, happening to see me, stopped and backed up to where I was parked. "Good morning," I said as a rather large farmer unlimbered himself from the front seat of an obvious farm truck. That is, if a truck covered with cow shit is any indicator of a dairy farmer.

The man sharply eyed me as he approached, saying nothing and smelling like his pickup looked. "What are you doing here, boy?" he barked as he warily looked me and my unmarked vehicle over.

"Well, I needed to clean my ducks before they spoiled, and this out-of-the-way place looked like the spot to do it. Is this is your land? If it is, I hope it is OK," I answered.

Ignoring my question, he said, "Looks like you got a few too many and of the wrong kind."

"Well, yeah. I guess you could say that," I said with false humility as I looked at the thirteen ducks laid out on my tailgate for all the world to see. "My shooting eye was on and my discerning eye as to species was somewhat off, one could say," I continued lamely.

"Where did you get them?" he rumbled.

"Down the way," I replied, trying to show outward calm for the casual outlaw effect. Over the years I had discovered that over 90 percent of the American people who find someone in violation of wildlife laws will say nothing to the authorities. I was banking on that historical experience in this confrontation.

"Damn, that's a nice bunch of mallards you have there," he replied. I detected a slight warming and dropping of his initial caution.

"Yes, I do," I replied. "Would you like a couple?" Now, there is no way in hell I could legally have given away any of my evidence birds. It seemed like a good chance to take in warming up this gruff bastard, but I was hoping he would turn me down.

"Naw, I will have plenty when the boys get home from their hunt on the ponds behind my barns," he replied.

"Is that where all the shooting is coming from across the road and down in those gullies?" I innocently asked.

Looking over his shoulder in the general direction of the shooting, he grumbled, "Yeah. I just wish they wouldn't shoot so damn much. That will just bring the damn game wardens down on them like a bunch of flies in my cow barns."

"Damn, you must have a fine bunch of teal over there if they are shooting up such a storm," I replied.

"Who knows? Them kids will shoot about anything that flies and is good to eat. They know their mom and aunt is a good cook, so they really get with it when they have the chance," he replied. Then, as if someone had shut off a switch, the shooting stopped. The farmer and I continued talking for a few more moments before I saw an all-terrain vehicle (ATV) coming from behind the rolling hills hiding the ponds and heading for the complex of dairy barns. It carried two riders, and even from my distance I could see what appeared to be one hell of a bunch of birds in the front carry basket. "Guess I better get back. Them two knotheads will be showing their kills off to anyone who will look. So I better get up there and put a stop to it by putting them to work milking cows. Besides, I don't want no damn game wardens sniffing around," he groused.

"Well, it was nice meeting you, and are you sure you don't want any birds? I will be happy to clean and share them, especially if you keep it quiet."

"Naw, them boys will have plenty. Your secret is safe with me. Just try to not have too many of them damn feathers blowing around. Don't want any game wardens sniffing around here either. If they do, one thing leads to another, if you get my meaning."

"Yes, sir. I'll pick 'em up, bag 'em, and take 'em home. Sure don't want any damn game wardens giving you or those boys any hassling," I replied. With that, he disappeared down the road in a cloud of dust and clanking sounds as I finished drawing my evidence birds. Yes, sir, I thought. Sure don't want any damn game wardens hassling you or the boys. ... Smiling, I picked up most of the feathers, leaving the guts, which I had tossed into the bushes for any hungry critters in the area. Throwing the gutted birds into my ice chest, I headed for home.

LEAVING MY PATROL TRUCK in a machine-shop parking area, I hoisted my pack of "possibles" onto my shoulder and headed for the shooting area I had discovered the week before. It was three in the morning, so I had time to walk the mile or so into the area, orient myself to the lay of the land around the waterways, hide, and give the ducks chased off by my presence an opportunity to return. When I arrived at what appeared to be the shooting area (based on the number of empty shotgun shells lying all over the place), I was surprised at the number of birds on the series of ponds. Ducks, a few Canada geese, killdeer (shorebird—a noisy one at that), and just about everything else with feathers found in that neck of the woods at that time of the year seemed to be gathered for the occasion. The numbers were suspiciously like those I had experienced in the past when working baited areas, where food items such as wheat or barley had been placed to entice the birds to the gun. There was a pit blind at one end of a large pond, with about three dozen decoys scattered on the water. No real waterfowl hunters here if the oddball decoy pattern was any indication of their prowess, I thought. In fact, several of the poor-quality rubber decoys were in danger of sinking, no doubt from having taken low-flying shot. Shining my flashlight through my fingers to reduce the intensity, I noticed bits and pieces of cracked corn on the ground. Damn! I thought. Don't tell me this place is baited! Sure as hell, a walk through the decoys brought up a large quantity of cracked corn in the mud sticking to my hip boots. Now my heart really raced. I had a great case in the making if I could only stay out of the way of the gruff bastard who owned the land. I hope his boys aren't the same kind and size, I thought. ...

Finding a small patch of brush at the base of a cottonwood tree at one end of the pond, about forty yards from the blind and in direct line of sight, I nestled in. Soon the area refilled with birds hurrying back to their corn-baited breakfast buffet. In about thirty minutes, the pond was again cluttered wall to wall with ducks and Canada geese happily lapping up the grits. Soon, over the lowing of Holsteins needing milking, I heard an ATV motor crank up. Within moments, over the hill came an ATV carrying two riders clearly visible through my binoculars. Damn! I thought. Here they come right for my hiding place! I quickly rolled around the giant cottonwood, putting it between me and the riders, and was shocked to have them hide their vehicle *right* behind my tree. Without a word, the two lads headed at a trot for the pond, amidst the alarmed calls and roaring wings of the hurriedly exiting waterfowl. Jumping into their pit blind, they all but disappeared. For the next thirty minutes, nothing moved in the area of the blind. That gave me time to move back to the far side of the tree for better cover. In fact, what better cover than hiding between their ATV and the cottonwood? I thought.

The ducks and geese came back in short order and soon were once again happily feeding by the hundreds on the cracked corn on the bottom of the pond. *Boom-boom-boom-boom — boom-boom-boom-*

boom-boom went nine shots. All hell broke loose. Ducks, geese, and shorebirds went every which way to get away from the exploding shotguns. For many more lying inert on the water, there was no escaping the fact that their greed had cost them their lives. The aerial confusion was soon accompanied by more shooting as frightened but hungry birds attempted a comeback into their "chow hall." Six more shots were fired in quick succession at birds winging in, and I saw two mallards drop out of the air and hit the water with soft *kerplops*. The pond area was alive with ripples of waterfowl kicking their last! It was all I could do to keep my field notes in a semblance of order. For the next fifteen minutes, the two men shot endlessly at the confused waterfowl as they circled the decoys. Nine more birds dropped, *none of which were teal*. ... However, since my lads were using unplugged shotguns and shooting over a baited area, anything killed was illegal under state and federal laws anyway. No matter how you cut it, these two lads were in a killing frenzy, not to mention in deep shit with the law.

Soon the flying bird numbers petered out and my two lads began collecting the birds floating dead on the pond. Through my binoculars I counted six Canada geese, eight mallards, two blue-winged teal, two green-winged teal, four widgeon, and one wood duck dead or dying on the water. Not bad for a "teal" hunt, I grimly mused. My lads threw the birds into their pit blind, jumped back inside, and started looking skyward for more targets. So that was where the cracked corn around the blind had come from, I thought. Walking in among the decoys, my two gunners had picked up the corn and mud on their boots. Then, jumping back into the blind, they had inadvertently knocked some of the mud carrying corn into the bottom of the pit.

To my surprise, a pair of yellow-legs (shorebirds that used to be market hunted for their excellent eating qualities) dropped onto the pond shoreline a short distance from the blind and began to feed in the mud. *Whoom* went a shotgun blast, and two happily feeding birds disappeared in a foam of water, feathers, and flying mud. Those bastards! I thought. Well, since yellow-legs were not on the list of migratory game birds to be hunted, the shooters were in for an additional surprise when I sprang the trap. About that time, three mallards winged over the pond, dropped straight into the decoys like birds used to feeding in a baited area, and upon hitting the water immediately tipped for the corn. Bear in mind that birds unaccustomed to feeding in a baited area will usually cautiously circle the area before descending, and upon landing will look all around for danger before doing anything else. All three were shot on the water straight away! That shooting spooked up several killdeer feeding on the edge of the pond, and only moments later they lay kicking their last as well. Again, good eating birds but illegal as hell!

That does it! I thought. I took the ATV key out of the ignition and put it into my shirt pocket, then headed straight for my two dingbats. At first they couldn't believe their eyes at seeing an approaching hulk that wasn't the dairy farmer. They hurriedly dropped back into their sunken pit blind as if hoping I would go away. Fat chance of that, lads, I thought as I approached to the sounds of plugs being quickly replaced in their shotguns. "Too late, lads," I said, towering over them as they continued halfheartedly reassembling their shotguns. You never saw such sick-looking folks in all your life. Truth be known, you probably never saw a happier man standing over such sick-looking chaps either. "Federal agent, lads. Unload and hand me the shotguns, butts first, please," I growled. Both lads complied, and once I had checked the guns for any remaining live rounds, I identified myself with badge and credentials as a special agent with the Fish and Wildlife Service. Their eyes were almost glued to the badge and credentials validating the identity of this image from hell. I requested their hunting licenses, duck stamps, and driver's licenses. As they started digging out the requested items, I had my first chance to really examine my two shooters. Both were over six feet in height, easily exceeded two hundred pounds, were stout as a couple of young bulls, and appeared to be in their early to mid-twenties. However, they seemed terrified, and I made the most of it.

Driver's licenses were handed up, and that was it. ... Neither had a hunting license or the required duck stamps! Shaking my head, I had them empty out the dead ducks and geese from their blind. Soon I had a pile of six Canada geese and twenty ducks (only four of which were teal). Then I had the lads retrieve the two greater yellow-legs and three killdeer from the pond's edge. Man, you never saw a glummer pair of lads. Something was wrong here, I thought, but I pushed that thought aside and went on with the business at hand.

"Gentlemen, as you probably suspect, we have a problem. As I see it, we have migratory game birds taken during the closed season, migratory nongame birds taken during closed season, use and aid of unplugged shotguns, no hunting licenses, no duck stamps, and taking migratory game birds over a baited area. Did I leave anything out?"

"No, sir," came their dual, depressed replies.

"Well then, gentlemen, let's get down to the paperwork. Hold your questions until I am finished, and I will be happy to clarify any issues you might have." With that, I began filling out the Field Information Forms, which took about forty-five minutes. During that time my two lads said nothing. Absolutely nothing! They kept looking at one another like a couple of trapped African meerkats. Man, something was odd with this situation, I thought, but I kept writing with a watchful eye. Once finished, I asked if they had any questions, and one of the lads asked if this was going to federal court and would he have to appear. I replied in the negative, informing them that they would be receiving bail notices in the mail and would have fourteen days to settle up with the clerk of the court or face issuance of a bench warrant for their arrest. One kid swallowed as if he had just eaten a rather large toad, poison glands and all, but said nothing. Now, I knew something was wrong from the way that kid looked at me and the way his cousin looked at him. But damn if I could put my finger on it. Maybe he was on probation or an escaped prisoner, was the only idea I could come up with. But I let the situation ride, figuring I would check when I was back at my radio.

They had no further questions, so I let them go. Watching them walk away, I gathered up and tagged my pile of evidence birds. Then I walked out into the pond and photographed what I could (the mud and corn on my boots, etc.), took samples of the bait, and sacked it in one of the sandwich bags I always carried. The sick-looking man returned and asked if I had the key to their ATV, which I had forgotten to give them during the heat of the initial contact. I returned the key and asked the lad if there was anything else he wanted to say. All I got was silence and the same sick look. Finally he said, "No sir, mister" and headed back for the ATV. Shortly afterward, I saw them drive away.

Gathering up my evidence birds and putting as many of the smaller ones as possible in my game bag, I grabbed the rest of my gear and evidence and headed for the road. I hadn't gone a hundred yards toward my truck when I heard a rattling pickup coming up fast behind me. Turning, I saw the truck sliding to a stop as the gruff old dairy farmer from the week before bailed out. It was obvious I was his center of attention. Facing the man, I let the gear I was carrying slide to the ground in case I had to use my hands for defense. "Are you the son of a bitch that just pinched those two kids?" he bellowed.

"Yes, sir. Let me introduce myself. My name is Terry Grosz, and I am a federal agent working for the Fish and Wildlife Service."

"Got any identification?" he growled.

"Sure do," I replied. Digging into my shirt pocket, all the while never taking my eyes off my mad dairyman, I showed him my credentials.

Surprisingly, he wilted. "What's going to happen to those kids?" he asked in a calmer, concerned tone.

"Well, I would imagine they are looking at a bail of at least a thousand dollars each before all is said and done. I don't think the issue of jail or probation is a problem, however. They were pretty contrite and well-mannered, so extra punishment shouldn't be an issue with the Denver magistrates unless their previous records show a lot of the same illegal behavior."

"Can you hold off filing those tickets for about a week?" he quietly asked.

"Why?" I replied.

"One of the boys you cited is a cousin to my boy. His dad was killed a month or so ago in a car wreck, and David just hasn't been able to get it all together since then. His dad was all he had in the way of close kinfolk, and now David is just lost. In fact, he is absent without leave from the army as a result of his dad's death. He came home for the funeral and just couldn't bring himself to go back. I am afraid if you file those tickets, the army will find out where he is and come after him. If they do that, it will destroy that young man."

Now the truth was coming home to roost, I thought. I never would have figured out the AWOL thing in a million years, though. I couldn't help but mull this one over for a few moments. The kid could easily have been destroyed if that had been my inclination. In fact, as a federal officer I was obligated to report the kid to the proper authorities now that I was aware of the problem. I did some real soul-searching in those moments. The kid could run, Terry, and then what? I asked myself. You could preclude flight by smashing him down even further with an arrest, a warrant, or time in the brig. No, I don't think that would be the right thing to do if this AWOL story is true. Why destroy a human being over a few dead ducks and geese? The farmer wasn't asking me to do anything illegal, just give him some time to try and get David squared away. I made up my mind.

"Tell you what. Have that young man turn himself in. That is the right and least destructive thing to do. If you guarantee he will do that, I won't send the army after him. But, you have one week to get it done, or else."

"Fair enough," said the farmer as relief flooded across his face. "Need a ride somewhere?" he added softly.

"Wouldn't mind one if you are in the mood. I have a ways to go, and carrying all these birds and my gear is a load."

"Hop in," he said, and shortly thereafter I was at my truck. "Thank you again, officer, for giving David a hand when he needed it the most. You won't regret it," he told me.

"I hope not," I replied. "He needs to go back and face the music. If he doesn't, he will hate himself forever, not to mention be looking over his shoulder for life."

"Don't worry. You are right, and I will see to it. I am all he has now, and I will do the right thing by him."

With that, we silently shook hands, avoiding each other's eyes, and went our ways.

I received a phone call from the dairy farmer two days later. David had turned himself in to army authorities. He asked if the federal citation could be sent to his address at the dairy. "That way I can pay the fine. That is the least I can do since I am just as guilty for letting that kind of activity take place on the farm. It won't happen again, officer."

"I will see to it," I replied, and having nothing more to say in a sad situation, the two of us hung up. As expected, the dairyman paid up like a slot machine.

Two years later, a smart-looking young man in an army uniform came into my office as I labored over another of those damn congressional responses for something one of my agents had allegedly done to one of the congressman's constituents. "Remember me?" he asked with a big grin. It took a moment rattling around in the recesses of my mind but finally the "sun shone on the manure pile behind the barn."

"Sure do. David, how the hell are you?" I exclaimed as I rose and shook his hand. Well the short of it was that David was finishing his first army tour and was going to re-up for a second one, then take the money from an army program and apply it toward a college education at Colorado State University in their Wildlife Management Department. I was damn glad to hear that and realize the young man had his head screwed on straight and was now heading down the road to a life of happiness. Today, I am happy to report, he is a waterfowl biologist in one of our western states, happily married, and the proud father of two young sons.

You can bet your bottom dollar that those two sons will be raised correctly, and when they go teal hunting with their father will know the differences between the waterfowl species and ... right from wrong.

It Takes All Kinds

PULLING MY PATROL TRUCK off the road, I hastily gathered up my gear for the day and raised the hood as if I had engine trouble. Part of that trick of the trade was a note under the windshield wiper indicating that I had gone to Greeley to find a wrecker. Trotting east along Colorado State Highway 34, I soon came to a dirt road heading north into several wealthy duck clubs along the Platte River. I turned down that road for a short distance, then headed east again, left the road, and began running along a set of railroad tracks paralleling the road. I continued at the same pace until I was about one hundred yards down the tracks and safely out of sight of any vehicles and their headlights before stopping to rest. It was two in the morning, overcast, and a Saturday, the second weekend of Colorado's teal season. Zipping open my hunting jacket, I let out the body heat because there is nothing worse than to sit at your stakeout spot in a cold sweat, trying to warm up for the rest of the day. With that, I began my long trek down the railroad tracks at a measured but ground-eating pace.

The weekend before, I had walked a length of the South Platte River, checking teal hunters on some of the area's fancy duck clubs as well as unattached hunters working the many springs and freshwater seeps along the way. In those freshwater springs was food aplenty, even for a duck as discriminating as the teal, along with many splendidly isolated resting and loafing sites. During that exploration of what the area had to offer in the way of teal hunting, I had come across a grim reminder of human greed and ignorance. Walking westerly along the river onto one particular duck club, I stumbled across some duck feathers that had drifted with the winds until they hung up on the bushes and weeds as if clamoring to be noticed by one carrying a conservation officer's badge and gun. Recognizing that many of the feathers were from closed-season species, I followed the trace of feathers north until I discovered a pile of breasted-out duck carcasses scattered on the ground—*and none of them were teal!* Thirteen mallards, northern pintail, wigeon, and gadwall made up the collection at the dump site. It didn't take long to backtrack human footprints to a well-camouflaged blind along the South Platte. Whoever had seen fit to kill those species during the closed season certainly felt comfortable doing so behind the locked gates and fences of their private shooting preserve. Well, Christmas was coming, and since I resembled Santa in size and shape, I thought I just might find out whether someone needed an early "Christmas present," if you get my drift. ...

Stopping to catch my wind and enjoy the inky blackness around me, I fired off a quick thank-you for my blessings to the Old Boy upstairs, followed by a request for my success on that day. Being my size, with all its inherent limitations, I don't take any chances—after many tough situations and hard-to-crack cases over the years, I have learned that I can *always* use extra help. Having caught my wind and mindful of the approaching daylight, I continued another mile or so east along the railroad tracks and the Platte River. It was a quiet, cool morning with only a hint of light because of the heavy cloud cover. There was a threat of rain, but I couldn't sense a whole lot of moisture in the air, so I decided not to worry about it. I continued at a fairly rapid pace until I came to the Coke can I had left alongside the railroad tracks the week before to mark my jumping-off point. Turning riverward, I shone my flashlight beam through my fingers to diffuse the light as I sought the way to the duck blind. Even using the light in this hard-to-spot manner, I frequently looked to the west, the direction from which I expected vehicles carrying hunters to the blind. I had arrived earlier then necessary in order to locate a good hiding place and also to allow ducks spooked off the river and freshwater spring areas by my bumbling presence time to return. That way, when my sportsmen arrived, they would in turn spook the ducks off their hunting area, leaving them with a feeling that they were the only ones in-country.

It was a great blind, as blinds go. It had been dug into the riverbank right next to the bases of some massive cottonwood trees. The designer of the blind had been smart enough to leave a dirt wall in front so arriving waterfowl would not detect anything out of the ordinary when they sailed into the decoys placed in a shallow pool at the edge of the river. Across the river from the blind was a marshy area about a fifth of an acre in size. It was one of those typical freshwater seeps so common along the Platte and was full of duckweed and every other kind of vegetation that delighted waterfowl. So my shooters had a wonderful pool area right in front of their blind and a duck's paradise in the marshy seep directly across from their decoys. If there were ducks in the area, they would be here. And speaking of ducks, the sound of whistling wings told of the feathered soon-to-be targets' return to their resting and feeding areas. From the calls, I could identify mallards, wigeon, several species of teal, and gadwall. Well, at least the table was set if my chaps cared to take a walk on the wild side!

Moving into a dense stand of brush just off the river with an unobstructed view of the shooting area, I made a "nest" and laid out my equipment. Then I reached into my pocket, took out my breakfast of a hard Italian salami and a Diet Pepsi. Savoring my breakfast and the quiet, I listened to Mother Nature rattle around in the pitch black surrounding me. The bark of a fox told me I had been "winded." It also told me the fox was probably enjoying a meal from last week's duck carcasses some forty yards away. The hoot of a great horned owl somewhere in the cottonwoods along the river signaled that all the "little people" had better be on the alert. No more efficient killer ever stalked the skies, except maybe the snowy owl. A pack of coyotes miles to the north "blew up," probably announcing a communal kill that would soon be breakfast. They set off just about every other coyote in the area, all wishing they had some of the same grub. Soon the "song dogs" lit up the airwaves, creating a smile on my sweaty, dusty face. Good old coyotes, I thought. Sure glad they ate the hell out of those goddamned "range maggots" (sheep, to you uninitiated). The continuing stream of whistling wings foretold a good shoot for my suspects, and the surprise of a cold, three-foot-long gopher snake crawling between my legs for the warmth they offered pretty well topped off my morning. Huddling deeper into my hunting jacket for the warmth it offered, I let my eyes close as my mind wandered through the annals of natural history for the area. I found that if I listened carefully, I could hear the grunting of a bull bison off in the distance as he happily rolled around in an almost dry buffalo wallow. He had better be careful, I thought, and keep it down. But a noisy set of Cheyenne dogs in an encampment upstream foretold an arrow later in the day. ...

Bouncing lights along a dirt road from the west announced my hunters, on their way for whatever adventures the day might bring. It took a while for the vehicle to carefully pick its way over the faint, dusty trail before it stopped some fifty yards from the blind. Soon dome lights went on, illuminating four figures. Their voices quietly wafted in and out to me on the morning's breezes as they took their shotguns from their gun cases and let out a single retriever. Good, I thought; the dog will reduce any bird losses and make it easier for me to recover all the ducks when I decide to strike. Checking for wind direction once again, I found the soft breezes favorable. There is nothing more frustrating than being scented by the hunters' dog and discovered before the work is done! But my location was far enough away and downwind, so all was well. The vehicle lights went out, and the dark mass of the hunters quietly walked to the blind and disappeared. Fleeing waterfowl confirmed that the men had reached the riverside. It was still thirty minutes before legal shooting time, so I lay back down and relaxed for a little while.

Boom-boom-boom—boom-boom-boom—boom-boom—boom-boom went ten shots in quick succession. Through my binoculars, I saw all four men rise up and blast away at ducks resting in the water among the decoys or in the marsh area at the river's edge. Numerous ducks fled the area like a swarm of bees as the largest hunter (who I could now see well enough to recognize as a loudmouth with political connections all the way up to the secretary of the Interior) commanded the dog to "fetch." Well, this might prove to be an interesting day, I thought. Knowing that chap the way I did, I figured there would be other, lesser "nobles" among his hunting partners. Checking my watch, I saw that they had initiated their shoot only two minutes early (legal shooting time begins one half hour before sunrise). Pretty smart move, I thought. No use calling the game warden's attention to early shooting if one is to have a bagful of closed-season species by the end of the day. Soon I was able to view and record the species carried by the retriever each time the dog returned, because he ran along the river before me and not twenty yards away. During multiple retrieves, I used the binoculars and counted two drake mallards, one diver, probably a red-head from the amount of gray and body size, and three blue-winged teal. Well, I thought, they just stepped into my arena with the three closed-season ducks. Now I wondered, just how far would they dip into the excrement in which they were already standing? The answer was not far off. As other shooting began up and down the river, the airways over my area filled with small flocks of fleeing ducks. A pair of wigeon sailed down the river and into the decoys straight away. *Boom-boom* went two quick shots from two shooters, and the wigeon soon joined their winged buddies in the blind. Then four green-winged teal poured into the decoys in typical green-wing fashion. Sensing something amiss before alighting, they shot vertically over the decoys at about forty miles per hour, and every shot loosed at them by my four hunters missed. Five more wigeon dropped over the treetops from upstream into the decoys and were killed in a blistering twelve-shot barrage. With all the lads shooting at the wigeon, my job just became easier, I thought as a large grin formed on my face. If nothing else, all could now be charged with taking migratory game birds during the closed season. This is teal season, boys, I mused, not open season on all ducks! Then a flock of ducks sailed into the decoys just as I got my binoculars back up. I didn't get to see what they were, but after seven more shots I saw the dog retrieve four blue-winged teal. The shooting was getting pretty hot and heavy up and down the river as more fleeing ducks filled the airways. A flock of eight mallards and one wigeon flew down the river toward my shooters. Sensing something wrong, they just kept the hammer down. However, not before three quick shots from my shooters dropped two more mallards, both hens. No conservationists here, I grimly concluded. A small flock of redheads zipped down the river just over the water, and this time my lads were ready. Five hit the water in final skids. Damn, I thought, slow down, boys. I'm having a hard time identifying the birds in flight and recording the numbers of shooters, numbers of shots, species killed, and time of shooting! Their hardworking dog was also having trouble keeping up. On one of his retrieves, he got snarled in a mess of decoy lines and had to be untangled. During those moments, several more small flocks of ducks arrived but quickly fled the scene upon seeing the men standing up and the confusion in the water around the dog. Once the dog was squared away and the decoys properly reset, the shooting recommenced. Six more shots accounted for two more teal, identified through my binoculars as blue-wings. Then things quieted down. Over the next hour, a lot fewer birds flew, and my shooters, like all the others on the river that morning, satisfied themselves with singles and doubles venturing into their decoys. However, they still managed to kill one more hen mallard and a drake gadwall.

About ten in the morning, two of my lads took handfuls of the closed-season ducks and headed over to the spot where I had discovered the carcasses the week before. They knelt down and breasted the ducks, stuffing the meat into plastic bags pulled from their hunting coats. How about a little intent there? I thought. Carrying plastic bags full well knowing they were going to break the law and have something to put into them. My duck cleaners walked to their vehicle, a black Chevy Suburban, washed their hands, and put the plastic bags of duck breasts into an ice chest. Then they returned to their buddies in the blind with a load of lunch fixings. For the next hour they had lunch and shot at the occasional duck venturing by. By now the flight appeared to be all but over for the day. However, my shooters killed two more blue-winged teal and a pair of northern pintail.

I could see they were tiring of the hunt, since the flights had all but disappeared, and were making ready to leave. Just then a flock of tiny green-winged teal roared into their decoys and, realizing there were four men standing up in the blind, did their usual vertical, high-speed climb in an attempt to get out of harm's way. However, four of them dropped stone cold to the tune of twelve shots. The dog got another workout retrieving the green-wings, and the shooters did a high five for the striking end to their day. Little did they realize they had forgotten to include one other chap soon to be intertwined in their day. ... They had killed thirty-six ducks in a little over four hours. Twenty-one of those ducks were illegal closed-season species! Hell, they even had an over-limit of teal. ... Their high fives had been a little premature.

Gathering up their gear and ducks, my four shooters started for their vehicle. I let them get partway before I rose up from my hiding place so I could circumvent the possibility of the illegal birds being tossed into the river. However, as soon as they spied me, two of the lads did a clever number by casually dropping those birds in the brush alongside their legs in the hope that they had not been seen.

I displayed my badge and said, "Morning, gentlemen; federal agent. I would like to check your birds, shotguns, hunting licenses, and duck stamps if I may."

To say the least, they were surprised and had little to say other than, "Where did you come from?"

Pointing in the general direction of the breasted birds, I said, "Over there by all those bird feathers and carcasses." Even the loudmouth was quiet and circumspect in light of my mentioning the carcasses. The two men unknown to me who had breasted out the illegal birds gave each other a look like their moms had just given them a table-spoon of castor oil. That's good, I thought. I am going to quickly take the high ground with these more than likely wealthy and probably politically influential chaps. If I have my way, they will never again get their feet under them for any hell raising!

"Gentlemen. I expect all of you have pressing business back at the clubhouse, so I will make this short and to the point. I have been here since before your arrival and have seen about all I cared to see when it came to killing ducks. You have taken closed-season waterfowl, twenty-one in number, shot an over-limit of teal, shown wanton waste of a pile of ducks, as evidenced over there in that clump of feathers, and transported migratory waterfowl without any means of species identification. That is for starters. Looking at your licenses, I also see that two of you do not have a federal duck stamp. Needless to say, you have a major legal problem by the time all this is added up. How close to the truth am I so far?" They all just looked at me and then at each other as if hoping someone would step forward with a good ex-planation and get their miserable carcasses off the hook. However, none cared to be that person, so I stepped forward again. "Gentlemen, I will need all of your driver's licenses so I might start the citation process. Also, I need the two of you who dropped the extra teal and out-of-season ducks in the weeds once you saw me approaching to go back and bring them here. Don't leave any because I have a count on not only the numbers but the species as well. Additionally, I need one of you to go over and bring me all those fresh duck carcasses that were breasted out this morning. And last but not least, I need the remain-ing chap to dig out the breasted duck meat from the ice chest in the back of the Suburban."

There was a slight pause, and then the chaps moved on my re-quests without saying a word. That generally is the case with violators when the bear trap is poised to snap shut around a portion of one's anatomy. ... Soon I had a pile of ducks in the round, breasted-out duck carcasses, and plastic bags of breast meat lying at my feet. The four rather quiet and thoroughly embarrassed men then dug out their driver's licenses and handed them to me. Moving over to the hood of their vehicle, I commenced recording the information needed to fill out the federal citations. Once finished, I handed back their driver's licenses and asked if they had any questions. The large one with the mouth, who was the owner of the duck club, asked if he could pay for all his guests' citations.

I said, "I don't care how these citations are settled. Just remember all of you will receive citations in the mail for the violations outlined today, and you will each have fourteen days to respond. You can forfeit bail as set forth on the citations, or you can appear and contest the charges."

"That won't be necessary," said the club owner. "We will just forfeit the bails, and I will cover all the costs. Any idea what the fines might run?"

"I expect you are looking at one thousand to fifteen hundred dollars each," I responded.

The club owner didn't blink an eye. How many of you readers could fork out $4,000 to $6,000 over a wildlife violation? "If that is all, officer, you are right. We all have pressing business to get back to and would like to leave if that is possible," he responded meekly.

"Be on your way, gentlemen, and have a nice day with what's left of it," I replied.

With that, they loaded up into the Suburban and left me standing there in a cloud of dust. What, no offer for a ride back to the main road? I thought, smiling. ... As they turned their vehicle around to leave, I noticed Trout Unlimited, Ducks Unlimited, Pheasants Forever, and several other conservation patches I didn't have time to read firmly affixed to the side windows. ... Oh well, it takes all kinds—and then some. ...

It took some doing to haul all my gear and evidence birds back to the truck. Once they were tagged with evidence tags, gutted so they wouldn't spoil, and placed in ice chests, I sat down on the tailgate of the truck with a Diet Pepsi and reflected on the day's events. Two Denver-area millionaires, one a big-time stock broker and one in real estate. The other two chaps were an out-of-state outdoor writer (I had wondered why he was taking pictures at times during the outing—notice

I don't call it hunting) and the other from an old family with money. All four of them were old enough to know better, I grimly mused. Under the cover of a teal hunt, killing anything that came into range because of their arrogance and greed. And two of them without even a federal duck stamp, one of those being the *well-known* writer. ... Monies from the sale of those stamps are almost in their entirety put back into wetland and nesting habitat acquisitions for the critters. No better government program than that one, I thought. Mornings like that indicated that the illegal killing of wildlife would never be controlled. I'm sure these thoughts have been shared by all my hardworking counterparts at some time or other during their careers. As I have been told by many of those counterparts, what occurred here in Colorado is a theme in other parts of the country as well during teal season, especially in the Southeast and parts of Texas. Not everyone hunting teal is like that, but enough are to keep state and federal officers in the fields of "battle," using their keen eyes and steadfast steps to hold the line.

I would bet a month's pay that the outdoor writer apprehended that fine day so long ago didn't spend any time writing a story about that hunt. I would imagine he simply tucked his tail and ran, hoping no one discovered his little secret.

As a postscript, on the way home that day I spied two lads jump-shooting ducks along an irrigation canal. I found them to be in possession of one blue-winged teal and four pie-billed grebes. Grebes, a pointy-billed waterbird, are totally protected under the Migratory Bird Treaty Act and state laws and truly do not look much like a duck. Here was yet another misidentification by two sportsmen who were supposed to invest not only their money but their time in the sport. That should mean, learn your bird life histories and identification. I wonder if their rather large fines for killing those grebes made them work a little harder on their bird identification skills? Somehow, I have my doubts.

That brings another story to mind. While working at a "wing bee" in 1970, where duck and goose wings (turned in by sportsmen) were identified as to species, sex, and age by state and federal biologists and law enforcement officers, a similar occasion arose. I had checked eleven packages that a gunner from Arizona had submitted, full of pie-billed grebe wings. All illegal as hell, but he didn't know any better.

He had attached a note to the last submission: "Dear Sir: Can you please tell me what kind of duck this is? It is found on small canals, submerges easily, and tastes like hell." Tastes like hell, but the shooter still found time to kill oodles of the totally protected critters and innocently submit them for identification!

That bad taste was kind of like the taste in my mouth when hunters don't invest time, thought, ethics, and like qualities in their sport. ... It is no wonder many of us in the wildlife law enforcement trade are watching more than ever for the natural heritage crash that is sure to come soon. We can only do so much. Without more help from the American people, we and the wildlife are lost.

In the meantime, one has to wonder about an early teal season. Biologically, it may be justified. But throw into that mix the problem a vast majority of the duck hunters have in identifying their targets, and one has to wonder about the management sense. Is this just another opportunity dreamed up by the states to earn a few pieces of silver from the sale of hunting licenses and state duck stamps?

Pronghorn, black bear, mule deer, bobcat, and white-tailed deer trophies that were illegally taken by poachers. These trophies were killed after two Montana outfitters supplied illegal guiding and outfitting services to nonresident clients. The subjects were apprehended after a covert multiagency investigation. (photo supplied by Special Agent Goessman)

Over-limit of big game taken down by poachers, which was discovered by state and federal conservation officers during an interstate wildlife check-station control operation. (photo supplied by assistant Special Agent in Charge Hartman)

A great horned owl illegally pole-trapped by a hunting club manager in an attempt to reduce avian predation on club grounds. Once trapped, the owl was then illegally killed. (photo supplied by Agent Bosco deGama, photographer unknown)

A gross over-limit of teal ducks taken by six poachers in Louisiana. A total of 198 teal was illegally killed. (photo by Special Agent Hall)

A total of 649 yellow-crowned night-herons that were illegally taken by four Vacherie, Louisiana, poachers. (photo supplied by Special Agent Mellor)

A total of 35 breasted-out ducks. The rest of the meat had been left to rot by "game hogs." (photo supplied by Agent Bosco deGama, photographer unknown)

A portion of the 27,000 migratory birds poisoned by a St. Clair County, Illinois, farmer. Furadan was the poison used by the farmer to keep the birds out of 18 acres of winter wheat. (photo supplied by Special Agent Santel, photographer unknown)

A Louisiana State Wildlife Officer and a U.S. Fish and Wildlife Service Special Agent with ducks and coots seized from the Vermillion Parish "High Sheriff" for shooting an over-limit over a baited area using lead shot. (photo supplied by Special Agent Siragusa)

A duck over-limit and a restricted species, northern pintail, taken in a closed season in the Bear River Marshes of Utah. Utah State Conservation Officer Larry Davis was the arresting officer. (photo by Warden Larry Davis)

Lesser snow geese, white and blue phases, taken by poachers from Louisiana in an illegal drive-by shooting. The shooters were apprehended by U.S. Fish and Wildlife Service Agents Simms and Ferguson. (photo supplied by Special Agent Ferguson)

A poached golden eagle taken by commercial-market hunters in the San Luis Valley of Colorado. The face of the officer is blurred to protect his undercover identity. (photo supplied by Special Agent Bosco deGama)

A total of 293 illegally taken ducks in the freezer of a commercial duck picker near Forked Island, Louisiana. (photo by Special Agent Siragusa)

Rare and endangered cycads, ancient plants, being held as evidence. These "fruits" of the crime were recovered after a lengthy covert operation. (photo by special agent McCloud)

Australian cycad "head" smuggled into the United States and intercepted by U.S. Fish and Wildlife Service Special Agents. (photo by Dave Martin)

Radiated tortoise, an endangered species, smuggled from Madagascar. This animal was seized by Special Agent Ken McCloud of the U.S. Fish and Wildlife Service. (photo by Tad Motoyama of the Los Angeles Zoo)

Illegal canisters of Compound 1080, a deadly poison, which had been amassed by a state employee in order to resell it to cattle ranchers and sheep ranchers. The poison is placed in animal carcasses on the range in order to unlawfully take mammalian predators. (photo supplied by Terry Grosz, photographer unknown)

Parts from a black bear illegally taken for the Asian food trade and jewelry market. Bear claws are used to make jewelry. (photo supplied by Terry Grosz, photographer unknown)

Illegally taken Pacific walrus ivory and marine mammal skins photographed in an Alaska storehouse. (photo supplied by Special Agent in Charge Mowad, photographer unknown)

Desert bighorn sheep that were taken illegally in California by commercial-market hunters. At the time this picture was taken, the State of California had protected desert sheep for the previous seventy-five years. (photo supplied by Terry Grosz, photographer unknown)

Illegally taken Pacific walrus ivory seized in Alaska by the U.S. Fish and Wildlife Service. (photo supplied by Agent in Charge Mowad)

Illegally taken walrus drying in preparation for entry into the ivory trade. (photo supplied by Special Agent Mowad, photographer unknown)

An endangered Bengal monitor lizard that was smuggled into the United States and intercepted by U.S. Fish and Wildlife Service Agents. This animal is only part of the overwhelming illegal trade flooding the country's borders on a daily basis. (photo by Dave Martin)

Smuggled Gray's monitor lizards. These animals, thought to have been extinct for 130 years, were seized by wildlife inspectors and special agents of the U.S. Fish and Wildlife Service. (photo by Tad Motoyama)

An endangered Bengal monitor lizard. This animal was smuggled from Asia through Canada and into the United States, where it was intercepted by agents of the U.S. Fish and Wildlife Service. (photo by Special Agent Leach)

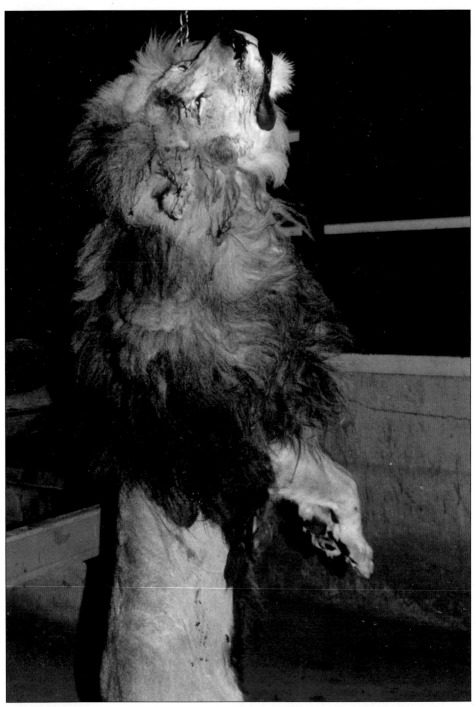

An African lion, one of the many tigers, leopards, and lions that are purchased from animal parks to be shot in captivity as trophies. A multistate undercover operation brought down a midwest ring that unlawfully purchased, sold, and killed many endangered cats under cruel conditions. Numerous indictments and prosecutions followed. (photo supplied by Special Agent Santel, photographer unknown)

three

A Weekend in the Arkansas Valley of Colorado

LYING IN MY SLEEPING BAG on the hard ground, I was mindful that dawn was not far away. Good old game warden's biological clock, waking me up before daylight, I thought with a grin. The early-morning air felt cool but good on my legs as I unzipped the bag, rolled over to my knees, and stood up. Thanking God for another great day and my many blessings, I unrolled a pair of cold jeans that had served as a pillow and slid my legs into them. Grabbing a clean shirt from my duffel bag, I quickly put it on as protection against the chill. Sitting down on an ice chest used for evidence birds, I put on my boots and looked east. From the look of the predawn light, shooting time was still a good hour away. There was a slight breeze, and I could smell the alkali dust in the air from the nearby heavily traveled dirt road. Rolling up my sleeping bag and brushing it off in the same motion, I stuffed it into the trunk of my patrol car. Then taking a gallon water jug from the backseat, I bent over and sloshed cold water over my face, hair, and hands. Damn, that felt good, I thought as the water droplets created small explosions in the dust at my feet. I toweled off the water along with yesterday's sweat and dust and combed what I had left for hair. A vigorous use of a toothbrush and paste signaled the end of my toilet. I opened my food ice chest and took out a Diet Pepsi and a stick of hard Italian salami. Opening the front door of the car, I took out a box of crackers, and my game warden's breakfast was now complete.

As I ate, the world around me began to awake. Off in the distance, I heard a rooster lustily crowing as he greeted another day. Occasionally a sleepy dove, disturbed by my presence, would fly out the far side of the row of cottonwood trees before me like a feathered, whistling rocket. (The whistling sound a dove makes when flying comes from a set of specialized feathers on the leading edge of the wing.) A pig squealed, and the slamming of a pickup door told me the owner of a nearby farmhouse, which had seen better days since it was built sometime in the late 1800s, was awake. Soon his pickup rattled and clanked down the dirt road along which I had camped, but he didn't see me or my vehicle, partly hidden behind another run-down, deserted farmhouse.

It was early September, the first day of dove season in Colorado. The afternoon before, I had driven down into the Arkansas Valley to see for myself what was available in the way of dove hunting and bad guy–catching opportunities. I was still new to my law enforcement district, and that area was on my list of places to explore and become knowledgeable about. My state counterparts had informed me that if the mourning dove were to be found anywhere in numbers worth hunting, that was the spot. The Arkansas Valley is located in southern Colorado and, but for the shallow, sandy Arkansas River, is pretty arid. Good water is few and far between, but the warm climate appeals to the dove population during early September. And if the dove were there in numbers, chances were humans would also be there with their shotguns, large pocketfuls of shells, and sweaty, dusty grins on their faces. They would need large pocketfuls of shells because the national average for gunning success with the dove ran about five shots per bird. The dove is a fast, erratic flyer and difficult to hit—in short, a real challenge to the shooting eye and skill of most gunners. Because it is basically a seed eater, the dove is considered a gourmet item by those who hunt it. It is hard to beat a batch of heavily seasoned, pan fried dove with thick white gravy, biscuits loaded with butter, green salad, and an ice-cold beer. The next day's lunch of leftover dove with another cold beer will lure even God to come down and join you for a bit of the good life. A large expenditure of shotgun shells is a small price to pay for such a challenging sporting event and sumptuous repast. In addition, dove season marked the advent of the long-awaited fall hunting season, giving one an excuse to be out and about, sharpening one's shooting eye for the myriad of seasons to follow. In some areas of the southeastern and southwestern United States, the opening of dove season has attained almost hallowed status. All of these things mean that there are some in the sporting community who get a little carried away. Shooting over illegally baited fields, taking gross over-limits, shooting behind gates locked to keep the game wardens out, spectacular cookouts, "paybacks" to local and national politicians in the form of a "good shoot," some officers of the law making sure they are on the other side of the county during those events, some officers of the law even *participating* in the illegal activity, rivers of liquid refreshment, and running from the law when discovered were among the excesses associated with the opening weekend of dove season. And an "army" of conservation officers patiently awaits that grim onslaught. Patiently awaits, yes. An "army," *no way*. There are about ten thousand conservation officers in *all* of North America protecting the world of wildlife that belongs to approximately 350 million people! From that ragtag, underfunded number, remove many of the supervisors and the sick, lame, and lazy, along with those sporting a political agenda, and you can readily see that conservation officers are few and far between. Not a good omen when it comes to protecting your national heritage, folks, but that's the way it is. ...

Enough wandering; back to the story at hand. Why was I sleeping on the ground? After all, I worked for the federal government! Plain and simply, I had bypassed any form of commercial sleeping accommodations because of a nonexistent budget. I had started the first day of the fiscal year months earlier, over thirty thousand dollars *in debt!* Figure that one out if you can. The very first day of the fiscal year, I was in the red and *had yet to spend one penny!* I didn't even have enough money in the till to pay the salaries of agents and staff already on board. It was a typical Fish and Wildlife Service leadership accomplishment: not enough money to pay salaries or fund any kind of viable law enforcement program for the whole year. Other divisions within the Service had money, but not the Division of Law Enforcement. It just seemed, year after year, that many of the Service leaders did not understand the value of a viable law enforcement program; did not understand how to use law enforcement as a wildlife management tool; were politically apprehensive of the program's ability to "reach out and touch" a variety of people (that is, even those from the political party in power); didn't really care whether the program survived; had been pinched themselves for doing something stupid; personally hated Clark Bavin, chief of law enforcement; or all of the above. Those negatives always seemed to be taken into account when it came to allocating the annual budget for the Division of Law Enforcement! We would have little or no money for the enforcement program unless we "tin-cupped" our way through the year among the wealthier programs. Hence, I could not afford the ten dollars required in those days for a night's lodging. But that was OK. The dove had to sleep in the trees and the rattlesnakes under old lumber piles, so I guessed I could sleep on the ground. My officers were doing the same thing. If they wanted to work, they had to scrounge the gasoline needed to do the job, carry their own food, and find lodging that cost nothing. You sure as hell didn't find personnel from other divisions sleeping on the ground when working for the Service!

The fat juice from the salami tasted good as I sat listening to the sounds around me. A mouthful of dry crackers and an occasional drink of Diet Pepsi rounded out the fare. Off to the immediate south, I heard a tractor start up, and a great horned owl, disturbed by the noise, fled my row of cottonwood trees. There was no sound, just the darkened shape of a silently flying killer to announce its presence. A smile slowly crossed my face. The heartbeat of Nature around me always brought me that particular kind of smile.

Realizing that I was burning daylight with my daydreaming, I hurried through the remainder of breakfast, cleaned up my camp, and slid into my patrol car. I headed onto the dirt road without headlights. I hadn't had a chance to scout out the valley for bait or dove concentrations (that lack of money thing again), so I would have to be satisfied with what I called "casting": nothing more than moving to the sounds of the guns. Lots of shooting, and I would be there. Little shooting, I would be elsewhere. Several miles down the dusty road, I found a nice hiding spot on the back side of a fresh haystack. Parking the car, I got out to look and listen. A quick glance at my map showed that I was just north of Ordway by the Colorado Canal. The soft popping sounds of shotguns greeted my ears from just about every quarter, announcing that dove season had begun in earnest. Standing there in the cool, soft morning, I listened to what the guns were saying. Sporadic firing told me I basically had run-of-the-mill shooters in the area. That was all right, I thought. They could shoot over-limits of dove just as easily as the next shooter if they could hit their hind end. Still listening for any heavier-than-normal shooting, I hoisted a healthy handful of chewing tobacco into my mouth. As I sloshed it around into my cheek, I finally identified a group of interesting-sounding guns to the south, about two miles away as the crow flew.

From the sounds there were just three guns, probably 12-gauge shotguns. Their shooting pattern was not really unusual, but it was constant, almost deliberate. That told me those chaps had a "honey hole" of some sort and were taking advantage of it. It also read methodical shooters, those who are such good shots that they don't need a lot of shooting to fill their game bags. Or it might mean a freshly harvested wheat field, a watering area favored by dove, a roosting area par excellence, or a mineral spring, which the dove family adores. Obviously it was a good place to start. Mentally marking the spot, I nosed my patrol car out and headed south. Cruising slowly along like a hunter looking for a place to shoot (we agents drove unmarked vehicles), I moved toward the suspected guns, listening all the way through open windows. After cruising about two miles, I spotted the location from which the shooting was emanating. It was a patch of unharvested field corn surrounded on three sides by a finely plowed field. Nosing into a patch of cottonwoods and brush to hide the car, I got out my binoculars for a closer look. Soon I made out three fellows concealed at the edge of the cornfield, each facing a side of the plowed field. They were pass-shooting dove as they flew along the cornfield and into the adjacent plowed field. My lads weren't bad shots, averaging about a dove for every one or two shots fired. However, one thing caught my eye. The dove appeared to be just loafing along over the plowed field as if looking for something. In some places, they were landing only to immediately leave when shots were fired at other birds. That was strange, I thought, until my binoculars located several wet areas running from the irrigated cornfield into the freshly plowed field. The dove had probably already fed and were looking for a place to get a drink before going to a roost site. Locating my shooters' transportation parked at the rear of the cornfield on a canal levee, I followed the road they had used with my binoculars until I discovered their entry point farther to the north. Making a mental note of the access, I continued watching the shooting. As near as I could tell from my notes, they were close to the limit of ten dove per man *just since my arrival.* Since they continued shooting, I figured I might have a damn good chance for an over-limit. Reversing out of my hiding place, I moved north back down the main road until I found the farm road the shooters had used to drive into their shooting area. Cruising slowly to keep down the dust (a dead giveaway), I pulled up behind their Ford van and got out.

My three shooters were to my left some fifty yards away and still shooting. Grabbing my gear, I took off along the north edge of the corn, careful to stay out of sight of the fellow shooting from that side of the field. I snuck to within twenty yards of my man and watched him retrieve and hide some doves before making my presence quietly known. Walking right up to my fellow on his blind side, I softly said, "Good morning." Surprised, he whirled, pointing his shotgun directly at me. Quickly stepping to one side, I said, "Good morning; federal agent. I would like to check your license, bag, and shotgun for a plug, if I may."

The man, still surprised as hell at my unannounced, silent arrival, said nothing for a moment and then blurted out, "You scared the hell out of me! Where the dickens did you come from?"

"From right there," I said, pointing toward the edge of the cornfield, my eyes not leaving the man.

"Damn, you shouldn't walk up on a man like that," he continued. "You might get shot one of these days!"

"That's why I am armed and maintain a distinguished expert rating with a handgun," I calmly retorted, my eyes never leaving his.

"What is it you wanted?" he asked, settling down some.

"I need to check your hunting license, birds, and shotgun to see if it is plugged" (capable of holding only three shells), I said.

Without fanfare, the man complied, and aside from being four dove over the limit, he was in compliance with the laws. The man's buddies kept shooting, obviously unaware of my presence because of the standing corn between us. That's good, I thought; I will be able to sneak up on at least one more of these chaps before the cat, or maybe I should say the dove, is out of the bag. Asking for and receiving my chap's driver's license, I asked him to sit down and await my return. Since he had exceeded the limit on dove, I also informed him that his hunting was over for the day, and he would soon be receiving a citation for the over-limit. He didn't say anything, just sat down heavily like there was now one hell of a load on his shoulders. I told him that to warn his buddies of my presence would be to invite a free trip to the nearest federal lockup. He just looked out into the field in disgust as more and more dove continued landing near him, now unafraid.

Sneaking across the front of the field, using two rows of corn for cover, I soon encountered chap number two. He too was very surprised to see me. I checked his license, shotgun, and doves and found that he too was over the limit by five birds. Other than that, he was in compliance with the hunting regulations. This chap was also very quiet, almost sullen but manageable. A little odd, I thought, but I figured I would soon get to the bottom of it, so I let the moment slide.

The third shooter, hearing that his two buddies' shooting had stopped, came over to investigate. He was also taken by surprise when I reared up out of the corn. In a few moments, he too was going through the field inspection routine to determine his compliance with the laws. I walked him back to his pile of dove, only to discover that, like his buddies, he was over the limit—again, not by a large number (four over), but an over-limit just the same. Getting my lads and their birds together at the end of the cornfield, I commenced filling out the Field Information Forms. Federal citations could be issued in the field, but many of us would take the needed information down on a Field Information Form, then, back in the quiet of the office, would issue and mail a professional-looking citation instead of issuing them in the field and having them covered with rain, dirt, blood, and the like. All the information was on the face of the citations, which were in the form of a specialized printed envelope. If the chap breaking the law wanted to forfeit bail, he made out a check to the clerk of the courts, inserted it into the envelope-combination citation, and mailed it back. With that, the violator was done with the federal justice system. However, anyone who wished to appear marked the box on the envelope signifying "appearance requested." Then the chap could have his day in court in the presence of the U.S. attorney and the officer, after which the magistrate (now called a magistrate judge) would rule on the issue and settle up with the chap who had received the citation.

Still puzzled by the odd behavior of my three chaps, I knelt in the plowed field and filled out their individual Field Information Forms using their drivers' and hunting licenses. Standing back up, I returned my first chap's driver's license—and *then the sunshine finally shone on the manure pile behind the barn*, in a manner of speaking. Stuck to the knees of my jeans were a few grains of wheat! Surprised, I looked

down into the freshly plowed dirt and saw that wheat had been lightly
sown all around the edges of the cornfield. I gave my three chaps a
"what the hell" look and noticed that they had turned the prettiest
shade of light green I had seen in some time. Gee, I wondered why
that was? Leaving them standing silently at the edge of the cornfield,
I took a "walkabout." All along the edge of the cornfield and out into
the plowed area for about twenty-five yards was what appeared to be
hand-sown wheat, not a grievous amount by a lot of standards, but at
least several hundred pounds. In and around the sprinkles of wheat
were three different sets of footprints. Having enough evidence of a
baited area, I walked back to my three now very quiet chaps.

"Gentlemen," I said, "your shooting area appears to be baited."
None of their eyes left mine, but they looked as if they wished they
could be somewhere else at that moment. I continued, "All around us
we have a plowed field, and surprisingly, in that area adjacent to your
shooting zones, we have wheat, a grain foreign to the plowed field.
Walk out into the field with me, gentlemen."

They reluctantly complied. As we came to each set of footprints
that I surmised belonged to those placing the offending kernels, I
asked each man to leave a footprint alongside. Before all was said and
done, every footprint in the field had been matched to one or another
of my shooters.

"That wasn't us," complained one of the men. "We made those
tracks when we retrieved our dove."

With that, I showed them how the wheat-spreading tracks were of
a different pattern than those made by running into the field to retrieve a downed bird (usually ending at a puff of feathers on the
ground where the dove had hit). More quiet followed that observa-
tion. "Now, gentlemen, why don't you face up to it and tell me what
happened?" I inquired.

For a few moments there was a lot of shuffling and looking down
at their feet. Then a man named Charlie said, "You got us, Officer. We
came out last Tuesday and put the wheat out to attract dove. We just
figured it would bring the dove in closer, providing us one hell of a
shoot. What is going to happen to us now?"

"First of all, I thank you for being a man and owning up to the
truth. As all of you seemingly know, baiting an area and then taking
migratory game birds over that baited area is a violation of state and

federal hunting regulations. Since you admitted to the violation after I deduced your involvement, I will issue each of you a citation for shooting over a baited area as well as one for your individual over-limits. In each instance, because of your cooperation, I will list only minimum bail. Now, you or anyone else shooting over this area before a ten-day period has expired after all the bait has been removed will be cited for shooting over a baited area as well. Do we have a clear understanding regarding that fact?"

They all nodded, and I got on with the remaining paperwork. I asked the lads to clean their doves so they wouldn't spoil, and they complied. In the meantime, dove continued to land in the baited area like there was no tomorrow, which I pointed out to further cement in their minds why this practice was so unsportsmanlike. Then I gathered up a bagful of the bait for evidence if the need arose and photographed the rest. Finishing the business at hand, I gathered my evidence birds and asked if they had any questions.

"How did you discover us?" asked one named Daniel.

"I just went to the sound of shooting and watched the behavior of the birds," I replied.

After some head-shaking in disbelief, they asked if they could go, and I said they were free to leave if they had no other questions. With that, we went our separate ways, they to ponder the quandary they were in and I to see what else I could dig up. Working in the Arkansas Valley was starting to pay some handsome dividends.

Moving out of the immediate area in case my three chaps told everyone they met to look out for the fed driving a brown Plymouth sedan (a vehicle no longer manufactured), I headed for an area labeled on the map as Olney Springs. It was getting hot, and dove tended to stay near areas where they could easily get water, so that looked like as good as any place to cast my net. I located a spot where I could hide my vehicle under the shade of some trees and listen without being discovered. There was still plenty of shooting in the area, but nothing that caused me to suspect anything other than run-of-the-mill shooters. Then I noticed a single hunter walking along a canal in the adjacent rolling hills. Having discovered over time that single hunters were usually good bets for over-limits and the like, I headed his way in such a manner that I could walk to him without being seen. Accompanied by a dog, he was a middle-aged man who seemed to be getting a fair amount of shooting, but many times his shots were groundward or aimed in such a manner that I couldn't tell what he was killing. But I found it interesting that he seemed to be getting a fair amount of shooting, since I didn't see much flying near him. When he walked behind a small hill, I used the opportunity to close the distance between us. Soon I was in intercept distance and, rising from my place of concealment, walked straight toward the man. His dog heard me approaching and began to bark. The man turned, and I hailed him. "Federal officer; I would like to check your hunting license, game bag, and shotgun if you don't mind."

"Sure," he replied and began walking toward me. When we met, I identified myself with my badge and credentials, which he acknowledged with a nod. Unloading his shotgun, he handed it to me and I checked it for a plug. It was plugged and in compliance with the regulations. Next, he dug out his license, and it too was up to snuff. Then he dumped out his game bag, and what a surprise it contained! Out tumbled the broken bodies of four dove, two meadow larks, one northern kestrel (a small species of hawk), one killdeer, three Wilson's snipe, and two rock dove (barnyard pigeons)! I couldn't believe what I was seeing!

"Where did you get all these?" I asked.

"All over," he replied. "Some down by the watered area and the rest around these hills."

"Do you know what you have here?" I asked.

"Dove," he replied with certainty.

"Well, these four are dove, that is for sure. But these others are not dove. Can't you see the difference?"

"Well, I thought some were adult dove and some were young birds," he replied hopefully.

Brother, I thought, this guy is a piece of work! Kneeling down, I took each species in hand and explained the differences to my obvious hunting novice. He nodded each time I identified a different species, as if gathering in the information. "Now," I said, "these six are legal." I laid out the dove and barnyard pigeons and explained why. "All the rest are illegal." Again I explained why. "How long have you been hunting?" I asked.

"Oh, about ten years," he replied.

"Have you been killing these types of birds during that ten-year period?" I asked.

"Oh yeah. In fact, except that one you called a hawk, they are pretty tasty eating," he innocently replied.

Oh man, I thought. Here we go! I went over the bird identification again and then informed him he would be receiving a citation for the illegal birds.

"Well, do what you have to do, Officer, but do I get to keep my birds?" he asked.

I answered partly in the negative. "Except for the six legal ones, they are my evidence of your wrongdoing." I requested his driver's license, took down all the needed information, seized the illegal birds, and asked if he had any questions.

"No, not really. If I done wrong, then I will have to pay the price," he quietly replied.

"I'll tell you what. You come with me, and I'll take you to a place where there are still some dove moving around and give you a lesson in bird identification. Then you can continue your hunt until you fill out your limit or run out of shells."

"OK," he replied happily, and the two of us spent the next two hours together, I identifying the birds on the wing and my novice happily continuing his hunt. He finally managed to scratch down his limit, and we parted ways, he feeling better about himself and I feeling not so sure. This guy had a ways to go, but at least he seemed to be catching on as to what he could shoot and what he couldn't.

By that time most of the shooting had died away as the day got hotter and the dove went to the shade of the trees to roost. Moving toward Cheraw, I pulled into an old abandoned farmstead for some lunch, peace, and quiet. Removing my ice chest from the car, I placed it alongside the house in the shade, took out a salami, Diet Pepsi, and some crackers, and sat on the ice chest, resting my back against the wall, to enjoy a quiet lunch. *Rattle-clank-rattle-rattle,* into the front driveway came what sounded like an old pickup. *Boom-boom* went two quick shots not fifteen yards away on the other side of the house. So close in fact that I instinctively pulled my head into my shoulders! Dropping my salami and Pepsi, I walked around the abandoned house just in time to see two chaps standing up in the back of a pickup, shooting two more times at a fleeing dove.

"Hey!" I yelled. The men in the back of the truck quickly put their guns down, looking like they had just swallowed frogs. The driver

hurriedly bent over and unloaded a shotgun lying beside him in the front seat. Out came the badge along with a yell for the men in the back to leave their shotguns and get out of the truck. A similar set of instructions went to the driver, who boiled out of the cab as if shot from a cannon. It was plain these folks had expected to find no one around the abandoned farmstead. Especially one so large, carrying a badge as big as a garbage-can lid! Getting them to one side of the truck, I made my approach, keeping an eye on the motley lot. They appeared to be Mexican Americans in bad need of a meal and bath. Probably several meals. "Federal agent. What the hell are you guys doing shooting from a motor vehicle?" I demanded.

There was a hurried conversation among the three in Spanish, and then the driver indicated to me that none of them spoke very good English.

"Let's see some drivers' licenses," I demanded. No one moved. Digging out my wallet, I took out my driver's license and in my best pidgin Spanish made clear what I wanted. They all shook their heads as if they were lost, and so was I at that point. Then I got pissed, feeling there was a whole lot of wool being pulled over my eyes! "All right, if I don't get some answers and pretty damn quickly, one or all of you is going to jail!"

Not one of my lads moved; they just stared at the large fellow standing in front of them. But the look in their eyes told me they understood and feared what I had just promised. Damn, I just knew that one or all of them spoke English. One more challenge just might do it, I thought. Taking my handcuffs off my belt, I said, "Either I get some answers right now or someone is going to jail." *Man, you talk about results!* It was amazing how fast my three lads "learned" the language.

"Wait a minute, mister, we don't want to go to jail. What do you want?"

"I want some damn answers, and I want them right now," I replied. "Let me see some hunting and drivers' licenses—now!"

For a second no one moved. Then the driver dug into his wallet and handed me his driver's license. The other two followed suit. All three chaps, according to their drivers' licenses, resided in Rocky Ford, Colorado.

"Where are your hunting licenses?" I asked.

There was a slight pause, and finally the driver indicated they had none.

"What the hell are you guys doing shooting dove if you don't have the required licenses?" I asked. All I got was a set of shrugs. "You guys come over here and sit down in the middle of the driveway," I ordered. After they sat down and I had control of the situation, I walked over to the back of their truck for a look. On the floor of the bed were two freshly killed chickens, four pheasants, and thirteen dove. Checking the shotguns, I found all of them loaded and without plugs. Emptying the guns, I laid them back down in the bed of the truck, pocketing the shells to avoid any subsequent unpleasantness. Walking over to the cab, I reached in and checked that shotgun. It was empty by then, but the five loaded shells on the floorboards told me it had been loaded just moments earlier. That shotgun was also unplugged. On the seat of the truck lay twelve rock dove, or barnyard pigeons, a legal species to kill without a hunting license. Some farmer had just lost all his barnyard pigeons, I thought. "Where do you fellows work?" I asked. I got the names of three different farmers from the Rocky Ford area. It was apparent that I had latched onto three very poor chaps out trying to get something for the pot. They all wore wedding rings, so I surmised they were rustling up some grub to feed their families. Another quick look at their shotguns showed one to be a Model 97 Winchester and the other two Winchester Model 12 pumps. All were in a bad state of disrepair. I doubted I would have shot any of them on a bet.

"Gentlemen. You are in violation of the state and federal hunting regulations. You two from the back of the truck were attempting to take a migratory game bird with the use and aid of a motor vehicle. And you, my friend, driving a vehicle to aid them in an illegal act is a violation as well. It is called 'Aiding and Abetting.' Additionally, there are four closed-season pheasants in the truck, which is a violation of state law. You two in the back have unplugged shotguns. No big deal except when you are trying to take a migratory game bird with them, which slips you into another set of violations, not to mention a state violation of possessing a loaded shotgun on a public way before you turned in here. All of you are going to be cited in federal court for the migratory bird violations. As far as the pheasants go, I will turn that information over to the resident state officer to prosecute. I can't do much about the pigeons because they can be taken at any time. As for the chickens, I suppose some poor dirt farmer is just out a couple of meals."

During this whole dissertation, they just looked at me like worms looking at a robin. I could tell they didn't have a pot to pee in and a window to throw it out of, but I would let the magistrate square that away (with some downward fine suggestions from me, of course, because of the obvious poverty of my culprits). Seeing no reaction to my statements, I took out my cite book and began writing out the information for later citation issuance. It was obvious they were scared to death and probably worried about being deported. I explained that taking care of the citations would square them with the U.S. government. If they failed to do so, a warrant would be issued for their arrest, and upon prosecution, they would be deported. That information lifted their spirits. With the paperwork done and questions responded to, I seized all their guns (to make sure they would take care of the citations) and bagged up their illegal birds. With many thanks and promises that they would pay their fines, off they went just as noisily as they had come. After cleaning their illegal birds to avoid spoilage, I headed for my evidence cooler to ice them down. Once that was finished, it dawned on me that my salami was gone! I looked high and low for that damn salami, but to no avail. I had left it on top of the cooler when my chaps roared in, only to have it ripped off by someone or something hungrier than me. No two ways about it, some critter had helped itself to my lunch! Probably a magpie or some damn feral cat, I thought. Settling for just my Pepsi and some crackers, I loaded up and headed east on state Highway 96. Man, I thought, this country is sure desolate. Overgrazed, hardly a tree in sight, and no watered areas for many a mile. I found it hard to believe the trappers of old from Santa Fe and Taos used to trap beaver around here, and that bison had happily grazed and gotten fat in this country. We must have had higher water tables and more grass in those days.

About then I passed an unoccupied car sitting at the edge of a gravel pit. Turning my patrol car around, I drove back to investigate. On the seat was an empty shotgun case and several half-full boxes of Number $7\frac{1}{2}$ shot. Looking around, all I could see was remnant short-grass prairie that was as barren as a billiard table. Then I heard a shot. Across the highway and down in a draw some four hundred yards away was a huge patch of wild sunflowers. The shot had come from there. Sunflowers were prime dove food, so I hurriedly gathered up my gear for a little hike and look-see.

Walking into the area carefully to avoid discovery, I settled into a shallow draw where I was out of sight but could watch the sunflower patch from higher ground. Pretty soon a pair of dove dropped into the sunflower patch and disappeared. Out from a draw below me walked a fellow I hadn't been able to see until then, slowly stalking the area where the dove had landed. Soon he jumped the dove, killing both before they got to speed. The chap retrieved the dove and walked back to his draw and disappeared, but not before taking a careful look all around. This activity was repeated several more times, with the shooter killing five additional dove in just a short period of time. Damn, I thought. What a great little hunting spot this fellow has. A single dove flew over and dropped into the sunflower patch to feed, and my man repeated his previous action, killing another dove. That time when he returned to his draw and sat down out of sight, I began my stalk. Moving slowly in a crouched position, I got to within twenty yards of my shooter before he realized he had company. Once discovered, I stood up and told him, "Federal agent. I would like to check your hunting license, shotgun, and birds if I may?"

My shooter stood up with surprise on his face but seemed cordial enough. Approaching, I could see a rather large pile of dove at his feet. Realizing I might see it about the time that I did, my shooter casually kicked his hunting coat over the birds with the tip of his hunting boot. When I got to within arm's length, I displayed my badge and commission, then replaced them in my shirt pocket. He quietly took out his hunting license for examination. It was in order, and I requested and received his shotgun as well. It was plugged and in accordance with state and federal laws. Then I asked to see his birds. He pointed toward a little cooler at his feet in which lay six freshly killed dove. Those birds, unlike the ones covered by the hunting coat, were all picked and cleaned. Then I innocently asked, "Is that all your birds?"

"That's it," came a rather strident response.

"What about those dove under your coat?" I asked.

The man froze for a second, and then collected himself and said, "What birds? You can see what I have is clearly not a limit."

Stepping closer and moving his coat with the tip of my boot, I said, "What about these?"

"You can't do that!" he exploded. "That is an illegal search. I am an attorney, and what you just did is a violation of my Fourth Amendment Rights."

"I don't think so," I coldly responded. "I saw you move the coat over those birds as I approached. Under the 'plain view' doctrine, that is not an illegal search. Besides, in a field inspection such as this when I find you hunting, I have every right to check your hunting gear, and that includes your hunting coat."

"Yeah, we will see about this in a court of law!" he stoutly retorted.

"I would like to see your driver's license," I said quietly.

Digging into his pocket, he withdrew his license and tossed it on the ground in front of me in a fit of anger. Ignoring this childishness, I stooped over, carefully watching him for any foul play, and picked it up. Getting out my citation book, I took the needed information and politely returned his property. He had twenty-six birds, or sixteen over the limit. When I issued him an evidence tag for the birds, he made it clear that this case was going clear to the Supreme Court in order to teach "jackbooted thugs" like me a lesson. I told him that would be fine since I got paid the same for field or court work. That really sent him into orbit, as it was meant to. Grabbing up his gear, he snorted his way out of the draw toward his car. I followed thirty minutes later after cleaning the birds to avoid spoilage. Once back at my car, I packed the warm birds in the ice of my evidence cooler, washed the blood off my hands, and grabbed a cold Diet Pepsi. Getting into my car, I saw that someone had torn off one of my windshield wipers. Gee, I wondered, who could have done that? I made a notation in my notebook regarding that bit of activity. Later, that incident was brought up for the magistrate's review and sentencing consideration in this matter. That somehow turned out to be a $500 windshield wiper!

The rest of the day passed uneventfully, and I got to see more of my new district. There was still plenty of hunter activity, so I decided to stay another day. Finding another abandoned farmhouse, I settled in for the evening. As it got darker and cooled off a bit, I sat on my ice chest enjoying a good Toscanni cigar. Dark closed in as I settled into my sleeping bag for some rest, anticipating what the next day would bring. Suffice it to say, it brought an unexpected but pleasant surprise.

Up before dawn the next morning, I had my usual breakfast, then loaded up and headed toward the sounds of several guns being fired along a set of railroad tracks. I had a feeling, common to many of us in law enforcement, that something special was going to happen that day. All morning long, however, nothing out of the ordinary occurred. I checked about two dozen dove hunters, and all of them were within the laws of the land. But that feeling was still there, so I kept an eye peeled.

Back in the Ordway area, I chanced across a freshly harvested oat field. Sailing into that field dotted by hundreds of oat bales were dove by the thousands. The first thought that crashed across my mind was that it must be a baited field! Jesus, the air was alive with dove from every quadrant of the compass. And partially hidden from view along the edges of the field were dozens of hunters, who were filling the air with puffs of feathers that moments before had been dove flying in for a meal and ending up with a faceful of shot. Damn! I thought. Terry, this is too good to be true—a *real* baited field full of outlaws waiting to be plucked. Quickly parking my car among other hunters' vehicles, I grabbed an empty shotgun in order to look the part and walked out into the field. The first thing I had to establish was that the field was baited. In a few moments, it was clear that it was not, as far as the regulations were concerned, even though the ground was literally covered with oats! The farmer had waited too long to harvest his field. Then when he hayed it, many of the overripe grains had fallen off the shafts, covering the ground with an unreal carpet of critter food. Since that was a normal agricultural practice, there was no violation. As I stood there, looking around and shaking my head, dove were landing everywhere, many just a few feet away in their hurry to feed on the free grits. Hunters were shooting and killing dove at the field's edge, and when walking forth to retrieve their kill would end up shooting other dove landing at their feet! It was an unreal scene that the hunters were exploiting to the fullest. Realizing there could still be problems with hunting violations, I made it a point to check everyone shooting around and in the field. Everyone was legal, showing that there are a lot of ethical hunters out there as well as those who have a tendency to "fall off the wagon." (My son Richard, now a special agent for the Service stationed in Bismarck, and I ran across a like situation in the Arkansas Valley some ten years later. In that instance, he got a good lesson as to why baiting is illegal as he observed thousands of crazy-as-a-loon doves falling into an agriculturally baited area. It was easy for him to see why the Service had outlawed baiting in the 1930s.)

By one o'clock, most hunters had left the fields. I still had that feeling something was going to happen, but I didn't know how, when, where, or what. The feeling was beginning to seem a little unrealistic in light of the near cessation of hunter activity. Getting bored and not wanting to waste gasoline, since I often had no idea where the next gallon would come from, I headed home. Stopping in Pueblo, I gassed up at a Bradley station, where gasoline was the cheapest. On the way back toward the interstate, I passed by a Motel 6 and happened to notice two fellows loading ice chests into the back of their covered pickup. Without even thinking, I whipped into the parking lot. Pulling into a vacant slot next to the two men's vehicle, I got out, opened my trunk as if I belonged there, and took out my evidence ice chest. I began counting my rather large "over-limit" of dove and other illegal critters out on a tarp for all to see. Soon one of my suspects came out with a garment bag and loaded it into the truck. Looking over at me and the critters on the ground, he said with a Texas drawl, "Goddamn! Boy, did you ever get into them!" He walked over to eye my stash in disbelief. "Jesus, how many you got?"

"Way more than I should, but you won't say anything, will you?" I asked with false meekness.

"Hell, no. But, I wouldn't be putting them out here in front of God and everybody if I were you," he responded as he guiltily looked all around. Then he spotted the pheasants. "Boy, I guess you had a good hunt. Pheasants as well, eh?"

"Yeah, might as well as get them when the getting is good," I said. "Come wintertime, they get so damn wild they are hard to find."

About that time his partner came out of the motel room with more gear for their truck. "Hey, Marshall," yelled the man standing next to me. "Come look here. This fellow had a hunt just about as good as we did." *Man, those were magic words for my ears.* Maybe a little thing called "probable cause" in the making, I thought.

Marshall walked over and took a hard look at my bounty. "By golly, mister, you did all right. Not as good as we did, but pretty damn well," he drawled.

"How can you say that?" I asked. "I have one hell of a pile of critters here, including a mess of pheasants and even some snipe."

My new "friends" just looked at each other and grinned. "Come here, boy, if you want to see a real haul," Marshall said. Walking to the back of his pickup, he dragged a large, obviously very heavy ice chest out on the tailgate. Throwing open the lid, he said, "How about that for a day-and-a-half hunt?"

By damn, he was right! I could identify picked and cleaned dove, ducks, pheasants, and what appeared to be quail (all the birds were skinned)! Yeah, he had a mess all right ... *in more ways than one!* "Where did you guys get these?" I asked in an amazed tone.

"Oh, we won't tell," replied Marshall in a smart-ass sort of way.

"The hell you say," I said as I showed the two now rather sick-looking individuals my credentials and badge. "Federal agent, gentlemen. And from the looks of it, you have a tad too many critters, not to mention a bunch of closed-season birds as well."

Man, you talk about two thunderstruck men. Well, after the fireworks had settled down, I counted 161 dove, 13 pheasants, 6 mallards, and 26 quail. As it turned out, both men were outdoor writers for their respective hometown newspapers in Texas. One owned a small ranch in Colorado, which was where they had had their hell of a shoot! My gut feeling that something was going to happen was now gone. After all was said and done, the magistrate was not pleased, and my two obliging fellows paid a small fortune for the errors of their ways for over-limits of dove and the illegal possession of closed-season species.

However, this episode didn't end there.

Several years later I hired an agent from the Southeast to be my senior resident agent in Lakewood, Colorado. His name was Joe Oliveros. I never saw a man more in tune with catching outlaws than that fellow—especially outlaws messing with migratory game and nongame birds. In fact, Joe's first year in the region found him rattling around the Arkansas Valley working dove hunters. Within two days he had filled up his ice chests with illegal birds taken from those all too happy to steal wildlife from you and me. As part of his cover, Joe had moved into a rather nice motel, posing as an outdoor writer (I had a few more dollars that year, which enabled my officers to sleep in a bed rather than on the ground). It wasn't long before the outlaws staying in the same motel took "Little Joe" under their wing (no pun intended) and were delighted to "show him the ropes"—ropes such as shooting over baited areas, shooting over-limits, and taking closed-season species. Well, after letting over one hundred outlaws have just enough rope to hang themselves, Joe dropped the trap door from under their collective feet. Two of those from that mess of unfortunates just happened to be *the same two outdoor writers from Texas* I had apprehended several years earlier.

Joe died from cancer years later before he really hit his stride, leaving many saddened family members, friends, and critters behind. No greater friend of the critters and many of us agents ever lived. I don't know where "Little Joe" is right now, but I will bet that if it ever becomes necessary, he will catch those two outdoor writers *once again* — and this time, instead of costing them an arm and a leg in the courts, it may cost them their "wings" in the clouds.

four

The Absaroka Range
and Ephraim

"JOEL SCRAFFORD needs to talk to you," advised Debbie, my secretary.
Picking up the phone, I said, "Good morning, Scraff, what's up?"

"You got a couple minutes?" asked a familiar gravelly voice.

"Sure do," I answered, even though I was up to my hind end in administrative matters. Joel was my senior resident agent or first line supervisor in Billings, Montana. He was the Service's senior law enforcement official for the states of Montana and Wyoming, which meant he was also in charge of my grizzly bear backcountry patrol program in those states.

"What's on your schedule starting this coming Friday and going through Friday of the week following?" he asked.

"Nothing," I said, lying through my teeth. As the Service's special agent in charge for eight resource-rich Western states occupied by at least one-third of the nation's hunting public (big-game seasons were open), I was always buried to my chin. I had one hell of a bunch of hustling agents scattered throughout those states stacking up the bad guys like buffalo hides alongside a railhead in the late 1870s, so there was never a moment of peace. However, when one of your hardworking supervisors asks for assistance, you had better be front and center to shoulder the load. I never had a problem piling work on their shoulders, or any problem helping them carry the load as well. That just comes with the turf when you operate under the maxim that what's good for the goose is good for the gander!

"Jim Klett's wife is sicker than a dog," Joel said, referring to the special agent in Lander, Wyoming, "and I need a replacement backcountry rider to ride with the Forest Service starting this Friday on a previously scheduled week-long patrol. Think you might be able to fill in for him?"

Now, Joel could be a little bit of a poop when he wanted to be, and my defenses went up in a heartbeat. When you rode with him on a backcountry patrol, he would have a horse that was six hundred hands high with the girth of a fifty-gallon barrel. Anyone who has ever ridden such a monster knows damn well what that does to your knees, not to mention the effort needed to keep such an animal under control. Then, Joel might take you thirty-five miles over some of the toughest country imaginable on your first day in the saddle, I guess to test your abilities as a horseman with a little bit of sheer orneriness mixed in. He might have wanted to demonstrate that he was a superior backcountry officer compared to a lowly office hack. In fact, he had done these things to my deputy, Tom Striegler, when I sent Tom to learn the backcountry ropes in order to help him become a better senior manager in addressing backcountry problems and issues. That was the last time Tom rode anywhere with anyone in the backcountry! After being sandpapered with the Joel Scrafford treatment, Tom cut short the patrol and came home, saddle sore and wiser. What kind of a horseshit detail could he have lined out for me this time? I thought. As I said, Joel could come from left field sometimes—was this one of those times, or did he really need help? Joel knew how important the grizzly backcountry patrol program was, both to the great bear and to yours truly, so my defenses went back down as fast as they had come up. Besides, Joel would be messing with the boss this time instead of a deputy. However, I don't think that boss thing ever mattered to Joel.... He was one strap-steel critter!

"Sure, Joel. Just give me some details as to whom I'm riding with, where I meet this Forest Service chap, where I will be riding, what kind of gear I should bring, and any other information pertinent to the detail," I responded.

"Great!" he said. "You will be riding with Dan Miller, a Forest Service Level IV law enforcement officer. He will be patrolling in the backcountry of the Absarokas. You will meet Dan at a Forest Service camp not far from the Triangle C Ranch and from there move into the Absarokas just below Toqwadee Pass. From there, you will patrol into the Crescent Mountain area in the Shoshone National Forest. I will get cracking and send you a map showing how to get to that Forest Service base camp. There are a number of outfitter camps in that area, and the plan is to camp out in an area that's central to them. You and Dan will take day rides to visit all those camps and check them for compliance with state and federal regulations. You will also advise everyone you meet in the camps or out hunting about our joint state-federal grizzly bear backcountry patrol program. The message I want given is to obey the laws, keep a clean camp, and if a bear is killed under any circumstances, it will be investigated like a homicide and prosecuted to the full extent of the law.

"Miller is an experienced backcountry officer even though he is quite young. The Forest Service will provide your horse and tack, but you will be responsible for your personals. The country is rugged and downright dangerous in many areas but beautiful. There is at least a foot of snow on the ground as we speak, so dress warmly. According to our biologists' radio-collar tracking system, Ephraim is still out and hasn't gone to bed. He is still trying to add on more fat since the white pine nut crop was so poor this year. That means unclean camps and elk and deer gut piles will be visited by hungry bears at every opportunity. So be on your toes, otherwise you will have a confrontation with him sure as God made little green apples. That would be all I need—a federal bureaucrat killing a federally protected species in my district! Keep alert and try to remain one step ahead of my bears, please."

That wasn't the problem, I thought. I had no intention of becoming a meal for "griz." If I had my way, they could eat the damn gut piles left by the hunters rather than eating "the grotz" (that's me). We exchanged other information and then went our ways, Joel to make some bad guy's day worse for wear and I to ponder my forthcoming adventure.

I had ridden a fair amount in Nevada while working for the Bureau of Land Management (a contradiction in terms ...) years before. But recently I had ridden little in snow and ice. Since I considered a horse an accident waiting to happen, the prospect was a little unsettling. However, I had started this grizzly bear backcountry patrol program by enlisting the assistance of other agencies to create a more coherent protection program. The program had already been going on in bits and pieces at the state and federal levels, but I had gotten everyone more or less together to provide a concentrated, unified front. So I would be damned if I'd be the one to sidestep the work just because I was a little concerned about my abilities on those damn beasts of burden. Nope; I would do my share and let the chips fall where they might. After all, I knew that if God killed me during such an endeavor, he would have to feed me. And weighing in at around 300 pounds, I wasn't likely to fit into His budget, so I would be OK. But damn, now that I thought about it, didn't He feed a multitude of folks with just a few loaves and fishes? I probably ought to zip my lip! I still had my two guardian angels. Damn, grizzlies eat guardian angels as well, don't they?

Friday found me on my way to the Forest Service base camp just north of Duboise to meet my fellow rider for the coming week. The weather was typically unsettled for late fall. The winds were sending dark clouds scudding low across the plains of Wyoming, with collateral cold temperatures. Great, I thought. Already a foot of snow on the ground, and the patrol is going to take you high up and into the Continental Divide country in the Absarokas in the dead of winter. There would likely be even more snow at that elevation, so things could get a little dicey atop the pitching deck of a horse! But it was late fall, the air was crisp, the trip through northern Colorado and Wyoming was spectacular even with the promise of bad weather, and soon my concerns melted into other thoughts—of mountain men, vast herds of wildlife, colorful but dangerous Native Americans, and the stark beauty of the lands around me two hundred years before.

Arriving late in the afternoon, I pulled into the Forest Service camp, which comprised a double-wide house trailer, a small hay barn, and several sets of corrals full of some damn fine-looking horses. I shook my head. Here I was having trouble paying for a drum of one-inch cotton lead rope for my guys because of financial mismanagement by senior Service officials, and the Forest Service had thousands of dollars' worth of horseflesh just standing around in the corrals. Oh well, sometimes you eat the bear, and sometimes he eats you. Ugh, I thought. Bad phrase to use here, Terry!

I walked over to the corrals and greeted a young fellow probably twenty years my junior. "Good afternoon. My name is Terry Grosz, and I am the one Joel sent to act as Jim Klett's replacement."

"Hey, good to see you," came a genuinely warm reply. "My name is Dan Miller. I'll be your partner in the backcountry for the next few days. You got here just in time, as we are about ready to go. Where is your gear?" he asked, looking nervously past me toward the truck as if expecting a load and a half based on my size.

"It's in the truck. Want me to go and get it right now?" I asked.

"You bet. I'll start packing the mules, and with a little luck we can make camp before it gets too late," he replied.

Walking back to my truck, I had to marvel. Joel had said this chap was a gunner, which was the same conclusion I was beginning to draw. Joel had also warned me not to bring any more than the bare necessities. It seemed that when Tom, my deputy, had gone into the backcountry with Joel, he had brought everything but the hot tub. I guess that embarrassed Joel in front of his National Park Service counterparts—*and Tom paid the price*. I had everything in just two military duffel bags. One held a heavy-duty sleeping bag, and the other was full of warm winter clothing. The bags were compact so as to be easily packed on a horse or mule.

When I hauled my gear over to Dan, he smiled approvingly. "Is this all you have other than what you're carrying? That's great," he beamed.

"You're looking at it," I said with a grin. It was always good to get off on the right foot with a partner one was going to be living with under tough backcountry conditions. Returning to my truck, I put on my heavy old U.S. Air Force insulated three-quarter-length bomber jacket and filled both side pockets with large bags of M&Ms (a genius move, I would soon discover). I strapped on my .44 magnum pistol, threw a handful of extra 250-grain soft-nosed cartridges into my front pants pocket, locked the truck, and headed for the corrals. I still had one concern. Every time I had ridden with Joel, he had had a horse for me that weighed at least fifteen hundred pounds. Remember the six hundred hands high and the girth of a fifty-gallon barrel ... but I'd be damned if I could see any horse in the two corrals even close to that weight. Oh well, maybe Dan had a bigger one on the way.

Seeing Dan struggling with the packing, I quit my daydreaming, stepped over, and gave him a hand loading a rather large mule with my gear. About then another Forest Service packer showed up, and the three of us loaded two more mules with the gear needed for an extended patrol. I soon discovered that a cook tent and a sleeping tent had already been set up in the camp up on the mountain. The new fellow commenced to saddle two horses and load another mule with bales of certified hay for the livestock.

"Where is my horse? I don't see one anywhere near big enough to carry this tired old carcass," I said with a worried grin.

Dan tilted his head to one side and fixed me with his eyes, saying, "Joel told me you knew how to ride."

"That's true, but Joel usually had a horse for me about twice the size of these."

"Well, if you can ride, that black horse with the white blaze on the forehead over there can carry you," he replied.

I was amazed. The horse was small-boned and of delicate build and didn't appear to weigh more than a thousand pounds. "Are you sure?" I asked nervously. "He seems pretty damn small to be carrying a three-hundred-pound carcass all over those mountains."

Dan smiled and replied matter-of-factly, "That horse will carry you anywhere you want to go. Sure, sometimes you'll need to get off and lead him to give him a break and rest your knees, but he is fit as a fiddle and can do the job."

Filled with doubt, I walked over to my horse, who was tied to the top log of the corral, curried him, then threw on a saddle blanket followed by the saddle. The saddle looked big enough for my lard ass, I concluded, but this little horse sure had me concerned.

"They are Tennessee Walkers," said Dan, realizing my still spoken and unspoken concerns. "They are great little backcountry horses with a heart to match. As long as you can ride and don't sit too far back in the saddle, that little horse will bring you home after the patrol." (Leaning back in the saddle places the rider's weight directly over the horse's kidneys, which can make the horse too sore to ride and leave you walking most of the way on foot.)

Still unconvinced, but not being a horseman or a judge of horseflesh, I continued saddling my horse and adjusting the stirrups to fit the length of my legs. Soon I was aboard and sitting easily in the saddle. Moving around the area while the other two made final adjustments to the pack animals, I found riding that little horse a dream. In moments I realized he was one of the finest horses I had ever ridden! He had a very smooth gait and was alert and sure footed (that particular dream would soon come crashing down)—just a real joy to ride. No jarring motion when he moved, just a brand of "smooth" that any rider could appreciate, especially after a long, hard day in the saddle.

Soon my two companions were loaded and saddled up. We walked our outfit along the shoulder of state Highway 26/287 for a mile or so. I brought up the rear, and man, what a pleasant start. The crisp fall mountain air, me comfortable in the saddle, off on another adventure, with my two saddle bags jug-full of large bags of M&Ms with peanuts. What more could a fellow want? Well ... I could think of a few things as my doubts regarding horseback riding in rugged mountains hove into my mind's eye once again.

Soon we arrived at a roughed-out parking area on the east side of the highway, adjacent to a trailhead. The area was packed with big four-wheelers attached to large horse trailers capable of hauling six to eight animals each. The ground was torn to smithereens from all the horse traffic, and it was easy to see why we were going into this area. With that many folks running around with itchy trigger fingers, and half of them new to the backcountry game, anticipated conflicts with old Ephraim could quickly become a reality. In those days we still had a world of distance to go in the educational department regarding the grizzly bear and the Endangered Species Act. Many—not all, mind you, but many—outfitters and guides would just as soon shoot a grizzly bear as spit. And since many were heavy tobacco chewers and spitters ... well, you get the deadly picture. With the basic backcountry outfitter maxim of "shoot, shovel, and shut up" still widely adhered to, a little government hand-holding was the word of the day if the griz was to make it back from the brink of extinction (there were about one thousand bears in the lower forty-eight states at that time).

The view of the country from the back of my steed was stunning. It was rugged in every aspect of the word, with huge rock formations and dense stands of old-growth coniferous forest rising to meet the sky. The well-worn horse trail headed up into the clouds, and we quietly followed it. It was now late in the afternoon, and the cool of late fall began to settle around us like a damp blanket. When we stopped to rest our animals, I couldn't help but be amazed. I could see for miles, and everything that met my eyes appeared to be as wild as it had been several hundred years before. The air was clear below the scudding clouds, yet the smell of terpenes was heavy in the air. Moose were in evidence at many turns in the trail, as were small herds of elk moving ever farther away from any human activity. Several blue grouse were observed pecking

at the undigested grains in the horse droppings left in the trail by earlier pack strings. They moved slowly out of our way, and life was good.
I may have been born one hundred years too late, but here I could pre-
tend it was *one hundred years before.* I could hardly believe the U.S.
government paid me to do this—but I was soon to earn that pay.

We climbed higher and higher. Soon we were close enough to touch
the face of God, and the air was heaven sent. It was crisp, cold, and
had the best smell imaginable! Still we climbed. Soon we were on top
of one of the many mountain ranges, and the ground began to level
out slightly. I began to notice that my horse enjoyed looking around
as much as I did. Now, that is not so good. ... A horse that isn't
watching where he is going will stumble a lot, which eventually leads
to one hell of a wreck! And this son of a bitch I was astride was beginning to stumble over every little rock and twig in the trail! Soon I
had to keep one eye on the trail instead of continuing to look around
in awe. When I spotted a hazard in the trail, I would rein my horse's
head around so he could see it and react accordingly. That would
work for a while, then back to his old habits he would go and the
"jerk and see" lessons would recommence. I had been tossed in the
past from horses that weren't too careful where they placed their feet,
and each time was a reminder of just how hard the rocks and ground
could be. The part hitting the ground first, providing you did not
break anything, had a tendency to turn black, blue, yellow, and various shades of brown. Using those spots to sit or lie on at a later date
usually brought one's eyes to dinner-plate size with vivid reminders
of the earlier event, if you get my drift.

It was almost dark now, and the cold began to manifest itself. On
one of our stops to rest the animals, I dug out my heavy gloves and
put them on. "Just a little further," Dan sang out merrily as we headed
into the dark timber, made all the darker by the onrushing evening.
After another thirty minutes of riding we arrived at the edge of a big
meadow. As we emerged from the dark timber into the twilight, I saw
a ten-by-twelve-foot wall tent lying on the ground, torn all to hell!
Fifty yards away at the edge of the meadow stood a nine-by-twelve
wall tent that was partially collapsed from the previous snows. Damn,
what the hell happened here? I thought as I stiffly dismounted. Once
I hit the ground, I stood by my horse for support as life slowly and
painfully came back to my legs and knees.

It turned out that a grizzly bear had discovered the cook tent with all its interesting smells and had taken it upon himself to go "shopping." Unfortunately, he had gone through the side of the tent, assisted by his rather large slashing claws. Everything inside was a shambles. Every can of food had been bitten into and torn to pieces. Every box and bag, or anything that smelled or looked interesting, had been torn asunder and scattered about. Every bottled item had been dropped and smashed, and most of the contents eaten, pieces of glass and all! In short, we had a real mess. Fortunately, a new tent had been included as an item on our pack string because it seemed the old one had leaked. Dan and the other chap began removing the old cook tent and erecting the new one in the fast-fading light. I was assigned the detail of getting the sleep tent up and running, fifty yards away. Why so far? Well, bears like cook tents because of all the interesting smells; hence, it's best to place the sleeping tent some distance from the cooking area. Then you should be careful to remove your clothes that smell of food items in the cook tent, change into others lacking such smells, and then move to the sleeping tent. That way, hopefully, if a bear pays a visit, it will invade just the cook tent and not the sleeping tent. If the bear does invade the sleeping tent, an exciting time is had by all. Just imagine three handguns going off in a sleeping tent, aimed at a bear a few feet away. And imagine what happens when those damn little popguns piss off old Ephraim! The same problem exists in backcountry cabins. The bear is tremendously strong and can rip his way into a cabin posthaste. Driving long, sharp spikes or nails through the doors from the inside out, as well as through the wooden window coverings, can prevent a bear from pushing on the doors or windows with all his might unless he wants to impale his sensitive feet on the spikes. Do I detect any readers getting a little goosey about going into the back-country with Ephraim? If not, you should be. The grizzly is at the top of the food chain. He has no enemies other than humankind, which he may eat with relish when given the opportunity. ... Well, he generally will leave part of the skull and pelvis.

Removing the snow from the roof of the collapsed sleeping tent, I got it reassembled and livable. With the aid of my flashlight, I took all our sleeping gear and laid it out on the dirt floor. Fortunately, the snow and damp had not permeated the floor of the sleeping area. Then I headed back to the cook tent to give the other lads a hand. They had removed the old tent and erected the new. I started a Coleman lantern for light and hooked it onto a limb by our livestock, then unsaddled the critters and placed the saddles over a previously erected log railing to dry. Those were soon followed by the pack frames and horse blankets. Then I got out the brushes and curried down all the stock, working out their matted, sweat-soaked hair. By then I could smell dinner cooking in the cook tent, so I hurried through feeding the stock with grain and hay. Bear in mind that these animals got us there and were needed for getting us home. It takes proper care and a lot of luck to see that mission accomplished without a whole lot of walking on your part.

Taking my lantern, I bent low and entered our new cook tent. The warmth from two other Coleman lanterns hit me head high as I entered, and it felt great. It was now about nine in the evening, and I began to realize just how hungry I was. Man, I could eat a horse! I thought. Excuse me critters. I didn't mean that except as a figure of speech.

"Your timing is right on. Soup is on," said Dan. We gathered around the small woodstove and filled up our plates with the good-smelling chow. When it was my turn, what a surprise awaited me! There might have been a cup of fried potatoes, a half cup of string beans, and two fried hot dogs for my first dinner in the backcountry! Now keep in mind that my boiler was as large as that of the ill-fated *Titanic*. To put that little bit of food into that cavernous hole would have created a riot between the big and little guts, as hungry as I was! Looking around, I didn't see any more. ... Not having eaten since six in the morning, I began to get a bad feeling about the amount of grub for the rest of this trip. The fellow responsible for procuring the eats was a little ol' stick, not much bigger than a mouse knuckle. I realized he had probably bought the grub for a man his size, not realizing someone else might be a little more of an eager eater. Oh well—I was starved and soon consumed my portion. I hoped that the dinner was scanty only because we had just met with a disaster, and it was so late at night and all. I was sure the next morning would be different, especially since we would be in the saddle from predawn until long after dark.

Wrong! I discovered the next morning that breakfast consisted of one fried egg, two strips of bacon so thin I could have read through them, two slices of toast (no butter, just jam), and coffee. *I don't drink coffee.* That was the breakfast menu for the next seven days. Suffice it to say, I started thinking that what I was carrying in my saddle bags might just be what kept me alive for the rest of this trip. And I wasn't wrong. The grub never got any better (lunch was a peanut-butter-and-jelly sandwich with a small apple), and I truly did live on several daily handfuls of M&Ms with peanuts for the rest of the trip. Lord help any grizzly, federally protected or not, who tried to help himself to that stash of M&Ms. ...

After retiring to our sleeping tent that first night, the three of us adjusted to our cold sleeping bags as they quickly warmed. Soon the tired, quiet snores of my two bedfellows told me I was the only one awake. With just my face exposed to the numbing cold, my mind began to wander back to the times of old and what the mountain men had gone through. You could bet they either ate very well, maybe six or seven pounds of meat at a sitting, when they had game, or not at all (kind of like me at supper) when hunting was unsuccessful. For sleeping provisions in country like this in November, they probably had several buffalo robes, a lean-to, and a roaring fire. Off in the distance, I could hear the plaintive hoot of a great horned owl, and in the tent a mouse, happy to be inside, scurried around. He'd better stay away from my M&Ms, I thought as I drifted off to sleep in the land of the grizzly and long-dead mountain men.

At three-thirty the next morning we were up, had a fire built in the stove in the cook tent, and were busy feeding the stock and saddling up. The third fellow was going back down the mountain with the pack string that morning, and Dan and I would remain until the end of the patrol. The air was crisp, about 10 above, and every star in the sky had to be over our camp that fine morning. It is really amazing just how many stars there are in the heavens when you're looking through an almost pollution-free atmosphere. Everyone should experience such a joy before the stars go out in their own eyes. Just before I entered the tent, I saw a large star slowly burn itself out in a brilliant streak as it entered Earth's atmosphere. That was always a good-luck charm for me, putting a smile on my face and in my heart. How soon that charm would be needed.

By four we were in the saddle and moving back down the trail we had traveled the night before. Part of our mission was to contact the outfitters, guides, and hunters to inform them about the new grizzly bear backcountry program. To do that most efficiently, we had to contact the groups in their hunting camps before they dispersed into the surrounding national forest. By leaving so early, with luck we would contact several camps before the hunters left. During the remainder of the day, we met them in ones and twos in the field. Then, late at night when they were back in camp, we'd seek out those we had missed in the morning. The backcountry riders followed this routine day in and day out. A sixteen-to-eighteen-hour day was the norm. As I said earlier, I would soon be earning my keep.

It was as dark as the inside of a dead cow on the trail, but the horses plodded along like it was an everyday situation. Riding horses in the backcountry in total darkness is a *treat*. You are always on guard so a low limb doesn't poke out your eye or brush you out of the saddle. The horses have remarkable eyesight and can see even the faintest of trails in the dark, and since humans can't see jack (you don't use your flashlight because it confuses the horse's night vision), it is definitely a memorable experience.

We came to a branch in the trail, and our extra man headed the pack string back down toward the trailhead as Dan and I headed up higher into the backcountry. Hell, we were already so far into the backcountry that the chickens had square faces. Speaking of chickens, I sure could do with a bucket of KFC about now, I thought. Extra crispy ...

In less than thirty minutes we entered our first camp. It was a large one, holding about fifteen guides and hunters. Greeting them from a distance so they wouldn't think the noise we were making was a bear, we rode into the light of their Coleman lanterns. There was great activity as everyone was making ready for the day's hunt. However, Dan and I finally got everyone gathered around and settled down to deliver our message. As we expected, there was a lot of grumbling about the "damn government bear," but the message was understood. There were several Fish and Game questions before the meeting ended and the guides hustled their charges away to their waiting horses. Soon they were off into the early morning, and we parted ways with their cook, who was to remain in camp. We hit one more large camp that morning and repeated our message before everyone hit the saddle leather en route to their little hunting "cherry patches."

Finally the sun danced over the high mountain peaks from the east, flooding the gray, hazy valleys below with tumbling rays of yellow. As if on cue, the gray jays, Clark's nutcrackers, red crossbills, and chickadees filled the air with their calls and movements as they greeted the day. With the sun's arrival, a slight breeze began to be felt and several elk disturbed during their breakfast clicked and crashed away unseen though the dark timber below the trail. God, it was great. Colder than all get-out, but what a view! We were on top of the world and watching it wake up. God only shares those moments with a few, and I was thankful to be among that number. The air was so crisp and clean, I couldn't suck it down in large gulps without freezing my "goozle." But what a day and experience. ... Even old Stumble Foot seemed to be enjoying himself. Soon we began to feel the welcome warmth as the sun crawled higher in the sky.

Dan had a map showing where every outfitter's camp was located, and as we laid our plans for the rest of the day, I casually looked back over my shoulder. Coming across the mountains behind us to the north was a billowing, fast-moving snowstorm. It quickly bulled its way over the ridges and then thundered down into the valleys, covering them in instant white. Then up the next draw and ridge it came with a determination indicating that we had best hang on to the willows! We quickly unrolled and put on the dusters (full-length waterproof coats) that were tied behind our saddles just as the first wet flakes touched our faces. I still have a picture on my wall of me sitting astride my trusty steed looking at that front racing toward me across the skies. That stirs not only old memories but old fires in this tired carcass. ...

For the next several days Dan and I crisscrossed the mountains and meadows, visiting the hunting camps with our message about the bear's survival. We were after compliance and figured education was the best way to start. We couldn't be everywhere all the time, and without support from the backcountry-using public, our program was dead. However, we made it very clear that times were changing and that the great bear was part of the ecosystem. For that bit of ecological history to maintain itself, we would all have to work hard for his survival and understand that the bear belonged there just as much as we did. There were some hardheads who grumbled and continued to illegally shoot grizzlies around their camps, but the hardworking state and federal officers were catching them in ever greater numbers, and in so doing making it a real challenge to illegally kill the bear and escape.

I noticed that all outfitters were very surprised to see us, and *every one* we contacted had a dirty camp: food scattered around the cook tent, horse feed placed carelessly around the corrals (grizzlies will eat horse feed, especially alfalfa cubes and grains), game carcasses hung too low (which allowed the bears to tear them down, usually getting themselves shot in the process), game trimmings left under the meat poles, and so on. Dan and I warned the guides and outfitters to have cleaner camps upon our return or there would be legal trouble. That warning was driven home as we crossed and recrossed several sets of large grizzly tracks in our wanderings. Aside from being dirty, the camps were in compliance with the state Fish and Game hunting regulations. Every time we contacted any backcountry users afoot or on horseback, I gave them the song and dance about the bear and clean camps and the warning that if bears were killed they'd better have powder burns on them, and what the Endangered Species Act penalties were. We also rode to the sound of the guns. Shooting usually meant someone had run into a deer, moose, or elk. Grizzlies, habituated to the sound of guns and the associated warm gut pile, also moved toward such disturbances. As I said, griz is at the top of the food chain, and with the winter snows coming and the need for more grub prior to hibernation, one hell of a wreck could occur if a hunter were not careful.

One day toward the end of the week, Dan and I heard a flurry of shots on top of a nearby mountain. To get there, we had to backtrack about five miles, grab another trail, and head back toward the place where we had heard the shooting (because of the dense stands of timber and blown-down trees, traveling across country is problematic with horses). We pushed the horses as hard as we dared in the snow. Twenty-one shots meant someone had gotten into a herd of elk and possible taken extras for everybody in camp who had not yet killed one. That would mean someone had taken an over-limit of elk, which would be a good case. It was snowing quite hard at that point, and we couldn't see more than forty yards. However, we kept climbing, following the rapidly vanishing trail. The climb in snow was troubling to our horses as well. Snow kept balling up in their hooves, causing a lot of slipping and sliding until the snow kicked free. It was nerve-wracking to say the least. Several times we lost the trail and had to backtrack. The heavy snowfall was really raising hell with the visibility, but we kept at it. Finally we arrived at the kill site after cutting across four fresh sets of horse tracks moving across the mountain and leading us to the area we sought. These tracks were later joined by six more sets of horse tracks, probably a pack string. Soon we also began to find blood trails. From my saddle, I spotted two cow elk with broken shoulders trying to navigate through the fallen timber. Then we found the place where the herd had been bedded down before the shootout. In short order, we found four gut piles and more blood trails leading into the dark timber. Damn, as far as we could tell, the shooters (notice I don't call them hunters) had killed four elk and crippled at least four more! Since our suspected pack string had a big head start on us, we pushed our horses hard in the climb. Up, up we went until we had gone several miles. They were moving at a good clip as well, as if they realized someone was on their trail. They left many blood smears or trickles from the packed and quartered elk for us to follow. As usual, my dumb damn horse had to smell and shy away from every one of them, not to mention stumbling over every limb or log under the snow on the trail. However, these things were easily overlooked in the heat of the chase.

Soon it became apparent that our pack string was heading for the other side of the mountain to another drainage and trailhead. As we sat there wet with sweat, like our horses, it became evident we were not going to catch them. In fact, they were heading clear off any of Dan's maps and into new territory. Dan tried to raise someone on our radio to head them off, but to no avail. It seemed there weren't many officers out working in this snowstorm. Realizing we were not going to catch those chaps and aware of the long distance (about ten miles) we had to go just to get back to our camp, coupled with the heavy snowfall and lateness of the hour, we gave up the chase—not without a lot of tooth grinding, but you must keep your head about you in the high country in the winter, or you will get your hair "lifted," if you get my meaning.

With a backward glance of frustration, we started back down the mountain, the trail all but erased by the continuing drifting wet snows. We carefully picked our way down as our horses slipped and stumbled on the steep slopes. I made sure just the toes of my boots were in the stirrups so I could kick out and off if my horse went down. I had been there before, and a wreck like that is not a whole lot of fun. That was all we needed, I thought, an injury this far back in the bush in a driving snowstorm. We carefully continued down for the next hour or so and then were delighted as the snow lightened up and finally abated. However, now the wind began whipping up, making the conditions even more hazardous. Coming to a rocky edge with about a thousand-foot fall to the rocks below, we stopped and let the horses blow. Man, let me tell you, I was not looking forward to the next hundred yards of the trail. One wrong slip and it would be spring before they could recover my body, if then.

"Dan," I said, "how about walking the horses across this next piece?"

"They have better footing than you or I," he yelled back over the wind. "We need to keep moving or we will be spending the night on this cold damn mountain. Their weight will allow them the best footing, so just give your horse his head when you start across."

By then the wind was coming up out of the canyon below, whipping around us at at least twenty miles per hour. I noticed that my horse was really starting to get nervous. He would snort and then dance rapidly around, no matter what I did with the reins. Then he would point his head down toward the canyon, ears forward, and snort and blow as he stomped nervously. Then he would skitter from side to side, never taking his eyes off something in the canyon, before spinning around once again. Dan's horse was doing the same, but not as badly.

"Let's get it done," he yelled and started across the rocky face. Moving slowly and carefully, his horse navigated the section without a problem. Now it was my turn. Looking one more time over the edge to oblivion ten feet away, I clucked to my horse to follow. Across that face my horse went, but he never once looked to see where he was going! He just stared down into that damn canyon like something was going to come up out of there and get him. I kept pulling the reins to the left to get him to watch where he was going to place his feet for the next step, but to no avail. However, with only ten feet to go, we had it made. Just as I began to relaxing a bit, I saw a limb lying in the trail under the snow. I jerked the horse's head around so he could see the hazard, but he jerked it right back. Then his hooves hit the limb under the snow, and he stumbled. Trying to quickly regain his footing, he went down on his left side, pinning my leg against the rock face before I could get it out of the stirrup. *Then the two of us slid down and over the cliff!* Jesus, my heart stopped as we hurtled downward, miraculously dropping only about ten feet onto a rocky shelf that was invisible under about six feet of loose snow. Then my horse went nuts! Lunging, kicking, and plunging in the soft, loose snow, he must have thought something had him. Pitching forward over his head, all the while trying to avoid those flailing hooves, I grabbed his head and "bull-dogged" him down. It took a few moments of trying to keep him from going over the edge of the ledge just inches away, but finally, except for a bad case of white eyes, flared nostrils, and ears going every which way, he settled down.

I could hear Dan yelling frantically over the pounding sound of my heart. *"Are you OK? Are you OK, Terry?"*

"Yeah, I'm fine. I'll probably have to clean out my shorts before I am able to ride again, but I think I'm all right."

"Hold his head, and I'll try to make a trail to you. I think we can lead him out if I can reach you," yelled Dan. A few minutes later I could see Dan neck-deep in snow, breaking a trail toward me. "Damn, I thought you were a goner when I saw that horse go over the cliff," he exclaimed.

"Me too," I said, still with a case of the big eye! "Let's get the hell off this ledge before this horse gets any more ideas!"

I began to lead my horse up the trail Dan had forged. Moments later I was standing by Dan's horse, and the two of us let our hearts get back to normal before continuing. That took a while!

The rest of the trip back to camp was without incident other than more snow, howling wind, and wet clothing. My damn horse now paid attention to every bump in the trail. It was apparent that he had learned a lesson. I never did figure out what was spooking him, but whatever it was, it had been cause for serious concern in his world. Another thing I noticed was that Dan's horse appeared to be laughing at my horse, "old Sure Foot," and my horse seemed to know it! You talk about an embarrassed horse—I now sat astride one. Thank God for my lucky star and my two guardian angels. *However,* they could have moved that ledge a little higher up so we wouldn't have dropped so far and landed so hard. My damn head was still ringing, having bounced off numerous rocks before going over the edge, and my left leg was starting to get pretty damn stiff. Oh well, that's all right, I thought. I have another leg on the other side. ...

Back at camp I went about the chores of caring for the horses while Dan cooked our "magnificent" supper. ... After dinner I went to my dwindling M&M stash and gobbled two handfuls. I added two full-strength Tylenol to the mix. About then a full-grown bull moose sauntered right through camp as if he owned the place (hell, as much as he weighed, *he did*). Our two horses went nuts! Grabbing both by the reins, I held on as they reared and plunged until Dan got there to give me a hand. A couple of hollers sent the moose on his way, and the horses finally settled down—not all the way, but at least their eyes had shrunk from the size of dinner plates to normal-sized saucers. Damn, they were behaving just as they had back on the mountain. I pointed that out to Dan, and he said horses didn't much care for moose. He thought it was the fear of being mounted by one. I guess I would be a little nervous and have a bad case of the big eye as well if a moose tried to mount me. ... And he'd better bring a lunch, because when it was all over I was going to have one hell of an appetite.

The next day the snow finally stopped, the sun came out, and the country was once again gorgeous beyond human powers of description! I could see why a lot of mountain men never came back from the mountains. Why should they? They had heaven right there in their own backyard. This was also the historical home of the fierce Blackfoot Confederacy; those tribes may have accounted for the disappearance of some of the mountain men as well (history relates that about 25 percent of the mountain men who entered the wilderness failed to return in any given year). I guess hell can come in some of the same colors as heaven, huh?

The next day Dan and I left our campsite and ventured into another outfitter's area. We found the campsite filthy and deserted, with fresh grizzly tracks all around. I guess the snow and the promise of more to come, along with the presence of griz, had made them move their camp to lower elevations. Dan discovered a half-eaten bale of hay that proved to be native hay from another part of the country, based on the floral types it contained. That kind of hay was not allowed in our national forest because of the harmful weeds it carried, so he got hot. You could tell from the tracks that the outfitter had beaten a hasty retreat down the mountain. Dan, feeling he may have taken the last load from camp and might have some of the illegal hay with him, wanted to pursue. After a hurried conference, Dan took off down the trail in pursuit and I took off laterally across the mountainside. Figuring I was finally even with the trailhead thousands of feet below, I kicked my horse in the flanks and started down. However, he misunderstood that little kick I gave him, *big time!* Thinking I wanted a race, he broke into a full gallop! Down that hillside, leaping over boulders and other obstacles, we hurtled through up to two feet of snow. There was no way I could rein him in without a slippery, head-over-tea-kettle wreck. Having had one of those the day before, I settled on letting him have his head, merely hoping he wouldn't slip and kill the both of us. Down, down we hurtled, jumping over logs and boulders too difficult to dodge. Then I became aware of something through the thrill and danger of the ride. This ride was one of the smoothest I had ever taken! This horse had an easy, gently rocking motion, and if it hadn't been so damn scary, what a beautiful ride it would have been. After many anxious moments galloping and sliding down that snow-covered mountainside, we crossed the main trail just above the trailhead and I finally got up enough nerve to stop my horse in his mission. I reined him in, and we skidded a ways as he planted his ass in the snow but finally and safely stopped. I swear that horse had a satisfied look on his face. Kind of like he had atoned for the slide over the cliff the day before. With a grin of relief, he walked back up the hill to the trail. Standing there, we both gathered our wind and composure—he out of exhaustion from having run several miles and I out of joy at being alive and not all broken up.

Looking down at the trailhead, I didn't see anyone near the parked rigs. Good, I thought, we are ahead of the bad guys. I looked back up the trail, and lo and behold, here they came. Two men were coming at a fast trot on their horses, each leading three mules with *bales of hay on each mule.* The men were looking back as if they were aware someone was on their trail. I was sure it was Dan. One of them looked down the trail toward me, making sure the way was clear before looking back over his shoulder again. All of a sudden, he realized there was someone blocking the trail. He skidded to a stop, and the chap running hard behind him violently crashed into the front pack string. It took a few moments of hollering and braying of mules to untangle the mess. Then down the trail they continued as if nothing were out of the ordinary, but now at a more respectable pace.

"Where the hell did you come from?" the lead man uttered as I held up my badge for them to see.

"Up there." I nodded toward the mountain's face.

"Did you gallop all the way down?" he asked.

"Sure did," I proudly replied.

"Goddamned fool," was his response.

Ignoring that probably correct statement, I said, "You gentlemen will have to wait a bit until the Forest Service gets here."

"What for?" demanded the man in the lead.

"There is some question regarding the legality of unregistered, out-of-state hay being brought into and used in the Shoshone National Forest, and also the matter of a dirty camp," I replied.

There was some grumbling, but with me blocking the trail before them, they complied. About twenty minutes later, Dan arrived on his lathered-up horse.

"Terry, how the hell …" His voice quickly trailed off. I pointed up the mountainside with a nod, and he just shook his head in amazement. By now I was beginning to realize how lucky I was just to be alive.

Dan confirmed that the hay the two guides had was illegal, and the appropriate paperwork was administered along with a warning about the dirty camp. We moved the entire pack string down to the rigs at the trailhead and seized the illegal hay. Dan called in and had it picked up at the trailhead to be used as evidence if necessary. Then back up the mountain we went to our camp. This time the ride was uneventful. It was our last day of the patrol, and another Forest Service hand had delivered two mules to our camp earlier so we could bring down our gear. As it turned out, we brought all the gear off the mountain on two heavily laden and complaining mules. When Dan met the other Forest Service chap at the trailhead during the hay detail, he was instructed to come off the mountain fast. There were several days' worth of storms heading our way, and with those the bears would more than likely head for their dens. So out we came, heavily loaded with gear, done for the season. To be frank, I was ready. Besides being too damn old for this kind of vigorous work, I didn't like the idea of falling off more mountains in heavy snow. True, we had contacted over sixty backcountry users and used the opportunity to inform them of the purpose of the grizzly bear backcountry patrols. We had gotten across the message that to shoot a grizzly bear for any reason but self-defense would land them in deep shit. The fact that we didn't have any bear killing on that trip spoke to another success. We sure had the bear out and about looking for food, but no run-ins, so that was a victory of sorts as well. Plus, I had had an opportunity to experience the rigors of this kind of work and gained additional respect not only for my Service horsemen but for all the officers on the joint teams working the backcountry on behalf of the bear.

Coming off the mountain that afternoon was a treat. It was quiet except for the clicking of the horses' hooves against the rocks. Moose and elk were still in abundance, and I couldn't help but appreciate the plain raw beauty of the land. God had really worked His wonders in that neck of the woods, I thought at one point as I sat still in the saddle drinking it all in. Just as we got to the bottom, it started to rain, then turned to a heavy, wet snow. We had gotten off the mountain just in time. The highway was icy as all get-out. This time, in the face of danger, I got off and walked my horse the several miles to our corrals. As predicted, my little horse had taken me everywhere I wanted to go, and one place I didn't. Once at the corrals, I curried and grained the animal. He had worked hard dragging my carcass all over that mountain range, and I was a better man and senior manager for it. Sore and hungry, but a man with a better realization of what went on and what was still needed if the program was to be safe and successful.

Thanking Dan for a great time, I loaded up my gear and headed for Duboise. It took awhile to get there because of the snow, but it felt good riding in a means of travel that did what it was told. Plus, I didn't see many limbs on the highway. ... I don't remember the eatery on the main street of Duboise, sort of a Western motif out front as I recollect, but after settling my tired frame into the dining room chair, I ordered two complete steak dinners! I advised the wide-eyed waitress that when she saw I was about two-thirds finished with the first, she should bring on the next. Two whiskey doubles seemed to get some of the kinks out as well. Walking back to my motel room with a hitch in my giddy-up, I took off my dirty, strongly horsy-smelling clothing and headed into the shower. I let the hot water run over my frame for at least half an hour. Getting out and toweling off, I had a chance to examine my tired, old carcass. I was black and blue from the waist down, especially on my left side where the horse had slid over the rock face with me partially pinned underneath! After I had sailed over his head, the flailing hooves had done a number on the front of my legs as well. As I stood there looking at my tired, unshaven self, a grin formed on my windburned face. Aside from my body of many colors, I had gone into some of the grandest country on the globe. I had seen and learned, not to mention survived what could have been one hell of a horse wreck. For an old man, that wasn't too bad. Hell, I would bet even Joel would have been proud.

If I remember correctly, Joel did call Dan and asked how I had done. Joel had a lot of pride in his grizzly bear program, and supervisor or no supervisor, it had better be done right! Dan gave me an "A" and told Joel he would be glad to have me along as his partner on a back-country patrol anytime. I guess that sort of put a cork in Joel's bottle.

Damn, did I sleep well that night. … However, getting everything moving the next day was a horse of a different color. Thank God the rest of the way home was in a mechanical horse. I hope the damn grizzly bear appreciates what a lot of good people went through to keep them from the black hole of extinction. Truth be known, I would bet he doesn't give a damn. Just wonders where his next meal of yellow-bellied marmot, dirty camp leavings, backcountry hiker, or gut pile is coming from.

As a postscript, the grizzly bear in the lower forty-eight *is back!* It is now not uncommon to find the grizzly bear in areas of his range where he has not been seen in the last seventy years. He hasn't reached his historic greatness—he will never be there again. But biologically, he is in better shape than he has been for years, thanks in part to the hard-riding backcountry officers, state and federal criminal investigators, prosecutors and judges, and those backcountry users who finally grew up and realized the great bear is part of them as well.

five

Operation SLV

NESTLED ALONG THE EASTERN SLOPE of the Rocky Mountains in south-central Colorado and north-central New Mexico lies the San Luis Valley. Historically, it is a land of immense natural resources: rich soils, seas of grasses, abundant waters, coniferous forests along its mountainous edges, and a climate that enriched the land. Along with those riches came great lumbering herds of bison, speedy pronghorn, stately mule deer, majestic elk, and many other North American ungulates. Following these great herds of "hay burners" were packs of gray wolves, coyotes (known as "song dogs" in the American West), and mountain lions and black bear along the fringes of the high country. At the top of the food chain wherever it decided to roam was the fearsome grizzly bear. Interspersed among these natural wonders was every other kind of site-specific aerial, arboreal, and creepy critter, including a rather insignificant-looking mammal called "man." At first humankind was represented by the ancient ones who lived in harmony with the land, eating as much as they were eaten. They were followed thousands of years later by Mexicans moving northward, looking for better lands. In the sixteenth century, Spaniards led by the "Black Robes" traveled into the valley from Mexico, weary from the rigors of travel but ever alert in seeking the land's mineral wealth as they conquered and converted its peoples. Finally came other Europeans, represented by explorers, traders, and fur trappers. They were followed by those seeking new lands for the plow and grass for their great herds of cattle. Interspersed throughout were those scouring the lands on foot, dreaming of great riches to be found in motherlodes of gold and silver.

All who came lived off the land, whether the largely untapped fisheries struggling in the fishermen's nets; the great herds of bison ambling unawares within rifle shot, soon to be killed and skinned, the meat largely left to rot; fur-bearers supplying the insatiable Eastern coat and hat markets; flocks of birds blackening the skies and fields of sage, destined to be salted or iced down for local consumption or transported to protein-starved local gold fields, or later by rail to faraway western and eastern markets; lands untouched by wooden or iron plows, soon to be turned, with their topsoils blowing clear to Texas; or cattle herds grazing the rich grasses in such numbers that original primary plant species began disappearing. All of this was surrounded by the ringing of axes and "singing" of cross-cut saws felling timber for all manner of needs, and bringing scars to the lands and erosion to the lowlands and waterways for hundreds of years thereafter as part of the legacy of their thoughtlessness.

Amid all those "westering" activities came statehood in 1876. Soon after came the infrastructures of local and state governments, which began regulating the movement and methods of humans on the early frontier. As the infrastructure matured and time passed, citizens realized in alarm that the wildlife populations so important to their growth and survival (turkeys, bighorn sheep, beaver, elk, mule deer, river otter, black bear) were disappearing at alarming rates or were already gone. A governmental conservation agency was created to address the taking, sale, methods of take, seasons, and bag limits of the land's wildlife populations. Initially, efforts to regulate the taking and use of natural resources were limited or unenforced due to lack of manpower or funds, human greed, history, or shortsighted wildlife management practices. Much remained unchanged, especially in the outback areas of the new state, such as the San Luis Valley. The inhabitants of the valley traditionally depended on the land's largesse for survival and paid little or no heed to the fledgling wildlife laws. This dependence had been their "right" for hundreds of years, and the desire to continue that way of life was almost unstoppable. The idea that there was always more over the horizon was their philosophical mainstay. However, the excessive killing and overuse of the land's vast resources were creating major signs of wear and tear. Species such as the bison, gray wolf, grizzly bear, many commercial-grade big fish species, bighorn sheep, elk, turkeys, mule deer, beaver, river otters, and many others paid the price of those unmitigated slaughters. Civilization was coming to "Dodge," and it was just a matter of time before

the citizens of the land were forced to adhere to the state's wildlife resource laws. But it was a bitter battle that took many years to fight. In
fact, right through the twentieth century, many of the people of the
San Luis Valley, in part because of its isolation and in part because of
the local culture, continued to take the resources of the land, particularly wildlife, as they saw fit and whenever the need arose.

Soon the illegal killing, sale, wanton waste, and overall destruction of
the valley's wildlife resources began to get the attention of the people
of Colorado and the Colorado Division of Wildlife. Conservation officers were moved into the valley in growing numbers. But change did
not occur without tremendous growing pains and strong, sometimes
violent opposition. Many of the valley's people continued to ignore
the conservation laws and harvested the natural resources as their
ancestors had. Many considered it a God-given right and anyone
interfering with that activity had best consider the possibly lethal consequences. However, society was changing, and civilized thought regarding wise use continued to evolve. Changing economics meant that
life as it had once been known in many agricultural and backwater areas
was soon destroyed by tremendous levels of unemployment, the breakdown of the family unit after World War II, heavy drinking, and disregard for authority. And now, on this ever-changing scene of misery,
appeared the new threat of drugs.

Along with those societal changes, the Division of Wildlife battled
the lawless elements in the valley in a vain attempt to save the resources for future wise use. The Division's efforts in the face of such
strong local resistance were almost too little, too late. Insufficient
budgets, lack of manpower, poor equipment, courts not supporting or
recognizing the value of wildlife enforcement, weak supervisors,
crooked politics at the highest state levels, lack of wildlife law enforcement support from the populace, physical abuse and threats to the enforcement officers and their families, and the historically strong
cultural support for the slaughter of wildlife finally brought the issue
of illegal market hunting and commercialization of the valley's wildlife
to a head in 1981. With the valley's long and storied history, it became
apparent that normal wildlife law enforcement efforts to curtail the
lawlessness was not working. Something drastic had to be initiated, or
the wildlife would continue to be lost until its reduction in numbers
would be reminiscent of those among animal populations around

large cities and gold fields in Colorado at the turn of the century. That "something" was in the wind.

A new "sheriff" came to Denver for the U.S. Fish and Wildlife Service in 1981, one possessing experience in overt as well as covert operations ranging from gill-netting and snagging salmon and sturgeon to the illegal interstate commerce of wildlife and their parts and products. That arrival, along with the right personality chemistry between Service officers and the Colorado Division of Wildlife, provided a new "ill wind" for the commercial market hunters and despoilers of wildlife in the San Luis Valley. The killers' and market hunters' time had passed. Their illegal and deadly practices would bring down the skilled wrath of agencies mandated to "protect, preserve, and enhance" the wildlife populations within the scope of their authorities. Like the sunrise, that retribution was now just over the horizon.

In the 1980s, a two-and-a-half-year almost picture-perfect covert investigation into the illegal killing and commercialization of wildlife in the San Luis Valley was conducted by the Fish and Wildlife Service, in concert with the Colorado and New Mexico Fish and Game departments. That investigation, code named "Operation SLV" at that time, was the Service's largest commercial-market-hunting investigation in the seventeen Western states. By the time it ended, the investigation involved 108 criminal subjects, calling into question not only those individuals' morality and actions but the ethics and conduct of many politicians. Sadly, that shameful mantle of questionable ethics and conduct included almost the entire media industry along the Front Range in Colorado as well.

The covert operation was huge by any standards, and decidedly necessary in light of the abject lawlessness and great size of the market-hunting industry and wildlife commercialization in the San Luis Valley. The killing was so gross and wasteful that many resources from one federal and two state agencies would be needed to accomplish the short-term goal of wildlife law enforcement. A secondary long-term goal was to bring about a renewed cultural awareness and pride among the valley's population once the out-of-control lawlessness was drastically slowed or curtailed. However, political interference and a media that sought only the sensational point of view meant that the larger project of bringing the law back to the land and providing a means for future cultural change was all but destroyed.

In May 1981 I was promoted to the position of special agent in charge in Denver, Colorado, the Service's senior law enforcement official over the states of Montana, Wyoming, Colorado, Utah, North Dakota, South Dakota, Nebraska, and Kansas. To enforce the myriad federal wildlife laws in such a wildlife-rich environment, I had twenty-four special agents and a small administrative staff. I also had the resources of the state Fish and Game departments *if* I could get them to cooperate with my agency. I say "if" because the Service's hierarchy had a dismal track record in assisting the states with their wildlife law enforcement problems.

That began to change as I set about establishing closer working relationships with my state counterparts. The state's historical expertise and collective numbers of conservation officers packed a punch far greater than the poachers or illegal commercial-market-hunting interests, or my small division of officers, for that matter. It soon became apparent that the state had a vital need for what the Service and the federal court system could offer (the Service could cross state lines, and federal courts were usually tougher and less inclined to be swayed by state politics).

As part of my cooperative state-federal fence-mending effort, I visited the central office of the Colorado Division of Wildlife to introduce myself. Kris Moser was chief of law enforcement in those days, and after a morning's discussion I could see that we were going to get along famously. He was soft spoken, introspective, and serious about protecting the resources of Colorado. It was almost like meeting a gunfighter of old because Kris exuded an air of confidence and a quality that quietly proclaimed that *if* it took running along the edge to get the job done, so be it (as long as it was legal). Having a state chief of such quality in my backyard was a blessing.

Kris's deputy, David Croonquist, I judged as a bit of a maverick. He moved with the smoothness and practiced grace of a jungle cat, and when his eyes were on me, I could tell his mind was working overtime. He was trying to figure out my direction, then running ahead of my thoughts to see where his law enforcement division might best fit into that picture. Dave, like Kris, was extremely intelligent and always ready for a challenge. He too was totally dedicated to the resources and quietly exuded a high level of energy. As expected in such a meeting between old-line officers and new friends, we talked away the morning until I had to leave for another meeting.

As Kris walked me out the door, he mentioned with a twinkle in his eyes, "When you have time after you get your feet on the ground, we need to talk about the San Luis Valley."

Still unfamiliar with my region, I said, "What and where is the San Luis Valley?"

"Oh, nothing more than a wildlife-rich region in south-central Colorado and north-central New Mexico, where wildlife has been and continues to be plundered by its residents."

I should have understood the meaning of that twinkle in his eyes (a look that happily welcomed the arrival of a new partner who could possibly help in this matter) and been forewarned, but it went over my head in my haste to get to my afternoon meeting. "Let's discuss it sometime after I've had a chance to learn my district," I casually threw over my shoulder. From where I stood looking into my own backyard, I had a hatful of problems: fiscal, logistical, personnel, administrative, and operational for starters. Damn if I needed to open another Pandora's box before I got to the bottom of my own nest of snakes! However, I figured Kris wouldn't have mentioned this San Luis Valley thing unless it was important. Oh well, I thought; I will get to that issue if and when I can.

Months later I was back in Kris's office discussing other mutual law enforcement problems when he again brought up the San Luis Valley, which was seemingly burning a hole in his pocket. Based on about ten years of raw intelligence (unsubstantiated information from many sources illustrating illegal acts of poaching, gross illegal take, and commercialization of wildlife, gathered by the Division of Wildlife and many others), Kris was convinced a major covert investigation was needed in the valley.

However, Kris had discovered he faced some insurmountable hurdles. The files showed a preponderance of Hispanic American families illegally involved in old-fashioned market hunting, commercialization of wildlife, and wanton waste. He did not feel he had anyone with the right kind of background and experience to break into a somewhat closed local culture and society. In that department, he also lacked an officer he considered developmentally ready. Finally, he felt that such an investigation would quickly be stymied by petty politics, outright betrayal, or inadvertent exposure because of the unreliable political atmosphere within his agency. In short, he was looking for a Hispanic officer with solid covert experience from outside his agency.

I mulled over the significance of what Kris had just said. My first thoughts were that an investigation of such magnitude could cost as little as fifty thousand or as much as a million dollars when all the state and federal pennies were finally counted. Service regional funding for such an operation was out of the question. My agency had seen to it that the Division of Law Enforcement remained underfunded for years, and my current regional budget was no exception. Also, I did not have a Hispanic officer in my squad at that time. But the more Kris detailed the intelligence regarding gross illegal taking of wildlife, interstate commerce, and rampant intrastate commercialization centered in this area, the more intrigued I grew. If what he said rang anywhere near true, a massive number of federal violations under the Lacey Act, the Bald and Golden Eagle Protection Act, the Migratory Bird Treaty Act, and possibly the Endangered Species Act could be uncovered in such an investigation. Those would pale in comparison to the potential Colorado and New Mexico Fish and Game violations. It would be a slew of state and federal offenses, including a pile of felonies, of a magnitude unheard of in modern-day wildlife law enforcement! The *look* of an operation of that magnitude had such allure that it was like being dragged around on the end of a fishing line by a well-hooked monster white sturgeon. (In the late 1800s, it was common for those fishing the larger river systems along the Pacific Coast to hook a team of horses to a line with a hooked sturgeon on the other end to assist in beaching the giant. There are many recorded instances in California newspapers of hooked sturgeon so large that they dragged a team of horses into the water!)

Looking at Kris, then Dave, I said, "All right, bring me your files and let me take a look." Dave got up in one fluid motion, as if he had anticipated my taking the bait, and left the office with a sinister, knowing smile before I could change my mind. He returned with a stack of papers at least three feet high. The width of his smile at the thought of being able to work such a flagrant mess damn near matched the size of the material he carried! Being eager to please and loving to catch outlaws, I lowered my guard. Between the devil, Dave, and that investigative possibility, I was hooked! Laying those documents on a coffee table in front of me, Kris and Dave sat back in their chairs and waited. Thumbing through that pile, which ranged from case reports to scraps of paper from highway patrol officers who had stopped individuals in the valley only to find illegal game in their vehicles, I read on with increasing interest. The documents I skimmed during the next few minutes pointed to many folks from the valley illegally taking, possessing, selling, or trading wildlife under every conceivable circumstance: wildlife possessed or taken during the closed season; over-limits; wrong species taken under the license issued; game taken while trespassing on private ranches; game taken using someone else's license; sale of wildlife in local bars; purchasing licenses for everyone in the family and then selling those licenses to the highest bidder; sale of wildlife to less successful out-of-state so-called hunters; sale of wildlife in general to anyone trustworthy enough to keep their mouths shut; sale of wildlife or parts to family members or relatives in distant towns; taking and sale of totally protected species (eagles, hawks, owls); wanton waste; sale of trophy parts; illegal sale of fur-bearers; wildlife taken with the use and aid of a spotlight; wildlife illegally transported across state lines; wildlife shot from motor vehicles; wildlife killed only to cripple it or watch it die—and on it went with sickening and numbing regularity.

Liberally sprinkled throughout those documents was information relating to the insidious stain of illicit drugs. Illegal wildlife was being traded or sold to purchase drugs, not only in small amounts but in any volume or type of "poison" the heart desired. There were even *darker* overtones. The material indicated that some local law enforcement officials were using their positions and offices of trust to perpetuate the lawlessness in the valley. That alone made the hair stand up on the back of my neck. The information pointed toward not only the illegal killing of wildlife while on and off duty but participation in illegal transport and sale as well. There were also bits and pieces of information regarding wrongdoing by elected officials, judges, and state and county employees as they knowingly accepted meat from poached animals. It was absolutely overwhelming, even to an officer with my years of experience!

The intelligence files covered a period of about ten years. I wondered how long this had been going on and the numbers of wildlife illegally taken *before* that file had been compiled? The historical numbers had to be monstrous! For a valley portrayed in the local media as full of poor but hardworking souls, those files darkly told another, albeit unsubstantiated, story.

Realizing this was going to take a mountain of work, starting with a detailed examination of the materials laid before me, I said, "I'll need some time to make heads or tails of this mess. If I feel I *can* get this off the ground, I will start looking for a Service officer capable of doing this kind of work. In the meantime, you guys need to figure out who in your organization can be trusted during such an investigation. Keep in mind, many people in the valley seem to be related to folks in Denver. My office is a classic microcosm of that social and population dynamic. I have three people on my staff out of seven who have very close family ties to people in the valley, and I am sure you will have like numbers. With Colorado possessing such a large Hispanic population, it should not be surprising that this family ties thing potentially poses a major security problem. Especially to a man buried on the inside, with the possibility of having his cover blown. Keep in mind, a leak could come from any corner and at any time—an auditor of the undercover books discussing the investigation with his wife, a division secretary typing case reports and seeing her brother's name, the wife of a loose-lipped officer with relatives in the valley, or the like. If that happened, because of the historical openly hostile attitude against law enforcement by many of the valley's folks, especially the violators, we may have a dead or seriously injured operative on our hands." I let that sink in for a moment because I wasn't sure if my state counterparts had worked this kind of investigation before and understood the complexities and potentially deadly implications. If they hadn't, it would be all too easy to make simple mistakes devastating to a covert operation and possibly the officer under cover.

I had worked over thirty simple to complex covert operations at the state and federal levels throughout my career as an operative, assigned case agent, and case management supervisor. I had discovered early on that much could go wrong and regularly did in any covert investigation. If you were not prepared for the worst-case scenario, you could get lumps on your head rather quickly, and big ones at that! However, I could tell from the looks I was receiving that my state lads were the professionals I expected, even though basically new to deep-cover wildlife law enforcement operations.

I continued, "No guarantee of an investigation, mind you, but let me examine the files in detail."

Croonquist gave me a Cheshire cat smile but said nothing. Hell, he didn't have to. He was a damn good fisherman and recognized when he had a big one on the line. Finished with the business at hand, I gathered up the armload of files and walked out the door with visions of bad guys in handcuffs dancing in my head.

Throughout the following year, I plowed through those intelligence files. It took awhile, not for lack of interest but because I had a struggling law enforcement district of my own to get to a level I considered truly operational in light of the district's federal demands. I spent a lot of time not only setting up my district's infrastructure and operational direction but begging for money from other, wealthier Service divisions so I could function at the most basic level. That aside, every chance I got I dug into the pile of intelligence documents looking for patterns, clues, or familiar names at a level that would support such a complex investigation. I also kept an eye peeled for methods of operation, transport routes, locations of middlemen, names of those operators considered dangerous, points of sale of edible portions or inedible parts (such as antlers, hides, capes, eagle feathers), and collection points for further distribution. I kept a detailed notebook of names, dates, places, and events. Slowly a picture of a massive, out-of-control killing field in the San Luis Valley began to rear its ugly head. There were hard-core individuals as well as loosely organized poaching rings made up of friends, farmers, store owners, those out of work looking for something to do, those looking for the excitement such activities would bring, or family members, all killing the hell out of deer, elk, black bear, ducks, birds of prey, eagles, and antelope for personal consumption or sale or trade. Many of the critters illegally taken for the markets would be sold to eating places in Denver, Pueblo, Colorado Springs, and cities in New Mexico. In a surprising number of documents were reports of trophy animals being killed for only the capes (the skin from the head, neck, and shoulders) and antlers, the rest being left to rot! Wildlife in many other instances was openly traded for drugs, goods, or services (tires, alcohol, weapons, ammunition, vehicle repairs). A lot of meat was consumed by those doing the shooting, or was used to pay off gambling debts to others who liked the taste of venison. I could see that the bounty wildlife offered was frequently substituted for the coin of the realm in many parts of the valley.

The ugly tales of dirty cops involved with the killing and commercialization or cover-up ran like a heavy red thread throughout the reports. Ultimately, that problem had become part of the cloth of poaching spread throughout the valley. Not all valley law enforcement officers were involved, mind you. Many were damn fine officers, upholding their oaths of office as they served their neighbors. But there were enough crooked officers, especially from the eastern side of the valley, to cause grave concern. Reports were replete with information of officers poaching game during the closed season, using patrol car spotlights to take game at night or to transport illegal game, selling wildlife from their patrol cars, and using their knowledge of ongoing law enforcement actions to provide an early warning system to their poaching or drug-dealing friends. The files showed that many of the decent folks in the valley were frustrated and oppressed because there were limited ways for them to report poaching without word getting back to the outlaw populace.

In reviewing those files, I eventually isolated the names of fifty-eight people, all but one possessing Hispanic surnames, who through constant documentation, with occasional arrests and prosecutions, were key suspects contributing in a major way toward the illegal killing and marketing of the valley's wildlife. Don't get me wrong; there were a passel of opportunistic killers throughout the valley, but fifty-eight were constantly mentioned as heavily involved in commercial-market hunting. I decided to focus on those folks for removal from the scene with a covert investigation and a subsequent ride through the state and federal judicial systems.

Some of you quicker readers may already be asking, why not just increase overt enforcement efforts instead of initiating a costly and potentially dangerous undercover operation? Good question. For years the states of Colorado and New Mexico had done just that. They had flooded the zone with extra officers whose identities were unknown to the locals; they had instituted surprise roadblocks and numerous dawn-to-dusk patrols. They had caught many of the "dummies." But the hard-case killers were generally too smart to be apprehended and put out of business by such overt tactics.

The other problem with increased overt activities in the valley ran much deeper than the casual eye discerned. The entire San Luis Valley had been largely populated with families of Hispanic and Mexican descent since the 1600s. Long-standing relationships and trust developed among those families, so it was very difficult for outsiders to obtain information about clandestine illegal acts such as commercial-market hunting or outright poaching. That closeness and secrecy coupled with the remoteness of the area made it dangerous for anyone to complain to the authorities. There were ample recorded instances of those unfortunates who did. They paid the price through savage acts of revenge against them, including personal violence (such as shooting into their homes with rifles while they slept), theft of their property, threats against their children, or arson. That code of silence enforced by the local culture, a few crooked law enforcement officers, and fear was so pervasive that in the seventeen years I served as the Service's senior law enforcement supervisor in the area, not one individual of Hispanic or Mexican descent stepped forward to finger another for a violation of wildlife laws in the San Luis Valley.

Successful overt enforcement has its place when the population routinely assists or supports officers in the work at hand. Remove the helping hand of the populace, and your enforcement program becomes extremely limited or doomed. Overt wildlife law enforcement aimed at the serious criminal was generally not possible in the San Luis Valley, when you worked openly with a smile on your face, wearing a uniform and showing the Great Seal of the State of Colorado or New Mexico plastered on the doors of your vehicle. Wildlife agencies faced with the unusual eventually had to resort to the unusual themselves in order to rein in the spoilers dominating those around them, both wildlife and human.

I ended my examination of my diminishing pile of raw intelligence on a rather gruesome note. Two fellows who were among my group of fifty-eight had allegedly poached two massive bull elk on a private ranch and removed the heads and capes, leaving one thousand pounds of meat to rot! That kind of arrogance, greed, and stupidity fairly leaped up from the pages of the intelligence files, leaving me cold and angry to the core. I just fumed! I still wasn't logistically ready to tackle the San Luis Valley, but *enough was enough!* Closing those last files with finality, I made up my mind. This was one challenge that had to be met or the needless slaughter would continue. But setting that kind of an operation in motion presented me with an endless line of hurdles. First and foremost was the undercover officer needed for such an operation. He or she would have to be mentally tough as a horseshoe nail; self-sufficient; in excellent physical condition; highly intelligent; honest; loaded with common sense; and very familiar with all the statutes, policies, and procedures relevant to such an operation. There were several officers in the Service's pipeline with a good "covert look," and I began to mentally look over the lot. One kept rising to the surface based on performance and experience. I felt he would be the right man for the job. Now I had to see if I could entice that fellow, George Morrison, to move to my region. With extra help from the states, monies scrounged from sister divisions coupled with my meager budget, some equipment to create the covert look, possibly a cooperating private citizen to assist, and special funds from Washington, we would be off and running. Boy, does that sound simple now that I look at the words. Well, hang on to the willows for one wild ride because the devil is coming, and he is riding a black horse. ...

I didn't have one plug nickel even to move my chosen officer from his current residence to Denver, a problem that threw me back on my haunches for a moment. Then my "begging" light went on. It took me the better part of an afternoon to get Marv Plennert, assistant regional director for the Refuge Division, to give me the money from his vast regional hoard of silver to pay for the move. Marv was a man small in stature but big in heart and vision, not to mention long on fight. With $46,000 of Refuge funds, I began moving my division into the vanguard of battle with a vengeance. When the states of Colorado and New Mexico and the Service finished with the San Luis Valley, there *would* be a dent in the killing and pride of those who chose to walk on the wild side in the world of wildlife, I thought. A smile slowly crossed my face as I picked up the gauntlet laid on the coffee table many months earlier by Deputy Chief Croonquist. Yeah, he had a big fish on the line—one the size of a green sturgeon. Dave had better go and get his team of horses. ...

I had just taken the first of many steps in setting up what was potentially one of the largest covert operations investigating illegal take and commercialization of wildlife in my career. Where it would take me only time would tell. Truth be known, it would be a wild ride for all concerned before the smoke cleared. A ride I would gladly take again if the opportunity arose because wildlife dies without making a sound. Many times the only voice it has is that of the officers who have sworn to protect it. And if the officers are not squalling like smashed cats, then they are part of the problem. In fact, they are no better than the poachers.

Walking into Kris's office the morning of my decision to go forward, carrying a weight of seriousness heavy enough to sag the shoulders of Atlas, I beckoned for him to follow me out into the hallway, where we could talk without being overheard. I told him of my decision to initiate the San Luis Valley investigation. I also informed him of my tentative covert operative selection, then brought him up to speed on the fast pace the planning was taking on my side of the fence. I told him I had just received $46,000 from Marv Plennert to pay for the operative's move. Kris got a big "here we go" grin on his face and said, "You know, this has the potential to be a big one. Bigger than anything I ever worked, and surely a big one for you. What can I do to support what *we* have just set into motion?"

"Well, the first thing I need is money to buy evidence. Let's say $10,000 from Colorado for starters. With $10,000 from the Service and a like share from New Mexico, I would think that $30,000 to purchase illegal wildlife flowing in commerce in the San Luis Valley would be a good starting point. It will take a week or so for me to get $10,000 from our Special Funds account in Washington, but if you could quickly get $10,000 Colorado money into my hands, we could use that as a crowbar to get that process in Washington off and running. There is nothing like good faith on the part of my partners in this endeavor to broaden the narrow thinking of those in Washington. And I think a $10,000 chunk of change from a state counterpart is just what the doctor ordered if speed of movement from those folks is of the essence."

"Well, never having done this before, I will have to go to Director Jack Grieb and see if he will go along with the $10,000," he eagerly replied.

"I suggest you get cracking because this operative I have in mind will want to hit the ground running. He isn't Hispanic, mind you, but he is a damn good officer. His track record looks pretty good, and his potential, according to those around him whose judgment I trust, is outstanding. He had time as a game warden in Ohio and would probably be able to slide right into our detail. However, I plan on giving him some smaller covert details in the region first to see if he has the right stuff. If he does, and with his consent, we will swing him into our valley operation."

Kris got another big grin, and I could just see years of deep frustration beginning to melt away. Not so fast, partner, I thought; we have years of hard work ahead of us. But I had to admit my grin was just as infectious. I continued, "I still need to meet with a pile of federal attorneys, get Washington office approval, start lining up my officers to provide logistical support to the operative, set up a meeting with New Mexico to get them on board, put together several cooperative agreements between the Service and the states, acquire several walk-in freezers for evidence preservation, procure needed undercover equipment, figure out when to get state of Colorado and New Mexico attorneys into the loop because of the security issues, convince my choice of operative he wants to work in Region 6, and work on finding him a partner. And lastly, finish detailing where I would like the operation to go for it to satisfy state needs as well. But other than a few simple things like that, ain't life grand?"

Kris grinned like a trapper of old looking into beaver-rich ponds on a mist-laden September morn in Yellowstone. "I will set up a meeting with Director Grieb. How about a luncheon meeting with him at the restaurant up the road from our office, say, tomorrow?"

"Sounds good to me, but I don't know Grieb. Can he be trusted to keep his mouth shut? If one word of what you and I want to do gets out on the street, you can kiss good-bye any covert work in the valley for the next several years."

"I think so," he replied. "I have known Jack for a long time and am sure he can be trusted. He has always been for the resources of the state and her peoples. I can't see him changing horses at this point in the game."

"Let's do it, then. I will meet the two of you tomorrow at eleven in the morning, and by then I should have my final operational thoughts in place."

Kris stuck out his hand, and we shook on the deal, two officers and friends about to embark on a mission that would take us through many twists in the road before it was over. In the process it would change many lives forever, including ours.

Ten-thirty the next morning found me standing in Kris's office waiting for him to get off the phone. Finishing up with business, Kris strode over to me, warmly shook my hand, and said, "It's all set. Jack will meet us at the restaurant up the road at eleven. Jack wanted to know what was up my sleeve, but I told him he would just have to wait." Another big grin of excitement spread across his face.

"Damn, Kris," I said with a grin of my own, "you keep grinning like that and your face will get a permanent case of the 'uglies.'"

Using the time to our advantage, I discussed my plans with Kris so he would not be blindsided at the luncheon. Then off we went to the restaurant to meet Director Grieb. We chose an isolated table in the back. Soon a balding man of medium stature walked into the room. After locating us in the dim light and greeting us with a wave, he headed for our table. Kris introduced Jack to me, and the three of us sat down to our meeting, the consequences of which none of us would soon forget.

After a few moments of pleasantries, we gave the waitress our orders. Then Jack said, "All right, Kris, you called this meeting; what is it about?"

Kris gestured to me and said, "Terry, it's all yours."

I said, "Jack, when I first met Kris, he mentioned a wildlife killing and commercialization problem in the San Luis Valley. He asked if the Service could help. After reviewing the intelligence documents your agency has accumulated over the past ten years, I also concluded there were serious state and federal wildlife violations occurring in the area. After months examining those documents and looking for just the right kind of officer to be our covert operative, I am damn near ready to address the problem. I would like to suggest that Colorado, New Mexico, and the Service team up in a joint covert investigation to address this commercial-market-hunting problem. We won't be able to start this minute because the officer I have in mind has yet to be selected and moved. But that is small potatoes compared to all the other preparation needed. I need to meet with New Mexico and get those folks on board, not to mention contacting a pile of state and federal attorneys for their approval and guidance. However, once in operation, the Service would supply the covert operative, provide his salary, pay for his move to the region, pay his per diem, and supply his other needs, such as a place to work. We would also supply one-third of the $30,000 anticipated buy money needed to purchase evidence associated with this investigation. I suggest that the states of New Mexico and Colorado pony up $10,000 each for evidence procurement, be responsible for appropriate logistical assistance during the investigation, and supply major manpower for the search and arrest portion. At the end of the operation, I would refund any unused monies equally to both states. We still have to work out which attorneys would prosecute what, but as long as we have strong state attorneys and judges, my plan is to let them carry forth. That way the local deterrent effect would be greater and longer lasting. When we have someone who is politically too hot to go through the local prosecution avenues, the feds will pick up those cases. We would also pick up investigations where federal interests are largely at stake, such as those involving the Eagle Act and the Endangered Species Act. I also propose that if this investigation turns to crap, the feds will pick up the credit for its initiation. However, if it turns to gold, then I would like the states to step forward and further strengthen their programs. This should also give the states a leg up in initiating their own much-needed covert agendas. If that occurs, I can move my limited number of officers into other arenas and let the states carry their own water into the twenty-first century. I realize the details are sketchy at this juncture, but once we get your blessing, we will be off and running, defining the operation even further."

After I finished, I sat back in my chair and waited. Jack sat there looking first at me and then at Kris, mulling over the proposal. "Kris, is this something we need to do, or for that matter can do?" he asked.

"Yes, sir. I asked Terry to look into this when he first got here, and after a time he has located a covert operative and agreed to do it. As you know, the folks in the valley have had their way with the wildlife for years, and we haven't been able to get a handle on those illegal activities. So I figured we would ask the feds to give us a hand."

Jack continued to look closely at his chief of law enforcement and then said, "Let's do it! Start it up and keep me in the loop, but not to such an extent that I am aware of every turn. Just those things you feel I should know. I will authorize the expenditure of funds, and if you have any trouble with their procurement or security, call me. I figure you enforcement types know what needs doing more than I, so get cracking." He paused and got a different look in his eyes, like the old trapper in Yellowstone when he realized the beaver *were all gone.* ... Speaking slowly, as if weighing every word, he said, "Those folks in the valley have had their way for years with the people's wildlife. It is about time we leveled the playing field. Yes, this needs doing. Ever since I was a kid, I've heard about the slaughter of game in the valley from my dad and uncles. We need to grab someone by the hind end and bring this illegal killing to a stop."

About that time lunch arrived and Jack stopped talking while the waitress was present. When she left, we resumed our conversation, mostly discussing the mechanics of the operation and what we ultimately hoped to accomplish.

After lunch, Kris and I returned to his office, brought Dave into the discussion, and went through Colorado's manuals on administrative policies and procedures. First, I wanted to make sure Colorado had the authority to undertake such a complex investigation. Second, I wanted to ascertain what hoops we had to jump through at the state level to acquire and spend their monies for such an operation. Third, I wanted to set up an audit process so the state could monitor its monies and expenditures in conformance with its laws. And fourth, I wanted to examine what avenues we would have to move through to ensure total security. Dave, in light of a possible three-year investigation, brought up the issue of the state statute of limitations. If we went the planned full three years, some of the state misdemeanor charges would drop by the wayside, though state felony cases would hold. We decided in such instances to write off the suspect or turn those cases over to the Service because our statute of limitations was more liberal.

Here we go, I thought. We haven't even started up the investigation and already we have a rock in the road. Thanks to Dave's acumen in the legal policies and procedures arenas, we caught a key problem early on and worked through it. I could see that Dave wanted to hang every miserable son of a bitch that needed hanging, and I couldn't blame him for his code of frontier justice. Hell, the poor critters in the valley had been hammered since the arrival of humankind. Now it was the critters' turn. In the spirit of getting the job done, Dave relented on prosecuting short-term investigations in exchange for an extensive investigation gathering in the worst of the worst. I had to give him credit. Dave was, and remained throughout, one of the major founders of Operation SLV. He was in the forefront of just about every investigative aspect and provided nothing but sterling support. As the investigation wound down and the prosecution demands reared their heads like the fabled Hydra, Dave continued meeting and exceeding the challenges. As I said, he moved with the finesse and finality of a jungle cat.

Speaking of rocks in the road, before this investigation would run its course, another issue tripped us up. Jack Grieb, the director who set the whole show in motion, would be replaced by two different state directors! Jack moved on because of health issues (may he rest in peace), and the other two came and went in the normal course of political evolution. In each instance, the newcomer had to be brought up to speed on the operation. During that initial briefing, we had to emphasize the issue of security in order to protect not only our covert operative but the reputations of those being investigated as well. Then we had to ascertain what angles or prohibitions the new director might throw into our path. Fortunately, the investigation had been planned in such careful detail that we had to make only minor adjustments each time. Small obstacles, but a portent of ill winds yet to blow.

Leaving Kris's office that day, I headed back for the boar's nest of work before me in setting up Operation SLV. I walked into my office with my head in a whirl and called Bob Miller, U.S. attorney for Colorado, to set up a meeting. The U.S. attorney was one of my bosses in a federal investigation, especially as it related to criminal matters prosecuted in federal court. Getting Miller on the phone, I gave him a thumbnail sketch of the planned investigation and requested a meeting the following week. I found him to be extremely competent and well-schooled in his profession. Best of all, I liked the man personally. He was honest, forthright, and possessed an ethic of the highest caliber. Not only that, he had guts. I have to say, Bob was one of the top three U.S. attorneys I worked with during my twenty-nine-year federal career.

Operation SLV roared out of the chute like a Brahma bull. Ten days after our meeting with Grieb, Kris walked into my office as I was on the telephone. Placing $10,000 cash on my desk in a big wad of bills, he turned to walk out. Putting my call on hold, I said, "Whoa, Kris; I need to give you a receipt documenting this transaction."

Kris turned and said, "Not necessary old man. I trust you."

I ended my call and beckoned Kris back to my office. As he returned, I thought, I am going to have to watch my state counterparts more closely. They were *great* to work with, but they were new to this covert thing, and I needed to make sure every action followed the law, policy, and administrative procedures. I advised Kris we needed to document every action because that paper trail would be required in a court of law, and would have to be legally available to defense attorneys under "discovery." Dragging out a blank case report, I recorded the date and the amount, serial numbers, and denominations of the cash transfer. Then I executed another document in which Kris released the money to me. Kris got a copy for his files, and I put the money into my office safe. Then I completed my case report under the assigned investigations number and sent it through the system. This moment did nothing but reinforce in me the determination that everything in this investigation would be done according to the letter of the law or the case could just fold under its own weight! Thank God I held that line of reasoning.

Then came the first of many shocks in Operation SLV. Kris resigned his position as chief of law enforcement in July 1984. Accepting a promotion, he moved to Idaho as a regional manager for their state Fish and Game Department. At first I thought, There goes the operation. However, Deputy Chief Dave Croonquist assumed temporary command. Dave was easy to work with and totally dedicated to eliminating the wildlife commercialization problems in the valley. So for the next several months development of the covert operation moved along without missing a beat.

Then in March 1985, Fran Marcoux was selected as the new Colorado chief of law enforcement. Not really knowing the man and fearing a hard sell along with a loss of time getting the new chief up to speed, I headed over to his office with some trepidation. However, Fran not only became one of my best friends over time but proved to be an outstanding wildlife professional as well. A Colorado officer long on field experience, he recognized the problems in the valley. In a short period, he was up to speed on the covert operation thanks to Dave's coaching and his own hard research, becoming another of the investigation's strongest supporters. No matter the degree of difficulty in bringing off the operation, he was always there taking the hits as well as dishing it out. He turned out to be one of my better advisers and was always ahead of his time when the two of us got together to discuss business. Our friendship has lasted through thick and thin to this day.

Also in 1985, I brought into my employ George Morrison, the young, single officer I had my eye on as a covert operative. George was showing a lot of promise in covert investigations in the state and federal arenas, fortified with a lot of damn good common sense. Shortly after his arrival and in accordance with not only my plan but that of his senior resident agent, we let him run covertly in the region to see what he could do. In no time he did what most young under-cover officers did: worked himself into an overload of damn good investigations. He zeroed in on a Korean businessman in Denver who was illegally involved in the bear-gall trade, not to mention the business of white slavery. He was also working on several people taking and smuggling endangered cats from Mexico and Central America into Colorado. And for dessert, he worked his way into a meat-processing plant in Duboise, Wyoming, whose owner was processing and selling illegal, sport-shot venison sausage.

Seeing that Morrison had the "sand" I needed to go forward with Operation SLV, I called his supervisor to run my proposal of a covert operation in the valley by him for the first time. He was stunned by its potential magnitude and duration, but after some thought, agreed that Morrison was certainly the man for the job. I asked him to have Morrison stop by my office for a chat but cautioned him to make sure there was no forewarning regarding the subject. I wanted to see how Morrison reacted when thrown unexpectedly into a lion's den.

Two days later, Morrison walked into my office. "Sit down," I told him, which he quietly did. He was a tall, muscular drink of water with not more than 4 percent body fat on his lean six-foot, five-inch frame. He had a full head of tousled blond hair and was ruggedly handsome with a shy smile that said more than caught the eye at first glance. To the casual observer, he was just one of the boys, but to one looking for traits that are commonly present under uncommon circumstances, his presence spoke volumes. When he moved, it was with the deliberate energy and practiced smoothness of an anaconda. He had an air of confidence with just a trace of arrogance. His eyes quickly assayed everything around him, and that was an important quality because that kind of alertness was required to succeed in and survive covert operations. His dark blue eyes were constantly gathering information. I sat quietly and examined my officer as he sat there doing the same to me. What I had in mind for this modern-day warrior would not be easy—in fact, it would be downright difficult with a hint of deadly thrown in daily for good measure. That was a lot to ask of anyone.

Finally, without taking my eyes off his, I said, "George, I have a proposition for you. I want to initiate a covert investigation into the illegal killing and commercialization of wildlife in the San Luis Valley of Colorado, which before all is said and done will probably extend into northern New Mexico." Morrison's eyes never left mine, nor mine his. He was a cool customer, I thought as I continued, "It would require that you sever all but the most necessary ties with your fellow officers because of security issues. Being seen with a known law dog is a sure way to wreck your cover and the investigation, and possibly get you killed. You will not be allowed in this or any other office of the Service except under the direst of circumstances for the same security reasons. You will be required to develop an identity that is fail-safe because before this is over, we will have some crooked officers check-ing you out through all known law enforcement means and files.

"If you are to be successful, you must penetrate the local Hispanics' culturally based shield of silence. They are especially closed to outside people, and that shield is as impressive as it is oppressive. The outlaws I have identified by going through reams of intelligence files from the Colorado Division of Wildlife have a rough, sometimes deadly repu-tation. If your true identity is discovered, there's a good chance they will take you on in numbers or from afar with a rifle in the dark of the night. Arson to your property or physical attack is definitely within the realm of possibility. Because of the nature of this assignment, we will not be able to provide any protective cover without giving you and the investigation away. So if you get involved, you will have to survive using your own wits, common sense, and 'top cover' of the god of your choice."

Pausing to study his demeanor and meeting nothing but an inter-ested, steely look, I went on, "I would plan on at least a two-and-a-half to three-year investigation. We have identified fifty-seven Hispanic-surnamed chaps and one Anglo heavily involved in plain old-fashioned commercial-market hunting. Many whom I consider major players have previous felony convictions for offenses that in-clude arson, child molestation, robbery, rape, homicide, and battery. This group is taking mainly deer and elk, but it appears to be taking anything that will garner a few pieces of silver. It appears that many of the valley's general population are also involved to a degree with the illegal killing of wildlife for sale or subsistence, but if we go on with this, I want you to concentrate on the big commercial killers and let the little guys go if at all possible. I'm not saying the little guys are immune, but if you have the opportunity, set up the program so it will snare those needing it the most. Concentrating on the real heavy hitters is important because that is where the serious drain on the wildlife resources is occurring. Plus, when it comes to trials, everyone and his uncle will be claiming the killing was done only to feed starving members of their families. To counter that, I need you to document everything these killers say and do, really establishing their predisposition to violate the laws—especially any loose talk on why they are involved in market hunting.

"I want to know how many illegal animals they are taking and have killed in the past. I want to know their marketing routes. I want to know who they are selling to, and I want you to ask every one of them what they plan on doing with their pieces of silver acquired from the sale of wildlife. Is the money going to help their kids and families, or is it going for drugs, booze, women, paying bills, ammunition, or the like? This may be a political hot potato because of the large number of Hispanics involved. I feel certain the general Hispanic population will raise hell once the hammer drops, citing racism as the main issue while minimizing or justifying the illegal killing and selling of wildlife. You take on a pile of folks like that and you may have the whole population yapping at your heels thinking you have challenged their manhood. But I will just have to try and keep a lid on that kettle if and when it starts to boil.

"I'm sure Washington will have some problems with this undertaking because of its size and potential length. That is another reason I want you to take extraordinary steps in taking out the major shooters regardless of who they are and documenting everything that occurs. When the shit hits the fan, and it will, I want to be able to pull out a case report and advise any accusers that they are wrong, and here is the evidence showing why.

"As is the case in any investigation of this magnitude, there will be a lot of adjustments as we go, but that is the nature of the beast. I suspect we will be looking at numerous state and federal felonies. That will require a lot of coordination with state and federal attorneys in several jurisdictions. It will be an expensive operation to fund, raise a pile of new and 'First Law' issues, and require a mountain of logistical support. If you manage to get the evidence on the worst of the worst, I think just trying to get together at least two to three hundred officers for the takedown will be a challenge of major proportions.

But that number of officers will be needed in order to safely execute all the state and federal warrants I feel this investigation will generate.

"There are a ton of good folks in the valley who do not support what is being done by some of their neighbors, but they are fiercely maintaining their silence because of their cultural constraints and fear of reprisal. To me, that is almost like having some of your freedoms removed. Through this operation we should be able to give back to those innocent folks a modicum of their self-respect and to free them from this tyranny. If you decide to take this assignment, you will essentially be hunting the lawless. Every one of them has a set of teeth, a rifle, the know-how to use it, and in some cases the willingness to use the killing end on a man as easily as on a beast.

"As if that were not enough of a load, as in any segment of our society, we have a raging intertwined drug problem. If that gets bigger than the illegal wildlife issue, we will have to stop our operation before its time in order to let the Drug Enforcement Administration address the situation. If you get a handle on a large drug shipment, there is no way the attorneys are going to let that poison pass. So as you can see, there are a lot of variables with many more waiting in the wings that I cannot even visualize at the moment. Before we even turn an investigative wheel, I need to meet with the attorneys and let them know of my intentions to get their approval, get Washington's approval, get the final approval of Colorado and New Mexico Fish and Game on the direction of the investigation, raise the money to fund the operation, arrange for the appropriate levels of security within my office and in the field, and make sure my regional director signs off. There are also the issues of procuring money from the Special Fund for evidence buys, arranging for the handling of evidence so you are not bogged down with those duties, coordination with our partners, and gambling on our division getting enough annual funding to make a three-year go of this operation in case my other sources of funding fail."

About then I ran down; looking intently at Morrison, I tried to read how the information had played. George looked intently at me for a moment as if waiting for more and then let a slight smile play across his face. Not one that most people would readily notice, but the kind of smile that revealed how the challenge just laid at his feet was about to be acted upon. I didn't have a psychotic sitting in front of me but a damned fine officer tuned in to covert work, with an excellent state and federal track record. Here was an officer carefully calculating the potential assignment and measuring his abilities against reality. Morrison sat silently for a few moments as if putting all into play for balance, then said, "I would need to closely manage my ongoing covert operations with this one, but you have a deal." He was already showing some unique qualities in managing to complete those ongoing operations on one hand while preparing for the much more complex detail on the other. I was to discover many more fine qualities about the man over the next two-and-a-half years and was not disappointed.

We spent several hours discussing where he would be located, how the operation would be set up, how evidence would be transported and cared for, and considering all who would have to know about the operation (not even the local game wardens would know). We also spent time talking over what his cover might be, who would be his immediate supervisor, and how the case reports would be processed. We considered the legal challenges we might face from defense attorneys, such as creation of a market, egregious government behavior, illegal search and seizure, and entrapment, just to mention a few. I also wanted to send Morrison to a language school so he could understand the Spanish language spoken around him as he worked. There is no better protection against a wreck being planned against an operative than his secret knowledge of the bad guys' language. A six-week CIA Spanish school took care of that concern.

I handed Morrison the Colorado intelligence file I had been laboring over for so long. Not once did Morrison show any emotion other than his ill-concealed enthusiasm; just eagerness to get under way. Little did either of us realize the full implications of the challenge we were about to undertake. Little did anyone understand, for that matter. ...

Morrison got up, saying, "This is going to be a good one, Chief. I wouldn't want to be in your shoes when the stuff hits the fan, but I can't think of anyone better able to handle it. I have a ton of work to do, so unless you have further need of me, I'd best get moving." With a wave of the hand, he left my office as if nothing more unusual than a casual discussion of the price of crowbars in Korea had taken place that morning. That casual discussion had locked up the next two-and-a-half years of his life and would expose him on a daily basis to some of the worst sides of nature and humankind.

I must now digress back to a time shortly before Kris and I began *seriously* planning Operation SLV. One day my secretary walked into my office and said there was a man waiting to see me. She asked if I had time to meet with him. I advised her with a wave of the hand to send him in. I was in the middle of a congressional letter, but as I finished getting my thoughts down on paper, I became aware of someone standing quietly in front of my desk. I looked up and saw a man small in stature but, as I was to discover, with the heart of a lion. At that moment he looked like a sparrow in a winter snowstorm, but the look on his face clearly indicated that he had something to say.

"Remember me?" he asked in a strident tone, extending his hand in friendship.

"Sure do," I replied. Standing up, I reached out to take his hand and said, "Jim Bensley, what are you doing in my town?"

"Bonnie and I live in Fort Collins now, and I wanted to stop by and see you. You see, I still feel bad about my part with Swanson." The Swanson investigation was one I had assisted on as a rookie U.S. game management agent some twelve years earlier in California. The ringleader, Gary Swanson, at the time a taxidermist in the Los Angeles area, was involved in a unique and highly profitable illegal wildlife commercialization scheme. He had in his employ an Indian guide named Ray Poctah who guided shooters out into the deserts of southern California, where they would kill the totally protected desert bighorn sheep around the waterholes where the thirsty animals came to drink. The cape would be brought to Swanson while Ray kept the head and horns for cleaning and drying. The rest of the animal would be left in the field to rot. Gary would send the cape to a tannery run by the man now standing before me. Jim would illegally tan the cape and return it to Gary. Gary and a woman named Pearl Prudholme would then fashion the "trophy" (skull, horns, and cape) into a first-class mount and send it off to the shooter for display on the wall of his trophy room.

A desert bighorn sheep is considered one of this nation's top big-game trophies by the sheep-hunting public. These sheep are very limited in number and located primarily in the southwestern United States and Mexico. In order to complete what is known in the trophy world as a Grand Slam, one needs to take a Rocky Mountain bighorn, desert bighorn, stone sheep, and Dall sheep. The Rocky, stone, and

Dall sheep licenses are not terribly hard to get; they just take time and money. But one needs to get a permit to take a desert sheep, and very few of those permits are issued in the United States, with a few more in Mexico (legally and *illegally*). So it is not uncommon for the trophy shooters, driven to distraction, to forget what is right and take these animals unlawfully. Not everyone takes their desert sheep illegally, but enough do to keep the Fish and Wildlife Service and respective state Fish and Game agencies interested.

Since no permits were available for California sheep (then totally protected since 1898), the heads and other parts were pure contraband. However, with Swanson providing what hunters thought was a totally secure, one-stop illegal sheep-killing service, takers of desert sheep were many. Swanson and his cohorts would go so far as to assist the California Department of Fish and Game in the locating and building of sheep watering holes in the desert mountains. Then they would send Ray and the shooter out in due time after the sheep had located the waterholes. Only the voiceless sheep were the wiser. ...

The Service got involved in the Swanson investigation when one of the finished "trophies" was accidentally discovered by postal inspectors. It was a Lacey Act violation (illegally taken in violation of state law and transported in interstate commerce), and subsequently through a covert investigation the Service rounded up seventy-nine defendants from twenty-three states, Canada, and Mexico. When we went through documents procured under search warrants, we discovered we had just missed a very famous *sitting* Southern state governor who had sent in his money and was supposed to go on an illegal hunt three days *after* we arrested the Swanson gang! Oh well—sometimes you eat the bear, and sometimes he eats you.

Coming back from my memories of the investigation, I asked Jim to sit down. I harbored no malice toward the man even though his participation had cost the desert bighorn sheep population dearly. He had paid his dues to society, and now I was curious to hear what he had to say.

"Terry, what I did with Swanson was wrong. I knew it then and know it today. I needed money in those days and just let that fact override my common sense. I have gone straight since that day and will continue to do so the rest of my life. I don't know if I can ever make up for my wrongs but sure have been giving it a try these last few years. and that is why I am here. First of all, I want you to know you will never again have to worry about me violating the wildlife laws. I will continue my tanning and taxidermy business, but if approached to do anything illegal, I will call you. Second, if you ever need me to help you guys on any kind of project, I stand ready to give you a hand, even if it means quitting my current job. Then maybe, just maybe, I can truly help the wildlife and myself in some small way."

I was impressed with the man's contrition. It appeared to be genuine and from his soul. "Jim," I said, "you have long ago paid your debt to society."

"Maybe according to society, but I don't feel I have done so yet for the wildlife I helped slaughter," he said. I could see the tears well up in Jim's eyes, and it became apparent this man was on a mission.

Jim is a talented taxidermist, tanner of hides, butcher, sausage maker, all around handyman and the like. His experience and business acumen could provide an up-front, credible working cover for an operative, I thought; such cover was *always* a weakness in covert operations. And when Jim spoke, he was believable! How my imagination started to spin with the huge opportunity Jim represented relative to the San Luis Valley. Thanking Jim, I told him if I ever had such a need, I would give him a call. That seemed to please him. After leaving me his phone number and address, he left the office a happier man for having gotten years of built-up misery and guilt off his chest.

I could not believe how many times the grace of God had manifested itself during my career. Here was a bird nest on the ground if Operation SLV ever got going. Just think what could happen if I hooked Jim up with my future operative and the two of them developed a trust and working relationship. That would fast-track the investigation because of the very *real* cover we could exhibit. I shook my head as a grin spread from ear to ear. Talk about timing: this had the potential to be a Rolex moment instead of a Timex moment!

A little while later Jim called to alert me to a significant case. It seemed that two doctors named Hagar and Hampers had contacted him regarding some endangered cat skins they intended to smuggle into the United States; they wanted Jim to do the taxidermy work. I was trying out Morrison on covert operations, so guess who got assigned Jim's case? At first Morrison was not keen on working with a non–law enforcement type, especially after I filled him in on Jim's history. But he agreed to meet with Jim and Bonnie (Jim's wife, may she rest in peace) to see if they could come to a working arrangement. I really hoped this "marriage" would work. If it did, my long-term valley plans would surely get a jump start.

Sometime later, deep into the planning and development of Operation SLV, I got Jim on the phone and asked if he was interested in working with the Service on another major covert investigation. Without hesitation Jim replied he was more than ready. I told Jim I'd send Morrison up to meet with him, and if Morrison felt they would make a good team for *this* operation, he would fill Jim in on the details. With that, Jim could decide if he was interested, and if so I would start the administrative process of bringing him on board. Damn, was he excited and raring to go.

"Just relax," I told him. "When Morrison gets in contact, we will let nature run her course." Jim agreed, and after hanging up, I called Morrison. At first Morrison was somewhat cool toward the idea of having a private citizen as a possible long-term partner in such a dangerous situation. But after reminding Morrison of Jim's attributes and abilities, I could sense his realization that Jim's background as well as his all-around good nature would strengthen the cover and investigation. Morrison agreed to get in touch with Jim and set up a meeting. Having a meeting of my own to run to, I asked Morrison to keep me in the loop, hoping my plan would not only have merit but that the two of them could get along as partners.

A month later Morrison told me his previous covert activities were progressing nicely. He also reported that he was within sixty days of obtaining a new identity that would hide his real background from anyone's view even if they ran an FBI check on him. Because some of the raw intelligence pointed to several law enforcement types being illegally involved, I wanted Morrison buried so well that even a grave digger could not locate him! Morrison told me that even his parents were not aware of his future plans; he had just told them that he would be so busy that they might not hear from him much for awhile.

Then he broached the subject of his meeting with Bensley. "Chief, we have a winner. I spent the last several days with Jim and Bonnie just looking the man over and making sure his wife understood and approved what they might be in for. I don't have any security problems with either of them and think they could be key to the operation.

He is not only a man I like and respect very much, but his wife is a jewel. They are both down-to-earth folks, and let me tell you, Jim is a wonder with his hands in anything he does. He is a great all-around handyman, and that will help if something breaks down in the shop or needs creating. He is also an excellent taxidermist, butcher, sausage maker, tanner, and just about anything else associated with the trade. Plus, he really looks the part. There are no two ways about it, he is a real asset to help front a covert operation, especially the type we are looking at initiating."

Man, you talk about skipping along; my feet hardly hit the ground! In Jim we had a man who would add greatly to our operation. Not only that, I could tell from the tone of Morrison's voice that he had a newfound friend. In the end, both men benefited from the relationship. Let me elaborate. The role of a deep covert operative is extremely stressful, lonely, and dangerous. If an operative becomes overly isolated in the work *and himself*, he sometimes develops a feeling that he is all alone, that no one else really knows what is going on or cares, and with that comes paranoia. The operative will sometimes develop tunnel vision, which leads to feeling even more isolated, which can lead to investigative mistakes or omissions. I wasn't worried about Morrison based on his track record, but any supervisor worth his salt will try to make his subordinate's life a little easier. I wasn't always successful, but I sure kept after it. Therein lay the core of my strategy for including Jim as George's partner and friend.

As I said, a supervisor worth his salt will go to great lengths to preserve the heart and soul of an officer by not letting him fall prey to the dangerous stresses of the investigation. Bear in mind what this officer would see every day: destruction, waste, cruelty to animals, corruption, individuals who represented nothing but the mean spirit of humankind, people who cared little about tomorrow and were full of greed and ego. There would be nothing pretty in those elements facing him on a daily basis. Throw in crooked law enforcement officials, weak judges, self-serving politicians, and the like and it is no wonder one has to fight off the demons to do the job. Add in bureaucrats and know-nothings in high places overseeing your investigation and the lousy food, long hours, isolation, danger, foul weather, and terrible living conditions, and you have the makings of a witch's brew. Having a friend alongside means the operative will last longer and do a better job protecting the critters for the American people as well as protecting the rights of those he is pursuing. Once the operation was under way, almost every night that Jim was not with George, he maintained contact via telephone to make sure his friend was all right. That contact gave George a small outlet from the everyday pressures and a small, personal link to the real world.

Pleased that my friend and covert operative had found a friend who would further the success of the operation, I said I would get Jim all the necessary clearances. Hanging up the phone, I sat back with a smile, only to have it quickly turn to a frown. I wondered if Morrison understood what truly awaited him in working that closely with a co-operating private individual. Morrison would be responsible not only for his own life but for his partner's as well. He would have to guide Jim in everything he did so as not to jeopardize the investigation. That would be especially true during any trials originating from the investigation because government attorneys would have to deal with Jim's past when using him as a witness. That background problem would double when the defense attorneys had a go at Jim on the stand. I wondered if either of them realized what a ride they were in for.

Among the many meetings to occur were those with U.S. Attorney Bob Miller and Jim Allison, his head of the Criminal Division. During those meetings, I brought everyone up to speed on the investigation now that the direction of the operation had been planned and it was being put in motion. Bob Miller listened intently to every detail laid out for his information and review. Periodically, he would interject ideas on how he wanted certain parts of the operation to proceed or be changed, especially regarding points of law defense attorneys normally raised in their smokescreen issues to blind the jury. Issues such as illegal search and seizure, creation of a market, entrapment, egregious government behavior, and the like. Bob would bring everyone in the room up to date on the various defenses, any associated case law, and his understanding of what each definition or investigative dimension meant. This was not a rigid legal view or politics but a genuine concern for doing it right. And since he was the U.S. attorney, he was the boss!

Toward the end of the investigation Bob introduced his final choice of assistant U.S. attorney who would be our adviser for the remainder of the case as well as our chief federal prosecutor. He wasn't much at first glance, compared to the size of my covert operative or some of my larger officers, but looks were deceiving. We were soon to find that he was as rough-and-tumble as any Irish street brawler. He was fearless and, we discovered, a gifted prosecutor with a towering intellect. He was a stickler for detail and had absolutely no bedside manner when it came to getting what he wanted. You either produced what he felt was needed for prosecution or you went back to the drawing board. He was so intense that you didn't show up unprepared more than once.

At first I found that my men were somewhat intimidated by him and exasperated at the amount of what they considered nitpicking detail work dumped on their shoulders. However, I soon saw them evolving from overworked and pissed-off agents to better case managers totally dedicated to the man. I am convinced Assistant U.S. Attorney Dave Conner had been with the Greeks in the Battle of Thermopylae in an earlier life. He was one of the greatest adversaries one could go up against, and as a result of his preparation and foresight, *the case had no legal flaws when it was finally presented.* Or, now that I think about it, he might have been Doc Holliday of OK Corral fame. … It was during this agent-attorney interaction that some of the special talents of my deputy, Neill Hartman, came into play. Neill is a gifted officer with a tremendous capacity for all things legal. It was Neill who, in addition to his other duties, stepped forward to deal with and manage the issues Conner found to cuss and discuss. On Neill's shoulders fell the tasks associated with all the prosecution preparations, affidavits, and arrest and search warrants, not to mention handling the frustrations of an assistant U.S. attorney who realized he had a good one that could run if properly managed. Looking back on all that now, I realize I was blessed with the finest assistant special agent in charge in the Service, bar none!

You can begin to see that covert operations aren't planned, executed, and wrapped up in thirty minutes, as in *Law and Order* on TV. The big ones take tons of preparation, fine-tuning, a world of time, a bucket of money, and a lot of blood, sweat, and tears. Years were spent in planning this investigation, and it took another two-and-a-half years to complete it once initiated! Those pundits who later insisted that this was a fly-by-night operation designed to hammer the Hispanics should have taken a closer look at what had gone on behind the scenes.

In May 1986, enforcement personnel from Colorado and New Mexico met with Service representatives, worked out the final particulars of the investigation, and signed the Service's required cooperative agreements. Finally we were on the verge of beginning actual field investigations. In the fall of 1986, we established a false cover business named the Bear River Trading Company in Woodland Park near Colorado Springs. The reason for setting this up outside the valley was simple: we had no idea what to expect if we tried to put it in the very heart of the killing fields. Also, I was using an "outsider" to work among the multitudes linked by family and other bonds of trust in the valley. Their acceptance of George would be highly questionable under those circumstances. Finally, I was concerned about security and chose to start the program outside the sphere of the heaviest criminal influence in order to ascertain the degree of danger before George moved in among those needing his attention.

The business was basically a combination taxidermy and sausage-making operation with a fur-buying route (that is, travel among the valley towns setting up fur-buying stations) on the side. The taxidermy side of the business was for both the legal hunters and the outlaws, in hopes of attracting those needing more than just taxidermy services. Once illegal shooters determined that the shop was available for illicit taxidermy work or trade, we would be off and running. The sausage-making aspect was a natural. Getting rid of or disguising the mounds of meat from their ill-gotten gains was a problem for poachers, so converting telltale critters into innocent-appearing, tough-to-regulate game sausage was a natural direction for the business. We could meet a lot of folks with illegal meat on their hands and provide a bankroll for those willing to sell their booty to the "friendly" sausage maker. The fur-buying route was designed to provide a liberal supply of rope to all who wanted hanging. That aspect was innocent enough. It was set up to process *legal* wildlife but, in the offing, provide those predisposed to violate the law with an outlet for the illegal sales of other wildlife parts and products. This angle gave George the freedom to move around as a legitimate businessman making acquaintances under a nonthreatening business mantle. This was our Trojan Horse, and history was to repeat itself in disaster for those who were fooled! For outlaws wanting illegal sausage or trophies processed, Morrison would be their man because he would always be around. He could alleviate their concerns by receiving and transporting their illegal meat to market, hence taking all the risks. As you can see, the net was thrown far and wide for those foolish enough to "buck the tiger" (a term from the days of the Old West meaning to take on tough odds such as gambling at the faro table—known for being rigged) in this very real game of chance. Here again, Jim Bensley was the man of the hour. He really knew his furs and provided the knowledge and cover needed to pull the wool over the killers' eyes.

Morrison set up two fur-buying routes designed to give him maximum exposure and coverage in the areas of greatest concern. One covered the towns of Walsenburg, San Luis, Alamosa, and Saguache in Colorado. The other covered the towns of Las Vegas, Mora, Taos, and Questa in New Mexico. After we opened our undercover store in Woodland Park, Morrison and Bensley circulated in those towns, meeting the people and handing out flyers announcing the Bear River Trading Company's fur-buying schedule, which soon generated business both good and bad.

In the early stages of operation, Morrison would front the taxidermy and sausage business as well as the fur routes. However, since Morrison was not an expert in those endeavors, all orders for taxidermy work or sausage processing went through him to Bensley and then back to Jim's home in Fort Collins. There Jim would process the meat and perform the taxidermy work, using his personal equipment. Those items were then returned to Morrison, who would reenter them into commerce through the storefront or take them back to their owners, thereby closing the ring. This procedure continued until the investigation progressed far enough that Jim was able to move some of his equipment and himself into the storefront. Throughout the rest of the operation, Jim and George worked in tandem. With beards, grubby looks, bloody hands and arms, and ready smiles, they made two fine "businessmen," and the outlaws flocked to the pair, believing them to be among "their own."

The American people, especially the resource-loving and decent residents of the San Luis Valley, owe a debt of gratitude to people like Jim Bensley, not only for donating part of their lives in hopes of saving a slice of heritage for the American people but for walking into a dangerous situation, knowing full well the possible consequences. Jim more than repaid any remaining debt to society he had incurred in his earlier days. In fact, *paid in full* should be the word of the day from a grateful American public to that hardworking man!

Soon the business was rocking along. Seven-day weeks and sixteen-hour days became the norm as Morrison and Bensley filtered through the valley's poaching rank-and-file. Many poachers known to Morrison through Colorado's intelligence files began to meet and scope out the new taxidermy-sausage-fur businessman as he became better known throughout the valley. This earlier-identified core group of killers began warming to George and Jim's personalities, believability, and business acumen. That relaxation soon resulted in loose talk regarding ongoing illegal events.

In fact, those in the business of extinction were so ready that one man, Bobby Romero, approached Morrison on his *first* fur-buying stop in San Luis and asked if he wanted to buy some illegal elk meat! Soon the illicit trade came like the rush from a spring-fed river! Morrison, as instructed by me and the legal beagles in the U.S. Attorney's Office, was very careful not to create a market by waving fistfuls of money under the noses of his targets. Having identified the fifty-eight from the intelligence files, he selectively purchased illegal wildlife running from bear meat to eagles in just those amounts necessary to guarantee a conviction in state or federal court. Then he would move on to the next individual eagerly standing in line. Included in this careful attention to detail was Morrison's use of the taxpayers' money. Never did he pay what the outlaws were asking for their ill-gotten gains. Morrison was a shrewd businessman and many times purchased the illegal goods for up to 60 percent below the asking price! Many times he would purchase just a small part of the wildlife being offered and pass on the rest. That way no one could accuse him of creating a market in an economically depressed area of Colorado or New Mexico. Not one defense attorney who subsequently accused Morrison of creation of a market made the charge stick in any court of law.

After several months of hard work I had a chance to meet with Morrison and evaluate the progress of the investigation and the health of my friend and operative. George was in excellent spirits and even better physical shape than when he had started (he even played on a local basketball team when he had time). He seemed to be weathering the long days and dangerous working conditions well, and I began to relax. With a twinkle in his eyes he said, "You were wrong, Chief;

there aren't fifty-eight hardcore market hunters in the valley. There are fifty-nine!" Suffice it to say that his supervisor, even though upstaged, was more than pleased!

I reminded Morrison again to continue gathering information in each and every transaction regarding what the money for illegal contraband was being used for. During the time Morrison worked in the valley, those monies went almost exclusively for the purchase of drugs, booze, and more ammunition, in that order, as reported by the willing sellers. Very few said the money would be used to feed or support their families!

A new challenge hammered into view in June 1987. The owner of our building in Woodland Park served notice that we must leave because he had other plans for the property. This required a meeting between officers in New Mexico, Colorado, and the Service to determine our plan of action in light of the impending move. We had been rocking along at a good pace, and now did not seem the time to change horses midstream. After much "cussin' and discussin'" we decided Morrison had been so well accepted by the people in the valley, he would move his operation into the eye of the storm and reside in the valley in Fort Garland. However, I had some concerns about Morrison's quality of life in such proximity to the outlaws and his undercover business. His time for resting between bouts of activity would be severely hampered; he would have no peace or life of his own and would have to be doubly careful around those being investigated as their lives and illegal activities constantly ebbed and flowed around him. Additionally, leaving the area to do reports or transport evidence could elicit suspicious questions. But the New Mexico and Colorado supervisors ultimately felt it would be best in light of the solid relationships Morrison had cultivated. Morrison also felt confident enough in his talents and past successes that he seconded the move. However, that move brought about another unlikely twist in the road.

We thought that picking up a business and moving it into Fort Garland, Colorado, a very small, close-knit community, would be problematic, but our concerns about lack of living and business space in such a small town turned out to be a nonissue. In fact, we found a diamond in the rough. On June 25, we located and leased a suitable building from Deputy Sheriff Robert Espinoza, *a prime target in the investigation!* In fact, during a taped phone call between Morrison and

Espinoza regarding the building lease, Morrison mentioned that everything he did was not totally legal and that he sometimes bought "stuff" from poachers. This remark was an investigative tool to determine Espinoza's culpability. Espinoza replied that that kind of activity was Morrison's business, and later in the same conversation told Morrison that the suggested kind of illegal activity was fine with him. Only six months later, in Morrison's presence, Espinoza shot at and missed a bald eagle, a violation of the Bald Eagle Protection Act and the Endangered Species Act. A short time later the same day he spotted another bald eagle sitting in a tree and killed it with one shot from a 22-250 rifle! Espinoza sold the eagle to Morrison for $110 cash and $100 worth of taxidermy work on a big-game head he wanted mounted.

Morrison moved into his new place of business in Fort Garland, and if the river of illegal wildlife had gushed before, it now became a flood. Pure and simply, it was commercial-market hunting at its worst without an ounce of concern about the loss of resources. Hawks, owls, eagles, fur-bearers, deer, elk, bear, antelope, and their parts, all taken illegally, moved across Morrison's doorstep in an ever-increasing volume. True to program direction, anything he purchased was collected in midnight runs and spirited off to evidence lockers miles away. Again, to avoid charges of "creating a market," Morrison selectively purchased just enough illegal wildlife from each market hunter to cement his case and then moved on to the many others standing in line. However, he could not always be so circumspect—for example, if he were buying an elk from a first-time defendant and a previous seller arrived at the same moment with parts of another elk to sell. Buying an elk from one man but claiming not to need any more from the next seller would fly in the face of common sense and alert a suspicious outlaw. In that kind of situation, Morrison would purchase some parts from the later-arriving subject for show and to preserve the investigation. But first he would attempt to convince the second arrival that he was just now full up with illegal meat.

To illustrate this legal point further, in the two-and-a-half years of investigation, Morrison was offered or was aware of 547 elk, 2,005 deer, and 92 eagles over the number he purchased that were moving illegally elsewhere in valley commerce! That fact later nullified allegations from people in the valley that there had been no commercial market or only a small one before Morrison arrived. Following the constant legal guidance of state and federal attorneys plus a generous helping of his own common sense, Morrison ended up purchasing only 96 whole animals or their parts during the entire period in order to make the cases he did! As you can see, creation of a market was never an issue. But *imagine how much wildlife actually traveled illegally in commerce since we did not see or know of all that was moving during this short investigative time frame!* Then add the string of years before our arrival and imagine the number of animals illegally killed and moved in commerce! That number had to be staggering and a blot on the souls of those involved in the destruction of this portion of our national heritage!

But on they came, hungry to move their illegal wildlife into the commercial markets so they could be off spending the money "earned." Bobby Romero offered to sell Morrison four elk; Bobby Romero sold Morrison a hawk for $40; Robert Espinoza killed and sold a bald eagle to Morrison for $110 dollars and taxidermy services on a trophy; Dale Vigil called Morrison on the phone and offered to sell him an elk for $200; the next day Jess and Clarence Vigil sold Morrison an elk for $250; Bobby and Ron Romero contacted Morrison just before Christmas to tell him they had just killed three elk; Clarence Vigil offered to sell Morrison one elk leg; Robert Romero offered to sell drugs to Morrison, in the process mentioning that he had just snorted two lines of cocaine; another time, Robert Romero offered to sell Morrison some "weed" for $1,500 per pound or a kilo of cocaine for $40,000; Chico Romero sold Morrison twelve elk ivories for $35; Robert Espinoza offered to use his position as deputy sheriff to warn Morrison of any impending raids; and Robert Espinoza told Morrison that he had gotten caught with an illegal deer. He added that he had shot four elk, taken the meat to Denver, and sold it to pay for his legal expenses. Robert Espinoza and Morrison went to Amos Medina's house and picked up an illegal elk Espinoza had killed earlier. Espinoza paid Medina $10 for keeping the elk. Robert Espinoza sold Morrison four nonresident deer and elk licenses belonging to Thomas Row, Gary Straach, Byran Gordon, and Gary Ketter for $31.50; Gary Straach and Thomas Row left a deer taken during the closed season with Morrison for processing; Robert Espinoza sold Morrison ten eagle talons for $50; Robert Espinoza took Morrison poaching in his patrol car. Under Robert's direction and insistence, Morrison shot a deer from the deputy sheriff's patrol car (the only animal Morrison had to kill during the entire investigation). And on it went.

Meanwhile, Morrison and Bensley were living in dreadful conditions. The roof in the building they occupied leaked like a sieve. Since both men were sleeping on the floor, they and their sleeping gear were often soaking wet. Those articles had to be dried nearly every day. Then the heating system wasn't much, and the snow would blow in through the wall cracks and stay for weeks on the floor. Finally they moved into a ramshackle trailer alongside their building, where it was so cold that they slept with all their clothes on in their sleeping bags in order to avoid freezing to death! So much for the glamorous life of an undercover agent. ...

As is typical with a covert operation, God threw in a ringer now and then just to make sure everyone was paying attention. And man, one caught everyone by surprise. Two Colorado game wardens in the valley had been eyeballing Morrison, especially after hearing from some of the good people in the valley that he was up to no good in the world of wildlife. Officers Mark Cousins and Tom Raush had been gunning for Morrison for some time but hadn't been able to get the goods on him. Finally, after many frustrating months trying to catch him, the officers got enough information from an informant for a search warrant. Pete Comar, deputy DA in Alamosa (who did not know Morrison was working undercover), signed off on the affidavit and presented it to the judge for a search warrant. It seemed the officers' informant had sworn that he had seen an illegal elk hanging from a rafter through a back window of the taxidermy shop in Fort Garland. The only problem was that what the informant had seen was in fact a legal coyote hanging from the rafter waiting to be skinned. Anyway, the state search warrant was served, and eagles, sea otters, and other illegal items were eventually discovered in freezers in Morrison's shop. As a result, Morrison was arrested, handcuffed, and booked in the Alamosa County jail.

This presented me with a *major* bump in the road. Department of Justice (DOJ) policy, based on an earlier court decision, was that a federal undercover officer was not allowed to give any false information or deceive any judge, court officer, or court clerk. In other words, Morrison could not appear in court to plead his case under his alias without violating that policy and subjecting him to further criminal prosecution. Additionally, Morrison could not deceive any member of the county attorney's office in Alamosa or Costilla County. The evening Morrison was arrested, he was smart enough to call me from his shop as the wardens circled the wagons outside. I advised him to burn the eagles in the hope that the smell of burning feathers as the wardens waited for their search warrant to arrive might cause them to stampede and enter his place of business illegally. If they did, we could have the search legally discredited without any court appearance and possibly circumvent the encumbering DOJ policy. After I hung up, I called Bob Miller at home and set up a meeting for the next day to see if there was a way out of this mess that would allow us to continue the covert operation. Hell, we still had a nest of outlaws in New Mexico that we hadn't even touched!

Early the next morning, the meeting between the Service and U.S. attorneys' office was a hot one in light of Morrison's arrest and incarceration! Every assistant attorney strongly advised Miller that to continue the investigation would violate DOJ policy and subject Miller to criminal prosecution! Man, for the life of me, this arrest could not have happened at a worse time. Stopping the investigation would leave a lot of loose ends and outlaws still running wild. In short, it would not have the effect I needed to nip this kind of killing in the bud or give the good people of the valley back their pride once the outlaws were removed. As I argued, Bob just sat there listening to both sides. Well, I didn't get as big as I was for being last in line, so I launched into Plan B for all to consider. It was a wild gamble, but a drowning man will try to catch even a spear thrown at him. If they bought it, we could continue the operation and none of us would do jail time for violation of a government policy that in my opinion did nothing but hinder legal investigations. Covert operations in the Service were run damn close to the vest by the Office of the U.S. Attorney, the county attorneys involved, and the investigating agencies. As long as the operations were run by the book, why the need for such a goofy policy? I guess that attitude was why I was just a "grunt" and not a "superchief."

I suggested that I go immediately to the valley and personally meet with the two arresting officers. Since they had no idea who Morrison was and knew nothing of the investigation, I proposed that I be allowed to try to convince them not to follow through on the arrest charges. Instead, I would persuade them to just issue citations by convincing them that if they did that, I could slap Morrison with a slew of federal charges based on the evidence they had procured under their search warrant and, between our two entities, break him financially and force him to leave "Dodge." Then, I quietly reasoned, we would move Morrison out of Fort Garland to Costilla, New Mexico, and collect that area's bunch of killers. What better cover, I reckoned, than being arrested in one state and fleeing to another, setting up business once more as if nothing out of the ordinary had happened? All the assistant attorneys (except the one assigned to the investigation) squalled at that suggestion and again beseeched Bob to stop the investigation, in essence calling it quits and proceeding through the courts with what we had.

Miller sat for a few moments thinking over my proposal, then said, "If you can do what you say you can, I don't feel that tactic will violate Department of Justice policy. However, if you deviate one inch from that plan, I will personally see to it, Terry, that you are criminally prosecuted for violation of that policy. Do we have an understanding?"

Well, that was pretty damn clear; plus it got Bob off the hook from being prosecuted by his own agency if the process wasn't followed to a T. "You have a deal," I said. Thanking Bob for the latitude, I hurriedly left the meeting before anyone could change his mind. Suffice it to say, my exit from that meeting was punctuated by the din of many assistant U.S. attorneys still arguing with their boss over the wisdom of his decision.

Some of you might ask, "Why not just tell the wardens of the investigation?" Well, officer safety was our primary concern—not the number of bad guys we could catch but bringing George home alive at the end of the detail. That meant the fewer who knew about the operation, the safer it was. That formula of only informing those who needed to know had worked successfully for years in covert operations of this nature, with a man's life on the line and no physical way to protect him. So we just worked around the rocks in the road.

I telephoned Morrison and outlined my plan so he would be prepared for the events to follow if I was successful with the two arresting officers. Next I called Colorado's Chief Marcoux, briefed him on my plans, and requested that he set up a meeting between me and his two arresting officers. Fran agreed, and several hours later I was in the company of two officers still riding the high that comes from apprehending what they thought was a real outlaw. After greetings and congratulations for catching such a fine "son of a bitch," I sat down with them to explain my need for such a posthaste meeting. Before I could say a word, Officer Tom Raush, possibly smelling a rat but unable to put a finger on the species, asked, "Is Morgan [George's undercover name] part of an undercover operation?"

Without batting an eye or showing any sign of emotion, I said, "What a coup it would be to get an operative here in the valley to catch these killing son of a guns! No, I can only wish for such a gift at this point in time."

That seemed to satisfy both officers, and they immediately launched into a description of catching the hated outlaw the evening before. I patiently listened as they told the story, wishing all the time they had just left things alone. However, I figured we had a silver lining to this cloud, especially if I could pull it all together and use it to our advantage.

"Gentlemen," I interrupted, "I have a proposal that may make your day. Let me talk to Morgan and see if we can get him to talk. Since you guys have him over a barrel, we may have just the opening we need to break him from sucking eggs in your backyard. Let's whipsaw the bastard between our two agencies and see if we can get him to give up the bad guys. Barring that, through multiple prosecutions at the state and federal levels we can make his life so miserable he will get the hell out of 'Dodge.' That way you can get back to the business of chasing the remaining outlaws in the valley and not have Morgan to worry about. Unbeknownst to Morgan, we have some federal charges on the eagles and sea otters that can be filed as well. If you guys agree to drop the arrest charges, maybe we can get him to pay for a slew of state tickets. If he goes for that to get out from under the gun of an arrest record, you guys can take him to the cleaners with multiple citations. Then, without him knowing when the next shoe will drop, we will hammer him from the federal side after he settles up with the state. Maybe that will be enough to break him financially and cause him to give up the rotten business he is in, or at least get him to fold up his tent and leave. Just think, between the two of us, we should be able to set him back by at least five to ten thousand dollars."

I could just see the wheels going around in the two officers' minds as they tallied up what the fines would be if they heaped a slew of citations on Morgan. Looking at each other with grins as wide as a football field, they quickly agreed, sensing the demise of Morgan and everything rotten in his henhouse. Plus, they could write a bushel basket of state citations, be out from under any other court work, and have at least a month's worth of bragging rights for such a fine catch.

Half an hour later found the three of us at Morrison's place of business in Fort Garland, where he was working on cleaning some hides after posting bond. Tom introduced me to Morrison as the federal agent in charge in the area and said I had some questions. Damn, you talk about hard! Try to interview one of your own kind and a close friend to boot without letting the cat out of the bag by inadvertently using his real name. I had to speak slowly, thinking out every word, to be sure not to give him up in any way. Morrison, trying hard not to break out laughing, just kept his eyes on the floor as I flooded him with pointed questions (more so than normal to throw the two game wardens off the trail) regarding his illegal activities. Morrison had consumed a jillion cups of coffee prior to our meeting to further the charade, leaving him with a case of the shakes to support the effect of being nervous. This song and dance went on for about thirty minutes, and I think Morrison and I were both sweating bullets in our attempts to hide the truth from the two closely watching game wardens.

Morrison did not roll over on his outlaw friends, saying he was afraid of what they would do to him if they found out he had talked (a damned good excuse). However, he agreed (surprise, surprise) to accept any citations the officers sent his way if they would just drop the arrest charges. Morrison made it abundantly clear and convincing that he did not want to spend any more time in jail. My two game wardens registered big grins over finally being in the driver's seat instead of that "scumbag" Morgan. Hell, I couldn't blame them. Morrison had made their lives miserable, and now it was their turn. If I had been in their shoes, I would have had a big grin too. Thus ended the interview, with a warning from me that to continue violating wildlife laws would bring the full force of the federal government down around his ears. Morrison, keeping his eyes on the floor, said he understood and wanted no more trouble. With that, the three of us walked out, leaving him to "ponder his fate." Once out of earshot, the two officers agreed on what citations would be issued and I agreed to wait until he had paid in state court. Then I would drop a mess of federal charges on him as well. We had lunch together, which I paid for in celebration of their "catch of the day," and then parted ways, two game wardens with grins on their faces and light hearts and I with a slight hitch in my "giddy-up." But I also had a grin on my puss plastered there by the devil because of my knowledge of things yet to come in the lives of some deserving poachers and market hunters in New Mexico.

Morrison paid for his state tickets with money out of the business funds. In the end, it cost the U.S. government $2,770 to settle up with the state of Colorado and maintain our charade. After that I "filed" federal charges against him, generating false prosecution documents in case anyone checked the system. That "bill" came to another $3,000 in fines. When that was done, I sent a nice letter from my office to Chief Fran Marcoux, informing him of the outcome and thanking him for his officers' outstanding work. In this final chapter of pulling the wool over the officers' eyes, I hinted in the letter that I would have a man available after December of that year for some covert work in the valley, suggesting that maybe we could work this man in on Morrison if he were still in Fort Garland doing business. I figured Fran would forward my letter to the officers along with the federal sentencing documents, and that would throw the two officers off Morrison's trail. Officers will often back off an individual if they think their agency is going to make a covert run on that person. If they keep away, the subject may get sloppy and overconfident, thus making him an easier investigative target.

Morrison folded up his tent in Fort Garland and moved to Costilla, New Mexico. There he rented several houses, opened for business as he had in Fort Garland, and was met with open arms by the local outlaws. What better badge of honor in their eyes than being arrested in Colorado for wildlife violations, hammered in state and federal court, and then moving to New Mexico to continue in the business of extinction in the teeth of the law? The outlaws accepted Morrison with visions of silver for their pockets, and in no time illegal wildlife was once again moving across Morrison's doorstep. Again closed-season elk, deer, hawks, owls, eagles, fur-bearers, and other wildlife parts and products flowed from the hands of the outlaws into the coffers of the investigation. Again conspiracies to violate state and federal laws were as common as sagebrush. Here again, the money "earned" from the sales of illegal wildlife went for drugs, booze, and more ammunition. Nothing, according to the culprits, for poor starving families. ...

However, a combination of winter weather, lousy living conditions, poor food, almost constant involvement with the criminal element every hour of the day and night for over two years, continuous massive agency legal and reporting requirements, and every other form of stress was beginning to manifest itself in George. Jim was able to go home on occasion, thereby relieving some of his stress, but someone had to mind the shop, and that task rightly fell on George's shoulders. He was wearing down. He had lasted in deep cover longer than most. I attributed his survival to his excellent physical condition and positive frame of mind. However, everyone is human, and I began to see the ragged signs of wear. About that time a man as close in temperament to a wolverine as humanly possible ambled into the picture. Tim Baraclough, assistant area supervisor for the Northeastern Area of the New Mexico Department of Game and Fish, sensing George's condition, stepped into the picture big time and provided the support needed in keeping the final days of the investigation and Morrison operating in top form. Any time of the day or night, Tim was quietly and secretly there for George, be it a drink of fine whiskey shared with a friend in an out-of-the-way place, someone to move evidence out of George's hands into an evidence lockup, or just someone to share a quiet, secure evening and dinner as George tried to rejoin the human race. Tim was as tough as a horseshoe nail, driven as if by the north wind, and as professionally dedicated as any man with whom I ever shared a campfire. With George and Tim in the saddle, the bad guys didn't have a chance. Tim went on to shepherd the investigation's takedown activities in New Mexico, and never did I have any better guiding hand than that man's. The critters, George, and I lost a very real friend when he retired.

In his new location in New Mexico, Morrison continued his strict investigative discipline. He documented amounts of wildlife purchased, set about establishing predisposition on the part of the market hunters and run-of-the-mill killers, and whenever possible documented conversations through tape-recorded phone calls, as he had done in Colorado. Following my explicit directions, George continued to dodge the little guys whenever possible but drew down hard on those with a track record of market hunting. As a check and balance to the system, many almost weekly meetings were now being held in Denver and Albuquerque with the U.S. attorneys and county attorneys from the major cities in Colorado and New Mexico germane to the investigation. We were getting close to the end and needed to start preparations for the extensive legal actions to follow. Those meetings made sure we were all on the same page and helped us direct the investigative traffic. We would bring the officers of the court up to speed on what had occurred since our last meeting and then discuss the actions planned for the remaining days. They provided input, many times redirecting parts of the investigation, suggesting a new plan of attack on a particular facet of the case, tightening an existing case, or adjusting our plans to meet new DOJ policies. Those instructions would be transmitted to Morrison if he were not at the meeting. I figured that with such a complex investigation, more heads were better than just the few of us closely surrounding the operative. Not that Morrison didn't know what to do. However, if attorneys are involved in every detail, they are much more inclined to fight harder in the end. As all those loose ends germane to an investigation of this magnitude swirled around our feet and heads, my ever-faithful deputy, Neill Hartman, continued to spin his magic in the U.S. attorneys' office, including seeing to it that all the detail footwork required by a very demanding Dave Conner was addressed. It was a thankless job but one that needed doing, and Neill did it in outstanding fashion.

As if the busy New Mexico traffic were not business enough, many of the illicit wildlife dealers from Colorado followed Morrison to New Mexico. In so doing, they willfully crossed state lines with their illegal game, further violating the Lacey Act (which makes it illegal to take wildlife and transport it across state lines). Of course Morrison, their friendly wildlife dealer, was there to *selectively* provide his goods and services with a smile and a bear-trap mind for detail. Soon Morrison had twenty-two eager poachers from the local scene moving their ill-gotten gains in commerce and joining the rest of the San Luis Valley outlaws soon to be enshrined in a "Hall of Shame."

Not to be snookered, God decided that since I had let Morrison's Colorado arrest slide off like water from a duck's back, He would proffer another challenge. Bob Miller, the stalwart U.S. attorney in

Denver, was replaced without warning! This political move could not have come at a worse time. Miller had been involved since the beginning and was now replaced with another man who, no matter how good he was, did not have clue one as to the complexity or history of the investigation! This type of change can be one hell of a hurdle in getting the new man to "buy into" an existing operation, not making any radical changes in the investigation's direction at such a late date, keeping the assistant U.S. attorneys previously assigned to the case ... and the headaches went on. Eventually we discovered that the new man was Mike Norton, who was rumored to be without any criminal experience in the prosecutions arena and considered likely to "politicize the office" by some attorneys. However, we got a break! Mike, in his inexperience, deferred to the assistant U.S. attorneys already running the investigation and just stood back to watch the events swirling around him. However, after that personnel change, I never again felt I had a *knowing* partner in the U.S. attorney.

Now, new U.S. attorney or not, a real second effort was beginning to take form in the planning involved in closing the commercial-market-hunting rings on those who had "opened" them in the first place. Morrison had touched most of those whom we considered to be the major killers in the valley. With that, I began the arduous task of lining up the 275 officers I felt were the minimum number needed to safely carry out the many aspects of the takedown. Simultaneously, the investigation's supporting officers were consolidating evidence into several freezers for ease of display if necessary in a court of law. State and federal attorneys were beginning to gather up all the final pieces of the puzzle in their particular investigations, preparing for the trials that would follow. All the while these massive efforts were under way, Morrison continued to round up the last few targeted individuals needing his attention. Since it would take some time to organize the takedown, we left Morrison in-country to maintain his cover and the integrity of the investigation.

In the end, 108 individuals willingly walked into the trap laid by Operation SLV. Again, bear in mind that not everyone was targeted. Emphasis was placed on those doing the worst damage to the wildlife resources based on old and new intelligence and the individual outlaws' predisposition to violate. With that emphasis as guidance, Morrison stayed "in" until his work was completed and it was safe to extract him without raising undue suspicion. As it turned out, we brought Morrison out in January 1989 under the pretext that he was moving to Denver to begin a new taxidermy job on a massive African trophy shipment.

Then the third phase of the operation began. First, all case reports were completed, reviewed, and submitted to the appropriate attorneys. Then transcription of over 280 taped conversations was finalized for the New Mexico and Colorado U.S. attorneys and their state counterparts from four legal jurisdictions. Tape transcription work is terribly difficult. *Every* word or sound on the tape must be present on the transcript, or the defense attorneys have a field day raising objections. A good transcriber will spend the better part of eight hours typing a thirty-minute tape! Then there are the crazy attorney-driven time frames and security issues that accompany such work. Being cash poor, I resorted to having my top secretary from the Golden office undertake the challenge. And what a challenge it was! In addition to her regular duties, which didn't go away just because she was assigned other duties, Jean Dennis tackled this mammoth task. In such tapes, the recordings are often poor, the operative may be wordy, there tends to be a lot of background noise, the words used are less than civil, and the like. No matter how it's cut, it's a job of devilish proportions. However, like the trooper she was and continues to be, Jean went after the project with a vengeance and, according to the feedback from all the attorneys, did an outstanding job. Meetings were held between all legal entities with hundreds of charges examined and a determination made as to which jurisdiction would handle which charges. Bear in mind that the attorneys ultimately had over 1,200 misdemeanor and felony charges to review and choose from! In the end, only 850 of the most serious charges involving sale; willful destruction; illegal possession; closed-season take; over-limits; transfer of license; conspiracy; and violations of the federal Lacey Act, Endangered Species Act, Migratory Bird Treaty Act, and Bald Eagle Protection Act were selected for prosecution. Other charges were added later as officers discovered additional contraband in the field on the day of the takedown. Additionally, the attorneys faced the daunting task of closely reviewing over 1,200 pages of case reports on 108 subjects, then reviewing over 200 evidence photos and listening to more than 280 taped conversations, checking the tapes against the typed transcripts. Not quite like TV, is it?

Finally the attorneys decided there would be 57 state and federal arrest warrants issued and 23 state and federal search warrants executed. We were to seize 18 vehicles used in the commission of the crimes and issue a large number of citations for lessor violations on the spot. Add to that equation the fact that these law enforcement actions would encompass activities in 17 locations from New Jersey to Texas, with the majority centered in Costilla County in Colorado and Taos County in New Mexico. Another complicating factor was that federal prisoners arrested in Colorado could be incarcerated only in Durango, Colorado (the nearest approved facility for federal prisoners), approximately two hundred miles away from Fort Garland, and state prisoners could be held only in Alamosa, some forty miles away! Similar logistical issues faced the New Mexico officers. As if that were not enough of a problem, the planners had to consider additional evidence discovered through the search and arrest warrants (evidence discovered during the search, such as a freshly killed deer), prisoners to arrest and transport, vehicles to seize, inventory transport to Denver, officer security, crowd and family control, moving Morrison's household items from his place of business in New Mexico, dealing with a command center utilizing two radio frequencies, securing lodging in the valley for the raid teams, conducting interviews, coordinating with any media that happened along (because of federal DOJ media policy and officer security the press would not be informed in advance), providing for medical emergencies, positioning the special Colorado State Highway Patrol unit central to the most dangerous activity, and everything else including the "kitchen sink." Then came the imposing task of putting together 108 packets of information for the raid teams regarding criminal history of the targeted defendants, charges against the defendants, vehicles commonly used by the violators to be identified, location of their dwellings, potential family problems (e.g., a young teenager who might go for a gun when he saw his father arrested), and so on. Before all was said and done, we would generate over 130,000 pages in the raid packets alone (file on subject, arrest-search-cite instructions, location, policy, procedures, warrants, case reports, etc.)! Here again, David Croonquist rose to the occasion. It took a superhuman "hand" to bring all those pages of documents into print in a secure manner, and Dave made it seem like a piece of cake.

With the date of March 6, 1989, fixed for the takedown (searches, arrests, and seizure of evidence), the process of collecting the needed officers from around the country began in earnest. Keep in mind that my region, the one initiating the covert operation, had only twenty-four officers! Help would have to be forthcoming from every point on the compass. This was where my earlier program of working with my state counterparts bore fruit of the sweetest kind. I started making phone calls to my counterparts requesting assistance, and offers of help poured in. Service regions from Portland, Boston, and Albuquerque committed officers and resources. The National Park Service, Department of the Army at Fort Carson, U.S. Forest Service, Colorado State Patrol, credentialed officers from the Division of Refuges, Service regional office personnel, including the regional director, law enforcement administrative staffs, Colorado State Parks, and the like began to flood the rolls with names of those who could serve. State Fish and Game agencies from Colorado, New Mexico, Utah, Wyoming, Montana, South Dakota, Idaho, and Kansas answered the call, pledging the lion's share of officers. Soon I had 275 officers on call and ready to roll.

Then we hit a windfall. Neill Hartman, through his connections in the U.S. Customs Service, was able to obtain free use of a Black Hawk helicopter and crew. Why a helicopter? Simple. The "bear in the air" would provide additional officer security and a medical platform in case a citizen or officer needed to be airlifted to the nearest hospital.

No one was told any details other than officers with a need to know. Morrison was still in-country, and his life was at stake. All participants were told they were needed for a detail and instructed not to ask questions. We asked the chiefs of the Fish and Game organizations to tell the officers selected that they were going into a very serious training exercise, and that was that! Officers were told to show up at Fort Carson on March 4 with their enforcement gear, sleeping bags, personal gear, and food for a field exercise that would last up to four days (even then we had no idea how long the operation would take). Every outside agency senior supervisor contacted heard only the bare facts and the request for assistance. To an officer, they promised the most experienced assistance, and in the end everyone followed through. It was a real tribute to the men and women of those organizations, of whom the American people should be very proud.

Fort Carson was selected as a preraid briefing site because of its security and the lack of public accessibility. It was also a place where officers could quietly requalify with their weapons in order to meet federal firearms guidelines and brush up on federal arrest and seizure policies. Another reason for choosing Fort Carson was a mountain of a man named Tom Warren. Tom was the environmental director for Fort Carson, an imposing figure at six foot eight inches and tough as one of the fort's Abrams tanks. He was a devoted talent when it came to protecting the natural resources, and if that meant using some of the army's resources to further the fight against destruction of the nation's heritage, so be it. When I called Tom, seeking a safe haven to gather my "brood," I was not disappointed in his response and the resources he provided for this "gathering of the clan." That very able assistance included many of his own federally credentialed badge carriers.

Fran and I decided it was time to brief Governor Roy Romer of Colorado. Keep in mind that once you bring in the politicians, anything can and will happen. However, one does not arrest a passel of people in a given state without giving the governor a chance to share in the information so he or she is not blindsided on the day of the event. (The governor of New Mexico was not briefed because only twenty-two folks were to be apprehended in his state.) So we stepped straight into that bog.

The people selected *three days before the raid* for that briefing detail were Service Regional Director Galen Buterbaugh; Chief John Dempsey of the Colorado Highway Patrol; Chips Berry, director of the Department of Natural Resources; Fran Marcoux, chief of law enforcement for the Colorado Division of Wildlife; and me. On the day of the meeting, we assembled in an office linked to the governor's office. Soon the governor arrived and was introduced all around, and I began to speak, using a detailed set of notes so I would not forget any element of the investigation and takedown. For about twenty-five minutes I briefed a very serious and attentive man, who obviously had had no idea of the extent of illegal commercial-market hunting going on in his state in the San Luis Valley.

The governor interrupted me twice, once when I mentioned the number of officers required to safely carry out the takedown and again when I mentioned the helicopter. Realizing the governor was inexperienced in law enforcement matters and suspecting his questions were politically motivated, I broke down the officer numbers and need for air support. I explained that when a person is arrested and transported long distances to a lockup, it makes for good safety to have an officer driving the vehicle and another riding with the prisoner (57 arrests to be executed required 114 officers to transport). The seizure of 18 vehicles would require one officer to drive the seized vehicle and one to provide an escort, making sure family members didn't try to reclaim their property. That left few officers for crowd control, serving search warrants, and issuing numerous state citations. I think you can see that even 275 officers were probably not nearly enough! The helicopter was strictly a real-time safety issue. Given the vast distances between hospitals in the valley, it was important to have a safety valve in case anyone needed emergency medical assistance. I also explained the fact that in case of an emergency, the helicopter carried an additional five officers, including two emergency medical technicians, who could be quickly thrust into any law enforcement situation. After those detailed explanations, Romer seemed more than satisfied.

The governor asked John Dempsey if the Colorado Highway Patrol still had a special team of officers that could be lent to this operation. Dempsey replied that they had a team of sixteen that could be deployed anywhere for any eventuality. Romer asked me if having that team on hand in the valley would be of benefit, and I quickly answered that it would. With that, Romer asked Dempsey to make the team available. Dempsey concurred, stating, "Many times when we go down there on some law enforcement detail, we get our tail ends kicked and run out of the valley. Having this team on hand in case something blows up is a good suggestion." Keep in mind the governor's offer of *an additional sixteen officers* in light of his later accusations that we had "used too many officers."

We had no other issues for the governor or he for us, so he rose to leave. Standing at the conference table, he said, "Men, I won't have this kind of criminal element breaking the wildlife laws of my state. The wildlife is just too valuable a resource to be destroyed in such a manner. I commend all of you for a job very well done. Please be careful in all you do, and good luck." He started to walk away, then paused and asked, "Does anyone else on my staff know about this investigation?"

I answered, "No one else, Governor."

"Good," he said. "Make sure you don't mention this to Ken Salazar." Salazar was the governor's legal counsel. "He is from down there, and if you do, there goes the security of your operation." With that, he whirled and was gone. Fran and I were elated at the support and concern he had shown regarding the operation and its officers. We couldn't stop talking about our good fortune in dealing with the political side as we walked out of the governor's office.

With that behind us and faced with melding groups of individuals recruited from around the country into efficient raid teams, we hunkered down for the long haul. The mad rush of fulfilling last-minute attorney needs, logistical demands, and meeting administrative timelines and deadlines expanded our days from long to longer. But as is typical in such events, no one pulls less than their full share, and Fran's and my staffs were pulling like draft horses, as were the others invited to the "dance."

The officers began arriving at Fort Carson several days before the takedown. Rumors ran rampant because many had been given only two days' notice, but not one missed the call! For the next thirty-six hours their days were filled with team assembly, fixing problems, addressing new issues, reviewing assignments, requalifying with firearms to meet federal firearms standards, committing to memory their duties on the raid teams, becoming closely familiar with all their fellow raid team members, and working out any and all last-minute issues. Think about this stage of the operation for just a moment: bringing 275 individuals together, many meeting each other for the first time, and expecting them to function like a Swiss watch under tremendous stress, is asking a lot. Safely carrying out such an assignment *really* says something about the quality of those officers. And that they did! Everyone's rights were protected, and everyone on the badge-carrying side of the operation came home that night. But I am getting ahead of myself. Proud of the operation and those officers—*you're damn right!*

In such a major operation it is good business to introduce the covert operative to the officers after everything else has been covered and have that officer visit each raid team to discuss their particular case assignments. The operative discusses each target's emotional temperament and any other issues that might arise relative to officer and citizen safety (e.g., the target always carries a gun, has declared he will kill any officer who tries to arrest him, etc.). I clearly remember that moment in a Fort Carson movie theater reserved for our use. All the officers were seated listening to some last-minute raid-team policy and procedure information from their supervisors when it came time to introduce the operative. Morrison walked out front and center on the stage and, having been in deep cover for so long, *could not look the officers in the eyes.* He just kept looking at the floor! The man was utterly spent. Even among his own kind, he could not bring himself to make eye contact after two-and-a-half hard years of working undercover. That says something about the stress covert officers undergo. The task force officers, having previously read their assigned case reports and been impressed with the quality of the work, rose as if on command and gave Morrison a standing ovation that lasted for about three minutes! It was a very unusual but hard-earned accolade from hard-bitten officers who themselves faced long and dangerous odds on a daily basis.

Looking over at the two Colorado officers who had arrested Morrison earlier, I saw Raush slowly turn toward me after recognizing Morrison as the man. He mouthed the words, "You son of a bitch!" through an embarrassed grin. I had to grin back. He had done his job to the best of his ability; he had just grabbed the wrong brass ring. That happens sometimes when you don't know "who's on first."

For the next several hours after meeting Morrison and hearing what he had to say, everyone rehearsed their assignments once again, reread their case reports for the tenth time, and checked their gear to make sure they were ready to go. Morrison visited every one of the teams, especially those arresting a known hard case or violent individual, and gave them the latest information regarding their targets. Soon I noticed the teams coming together like well-oiled machines.

The team leaders had been assigned based on their grit, common sense, and experience in takedowns and overall law enforcement techniques. If things turned to crap, we wanted our best foot forward, and in the San Luis Valley takedown, with one exception, that was the norm. Rank made no difference on these teams; the best officer for the business at hand was the leader. In several instances an agent or game warden was team leader over his or her supervisor, whose specialty was something else. A classic example of blurring lines of supervision was the raid team to which my regional director was assigned. The regional director was just that—the supervisor of an eight-state region for the

Service, supervising over eight hundred professionals. However, he was also an excellent photographer, and that was his assignment. His team leader was Special Agent Joel Scrafford, a senior resident agent known for his coolness under fire. That would be needed in this situation because the person they were to bring in had bragged that he would kill anyone trying to arrest him. And he had the criminal record to back up his claim! As expected, Joel handled a sensitive situation beautifully, and the regional director, Joel's overall supervisor, took excellent evidence photographs. The other teams' composition was no less unusual. Everyone had been selected for some special facet that would strengthen the overall team, be it as a photographer, gatherer of evidence, good security person, or interviewer.

The day of the raid, March 6, 1989, everyone was up and ready to go by one-thirty in the morning. Most of us had gotten little sleep. Since it was impossible to feed all 275 officers in town at that hour without raising a lot of eyebrows, we ate a cold breakfast each of us had brought along. Then we headed for the assembly area. When all officers were assembled, final instructions were given on the last-minute locations of some of the targets, and then a convoy was formed. And what a convoy it was!

Out from Fort Carson we came with the local police holding open the stoplights so the convoy could stay intact en route to the freeway. Through town and onto I-25 south we headed. Soon over 150 law enforcement vehicles were strung out bumper to bumper in a line stretching about four miles! Talk about an impressive sight in the dead of morning. It seemed as if the headlights stretched for infinity! Along the way two truckers pulled over to look at the convoy, and one was overheard talking on his CB, saying, "Somewhere someone is in a world of shit!" When the convoy arrived at Lathrop State Park, just fifty miles from Fort Garland, everyone formed up into their teams. Those having the farthest to go were at the front of the line. Once organized and ready, off we went to face the morning's destiny.

Speaking of destiny, Morrison and several other agents headed for the command center. (Except in very unusual circumstances, the undercover officer is not allowed on the actual raid because his or her presence has a tendency to provoke the defendants, especially if the officer ate at the defendant's table or the like. Also, the officer is needed to testify at all the numerous trials, so if he or she is killed or injured during a raid, there goes the government's primary witness.) Driving their small but fast car was Agent Tom Riley. Tom was an ex-linebacker for the old Baltimore Colts NFL football team. He was built like a brick outhouse and drove in the same wild manner that he had played professional football. As they hurled across the valley, an unfortunate cow elk stepped into their headlights. Trying to escape the speeding car, she fell down in the highway, smack-dab in the car's path! Riley stomped on the brakes, and the speeding car began to skid out of control. Meanwhile, the elk finally got up and stepped out from in front of the careening car, allowing all to live another day. Just goes to show that sometimes the critters you're trying to protect will kill you just as fast as the bad guys. According to Riley, there was elk hair on the front bumper ... and on his front teeth!

A six-thirty "wake-up call" was scheduled for all of Morrison's friends who were heavy on the trigger and quick with the illegal sales of wildlife. There were several reasons for the early hour. Generally, everyone is home at that hour and still in the process of waking up as they prepare for the day. They are usually not expecting anyone at their front door that early in the morning, so surprise is complete. Also, striking that early gives the officers time to whisk the defendant away, minimizing family or outside interference and providing the time needed to conduct collateral searches, or if the target is not home to locate him before he is alerted.

At the command center on the Alamosa National Wildlife Refuge, the communications team waited expectantly for the officers to arrive at their individual destinations as they operated under strict radio silence. As daylight approached, the Black Hawk helicopter flown by the U.S. Customs Service rose into the air with its enforcement team on board. A Colorado Division of Wildlife Cessna 185 also rose into the air to act as a radio relay and forward observer. The Colorado State Patrol Special Emergency Response Team (SERT), commanded by Phil Tipton, had moved into an area central to the operation in the valley and waited for the dreaded call requesting assistance. This group included some of Colorado's finest, all as tough as horseshoe nails, very well trained, and expert in what they did. I personally knew one member of that team, Jess Gibson, and no tougher or better man ever crapped between a pair of boots. He was an ex–military man with a world of combat experience. Somehow I don't think flying bullets ever bothered him. ... It gave me a damn fine feeling to have such professionals at our beck and call. With the trigger pulled, everyone waited as the officers sped to their tasks while another glorious cold spring day dawned in the valley.

At six twenty-eight, the first arriving unit broke radio silence to announce that its subject was in custody. After that, in a quick running sequence, team after team reported its presence at the subject's residence with the individual safely in custody, or that it was commencing the execution of a search warrant. Shortly thereafter, more radio traffic came in reporting that the subject in custody was en route to the local state or federal lockup. It is always safer to move the arrested subject away from his home and other family members as soon as he has been searched and handcuffed to prevent family members or friends from thinking about it, boiling over, and starting something they can't finish. Soon the airways were full of announcements of successful operations, with the defendants safely in custody or the search warrants successfully executed. The operation moved so swiftly that in a period of about five hours, all the arrests were safely made, search warrants successfully executed, citations issued, interviews conducted, and seized vehicles loaded on truck transport for movement out of the valley to the Denver area! Not an officer had been injured, not a single subject arrested had to be physically constrained, not a single punch had been thrown or an escape tried; all searches were safely conducted and evidence described in the warrant located, and all vehicles were seized without any violence. In fact, the operation up to that point was picture perfect!

Then the best-laid plans of mice and men began to unravel! An ABC News team showed up at the command center at daylight. Word on the operation had somehow leaked out, and now we were faced with the media looking for a story. Since it is DOJ policy to try an investigation in the courtroom rather than in the press, the reporters were told that, "the investigation could not be confirmed or denied" (also DOJ policy). Truth be known, we had not counted on being so successful. Past history from similar penal code operations in the valley pointed to a whole lot more problems in accomplishing the enforcement tasks: problems in locating individuals, family members fighting to save those targeted for arrest, safety becoming a serious issue, outsiders intervening, and opposing numbers of local residents far surpassing the enforcement presence. And, those had been far smaller operations than ours! We had believed we would not be finished for several days with such a large number of defendants, so we were not prepared with a press release just hours after the operation began.

By ten in the morning, Governor Roy Romer's office began receiving numerous phone calls from family members and friends of those arrested complaining about how they had been treated. They complained of masked officers with machine guns wearing full camouflage gear entering their homes illegally and dragging them out of their beds. Allegedly, children had been mishandled and terrorized, naked women had been dragged from the showers and displayed for all to see, and other brutal forms of treatment were related. The Colorado legislature was in session at the time, and soon numerous wild calls were also being received by legislators from people complaining about unprofessional actions, with racial motivation or overtones as the main theme. In turn, members of the Hispanic caucus called the governor's office for information. Soon other journalists were receiving calls about the operation from the locals and politicians in the valley, causing them to hurry to the area in the hope of a story. What followed gave me a firsthand chance to observe a media feeding frenzy!

The governor feigned ignorance of the details of the event. None of us could believe what we were seeing and hearing emanating from his office! Realizing that he had a large voting bloc of tigers by the tail, he chose Ken Salazar, his legal adviser (the very man he had implied couldn't be trusted because he was "from down there"), a staff member, and two legislators to travel to Alamosa that afternoon and ascertain what had happened. They were to look into the allegations that the law enforcement operation was racially motivated and see if our procedures were heavy-handed and if we had abused the defendants and their families. Neill Hartman and Fran Marcoux took time off from their hectic schedules and briefed the governor's hurriedly assembled commission (I was guarding the loading of eighteen seized vehicles after a credible threat had been intercepted that many armed locals were coming to take the vehicles back). They shared as much information as they could, bearing in mind the DOJ policy of no admissions or denials regarding ongoing investigations. With many limitations, they kept the briefing on the particulars to a minimum but were still able to give a fair overview of that morning's operation and in fact flatly denied any accusations such as abuse of the public or racially motivated investigations and arrests. We had yet to receive from the teams then, *and never did,* any information as to the take-down actions being directed at anyone other than the subjects of the investigation. In short, race had played no part, and we sure as hell hadn't violated anyone's rights! That was made clear to the governor's team. However, Neill and Fran found themselves wondering if the commission members had *really* listened to anything that had been said. They later reported that it felt almost as if the four men had been sent on a political mission by the governor to alleviate his political "gas pains," and what we said to them mattered little. However, with all the action swirling around them, back to the task at hand they went without giving further thought to that meeting. After all, they knew I had personally briefed Governor Romer three days before the raid and he had voiced his strong support at that time before all concerned, including Fran Marcoux. Surely Romer's word was good. ...

As mentioned earlier, we had not prepared any information for the press on the day of the raid. First, we had believed we might not be done with all the 108 assignments, and officer safety and the safety of those we *touched* was first and foremost. Second, we had strict orders from the state and federal legal divisions not to discuss the operation with anyone outside the need-to-know arena without their specific approval. We had officers on assignments from New Jersey to Texas, not to mention scattered throughout the valley. Having the press underfoot and putting the outlaws in front of a camera can have a deleterious effect on the behavior of the targets or their families, and we weren't looking for any confrontations to unfold in front of the cameras for the five o'clock viewers. We didn't feel that we would have all the facts in such a short period of time for the attorneys to plow through in order to provide a fair but controlled dissemination of public information. However, the U.S. attorneys' office had scheduled a full-blown press conference for March 7 (the following day) at ten A.M., figuring the officers would be far enough along at that time.

However, on the day of the raid, because of the unexpected presence of the ABC News crew, the legal divisions hurriedly released a statement briefly outlining the history of the investigation. That statement also said that the county and federal attorneys would be holding a press conference in the Service's regional office the following day. With that, we got back to the business at hand of recording and documenting seized evidence, transporting seized vehicles to a secure lockup in Denver, arraigning our prisoners, completing all our case reports (122 case reports were completed by nine that evening), returning search and arrest warrants, transporting wildlife evidence to secure freezers, completing interviews, and issuing the remainder of the citations for lesser wildlife violations discovered during the law enforcement operations.

The next day was just as hectic as the day of the raid because of heavy follow-up work. When the press conference took place, the events of March 6 were still swirling around like an F-5 tornado. The Service's regional office conference room was filled with dozens of bags of wet evidence, trophies, animal parts, piles of antlers, dead eagles, and the like. At the request of the attorneys, Neill Hartman and other agents brought some of the evidence from the lockers via the Black Hawk helicopter and arranged it for members of the media to view while providing sanctioned photo opportunities. Walking around in the room before the press conference, I was amazed to discover that the credible outdoors reporters who normally covered such events were all absent! In their places were reporters I did not recognize, and as I listened to their questions, it became apparent that a bunch of rookies had been sent to cover the event. I even overheard several asking which were deer and which were elk heads! When they are that far removed from reality, you are in for a drubbing in the press, I thought—and how true that premonition was soon to become! This assembly showed that the media leaders were pissed. They had not been included in the operation early on, and they believed that ABC had been, which meant that the agencies and the story they had to tell were likely to get some rather unfair treatment. In addition, the media were predisposed to side with Hispanics over the government in a state heavy with Hispanic viewers. Such is the power of the media and some of the little people and minds that address the fairness doctrine through the print and airwaves.

As I returned to my place alongside U.S. Attorney Mike Norton, the conference commenced. It immediately became apparent that we were facing a hostile press corps. After Norton spoke, the questions from the floor dealt little with the actual investigation but probed the racism issue; unprofessional behavior of the officers; the number of officers used; the blatant display and use of machine guns; the scare and intimidation tactics; the use of a helicopter "gunship"; officers in camouflaged outfits slinking around, tearing houses apart during the searches, and terrorizing children and women; and on it went. Norton, sensing the negative direction the conference was taking, abruptly chose not to continue addressing a feeding frenzy and terminated the event. As he started to leave, one reporter hurled a sharply worded question at him about the misbehavior of the officers. Norton just kept going, but Regional Director Galen Buterbaugh, a man not known for jumping into this type of adverse situation, had had a gutful of the reporters' childish behavior, so he turned and responded. "Look," he said, "I was there on site and working with those officers. I saw none of what all of you are alluding to and find it shameful that you are carrying on in such a fashion. What you are doing is wrong!"

With that, we all left at the U.S. attorney's order and walked back to my office to discuss the morning's events. It was clear that the media was on the prod and on the side of the folks from the valley. We suspected that our treatment in the media would be less than fair or objective, partly because of the DOJ policy regarding not detailing an investigation in the press or any other public forum until the prosecution was settled and a judgment rendered. Those policies were sound and justified, but a "feeding" press interpreted them merely as an impediment to the five o'clock news, and we were treated accordingly. The judges in Colorado had also made it abundantly clear in other cases that to try a case in the press first would mean foregoing any access to their courts. So the only "news" coming out was from the folks feeling they had been "abused," and that type of story sold more print anyway, so the presses ran full tilt. There we sat between the devil and the deep blue.

During the following weeks, just about every form of media in Colorado and others from national programs feeding off local leads decried the behavior of the agencies involved in Operation SLV. They focused on the plight of the San Luis Valley poor instead of addressing the criminal issues or the massive destruction of wildlife. We heard nothing about the violation of state and federal laws in the illegal taking of hundreds of animals, just the plight of an economically depressed and seemingly downtrodden population beset by those from big government. Headlines screamed racism and heavy-handed government tactics. Many television reports followed suit. I remember one well-known TV commentator criticizing the government for keeping poor people like the Hispanics in the valley from killing wildlife to feed their families. "What are a few animals when one is trying to feed one's family?" he lamented.

I just shook my head. There were plenty of county, state, and church programs that saw to it one's family would be fed, I thought. Yet here was this airhead on TV denouncing the government's efforts to enforce the criminal statutes of the land.

And it only got worse. I remember one particularly bad example, a phone call I received from a reporter from the *Pueblo Chieftain*. I could tell by her voice that she was Hispanic, and she started right off wanting to know about the number of machine guns used in the raid. Wanting to set the record straight and knowing such information would not jeopardize the prosecution, I told her, "Six."

"That can't be true," she replied haughtily. "My sources informed me that everyone had machine guns and were waving them around scaring everybody!"

"Not true," I calmly replied. "Since I am the supervisor of the operation, it was up to me to authorize the use and number of machine guns. I authorized only six. Of those six, one was carried because the man whom my team arrested had bragged that he would kill anyone trying to arrest him, and he has a violent temper with a criminal record to back it up. However, that gun never came out of its case because the arresting officer had such good command of the situation. The other five machine guns were on the helicopter, and they remained in their gun cases throughout."

"That is not the information I have, and have chosen to print from my sources and not you," she brusquely replied.

I just shook my head at the "fair and objective" reporting about to be spawned from this source. Then it got worse.

"What about everyone being in camouflaged clothing and slinking around terrorizing people?" she stridently asked.

"Not true," I replied. "Everyone wore their issued uniforms so people would readily recognize them. Plain and simply, it was a safety issue. The only ones out of uniform were the agents from the Fish and Wildlife Service, and that was because we haven't been uniformed since 1973. They wore clothing in accordance with their assignments, which did not include the use of camouflage. As far as the camouflage issue goes, I am aware of only one person who wore camouflage pants, and that was an assistant county attorney walking out to look at the helicopter as it sat on the landing pad."

"I don't think you had a very good handle on your men, and I prefer again to use my sources on that issue," she replied. "What about naked women dragged out of the showers so they could be searched and then paraded nude before all the officers?"

"Again, not true. I heard that complaint and, just to make sure nothing of the sort happened, personally queried all my raid team leaders. It did not happen. And if something like that ever did occur and it were one of my men, I would take the appropriate action necessary to have that officer removed!"

"*Well,* I know differently and will again use my sources," she replied in a steely tone.

"Why are we having this interview?" I asked. "You seem to have your mind made up, and I see very little value in continuing."

"You are right," she replied. "You haven't been truthful the whole time, so I will just print what information I get from the valley folks."

I thanked her for her time, and she slammed the phone down. And so it went. Because we were unable to get our side of the story out, partly due to DOJ policy effectively gagging us, the media ran one side of the story instead of qualifying it with some balance from our side.

The governor didn't help much either, stating in one interview, "I did not know there was going to be this kind of force concentrated in one place." Hogwash! Remember the briefing three days before the raid? He continued to sidestep the handling of the raid instead of saying, "Look, folks, this is a law enforcement issue. Let's just wait and see how it plays out in the courts of law and then make our decisions on the professionalism of the officers and the merits of the investigation. If I find my officers are at fault, I will take appropriate action to address the issues. And if the federal officers are at fault, I will address that at the highest levels of government and see to it that those issues are corrected as well." But rather than facing the issue head on, he supported commissions and hearings into the matter, hoping that would solve this political hot potato the Hispanic community and media had thrust on him.

Then Mike Callihan, the lieutenant governor, knowing only one side of the situation—and very little of that—jumped right in as if he knew what he was talking about. "The sting operation was like swatting a fly with a sledgehammer. It is hard to escape the fact that this was heavy-handed and clumsy. If you create a market, you are probably guilty of entrapment," he announced. Damn, I sure didn't remember Mike participating in any of the law enforcement operations so that he would know what had gone on behind the scenes. ... By the way, entrapment (as is always the case) was raised as an issue several times by defense attorneys and was handily overcome in every courtroom by state and federal attorneys.

Then there was the entry into the fracas by lesser mortals in the political hierarchy, including several Colorado state legislators. Senator Joe Winkler, R–Castle Rock, and Representative Juan Trujillo, D–Pueblo, were quoted in the *Pueblo Chieftain* as saying "that it appeared to be entrapment." I wonder if the rest of the business they conducted for the citizens of Colorado was as carefully researched as those statements? On it went as many in the world of politics strained to jump into the pile and squeeze out a vote here or there. Most seemed to be trying to give direct comfort and aid to the poaching community if their comments in the press and on TV were to be taken seriously.

As if that were not enough of a load to carry, U.S. Attorney Mike Norton, a Republican, quickly found himself mired in the political morass developing around the investigation. At one point he buckled and called my office in a panic. "Mr. Grosz! What the hell did you tell that damn Roy Romer? We are getting zero support from that bastard, and it almost appears he is trying to torpedo us! Didn't you brief him? Because if you did, he sure didn't seem to get the message."

"Yes, sir, I did. I briefed him using a three-page briefing document so there would be no misunderstanding, and at the end of the briefing he voiced support for the program, even offering us an additional sixteen men from his highway patrol SERT team. He also advised he would not tolerate any kind of criminality like this in his state and told us to go get them but be careful to avoid injury in the process. There were four others in the room, including my regional director and Fran Marcoux, chief of law enforcement for the Colorado Division of Wildlife, who can and will validate what I just said if you feel it necessary."

"Well, something happened because he is acting like he is out in the ozone somewhere. I want you to send me a detailed report on the briefing, who was there, what was said, Roy's reaction—and I mean now! Don't leave anything out!"

"Yes, sir," I replied as he hung up. I immediately composed a letter regarding the briefing and the governor's response to it. The next thing I knew, Romer was complaining to my regional director about the letter I had written to Norton. I had not foreseen that Norton would send a letter meant for his eyes only to Romer as a political gesture, hoping to take the pressure off his own office. I just shook my head in disbelief. I had been perfectly candid, at one point pointing out to Norton that Romer had been very attentive during the briefing. When Romer called my boss, he groused in particular about that statement. "What did he think, that I was sleeping during the briefing?" he hurled at Galen before slamming down the phone. So in addition to having a U.S. attorney who appeared to be a standing invertebrate, I had an embarrassed, running-scared governor, which made continuing to work with my state counterparts a bit dicey. I know the good Lord only gives you as much weight as your shoulders can bear, but, I was clearly carrying a load.

Speaking of the good Lord, one of his minions now chose to throw his two cents into the fracas. According to the media, Father Patrick Valdez, a priest in San Luis, was frothing about the raid and what it had done to the people of his parish. Father Valdez was reportedly upset over the "small thing" of some of his parishioners illegally taking wildlife. "Times are hard here. Hunting year-round is a way to put animal protein on your table to feed your family," he championed. As I recall, the Ten Commandments include a prohibition of stealing. And poaching the national heritage from the American people is stealing. I wonder where the good father was when that part of the list was covered at the seminary?

Then there was another setback. Trying to protect Morrison as he provided testimony, we requested a venue change from San Luis to a larger city where he would have better protection from professional town officers. The judge ruled against us, and we soon found ourselves heading for court in San Luis, a hotbed of activity, with Morrison to testify. Talk about going into the lion's den! But we had nothing to hide and had done a good job, totally within the bounds of legality and common sense. I would be damned if we were going to be intimidated because of a hazardous ruling by a lower-court judge. Getting together with Neill Hartman, I had him assemble a team of officers who could be meaner than a snake or just as smooth as a schoolmarm's thigh, depending on the situation! We escorted Morrison to San Luis and had our time in court. Outside, crowds grumbled and threatened but went no further than that, not wanting to cause a lot of openings for fathers and older sons in their family trees.

Then state Senator Tilley Bishop, chairing a joint legislative oversight committee, called for the state and federal entities to meet and discuss Operation SLV, addressing charges of ethical and procedural abuses during the raid. Another goddamned event spurred on by the media's "objective and fair" treatment and a loose-cannon governor, I surmised. Walking into that meeting, we were met by about a hundred mad Hispanic bystanders all looking for blood. We sat before the committee and covered what we could address at that time. Senator Bishop impressed me as a fair man, and he ran the committee accordingly. However, there were lots of tough questions based on the erroneous information coming from the valley community and "yellow journalism." Again hamstrung by DOJ policies, we presented all the information we could share. I had a gutful from some of the sharply worded questions and the catcalls from the audience. Getting my dander up, I took the opportunity to let the committee know in no uncertain terms what a wonderful job the officers, especially those from the Colorado Division of Wildlife, had done. I didn't realize how high I got up on my soapbox, but after I finished, the angry crowd was a hell of a lot quieter. It was almost as if they had gotten the straight skinny for the first time, and respected us for what we had done. Almost ...

One interesting detail during this whole go-around were the phone calls and letters my office received. Over the weeks following the raid, I was deluged with hundreds of communications supporting the government's efforts at trying to stamp out the lawlessness in the valley: letters that suggested the locals had been killing since the 1600s and needed to be controlled; if you find my stolen rifle, serial number such and such, please return it; the place is full of outlaws and in-laws and I am glad you guys took them on; and so on. If I remember correctly, 831 letters, personal communications with citizens, reports from officers in the field, and phone calls came in supporting the investigation, with only two in dissent. And those two calls were from people whose cousins had been arrested in New Mexico.

Then another pissing contest reared its ugly head. This time it was begun by Congressman Bill Richardson, who joined Congressman Peter Kostmayer of the House Interior Subcommittee on General Oversight and Investigations to look into "wildlife conservation in the San Luis Valley in general." By this time I was getting really hot under the collar and disgusted at what I considered the unfair and one-sided treatment of our agencies. The meeting was set for July 29 in the National Guard Armory in Taos, New Mexico.

Realizing I was going down to testify and not having spent a lot of time with my wife over the past year, I received permission from John Spinks, deputy regional director, to take my bride with me in the government vehicle (legal in those days—not now). I saw it as an opportunity to relax until I had to testify, spending some time with my wife en route and letting her shop in Taos while I attended to business. When the day arrived, I left at three in the morning and headed down through the valley. When we arrived at the armory, Donna called a taxi to take her into the shopping district (one can't use a government vehicle for personal business), and I walked into the armory. What a surprise! There were hundreds of mad, howling local citizens out for blood! That changed my tone from relaxed to damn mad once again. These folks just didn't have a clue as to what had really happened thanks to the William Randolph Hearst style of reporting by the media. Now by damn, I was going to set that record straight once and for all! When I walked over to Bill Montoya, Fish and Game director for New Mexico, I could tell he was pissed as well.

"Bill, you carrying?" I asked.

"Got one on my belt and one in an ankle holster," he grimly replied as he eyeballed the angry crowd over my shoulder. Without a word, I opened my dress coat slightly so he could see the butt of my .44 magnum in a shoulder holster and then said, "And the .45 with two spare magazines is on my hip!"

"If this turns to crap, you take those on your right and I will take those on my left," he muttered through a grin.

Good old Bill, I thought. Just your quiet cowboy type, but don't seriously mess with him unless you're really in need of dying. ...

About that time, Congressman Kostmayer called the meeting to order as he, Richardson, and another congressman whose name I have forgotten sat down at the head table. Bill and I were seated in front of the panel along with representatives from the Bureau of Land Management (BLM) and the U.S. Forest Service. I had no idea why the last two government officials were there, and they soon washed out of the hearing as knowing nothing about the recent events; however, not before the BLM representative made an offhand remark for the record about how the operation "could have been handled a little better." I found that surprising coming from an agency nationally recognized as a weak sister in the law enforcement arena—and a contradiction in terms.

I just got madder and madder. I had headed up a classic undercover operation only to have a bunch of political and media limp-brained types turn it into something brown and viscous in the public's eye. Enough was enough! Bill testified first, accompanied by the hoots and jeers of the peanut gallery behind our table. He gave no ground on his agency's role in the operation, supporting it fully. The hoots and jeers seemed to lessen somewhat, but they were still there. Then it was my turn as I looked intently at Richardson. I suspected his part in this charade probably meant he had some shirt-tail cousin trapped in the San Luis Valley arrests. Before testifying, all of us were told that we had a three-minute time limit, and once the clock chimed we were done. I really bulled up my neck. You cannot get to the bottom of a complex two-and-a-half-year criminal investigation in three minutes! Who the hell did these guys think they were fooling? This meeting was nothing more than an excuse to placate Richardson and cast aspersions once again on the investigation. Well, when it came to my time, I was out of the gate like a 320-pound grizzly! The oversight committee got an earful, as did the crowd standing behind me.

"Jesus," whispered Montoya with a big grin, "don't kill 'em all."

That group of legislators wanted testimony; well, they got it! And when that damn alarm clock went off, I just kept running with the bit in my teeth, making sure all concerned knew about the operation and how carefully it had been conducted. I also pointed out that 100 percent of those who to date had been before the courts as a result of this investigation had been convicted, and I expected that all of the others would soon follow suit. Kostmayer kept pointing to the clock, but I ignored him. I had come many miles to testify and was going to do just that! I finished about ten minutes later, and all was quiet in the armory. Finally Kostmayer leaned forward and said, "Well, it is obvious you came to testify, Mr. Grosz." *He didn't know the half of it!*

There were a few questions from Richardson to which I responded, and then the hearing concluded. Walking out the door, I made it a point to look every person in the eyes who had the guts to look at me, letting him or her know I wasn't ashamed of what we had done. They ought to rejoice that someone had had the guts to take on such a shameful conservation issue. Most failed to make eye contact or looked at their shoes.

I said good-bye to Montoya, got into my truck, and headed to an eatery in Taos, where I met my wife and had dinner (use of a government vehicle for meals while on government business is allowed). Stopping at the nearest gas station after dinner, I filled up both tanks on the Dodge truck and headed home in order to save per diem. It made for a long day, but that saving on lodging amounted to two tanks of gas for my hardworking agents.

It had been raining, and as the skies cleared, the air was clean with the smell of rain on the pavement. Turning north, we headed home as the sun began to lower in a sky still dotted with angry gray clouds. Loosening my tie, I rolled down the window and began to enjoy life as the cool, fresh air flowed in around me.

Just north of Alamosa on state Highway 17, I noticed a newer-model Dodge pickup sitting about one hundred yards off the road to the east. The windows were all steamed up, but I just figured it was a couple of kids having a good time and let the image of it slip away like the miles under my tires. Then, coming out of the joy of being alive and in the outback, I noticed that same truck rapidly bearing down on me from the south. There was little traffic, so I surmised the driver was in a hurry to get his girlfriend home. Watching the road ahead, I was surprised to see the front of that truck disappear from my rearview mirror as he ran right up to my bumper. Piqued that he didn't pass and not amused at having his nose under the rear of my truck, I sped up to sixty. He did the same and once again stuck the nose of his truck right up to my rear bumper. Looking in the rearview mirror with a little more interest than the average bear, I could see three grim-faced Hispanic men in the front seat. Realizing these folks were more than lovers and possibly up to something stupid, I increased my speed to seventy. By now Donna was aware of my tailgating friend and beginning to worry. I also had some concerns. Having her along prevented me from speeding up, getting ahead of my pain-in-the-ass tailgaters, spinning around, and confronting them head on with the .44 magnum in hand as my Bible in a come-to-Jesus meeting. If anything happened to me, she would be at their mercy, so stopping was not an option. Besides, with a newer-model Dodge he could easily outrace me in the straight stretches. But I had an ace or two up my sleeve. Even though my truck had 200,000 miles on it (I didn't have much of a budget to replace four-wheel-drive vehicles at the mandated 50,000-mile mark), it still had a well-cared-for 360-cubic-inch engine, and I knew how to drive at high speeds on twisty mountain roads. I had just replaced my tires and brakes the week before. Fellows, grab your last part over the fence, I thought with a spreading grin. You are in for a wild ride! I figured I would just race along in excess of the speed limit until a highway patrol officer came along and stopped the both of us. With that, the odds would be more favorable, and *then* we would see where the cow crapped in the clover!

Grinning at the challenge before me, I put the hammer down and let the old Dodge have its head. It was almost as if it welcomed the challenge, humming along like a Swiss watch and slowly pegging the dial on the speedometer! It didn't stop there either. The old girl still had a little more in her, and slowly the speed continued to inch up until we had to be going over a hundred miles per hour! The new Dodge stayed right with me, but he was taking a bath from all the water left on the highway sprayed up from my tires. Man, were his windshield wipers flying!

The new tires had a tread that wrapped up onto the side wall about two inches, so sliding through a turn, even though the tires flattened out, still left valuable tread high on the sides to hold the road, *and hold the road they did!* I powered through many turns with a posted speed of thirty-five miles per hour doing seventy and better! Not once did I slide between my driving skill, the new tires, and the two hundred pounds of extra weight I had in the box of the truck for added traction. My followers slid through many a turn, and if the size of their three sets of eyes spoke of anything, it indicated that they were saying their rosaries as they hung on for dear life. However, in the straight stretches of the highway, here they came with a vengeance! Donna was terrified and not doing well as a passenger. I was rather liking the challenge, and the faster I could take a turn, the better. Dark was now upon us as I strained my eyes down the road far as I could see for the telltale glint of an animal's eyes. It would do me no good to hit an elk or deer at these speeds! Hell, even hitting a mouse at those speeds would have created a problem for the sphincter, not to mention the sheet metal on the truck! With my two guardian angels as backup, we saw nary a deer or elk—*or a damn highway patrol officer!* Zooming along from just north of Alamosa all the way to Fairplay, I didn't spot one highway patrol officer! Any other time, I would have run across a hundred of them.

Traveling at those speeds, fuel became a problem. My three big-eyed pursuers turned off the highway and slid into a gas station in Fairplay. However, I had filled *both* my gas tanks in Taos, and with the flick of a switch, the needle on the gas gauge rose from empty to the full mark on the second tank as Donna and I drove up over Kenosha Pass and home. That was the last of those three wild-eyed men, and as far as Donna was concerned, it was none too soon. I never did find out who they were or what they were up to.

About a week later I received a phone call from a supervisor in a sister federal law enforcement agency. He wanted a meeting between the Service and his agency regarding a series of terrorist threats he considered very real. Later that morning my officers and I met with the man (who shall remain unnamed as well as his agency) and were briefed on a ring of terrorists in the valley. Apparently those chaps, though not part of the recent sting operation, felt a need to get involved because of the heritage they shared with our outlaws. Many were sufficiently upset over the handling of their brethren during Operation SLV that they felt a few bombs in our mailboxes or attached to our vehicles were called for. The unnamed agency had firsthand information regarding the threats. With no reason to disbelieve this information, all of us in the Denver area involved with the raid took the proper precautions for the next six months. Nothing ever came of the threats, but they certainly were taken seriously. Again, this rumor was probably another spin-off of the wildly untrue media reports. As I said before, on any undercover operation, expect the unexpected or you will take it in the teeth. It was a good thing I still had all my teeth before we began this operation!

The media continued to fill the ink and airways with a stream of outrageous stories with headlines such as "Poaching Raid Leaves Bitter Aftertaste"; "San Luis Calls Wildlife Raid 'Extreme' Action"; "A Year After, Bitterness Remains over San Luis Poaching Raid"; "Sweep Briefing Packets Cited as Racist"; "Might Apparently Makes Right to Wildlife Officials"; "Invasion of San Luis"; "State Sponsored Terror- ism on the Lives of San Luis and Its Children"; or "Poaching Sting Scars San Luis Residents." There was nary a word for the thousands of animals that died illegally, for the laws of the land, for the national heritage of the American people, for the violation of rights of those unable to get redress because of crooked law enforcement, or for the legal process that was being followed to a T! It is easy to see why the statue of justice wears a blindfold.

When the government attempted to set the record straight, it was thrown back into our faces at every turn and the emotional tripe laid once again on the public's plate. The governor played to this contin- uing media hype and avoided taking a direct stand. In his bobbing and weaving, he created buffer groups or commissions to "look into the matter," distancing himself from the state and federal law enforcement communities he also supposedly represented. I found it interesting that when there was any written communication between the gover- nor's office and anyone involved with the operation, those missives were properly and professionally worded. It was obvious that Gov- ernor Romer understood the double edge of the sword when it came to leaving a paper trail. But when it came time to waffle for the pub- lic, he was in the bottom of the Mariana Trench with the best of them.

As things came to a head, the governor let it be known that he would be able to report his findings to the people no later than April 7. Hence, another request for a meeting between members of a blue-ribbon commission and my office worked its way through channels. In this latest probe into the "unprofessional behavior" of the law enforcement community, Manny Martinez, director of safety for the city of Denver, was tapped to lead the governor's cause. Interest- ingly enough, Manny had earlier said regarding the takedown, "That's not a sign of racism as much as a sign of ignorance of the cultural reali- ties of the San Luis Valley." Other commission members were John

Vanderhoof, a former governor; Paul Sandoval; and Tom Coogan, ex–chief of police for the city of Denver. Governor Romer's charge to Manny was "to review the alleged issues dealing with the number of law enforcement officers used, the number used in each community, that the operation was carried out without violence or injury to the peoples involved or there were no improper incidents, threatened uses of force, and lack of communication to the affected communities once the law enforcement actions were completed."

Neill Hartman and I set up a meeting with the commission around our busy schedules, and by now we were both steaming, to say the least. In addition to all of our other pressing work, we had to wet-nurse a gutless governor through another set of hearings designed to cover his hind end. Normally I might have told the person making such an outlandish request to bug off, but this time I could not. Even though all the charges were baseless and proved baseless as time and the trials went on, I had to consider my loyal Colorado state counter-parts, who were still under the governor's gun. Therefore, I stood and fought alongside them, destroying the credibility of these wild and baseless charges every way I could.

When Neill and I met with Manny Martinez and the other mem-bers of his commission, I perceived a coolness and energy of a mind-set against us and what Operation SLV represented. That perception was buttressed by a flurry of negatively framed questions that arose from the commission members almost before we sat down. Boiling mad but very much in control, I waved off their questions and, look-ing at Manny, said, "I think the best way to do this is for us to lay out the entire operation, other than people-driven specifics. Once fin-ished, we can open the meeting to any and all questions as long as the DOJ policy is not violated." Manny nodded in agreement, and I com-menced. In about half an hour Neill and I laid out the operation from the careful gleaning of ten years of raw intelligence, to subsequent spe-cific intelligence gathering by an experienced on-site operative, to the actual operation directed at the worst of the criminal element, to the final planning and execution of the takedown. We followed that with the fact that prosecutions were still running at the 100 percent convic-tion level! Liberally sprinkled throughout that briefing was information relating to the numerous meetings between state and federal attorneys for legal guidance and the governor's personal briefing before the raid.

I could almost feel the antagonism of the commission members slowly melting away as they learned of the amount of careful preparation and planning that had gone into the operation, especially the care taken not to abuse anyone's legal rights. When Neill and I laid out the tremendous numbers of wildlife being illegally killed and openly moving in commerce, the last vestiges of doubt seemed to disappear, especially in light of how little we had purchased from the huge illegal market and the attention we had paid to all the legal issues routinely raised by defense attorneys.

When we finished our presentation, the questions flew, but in a more orderly and professional fashion. Neill and I responded as fast as we could, and still they came. But we killed every "snake" introduced into the arena! Finally we could see support for the operation building in the surfacing questions. Toward the end of the session, Coogan said, "Hell, when I was chief, I couldn't send twenty guys to arrest one person without getting someone injured or killed. What you guys pulled off in the valley, a place known for a dangerous and violent element, is a miracle of law enforcement done as professionally as can be done. You guys and your officers are to be commended!"

Seeing there were no more questions, Neill and I got up to leave. Manny Martinez asked if he could speak to me for a moment, and we moved off to a corner of the room. "Terry," he said, "I need to know if the Fish and Wildlife Service ever had any other operations like this in which they used as many men?"

"Yes," I replied. " I can think of several operations, especially in Region 3 of the Service, which used 300 officers in one covert fur/fish operation, and on another 350 men to safely accomplish the mission."

Manny furrowed his brow and said, "Well, I am afraid in light of the information supplied at this meeting, I am going to have to tell the governor something he doesn't want to hear." With that, the meeting ended with handshakes all around. I have to say that Manny ran a very professional meeting and, his earlier statement notwithstanding, wanted to get to the bottom of the "hoorah" so he could fairly advise the governor. (As an aside, note that today's state-federal big-game check stations on the interstates routinely utilize from 250 to 350 officers.)

The governor was supposed to have his press conference at ten that morning after Manny Martinez reported back to him, and lo and behold, it was canceled. As I recall, that press conference was held some thirty or so days later, and during that event Romer said that the commission had found that "the operation tended to intimidate residents, polarize the inhabitants, and inflicted psychological damage on innocent citizens." The commission also "found no evidence supporting allegations that the motivation for the law enforcement undertaking and subsequent arrests were racially motivated" and "found that the undertaking was marked by dedication and professionalism by the wildlife officers involved." Makes me wonder how both sets of statements could have come from the same session?

The press of course, in its frenzy to continue feeding on the already badly chewed carcass of an honorable law enforcement program, again trumpeted the clarion call to arms against the heavy hand of government. Still little fairly reported distinguishing right from wrong, nothing on the careful legal work characteristic of the operation, nothing on the natural resources being slaughtered until the trials, nothing on the willingness of many of the valley's people to take wildlife illegally as they saw fit, nothing on the good people of the valley and their calls for help against what they saw as crooked local law enforcement. Again, the media had unlimited air waves and ink by the barrel, and I had only my voice, lost in the wind of broadcast media, and one ink pen ... that is, until a lone voice from the wilderness broke free and voiced his opinion in a short article buried in the bowels of the newsprint. Bob Saile of the *Denver Post* called it as he saw it. "Poverty as an excuse for stealing won't get you very far. ... That's what poaching is: stealing from you and me and all other citizens of this state who own the wildlife collectively." That pretty much said it all.

As if there were any surprises left, another reared its head. U.S. Attorney Norton in a letter to Governor Romer tried to placate the ghosts and demons raised by the investigation's dust swirls. Norton mentioned the commission's findings, then out of the blue informed Romer that he was requesting "the Community Relations Service of the U.S. Department of Justice to mediate through conciliation those aspects of the law enforcement undertaking." He went on to state that the Community Relations Service, "as you know ... was created by the Civil Rights Act of 1964 to provide assistance to communities in resolving disputes, disagreements, or difficulties relating to alleged

discriminatory practices based on race, color or national origin."
Here was the U.S. attorney, the man who had ultimately cleared and
authorized the operation, attempting to make amends for imaginary
racism, adding more fuel to an already one-sided firestorm! And that
was after the latest commission had reported that the operation and
takedown were not racially motivated! As was later determined by the
courts of the land, no one's civil rights had been violated. So why the
letter from a man who knew nothing of the kind had occurred?

Assistant U.S. Attorney David Conner, our chief prosecutor, had
had a gutful of the project and character assassination flowing
throughout the media. He wrote a letter to Secretary of the Interior
Lujan, stating it best:

> I am aware, as I am sure you are, that numerous allegations concern-
> ing possible entrapment of the defendants in connection with Operation
> SLV were made virtually the moment the prosecutions commenced. As
> part of my preparation for prosecution of the federal defendants in the
> District of Colorado, I had occasion to review *all* documents and re-
> ports connected with the entire operation. Additionally, I had occasion
> to listen to all of the 280 audio tapes taken by Special Agent Morrison
> during the course of the investigation. I can state to you in no uncer-
> tain terms that no defendant, whether state or federal, was entrapped
> by special Agent Morrison or any other agent in connection with Op-
> eration SLV. In fact, special Agent Morrison would only engage in ne-
> gotiations regarding the purchase and sale of illegal wildlife with a given
> individual *after* that individual had approached him and indicated his
> willingness to traffic in illegal wildlife. Thus, special Agent Morrison
> never induced nor encouraged any individual to break any law. During
> the course of the prosecutions in federal court in Colorado I also had
> occasion to do a great deal of research on entrapment and outrageous
> governmental conduct. Special Agent Morrison's conduct never ap-
> proached entrapment nor outrageous conduct. In fact, all seven crimi-
> nal defendants prosecuted within the District of Colorado, as part of
> the factual basis in their plea agreements with the government, affirma-
> tively stated under oath, that they were not induced, encouraged, nor
> entrapped by Special Agent Morrison nor any other governmental
> agent. They further affirmatively stated that they were unaware of any
> individual who was entrapped. Additionally, a federal district court
> judge has ruled with regard to one of the Operation SLV cases that
> there was no entrapment, outrageous governmental conduct or selective

prosecution. In that case the defendant, while testifying, stated that there had been a preexisting commercial market for illegal wildlife prior to the initiation of the investigation.

Special Agent Morrison is a fine man with a great love of wildlife. During the course of this investigation he declined to make many cases he could have by purchasing illegal wildlife. Many times Special Agent Morrison would forego making felony cases on individuals regarding the unlawful sale of golden eagles when it was apparent the individual would go out and actually kill an eagle to sell. Rather, Special Agent Morrison had the U.S. Fish and Wildlife Service provide dead eagles, killed by other means, and used them in connection with his dealings; thus, saving the lives of eagles, which would otherwise have been killed. Likewise, Special Agent Morrison was cognizant that his presence in the San Luis Valley might create a market for illegal wildlife. Before locating in the valley in an undercover capacity, Special Agent Morrison spent approximately one year verifying a previously existing commercial market for illegally taken wildlife. Additionally, the prices that he would pay for illegally taken wildlife were minimal, in an effort to keep individuals from killing additional animals while still documenting criminal activity.

Dave laid out the facts as he saw them from a position of knowledge. The more I think about it, the more I think Dave's earlier life must have taken him through the battle of Thermopylae. ...

As anticipated, defense attorneys tried every angle to discredit the government's witness or the investigation, all for naught. We had put together an iron-clad investigation under the astute guidance of our attorneys, and now all that hard work and careful attention to detail was paying dividends. After reviewing all the hard evidence against their clients, defense attorneys began to troop forward and lay their clients' heads on the block. Pleas were cut commensurate with the violations, with a lot of charges being laid aside in light of a defendant's ability to pay. Soon a flood of settlements issued forth in favor of the government's investigation. The media, now bored with the happenings and possibly embarrassed over their earlier lack of professionalism, moved on to other news. However, in support of the press, I found that fines, penalties, community service, and jail sentences following on convictions or plea bargains were accurately reported. There were no further comments regarding the investigation, just fairly reported statistics, and then they moved on. I found it interesting

that all the earlier charges laid against the government and the investigation just melted into nothing like the snows of spring. Many of
those making the earlier wild charges moved back under their leaf
litter. Not one of the earlier charges laid against the officers during the
takedown phases of the operation was ever substantiated! Not one
charge against Morrison for twisting or violating the laws was ever
found to be justified! That speaks volumes regarding a very tightly
run operation holding people's rights, both moral and legal, to the
highest standard!

As if not enough of the public's money had been spent running
down blind alleys, Congressman Bill Richardson, not happy with
the results of his hearing in Taos, made another run at the Service.
He got the idea that if he could obtain the operational cost figures
for the San Luis Valley Project, they would be so large that they
could be used to embarrass the Service and play to the Hispanic vot-
ers. On September 15, his office requested information on the cost
of the two-and-a-half-year operation. As required, the Service responded with those figures representing the *specific* federal involvement, minus salaries, benefits, insurance costs, and the like. Those
costs were associated with an agent position, working a covert project or not. What was left came to a paltry $47,126 for the entire op-
eration, including my federal takedown costs! The state and federal
monies received by the courts from the defendants for their violations surpassed that figure! That was the last time anyone heard
from Congressman Richardson on these matters. I hope he makes a
better governor for the people of New Mexico than he did a federal
legislator during the SLV Operation.

When all was said and done, of the original 108 defendants, 103 pled
or were found guilty! One was found not guilty owing to a judicial
error, and four cases were dismissed because the defendants were
found mentally incompetent to stand trial. In the end, a showcase
covert operation was publicly marred by politicians and media interested only in placating the public.

It has been many years since Operation SLV ran its course and to
this day people still ask me about it. Many still have no inkling as to
what happened except what they read in the papers during those tur-
bulent times, and that is sad. It just goes to show that the pen is might-
ier than the sword, and there is a greater responsibility that goes with

the ink flowing from that pen. Unfortunately, that responsibility is seldom recognized or valued in the media or political arena, or in many cases is simply ignored for personal gain or satisfaction.

Law enforcement contacts in the valley indicated that wildlife crime took a header after the investigation. For a long time it was hard to locate any serious wildlife crime in that area. Then, as is always the case, individuals previously involved faded out of the picture and newer ones out for the coin of the realm or the excitement illegal acts bring reared their ugly heads. Law enforcement officers today indicate that another covert operation is in order as the illegal killing grows once more among a new generation weaned on lawlessness. In Colorado and New Mexico, we had a perfectly executed law enforcement operation, organized by skilled officers, strongly overviewed by state and federal attorneys, melded with common sense and purpose, and all within the law of the land. Yet that investigation was portrayed as something evil. I wonder if the members of the media and public officials who took such license realized that they were just as bad as the poachers and market hunters! I hope they never have to answer to their children for the national heritage they helped tear asunder.

The results of Operation SLV, other than those directly tied to the investigation, sadden me. The political and media-driven aftermath was a bitter pill to swallow. So much work went into doing it right that it is just unbelievable how it was addressed once the investigation saw the light of day. Plain and simply, the responses from the irresponsible undercut the goal of fair play and valid processes of law enforcement. Nothing was presented to the public about the lawlessness of many people in the San Luis Valley. Nothing about the very real loss of part of our national heritage. Nothing about those people in the valley who desired a return of the law. Nothing about some law enforcement officers in the valley using their badges and office to intimidate those making an honest and legal effort to be good members of the human race. Nothing about the questionable politics sprayed like a cat scenting signposts throughout the community. Nothing but one sentence in a commission report about the professionalism of the officers attempting to uphold the laws of the land. Nothing about those lacking a voice, who died without making a sound. ...

   Those included in the story (and those I unfortunately forgot to mention due to the complexity of the investigation and the time that has elapsed since it took place), and there were many, were part of Colorado and national history. Operation SLV still stands today as an example of how to conduct a complex covert operation. And it patently held to the first rule of law enforcement: everyone came home at the end of their shifts — including those touched by the long arm of the law. Lessons were learned, but when all the chips were counted, it turned out that somebody had done something right.

six

The Elk, the Sage Grouse, and the Pickled Herring

"HONEY, I'M LEAVING," I yelled as I started out the front door.

"Just a minute," my bride called from the kitchen. A few moments later she was in my arms for a hug, gave me a kiss, and told me to have a good day at work. Her beautiful blue eyes and loving smile enhanced the honesty and love of her words. With that, out the front door of my home in the mountains of Evergreen I went, drinking in the cold, clean-smelling air. Walking to my patrol vehicle, I took a quick look at the tire tread on my old Dodge three-quarter-ton pickup, vaulted into the seat, and inserted the key in the ignition. *Vrrooom* went the 360-cubic-inch engine as it spun powerfully to life to meet another day. The gauges on the dash came to life and soon indicated that all was well with my truck's power plant. Easing the stick shift into gear, I moved out of my yard and onto Grizzly Way in my subdivision, waving to Donna as she stood in the doorway to see me off.

It was a few minutes before six in the morning and still dark. I smiled cynically as I remembered President Ronald Reagan's many brilliant statements about how lazy he had found government employees when he took over as this country's leader. I wasn't due on the job until seven-thirty in the morning. Yet, with my president's words regarding my poor work ethics ringing in my ears, I was already on my way to work. No extra compensation, Mr. President, just an opportunity to get in an hour or so of quality extra work before the phones in my office rang off the hook. I drove out of my subdivision onto state Highway 73 as much of the rest of the world slept.

I had worked for Reagan as a state game warden when he was governor of California. The former actor was as much an airhead then as now, I thought—a point that had been driven home when his office tried to interfere with several of my cases involving influential Republicans whom I had apprehended breaking the conservation laws. However, they were all prosecuted to the full extent of the law regardless of the tactics practiced by the governor's staff. Trying once again to erase my distaste for the man whom much of the rest of the nation thought was the greatest, I headed toward the small Colorado mountain town of Evergreen. Turning east from Highway 73 onto state Highway 74 in Evergreen, I headed for Interstate 70, which eventually led down the mountain to my law enforcement office in Lakewood, some twenty-three miles away.

Stopping at the traffic light at the edge of town on Highway 74 and Bryant Drive, I checked the gauges one more time to make sure everything was operating correctly. Everything was a go. The light changed to green, and down the hill I went, gathering speed rapidly as I quickly shifted through the gears of the four-speed, enjoying the morning's cool air through the open window and the power of the vehicle on a deserted four-lane highway. The truck didn't have a tachometer, so I had memorized the speeds at which to shift gears in order to not over-rev the engine. Looking down for an instant to check the speedometer as I shifted from third into fourth gear at fifty-five miles per hour, I was shocked upon looking up to find a huge cow elk running from the dark of the morning into my lane. At a distance of twenty yards with me traveling fifty-five miles per hour, she was headed right into my grill! I had a problem, and so did my two guardian angels as they scrambled out of the way in order to avoid messing up their feathers! With no time to brake (to do so would have lowered the front of the truck, making it easier for the cow to roll up over the hood into my windshield, killing me instantly), I jerked the steering wheel hard to the left. As my Germanic luck held (after all, we Germans haven't won a war since 1870), a pack of dogs I hadn't yet seen chasing the elk suddenly appeared and sent her scrambling across the highway, also to the left. She was moving directly into my path. Jerking the steering wheel even farther to the left, so much so that I feared the truck might roll if it held the road surface too tightly, I struck the elk full force with my right front fender. *Crrrash* went her left shoulder into the right front fender of the truck, the impact of which blew me across two lanes of traffic, thankfully empty at that time of the morning. *Plooom* went her head and neck through the right side of the windshield as the impact smashed and curled her body around the window post and into the side of the pickup. A million pieces of flying glass exploded inside the truck, sending shrapnel and elk snot throughout the cab and over my body as I frantically tried to manhandle the now skidding and careening vehicle. *Ka-whammm* went the seven-hundred-pound animal into the right side of the truck with such force that it almost tore off the passenger door as she smashed into the rear side of the truck with a violent crunch!

The elk and all the body work she was doing to my truck were secondary to my thoughts as I desperately worked to regain control of my three thousand pounds of flying metal on a mission destined for the far dirt bank at the edge of the highway. Fortunately, I had brand-new tires, plus many years of driving experience under just about every possible condition! Knowing what the truck would more than likely do under those circumstances saved my bacon. I turned the wheel hard to the right to avoid going into the embankment, and the truck responded with a 180-degree, wheel-scorching turn. The next thing I knew, it was quietly resting in the middle of the highway in the oncoming lanes, as if nothing had happened.

Pushing in the clutch, I just sat there for a moment gathering up my thoughts. Somehow the morning had gone from a pleasant hug from my wife to a metal-rending collision with a cow elk! I think I preferred the arms of my wife. Gathering up my mass, I thanked the Old Boy upstairs for my many blessings and then listened carefully to the sound of my engine. It was purring like a kitten. A scared kitten, but it was all right. Thank God I had been able to avoid smashing in my engine with a head-on collision. Damn, isn't that something? My first worry was about my vehicle, not myself. No wonder. My divisional budget was so flat that I could barely afford tires, much less vehicle replacement. What a hell of a way to run a show: just enough money to keep the agents minimally operating and none for equipment replacement. Kind of makes you wonder what those on high in the agency were thinking when it came to funding their divisions with their normal buckets of dollars, all the while letting mine twist in the wind.

I heard my two errant guardian angels sheepishly returning to the scene. That will teach them to sleep in the back of the truck instead of flying ahead of me, I thought. Carefully pulling off the road, I looked back at the elk lying in the middle of the road. She had not fared as well. In addition to being deader than a hammer, she was suffering the indignity of being mauled by four curs in the middle of the highway in front of God and everybody.

Until that moment, in over a million miles of driving I had had only one previous wreck with a government vehicle. Suffice it to say, I was *pissed beyond all else!* Especially now that I thought of all the attendant government paperwork I would have to fill out! Grabbing my Colt .45 from under the seat, I took my five-cell flashlight and headed down the still-darkened highway to do unto those dogs as they had just done unto me!

About that time I realized that another car was coming toward me. Terry, I thought, it will do no good for that driver heading down the highway this early in the morning, probably still half asleep, to suddenly see a huge, bear-like fellow in his headlights with a flashlight in one hand and a gun in the other! That would probably send him into such a panic that anything he did with his car would probably be considerably more spectacular than what I had just done with mine!

Putting the gun into the back pocket of my pants just as the dogs ran off, I grabbed the elk by her hind leg. Being so damned mad, I was able to pull her right off the road! Walking back to my still beautifully running truck and taking a first look, I couldn't believe my eyes. The hood was buckled upward in the middle and would have to be replaced. The windshield was blown all to hell and, needless to say, needed serious help. The right front fender was pushed back four inches and also needed to be replaced. The right front door was hanging by one hinge and bent almost in half like a horseshoe. Where the window from that door had gone was anyone's guess, but it was AWOL. There was a deep dent on the right-hand side from the cab to the tailgate. The tailgate was even bent on the right side! It was unreal the damage that elk had done to my once proud Dodge with 214,000 miles on it. That's right, 214,000 miles! I could not afford to replace it, so I had just kept driving it past the government's mandatory replacement mileage of 50,000 miles. I guess Mr. President might have said I was just another one of those useless piss-ant government employees who didn't try to save the taxpayers' money.

After tying the smashed door with a piece of rope, I took a whisk broom and swept all the glass off the front seat of the truck and out onto the road. I hopped carefully back in to avoid cutting myself or my dress pants on the remaining loose glass shards and headed down the highway as if nothing had happened. Well, not quite. The howling wind coming into the cab through the hole in the windshield and basically absent right front door let me know fall was in the air.

Pulling into a local service station where I usually had my truck's maintenance work done, I stepped out and handed the keys to the amazed mechanic standing there slack-jawed as he viewed the damage. "Fix her up, Robert," I stridently directed. "I will be back at 5:00 this evening to pick her up." With that, I sauntered away as if I had asked the man to fix my windshield wipers. After walking about twenty yards, I turned and looked back with a devious smile. Robert was still standing there holding my keys and looking at me in disbelief. Chuckling, I walked back to the man who was in more shock then I. "Well, what do you think?" I said.

"What the hell did you hit, Terry?" was his first surprised utterance.

"An elk at fifty-five miles per hour," I replied.

"Goddamn, are you OK, man?" he asked with concern rising in his voice.

"Other than my ego and arrogance," I replied, "I am fine. What do you think, Robert? Can you fix her up?"

He just looked at me and said, "I know you law enforcement guys are always broke, but how do I get paid on this one? Because it may take some doing!"

I said, "Robert, this is Monday. I need this truck no later than Friday noon of this week. The state of Colorado has requested all the help they can get for the opening of their grouse season, and I plan on giving them a hand in the Craig area. And you are right, we don't have much money. If you could just beat out a few dents, replace the windshield, and somehow fix that door, I would really appreciate it. In fact, it doesn't even have to be painted. Just leave it as is. That way, I will have an undercover truck par excellence, courtesy one very dead elk."

"Terry, you know I will do the best I can, but you have to give me some latitude in fixing this piece of junk." He gave me a look as if he had a few off-the-wall ideas, but I would have to trust him.

"Give it your best shot, Bob; just make her safe to drive." With that, I walked the remaining four blocks to my office. I still had a ton of glass in my hair and clothes, and there was the matter of talking with my two guardian angels, who were still complaining about all the flying glass that had lodged in their wing feathers. ...

I heard nothing from Bob as I drove another beater vehicle on loan from the Refuge Division until Friday noon. Then I walked down to the gas station and garage, hopeful that Bob had worked a miracle. As I got closer, I could see the good side of my vehicle parked outside the garage doors. That was a good omen, I thought. If it was parked outside, that meant Bob had it fixed up. As I got closer, I could see that my tan pickup had a proper hood without a huge bend in it, but that part was now primer black. Oh well, I thought, black and tan doesn't look so bad. Walking around to the front of the truck accompanied by a very worried-looking Bob, I discovered that my right front fender had been replaced. Not bad, I thought, but a *yellow fender* with a black hood and tan body? A French fashion plate I wasn't! But with my division as broke as it was, I couldn't be picky. Then there was the matter of the right front door. It was a *bright robin's egg blue!* Boy, you talk about a coat of many colors ... this truck had it all!

Turning, I got a look at Bob's face, and I just started to laugh. Bob got a smile on his worried face and then started to laugh as well. Soon the tears were rolling down both our faces. When we finally got control of ourselves, I commented that the windshield at least seemed to be color coordinated. After another laugh, I asked Bob what the "damage" was.

"Well," he said, "I got the hood from my brother off his old junked Dodge truck, and since it was red, knew that wouldn't do. So I took a can of primer and painted it black. I figured that way it would reduce the glare off your hood and be better for your eyes. My brother didn't want the hood, so you got that for free. Then there was the matter of the right front door. I got that from my cop buddies out at the police range before they shot up an old Dodge pickup they had placed there for bullet penetration tests. So that was a freebie as well."

I stood there and shook my head in amazement. My friend was just an old country boy trying hard to make a living. He did excellent work, and I had tried to help him over the years with a lot of government business, both mine and that of my local agents. Now all those helping times were coming home to roost in the government coop.

"As for the dent along the entire side of your truck, I couldn't get that out without spending a lot of money, and since your truck is ten years old, I just left it alone. Other than looking like hell, that dent isn't a safety issue. So you owe me for a spray can of black primer and a new windshield, and throw in a hundred bucks for labor. Oh, and I threw in a tune-up for free."

I just stood there and looked at him. I knew damn well he had more than a hundred bucks' worth of labor in the truck. "Bob," I said, "be realistic with me."

"No, Terry, you have been good to me over the years with all the government business when I was struggling. This is my way of saying thank you. Besides, it was fun fixing the old girl up once more." Well, Mr. President, it looks like another rotten move by one of your hardly fit government employees to save you and the taxpayers some money, I mused. Needless to say, the government business kept coming Bob's way long after he got on his feet and finally made it big.

Now that I had my truck of many colors back, I got down to the business at hand. I had arranged with Ray Rauch, refuge manager at the Rocky Mountain Arsenal, to loan me one of his badge-carrying, credentialed biologists for the weekend in the Craig area. As luck would have it, he assigned me a tall drink of water named Rich Grosz. That lad was six foot seven if he was an inch, weighed at least 275, and probably didn't have much more than 6 percent body fat on his carcass. He was a good runner, absolutely fearless, and eager to learn more about this thing called wildlife law enforcement. It seemed he had his eye set on becoming an agent someday (as this story is written, Rich is a special agent for the Service in Bismarck, North Dakota). The two of us met about two in the afternoon that Friday, loaded his gear in my goofy-looking truck of many colors, and prepared for another adventure.

Instead of asking what had happened to the truck, Rich just walked to the smashed-in side and removed a tuft of elk hair still clumped in the bent and broken metal by the tailgate. Rolling it in his fingers, he looked over at me and said, "Damn, old man, can't kill them with a rifle and fair chase, so have to use a truck, eh?"

There wasn't much I could say to that shot across the bow. He had a keen eye, and trying to explain what had happened would draw nothing but more chiding about my "elk hunting," so I just let it ride. Besides, I could just tell his mother and she would settle up with him if he got too far out of line.

Arriving late in Craig, we went to the A Bar Z Motel and unloaded our gear. Then downtown we went and loaded up several ice chests with soda pop, Italian salami, cheese, chips, pickled pig's feet, crackers, and other "healthy" game warden food. Then we purchased fifty pieces of fried chicken (all they had) at the Safeway deli and headed back to our motel room for our feast. There were only two pieces of chicken left when we went to bed that evening. ... In those days of our foolish youth, we could really "smash" chickens, as Agent Pat Bosco used to say before he went on a diet himself.

About three the next morning, Rich and I loaded up our food, guns, cameras, optics, and the like and headed for the hills northeast of Craig. Driving up onto a sagebrush-covered hilltop in the center of an extensive area historically frequented by grouse hunters, I parked my truck and we got out. Both of us just stood there a long moment in the silence of the dark before the dawn, quietly listening to the life stirring around us.

Off in the distance, we could hear a coyote announcing to the world of coyotes that he had caught breakfast, probably in the form of a blacktail jackrabbit. Down in a draw by a small dugout some hundred yards away holding muddy runoff waters from an overgrazed range, the plaintive hoot of a great horned owl told us he was celebrating his full crop and the dawn of a new day. Way off in the distance to the west, the telltale scream of a rabbit told us it had made a wrong turn from cover into the waiting jaws of death. The smell of dust was heavy in the air from our arrival, and the pungent smell of big sage crushed by our wheels topped off the morning's sensory tour. We stood there for about another ten minutes, and then I said, "How about some breakfast?"

"Sounds good to me, Pop; let's do it," came my partner's reply.

Breakfast that morning, like so many mornings in the past when we had worked together, consisted of a one-pound stick of Italian dry salami each, a bottle of Diet Pepsi, and a box of crackers split between us. That is what many of us in the business call good game warden food: it's high in fat (no wonder most of us die young with heart and circulatory problems), but it is a fuel load that will carry you many miles when the chance of hearing the dinner bell is remote.

With the dawn came many sets of headlights wandered around in the sagebrush below our high ground, looking for that favorite spot to hunt the always elusive sage grouse. The sage grouse is found in sagebrush habitats (especially big and black sage) and can be as large as a small turkey. Its meat has a fairly strong flavor owing to its food habits (grass, insects, berries, and leaves of sage, among other things), and if not gutted and iced down as soon as it's shot, it can be a real challenge to a cook and anyone's palate. Many dyed-in-the-wool grouse hunters have learned to identify the young on the wing and shoot only those because of their slightly better eating quality. However, I advise you die-hard sage grouse hunters to go ahead and shoot some of the "bombers" next time you are out. Clean them immediately, ice them down (inside and out), and when you get home, breast them out and remove the legs. Remove the bloodshot meat and shot, then slice the breast meat in half-inch-thick slices. Soak the breast meat and legs overnight in soy sauce, dredge it heavily in flour the next day, spice with Greek seasoning, and pan fry in hot olive oil. If you do, you will find yourself taking a few "bombers" every time you go out for the culinary delight just described.

The limits on these birds have historically been somewhat restricted due to their limited population numbers (no one seems to have a good handle on why the numbers are low other than destruction of their habitat by humans and range cattle and possible overshooting in some areas), with a daily bag of two or three usually being the norm. With such restricted bag limits, anyone who wanted to stray across the legal line would find it easy to do. If so, they would hopefully get more than they bargained for, if you get my drift ... especially that morning as two pairs of eyes aided by binoculars watched the hunters pursue their sport, punctuated by the soft *crumping* sounds of shotguns from all points of the compass.

Finally, a single male hunter with a female companion drew the attention of the two men using excellent Steiner optics a half mile or so away. That lad got a covey of grouse up and promptly killed two birds, the limit that year being three. The woman had no opportunity of shooting into that covey because of the distance of its rise from where she stood. As the man walked out to pick up his two birds in the sagebrush, two more birds got up at his feet, and he killed both of them as well. He had just shot an over-limit. Picking up his four birds, the man walked back to the female, and with the aid of a 60-power spotting scope, I saw him hand her three birds to hold as if she had killed a daily limit. Then, placing one bird into the game bag in his hunting coat, the fellow continued to hunt for more grouse. About twenty minutes later he jumped another covey in a dry creek bottom and promptly killed two more birds, making him now three birds over the limit. With the spotting scope, I could see him looking all around to make sure that no one had seen the deed. Satisfied that he was unobserved, he and the woman walked back to their vehicle and commenced to gut and pick the birds, all the while constantly looking around as if watching for a game warden.

Rich and I drove over to the couple as if we were other hunters cruising the area. Shortly thereafter and with little fanfare, we had seized the six illegal grouse and issued the man a citation for taking an over-limit. The rest of the day was pretty uneventful, and aside from our pure joy at being out and about in the world of wildlife, sharing a special moment and relationship, the day slowly and all too quickly expired. But not before the "Walt Disney paintbrush" stroked across the sky a sunset that was so spectacular that father and son stood in the sage in awe, quietly watching until it went the way of the Old West. There is something to be said for those moments when the great out-of-doors manages to burn itself into your soul. The yelping call of a lone coyote in the distance, followed by other coyote supporting singers, heralded the final end of the day. We loaded up in the pickup of many colors and headed down the mountain for another greasy repast of fried chicken.

The next morning found us standing on the same hillside, drinking in the sights and sounds of the dark just before the dawn. That morning there was a slight breeze heavy with moisture from the northwest, foretelling a storm to come. Snuggling deeper into the warmth of our insulated hunting coats, we appreciated the keenly accented smells of fresh dust, damp air, and oil of sage even more. There were fewer hunters that morning, and most we saw after daylight seemed to be hunting the long, sloping ridges and sagebrush draws to the north.

Slowly chewing a cold stick of salami and letting the fat juices mill around in my mouth, I noticed three hunters through the binoculars some three-eighths of a mile away, flushing a covey of about forty grouse. Numerous shots were fired, and several birds fell. The covey sailed over a ridge to the north, and after picking up their birds, the three hunters briskly walked up to that ridgetop. After a moment's hesitation, the three disappeared over the ridge. Moments later, there were more shots as if that group of hunters had again flushed part of the same covey.

Keeping that shooting action in the back of my mind, I fastened my attention on two hunters in the draws below us, who had flushed a covey of grouse, killing five in the process. "Dad," Rich said, "that guy in the blue jacket killed three grouse on that rise." The two of us watched those hunters, especially the one with a limit of grouse, who continued to hunt. They never did jump another covey, so we were unable to ruin their Christmas, so to speak. However, the group of three we had seen earlier before they walked over the ridge to the north continued to have a very good morning if the number of shots fired out of our sight was any indicator.

About ten in the morning, I told Rich, "Let's saddle up and head north and see how much damage those chaps have done."

Rich nodded, and a few minutes later we were slowly crawling the pickup up and over the sparse trails in the sage, angling our way toward the three chaps. Not finding any backcountry trails that would take us directly to them, we finally moved up onto the main dirt road and headed to where we had last seen them. As we drove over the top of the last ridge, we chanced to see the three lads walking down a small dirt road holding their shotguns and what appeared to be limits of grouse. Parked off to one side and near a set of corrals was a cab-over camper outfit. I had Rich throw one of our extra hunting coats over the law enforcement radio so they wouldn't get wise to us if they looked into the cab, turned off the radio, and then slowly drove up to the three men.

I noticed all three were nervously eyeballing my truck as we approached and rolled to a stop a few feet away. Keep in mind that Rich and I were dressed like every other hunter in the boondocks. There were even two shotguns in plain view in the front seat to perpetuate the ruse. I leaned out my window and said, "Good morning, guys. Looks like you guys got into them."

The sports were almost sullen at being confronted by two perfect strangers, but finally one of them said, "Yeah, we got a few."

"Man, I guess you did," I said, trying to act like another excited hunter impressed with their bag. "Did you guys get those birds over there?" I pointed toward a long sagebrush ridge stretching a mile or so off to the south.

"Yeah," replied the biggest man of the bunch. The rest remained mute as if not wanting to jawbone with a couple of idiots.

"Is that area state land or private?" I asked like a novice.

"Private," said the big guy. "But you can get permission if you ask the landowner, who lives over in Bow Bells."

The other two fellows still looked at Rich and me with suspicion, so in order to break through their quiet defenses, I popped the obvious question. "What's the matter with you guys? You look like you saw a ghost or something."

"Game wardens drive Dodges," one of the men said softly, without taking his eyes off me for a second.

"What," I said in mock surprise, "game wardens! You guys must be kidding. We are not game wardens." (I didn't lie; we were federal agents.) Jumping out of the truck to emphasize our innocence, I faced the three hunters and said, "Do any of you know anything about pickups?"

"Yeah, I do," said the heavyset fellow. "I'm a mechanic at the Ford dealership in town."

"Well, then," I said, "just take a look at this truck. Does it look like one a game warden would drive?" I swept my arm toward the truck to emphasize my point.

"Well," said the mechanic, "it is kind of old."

"Old!" I said, "Old … this truck is over ten years old and has over 200,000 miles on it."

The mechanic said, "Well, yeah, you're right, it is kind of old."

Then, reaching the crescendo of my song and dance, I stepped over to the far side, the one the elk had visited at fifty-five miles per hour, and said to the man, "Come here." Walking to that side of the truck, he looked at the body parts of many colors in silence. "Does that look like a game warden truck to you?" I asked.

"Jesus," he said, "what the hell did you hit, a train?"

"Well, to be frank, an elk, and I used the truck as a go-between at fifty-five miles per hour," I said.

The man just shook his head and then, turning to his partners, said, "This guy is OK. Ain't no way any game warden would be driving this piece of junk." He caught himself, turned to me, and said, "No insult intended."

"No insult taken," I mumbled, glad I had finally broken the ice. I continued, "I couldn't figure out why you guys were so hostile to a couple fellow members of the hunting fraternity. We were just looking for a place to hunt, and usually most hunters will share their good fortune with others."

"Well," said the skinny one, "as we said, game wardens drive Dodges, and we thought you was a game warden."

"What the hell difference does that make?" I innocently asked, suspecting full well why they were so cautious.

"Well," said the heavyset fellow, "Carl here had three grouse too many, and when we saw you coming, he had to hide them by that plum tree down the road for fear of getting caught. But now that we have really looked at your truck, we can see that no game warden in his right mind would drive that piece of junk." We all just belly laughed, three out of relief, and the other two at having pulled the wool over the eyes of the other three.

Reaching into my shirt pocket as the laugh continued, I pulled out my badge and, holding it up for all to see, said, "We can all laugh over this badge thing years from now too." For a moment there was a break in the laughter, and it was so quiet I could hear the sparrows calling to each other in the sagebrush. Then the large one doubled over with even harder laughter, and pretty soon his buddies followed suit. The large one said with a big grin, "You really had us fooled with that fake badge of yours."

I walked toward him and said, "Does that look fake to you now that you have a closer look?"

He froze, especially after getting a better look at my badge and the one Rich was now holding up for all to see as well. "Oh my God! This damn ugly truck and slick-talking son of a bitch just did us in, guys!"

"Gentlemen," I said, "we are federal agents authorized to enforce state laws, and it seems we have a problem here." Pointing to Carl, I said, "Carl, I need you and Rich to go back to the plum tree and bring the extra grouse here if you would, please." Turning to the two remaining hunters, I said, "While those lads are doing that, I would like you two gentlemen to show me your hunting licenses and empty your shotguns so I might check them."

Rich and Carl went and retrieved the three extra grouse while I checked the remaining two lads. They were in accordance with the law, so I was finished with them. When Carl returned with his extra birds, I asked for his hunting and driver's licenses and received both. After issuing Carl a citation for possessing an over-limit of sage grouse, I seized all six of his birds and returned his driver's license. Up to that moment, the group of hunters had been mostly silent, partly because of being caught and partly because of catching themselves, I suppose. Finishing up, I asked the lads if they had any questions, and they didn't say anything for a moment. Then the large one said, "Well, you caught us, uh, we caught ourselves fair and square. But tell me, Mr. Federal Agent, is that truck really yours or is it an undercover vehicle?"

"It is my issue patrol vehicle," I said matter-of-factly.

"Can't they buy you anything better than that?" he asked.

"Well, gentlemen, the truck runs well, gets good gas mileage, doesn't burn oil, and costs me very little to maintain. So why should the taxpayers go out and get me a new one just because this one looks a little rough?"

"Jesus," said the large one, "I can't hardly believe you can't get a better truck."

"Well, as I said, this one is fine, and I will keep it until it gets too expensive to run, and then and only then will I get rid of it. After all, you chaps don't pay me to piss away your hard-earned tax dollars."

Rich and I were turning to go when the large one beckoned me to stop with his raised hand. "Pardon me, Mister, I don't mean to be a smart-ass, but if all the government is that broke and using run-down equipment like you, if the Russians were to attack, they would get clear to the Mississippi River before we could stop them!"

With that, we all burst out laughing. Rich and I shook hands all around and left the men in a good mood, especially after I explained that all three of them could chip in on the fine and thereby lessen the financial impact on Carl. It was apparent it would be done among friends, one of whom had gotten greedy with the other two conspiring to assist. As Rich and I drove off, I could see the lads still looking at my truck of many colors and shaking their heads in disbelief. I could just imagine what they said to their buddies at work on Monday. Oh well, we catch the bad guys any way we can just as long as it is legal, I thought. Also, Rich had no more smart-ass remarks about my "elk-hunting" truck for the rest of the trip. Perhaps it was the thought of me telling his mother that he had bad-mouthed me or my truck. ...

The rest of the day was pretty uneventful, and we caught only five other lads at a motel loading up ice chests of grouse with no evidence of species. The season was open for several species of grouse at the same time, and Fish and Game regulations required that the hunter leave a fully feathered wing on the bird when transporting it so a Fish and Game official could determine which species of grouse you had in your possession and also determine if you had stayed within the daily bag limit for the species.

By afternoon, not unusually for the area, the weather had turned from pleasant to cold and rainy as portended by the northwest breezes. Soon Rich and I were slipping and sliding through the mud as we walked out to check the remaining die-hard hunters, in the process finding our shoes caked with twenty pounds of glue-like mud per foot. As the prewinter rains increased in force, we began to feel the bodily cold that came from working and sweating all day in the elements. By nightfall we were cold, wet, and short-tempered after walking at least ten miles in the boot-sucking mud. You might ask why the effort? In heavy rains, most game birds go to ground to avoid being soaked and losing a world of body heat in the process. They become very difficult to find and reluctant to rise to the gun. However, over the years, conservation officers soon learn that those who pursue wildlife through thick and thin, including bad weather, are often those dedicated to killing outside what the law allows. Hence, Rich and I stayed with those last few hunters to make sure they stayed within the boundaries of the law and common sense. There was also a little bit of showing the flag so they wouldn't think the lowly game warden went home when the weather got a little tough. Finally even the last of those die-hard folks gave up and headed home, but not before they all looked like chickens thrown into a stock pond and then dragged through the mud.

Come the end of that day, two rather large, badge-carrying fellows were *plenty hungry!* Now, when I tell you a 300-pounder and a 275-pounder are hungry, *watch out!* Whatever they choose for a meal, you'll find that item diminishing in fast order! The two of us in our soaked and cold misery began to envisage our evening meal. After discussing many mouth-watering ideas, from frog legs to flaming filet of yak, Peking style, we settled on a prime rib dinner with all the fixin's. Now, there was a restaurant on the hill across from the A Bar Z Motel where we were staying called the Hill Topper. A sign outside boasted that it featured the best prime rib in the area. The more we thought about a prime rib dinner, the more we set our hearts on that culinary conclusion as a fitting tribute to our great day in the field.

By the time we hit Craig around seven in the evening, we were famished and ready to eat a whole ranch of prime ribs *each!* Swinging into our motel, we cleaned up as best as we could and put our evidence birds into ice chests containing fresh ice. We walked across the highway to the restaurant with visions of prime rib, medium rare, baked potato with all the trimmings, rainforests of green salads, and gallons of iced tea dancing in our heads. By that time our big guts were eating the little ones, so there was a ton of room in our boilers for whatever we could shovel their way!

Into the eatery known for the area's best prime rib we stomped, muddy boots, big appetites, big grins, and all. Seating ourselves at a table, we surveyed the dining room. It was chock-full of Sunday-night diners, and then we spied it! A huge all-you-could-eat salad bar with a monster-sized pot of clam chowder, ready for the taking. Man, that was too good to be true, and when the waitress appeared, we were ready. When asked if we wanted any drinks, I advised that iced tea by the gallon would be just fine and that both of us would like their prime rib, medium rare, and the largest cut possible. "In fact," I told her, "if the cook could see his way to cut us each a three-pound cut, we would be more than happy to pay the difference." With that, I gave her a big but "hungry for prime rib dinner" friendly grin and was promptly hammered right between the eyes, in a manner of speaking!

"You two are the tenth people to ask for prime rib in the last twenty minutes. We don't have any left, and if you want some, you will have to wait an hour-and-a-half before any more is cooked!" The voice in which she delivered this edict was strained, grating, and out of patience, to say the least. Hell, lady, I thought, we just got here. What the hell did we do to deserve this kind of treatment? She continued, "If you wanted prime rib, you should have gotten here earlier."

Man, if that had been Kimberlee, my strong-willed Vietnamese daughter, speaking to me in such a manner, she would have gotten a swat across the backside right then and there for being so impertinent! I couldn't believe what I was hearing, and neither could Rich if his flashing dark blue eyes were any indicator. We hadn't done anything to upset this little miss other than order prime rib. And for that, she sure was on the prod big time.

Since there weren't any other prime rib eateries in the small town of Craig and it was getting later by the minute, we scurried through the menu while Miss Congeniality stood there impatiently tapping the table with her pencil and awaiting our decisions. Finding nothing else of culinary interest on the menu, Rich and I settled on the all-you-could-eat salad bar and soup choice. After about our tenth bowl of clam chowder and plates of salad, we began to fill up the cracks and feel a tad better. But we were still disappointed over our lack of a huge prime rib dinner with all the fixin's … and especially irritated over the treatment we had received.

Then Rich got a look in his eyes that meant only one thing: *trouble*, with a capital T. It wasn't the kind of look I would have fathered, being the gentle person I am—it was pure and simply from his mother's side of the family! "Dad," he said, "want any more clam chowder?"

"Yes," I said, "I could use one more bowl, and then I will be filled to the gunwales."

"Good," he said, "go and get it now." He said it with such finality that I knew something was up. And knowing my son the way I did, I suspected it was *big!*

I loaded up another bowl of clam chowder and sat back down at our table with a questioning look. With that, Rich got up just as casual as you please to get another plate of salad and bowl of clam chowder. I saw him fill a salad plate and then, with hardly a break in stride, load up in *the palm of his hand* holding the salad plate, a dozen or so large, dripping pieces of sour pickled herring. The way he held the plate in those big shovel-sized hands of his, unless you were looking for it, you wouldn't see the herring concealed under the plate. What the hell?

I thought! Laying his salad plate down but not the herring still hidden in his big old paddle-like hand, he commenced to fill up a bowl with clam chowder just like he owned the place. As he filled his bowl, I saw the pickled herring dropping into the chowder pot, but if I hadn't been watching, I would never have seen it happen. I told you, he gets that kind of behavior from his mom. Don't any of you readers give *me* those looks. ...

Bone tired as I was, I started to chuckle as my son casually walked back to our table with a straight face. The two of us had a hard time keeping from rolling around on the floor once our eyes met.

As Rich and I watched the clam chowder bucket, three ladies all busy jawboning went up to the pot, loaded up their bowls, and left. Nothing happened as they finished their chowder and went on to eat the rest of their dinners. Damn, we drew a miss, or those three ladies were so busy visiting, they could have eaten raw buffalo liver and never noticed the difference. Then a cowboy and his girlfriend got some chowder, and nothing exploded at their table either. I guess their thoughts were elsewhere as well.

"Damn, Rich, where did you put the pickled herring?" I quietly asked.

"It is in the chowder, Dad, just be patient."

Nothing happened with the next several groups of people, and soon Rich and I tired of waiting for the results of his little trick and went back to the remains of our dinner and plans for the morrow.

"*Aaaaggghhh! Uugghhh! Urrrppp!*" came a horrible gagging sound from a fellow seated at the table just behind Rich and me. Our fellow diner had obviously eaten some clam chowder and found something pickled, wet, squishy, and crappy tasting in his mouthful of food. ... Gagging at the foreign taste yet not wanting to spit it out all over his table, he fought it until it went down. "*Aaaaggghhh!*" he bellowed, standing up. The whole place went silent and everyone looked at him as he continued to gag and dry heave, attempting to hold down an overwhelming urge to broadcast puke across several tables! It was all I could do to keep from breaking out with laughter. It was so bad I couldn't even look at Rich or I would have given the whole thing away. With the rest of the evening crowd looking on in horror and the two of us breaking out laughing, imagine how long it would have taken to identify the culprits. So we just laughed in silence until we cried at our fellow diner's discomfort. *"Uggghhh!"* continued our lad, still gagging. Miss Congeniality came running over to see what was the matter, and when confronted with the peering face of the waitress, our retching diner blasted at it from about two inches away with, *"What the goddamned hell are you feeding us in this place?* I just ate something cold, wet, and slimy in the clam chowder that tasted like shit, and it is all I can do to avoid puking right here and now. What kind of crappy restaurant is this, anyway?"

He was furious, to say the least, and *pissed* to say the most. Here he looked like some poor damn sheepherder fresh off the range, in for a hot bowl of clam chowder on a cold, rainy night. And for his efforts to find something comforting, someone had ambushed him with a mouthful of soup that tasted like wet, fresh tripe! Still standing, he kept hollering at the waitress until the cook and manager arrived. They got their comeuppance as well. Meanwhile, the rest of the diners, except two men of monster size, continued looking on in horror at the incident unfolding in their midst.

This "hoorah" went on for about five minutes until the restaurant folks got the gagging sheepherder settled down by promising a free meal and unlimited drinks. The cook removed the container of clam chowder and soon arrived with another brimful of the good goop. The guy behind us kept periodically gagging and "urping" as an aftereffect of his horrible experience, and Rich and I kept silently shaking with mirth. Every time our eyes met, they began dancing again with laughter. I don't know what the fellow was so pissed about. The pickled herring I had eaten earlier was pretty damn good. ... Well, one thing was for sure, our waitress had surely gotten hers before that little show on the dining room floor was finished, I smugly thought.

Finally I was able to get over my laughter and could walk normally, having regained enough composure to get the hell out of there without being discovered. "Ready to go, son?" I asked with an ear-to-ear grin.

"Just a minute, Pop," came his reply as he got up and headed for the salad bar. Oh no, I thought, not again! Yep, there Rich went with his salad plate, picking up another handful of pickled herring and palming them so quickly that even if you were watching for it, that movement was hard to see. Over to the clam chowder container he went, and as he scooped out his clam chowder, I could see the pickled herring, one by one, dropping into the concoction. This time it was a *real* handful, mind you! I couldn't believe it! Coming back to the table, Rich finished up his salad and chowder as if nothing was wrong as three more couples went to the chowder pot and got soup. About that time the cook came out of the kitchen, looked in the chowder pot, and stirred it, missing the pickled herring as it swirled around with its kin the clams. Satisfied, he scooped out a bowl of the chowder and, walking over to our still faintly "urping" diner, placed it on his table with numerous assurances of its quality.

Not wanting to be a part of another wreck, and not sure my sides could stand another round of deep, silent laughter, I asked for the bill. When I paid it, I noticed that our waitress was somewhat nicer and seemed to have gotten her head on straight. Thanking her for the dinner and telling her everything was all right except the chowder, I started to follow Rich out the door. "What was wrong with the clam chowder?" she sweetly asked before I had taken two steps.

"Well," I said, "it just tasted funny," trying to hold a straight face.

"Oh," she said as Rich went out the front door with all the toothpicks from the bowl by the cash register.

"Have a nice day," I said, leaving her to the rest of the evening.

Nearing the door, I heard a loud *"Uggghhh! Aghhh! Uurrrrppp!"* … and that time, it sounded as if our sheepherder was bringing the pickled herring back up! Looking back over my shoulder as I went out the front door, I could see the fellow who had been sitting behind us standing up and this time successfully ridding himself of the pickled herring from his second bowl of clam chowder. People were scattering every which way, and if Rich and I had still been seated at our table, we would have been the recipients of the sheepherder's used clam chowder! You talk about timing. … I would bet a month's paycheck that after that episode, our sheepherder stuck to his Dutch-oven greasy lamb stew out on the range. Other diners were getting up and hurriedly leaving before the mad sheepherder began a rampage by throwing things around, including possibly the cook who had personally served him this latest bowl of gag special clam chowder. You talk about a circus. … Rich could hear what was going on in the diner even from clear across the parking lot and was laughing himself silly. I let the door hit me in the ass as I got the hell out of Dodge, to the sounds of breaking dishes.

That had been quite a week, I thought. First almost getting killed by a cow elk. Then making a hatful of nice sage grouse cases, including one in which I bet the hunters still tell their friends the tale of the truck of many colors. And last but not least, I had aided the migration of pickled herring from their cold plate into that warm clam chowder pot. Come to think of it, Rich and I never did get any prime rib on that trip, but we certainly ate our share of pickled herring whenever we got the chance. ...

seven

Roadblock

ONE DAY IN OCTOBER 1994, I walked into the office of my deputy, Neill Hartman, and sat down to wait for him to finish his work on the computer. While he addressed the computer issues, I quietly reflected on the background and character of the man sitting before me. Neill was a veteran officer of many years, and if I had to rate him among all other Service agents, I would be hard-pressed to find one more loyal or with greater professional excellence. He had worked for me in two separate Service regions and in both places his performance had been nothing short of outstanding. He was a block of a man, strong as a bull with cat-quick reflexes, yet possessed a gentle heart as big as all outdoors. He also possessed a latent, unmatched energy that when directed toward difficult or complex assignments was hell on wheels. That quality was especially in evidence when going after those with a bit of the larcenous devil in their souls and a liking for walking on the illegal side in the world of wildlife. I considered myself very lucky to have him as my deputy and close friend.

At that point in my thinking, he finished his computer work and acknowledged my presence. "What's up, Chief?" he asked with his usual big grin.

"Neill, I think it's time we bring Nebraska into the twenty-first century with a major interstate big-game road block. I would like you to get cracking on this one because it will take more planning than usual because of the uniqueness of Nebraska politics and it being the very first such 'animal' for those rather conservative folks. I want it planned down to the smallest detail, and I want you and Manny Medina to work hand-in-hand on this one." Manny was the Nebraska-Kansas senior resident agent. "I would also like Mike Damico to be the point man on the detail work." Mike was the North Platte special agent. "Mike has never done one of these, and the experience will serve him well someday when he makes supervisor. Set it up somewhere along I-80, maybe in the North Platte area, which will also provide adequate commercial lodging for all the assigned officers. That location should allow us to check hunters funneling into the interstate area from their hunting areas in Colorado, Wyoming, Montana, Idaho, and Nebraska as they head for home." Pausing to get more of my thoughts together and into play, I added, "Be sure and get the state Fish and Game agencies involved, including those outside the region as well as our regional sister enforcement and other badge-carrying Service management divisions. That way their officers can get in some first-class training on search and seizure, interviewing techniques, and criminal investigative procedures as well as providing us some damn good help. Also, see if any other federal agencies like the Park Service or associated state park systems would like to send some of their folks for the intensive interviewing and search training that will result. I figure three to four hard days of wildlife inspections will be all the opportunity we can get before the truckers, media outlets, and restaurants blow us and the element of surprise out of the water."

Truckers had a habit of advising the whole world through their CBs when they came across something as unique and big as an interstate roadblock. Couple that with the local media outlets, due to their starvation for *any* news, blasting announcements of our presence through the airwaves, and most wildlife outlaws would be off and running on the secondary roads hoping to avoid the dragnet. In addition, every eatery for a hundred miles around would have the roadblock on the waitresses' lips as the major topic of conversation for the day.

I told Neill I wanted the operation covered down to the smallest detail such as having free dry ice for the returning hunters to aid in the preservation of their game, working with a local county judge, and having ambulance or emergency management personnel on site if possible. That way I could eliminate the congressional letters growling about meat spoilage, and with a judge close at hand, I would have a way to settle issues on site if the offenders cared to do so. The presence of emergency management personnel and an ambulance is self-explanatory. "Have Mike contact the state patrol as well and make sure we get all the clearances necessary to shut down eastward-flowing traffic on I-80. In fact, invite those chaps to the party as well. I'll bet my bottom dollar they would love to do some of their own work—vehicle inspections, drug searches, DUI inspections—if given the opportunity."

"OK, Chief, I'll get on it," he replied with a big smile of anticipation. Good old Neill, I thought. Never a challenge too big or too difficult for him to tackle. Setting up a major interstate wildlife check station like the one I just described takes anywhere from six months to a year of preparation, requires about 250 officers, and takes about $75,000 to pay for the essentials (excluding salary, per diem, etc.)! Yet here was an officer ready to tackle a myriad of assigned problems, the weight of which would have buckled the shoulders of Hercules. As I got up to leave Neill's office for other fields of battle, I had to grin. Hercules and Neill had about the same build. ... No wonder Neill had never *once* let me down during the tenure of our professional relationship.

IN FEBRUARY 1995, I spent my weekends with a chainsaw cutting standing timber on a neighbor's mountain property. The work was hard, done in eight inches of snow and at an elevation of about 8,200 feet. However, I had cut timber as a young man for Meadow Valley Lumber Company in Plumas County in California and rather enjoyed the back-breaking work. It made me work many muscle groups I normally did not get the opportunity to exercise as a senior Service law enforcement administrator in the regional office, or a "tweed-backed bureaucrat," as John Cooper, my senior resident agent for South Dakota, used to call us desk-bound supervisors. I find his words of yesteryear ironic today. Cooper, as these words are written, is the director for the South Dakota Game Fish and Parks, or one of those same "tweed-backed bureaucrats" he always growled about.

Soon I had many trees down and bucked up, ready to be hauled up the mountain for my following winter's wood. A call to my two strapping sons, Rich and Chris, and son-in-law, Myles Jackson, brought the promise of help in hauling the wood from the forest to my home in Evergreen. An added bonus was my daughter-in-law Lisa, Chris's wife. She is a true outdoorswoman, and no stranger to hard work. She considers herself just another part of the family and as good as any man in it. If that included hauling wood up the mountainside, so be it. You single men out there should be so lucky as to land such a classy woman for your wife and best friend! Not to mention, Lisa is a crack rifle, pistol, and shotgun shot in her role as a hunter as well.

Come the day of the wood-hauling adventure, I had the whole clan at the house for a real lumberjack's breakfast. Fried spuds loaded with garlic and onions, seasoned side pork, vegetable and cheese omelets, homemade bread (my bride makes the best in the world), crispy bacon, orange juice, sweet rolls, milk, and coffee rounded out the fare. After breakfast, we headed up the mountain into the snow and the logs began to fly. The process was simple: place a wet, heavy, six-to-eight-foot section of log on your shoulder and haul it thirty to fifty yards up the mountainside to a waiting pickup. Load the pickup until the springs show signs of leveling out and then drive it down the mountain to be off-loaded in my backyard. This process was repeated numerous times until lunch, and then off the mountain came the "loggers" for a noonday meal even heartier than breakfast.

After lunch, back up on the mountain we went to hit it even harder. Now, in those days I was still a whole man, not falling apart as I am today. It always became somewhat of a contest for my two young sons, all six foot and six foot seven of them, to try the old man on for size. Of course, the old man would see that the challenge didn't go un-answered! With that, the two young bucks would get their come-uppance and I would sport a grin worthy of the "king of the hill." During one of those proving moments, I was hauling a green Douglas fir, butt-cut log, weighing in the neighborhood of 350 to 400 pounds. True, it was a *load,* but I was determined to show my young sons that old Dad still had it in him. The hillside was steeper than the side of a cow's face, the snow was troublesome, and the elevation was beginning to take its toll on my fifty-four-year-old, overweight, and out-of-shape carcass. But I was determined to carry the log to the truck or hell could freeze over. Both boys and Myles were eyeballing the old man, and I could see in their eyes the recognition that I still had it. Then, as if someone had thrown a switch, every ounce of energy left my body and I was forced to slump against a handy tree to keep from dropping the log. Baffled, I called out to Rich as he passed by and said, "Son, I just ran out of gas. Take this log off my shoulder, will you?" Without ef-fort he lifted the log off my shoulder and hauled it to the waiting pickup, some thirty yards away. I just leaned against the tree for a few moments, got my breath, and then headed for the truck, advising the crew that the wood-hauling was over for the day. It had been a hard day for all with a lot of wood (sixteen pickup loads) being moved, and the crew, including me, was ready for it to end. Without another word, the tired crew headed down the mountain. None of us realized the impact of that day, *especially me.* … In retrospect, I know that that moment of losing all my strength was none other than one of two heart attacks I have experienced to date … no pain, just no power. Welcome to the world of a diabetic, as I was soon to discover, when it came to heart pain or the absence thereof.

IN JUNE 1995, I underwent my annual law enforcement physical. Dr. V. J., my cardiologist, ran the usual thallium stress EKG test, and a cloud flew across his face as I performed on the treadmill. When I finished the stress portion of the test, he hustled me off to the second part under the machine that "dissected" the heart, taking pictures all the way. At the end of the test, Dr. V. J. told me he had seen a small abnormality in my tests and would be in touch once he got the final results from the images. Two days later he called to say there appeared to be blockages in the arteries leading to the back side of my heart and he wanted me to come back so he could do some more tests. The following day found me in the hospital undergoing an angiogram.

Lying on the table as Dr. V. J. explored the extent of the blockages, having gone up through my femoral artery, I can still hear his words. "That artery is 90 percent blocked. These appear to be clear. Let's see how the other one is. That one is 100 percent blocked. *We operate tomorrow!*"

"Whoa, Doc, I don't think so!" I said.

"Yes, I think so," he replied. "This is very serious, and if we don't operate, you are heading for a serious heart attack! With that much blockage you are asking for a heart attack every day you 'roar around' and delay the operation. I will put together a team to do the surgery, but it *really* should be done tomorrow!"

"This is the end of the fiscal year, and there is no way I leave an overworked administrative officer and a buried assistant special agent in charge holding the bag," I forcefully replied.

"Terry, I don't think you understand the gravity of this situation. You are a walking time bomb unless we operate and clear those blockages, *and do so now!* Also, now that you know the extent of the problem, you will stress out even more and place your heart and life at even further risk."

"Doc," I said, "I am *not* going to have surgery until I have my end-of-the-year fiscal affairs at the office in order, and that is that!" Well, to make a long story short, I signed some papers exonerating the hospital from any liability if I folded my tent, if you get my drift, and off to work I went. Dr. V. J. was right, though. Now that I was acutely aware of the problem, my body reacted accordingly, and come time for the operation I was exhausted and ready for the surgery.

However, I used the two weeks after discovery of the blockages and before the surgery wisely. In addition to clearing the administrative and fiscal backlogs, I found myself talking to my two guardian angels and the Fellow they referred me to for the ultimate consultation. I remember clearly that when I asked how things would go, a physical feeling of *absolute peace* swept over me as if I were being painted with a huge "caring" brush. I dismissed from my mind any concerns about the bypass procedure and tried to pass on that feeling of reassurance to my bride and best friend. However, she found it hard to relax and did not until I was ambulatory once again. Hell, now that I think about it, I don't think she has ever stopped worrying about my miserable carcass.

Come the day of the operation, I was at the hospital by seven in the morning after having a great night's sleep. I went through the usual procedure of being shaved—my entire body, that is, with a razor and no shaving cream. Damn, in those days, I had enough body hair for a mountain gorilla, and the shaving exercise was just a prelude to the unpleasantness to come.

Then I met Dr. Young, my highly recommended heart surgeon, for the first time. He was an older chap who shook my hand and then with little fanfare commenced delving into my extensive Service medical records. After a few minutes I said, "Doc, I have to be up and out of here in less than two weeks. I am heading up a major roadblock in Nebraska next month with over 250 officers, and I need to be there. Given the innate sensitivity and uniqueness of that law enforcement operation, it's not something I want to leave to my subordinates, no matter how good they are." Of course, my deputy could have handled it without a pause in the process. He was that good! But when you put a state government in harm's way with an interstate roadblock and all its "warts," you want to have every base covered. If the crap hit the fan, I wanted to be there to iron things out and not dump that problem on my deputy.

The good doctor never moved as he continued reviewing my medical records. I continued, "This is the first time the state of Nebraska has ever undertaken such a large and complex enforcement operation. If things blow up, politically or otherwise, the senior officer needs to be on site because that is where the buck must stop, and I plan on being there."

A few more moments slipped by as the doctor continued examining my medical records as if not hearing my comments and then said without looking up, "That is impossible. You are fifty-five years old, overweight, diabetic, and facing major bypass surgery. I suspect you are looking at a week in the hospital and another six weeks of intensive stay-out-of-the-mainstream-of-life rehabilitation. And that is only if everything goes well."

Feeling the frustration of that revelation wash over me like a wave on a Pacific beach, I made another run at the problem. "Doc," I said with a big yet hopeful grin, "if you were anything but a large animal veterinarian, you would have me out of here in five days and on my way to recovery!"

He looked up from my records over the tops of his half glasses at the big-mouthed shaved rat lying in the bunk before him. Staring hard but with a twinkle in his eyes, he got a big grin and said, "All right, if you want to be wired for sound I will see you get your wish. And you will remember this day and that smart-assed remark every time you attempt to go through a metal detector at an airport because you will set off every bell in the place." With that he grinned, as did I. At least we had an understanding, up to that point anyway.

ANOTHER DOCTOR placed a shunt in my left shoulder just moments before they wheeled me into the operating area, as I waved to my bride and told her one last time that I loved her. I have never seen her look so worried and forlorn. As the nurse wheeled me into the operating room, I noticed it was at least 20 to 30 degrees colder than the rest of the hospital. The room was a beehive of activity. Several doctors shifted me from the comfort of the gurney onto an operating table. That was a trip! The actual operating table was nothing more than a cold plastic table not more than eighteen to twenty inches wide and raised at the sides to keep one from sliding off, *or the slippery blood from dripping onto the floor!* My rather generous frame hung over on both sides as I tried to center my mass and hold on to my dignity. As someone fussed over the shunt in my shoulder, I wisecracked to one of the nurses that they had better get more operating tools than what I saw lying on the nearby table. I suggested a chainsaw, shovel, and maybe even a crowbar. That was the last goddamned thing I remember! The chap fooling with my shunt must have given me something to knock me out, and he did! There was none of that counting back from ten, just blackness, and I do mean right now!

The next thing I remember was total blackness and an awareness of what seemed like thousands of tubes crammed down my throat, making it so difficult to breathe that I had to tell myself to take it easy and not gag. If I did, I was in a world of hurt with no place for the tubes and puke to go at the same time. Then I remember the sensation of my hand being held by my wife and her soothing voice telling me to lie still. Still unable to see anything except black and continuing to struggle slightly with all the tubes down my throat, I heard her ask, "Is anything the matter?"

Knowing I couldn't speak, I raised my arm and made a writing motion with my hand.

Donna said, "What does he mean?"

I heard my son Chris say, "He wants something to write on."

Damn, I thought. I hadn't wanted any of my kids present during the operation or my time in the recovery room. They didn't need my worries on top of theirs. I had told them all to stay at home and let their mom fill them in on the details. Yet there was Chris. He had just changed law enforcement agencies, and I knew he had not worked long enough to accrue any leave. I discovered later that Chris had a supervisor named Lt. Bill Black who, when approached by Chris with news of his dad's rather serious impending operation, told him to go to the hospital and be with his family because he would be no good on the street if his mind was elsewhere. They would work out the leave situation afterward. That supervisor sure knew what he was talking about and understood the science and art of supervision. Chris would go down the lit barrel of a cannon for that man today without a backward glance.

I felt a pencil thrust into my hand and a tablet placed under the pencil. Writing in the "dark," I made the symbol for oxygen, "O_2." I was still gagging on the tubes placed in my throat and continued to find myself struggling to breathe, so much so that I was concerned I would overload my just-repaired heart with my struggles for air. I heard Donna say, "What does this mean?"

Then I heard the unmistakable voice of Fran Marcoux, chief of law enforcement for the Colorado Division of Wildlife: "Oh, he is making the chemical symbol for oxygen. He is saying he needs more oxygen."

How the hell did Fran get into the recovery room? I thought, surprised at his presence. He was not a family member but a very close friend. Not that I cared, mind you, for he was and continues to be one of my best friends. But I understood hospital rules, and they just didn't let anyone in the recovery room after major surgery unless they were family. I found out later that Fran had told the doctor he was my brother. How is that for a dear and close friend? He wanted to be sure he was there for Donna because he knew of my wish not to have my kids missing work to be there. Donna and I have not forgotten that act of generosity, and to this day Fran and his wife, Di, are among our closest circle of friends!

Donna quickly asked the nurse if I could have more oxygen, and she answered that I was getting 100 percent at the time and could receive no more. She told us this gagging reflex was normal and would soon pass as my body began to recover, and it did as my vision gradually returned. I reassured my wife and supporting crew that I was well and ready to go, using my eyes and facial expressions. Fran and Chris thoughtfully took Donna off to get some food and rest, and I began to examine my surroundings. I was in a large room tended by at least two very attentive nurses. Looking over my feet, I could see a woman in another bed who appeared to be struggling, if not starting to die. Another chap who had also just had heart surgery was to my immediate right. He too appeared to be struggling with the tubes in his throat and was moving around in pain in his bed. Farther to my right was another man fresh out of surgery who appeared to be doing all right. Then I noticed the woman whom I could see over my feet struggling once more, with fountains of blood foaming out her mouth. Both nurses rushed to her aid, but to no avail. She passed over "the great divide" and was soon wheeled out of the room. Then the fellow next to me started going wild and jerking around in his bed. Since there was a curtain between the two of us, I could not see what his problem was, but he was soon rushed back into surgery, and that was the last I saw of that chap.

Man, I didn't like this place, and just as soon as the nurse removed the tubes from my throat so I could talk, I gave her an earful. "Get me the hell out of here, please. I don't like this place with all the dying and struggling going on."

She just smiled and said, "Just as soon as you get out of bed so I can change the bloody sheets and then get back into it, you can be on your way."

Hell, that was no problem I thought; out of my way, lady! *Wrong!* Remember that my chest was split open from just below my Adam's apple to just inches above my navel. After the operation, that mass of spongy bone and tissue representing the chest had been sewn back together, and there I lay with two tubes hanging out of my belly that had been inserted into the lower portions of my lungs to act as drains. Without thinking, I started to prop myself up using my arms as I normally would. *Wrong!* In an instant pain shot through my chest, regardless of the morphine, as my arms pulled on the stitches from the incision. I felt the recently separated bone grating and the stitches starting to separate! Man, you talk about letting go and falling back into bed. *Wrong again!* After heart surgery you don't just let yourself fall back into bed, jarring the incision and loose-fitting bones. Damn, I was in so much pain, it even hurt to breathe! I found myself too weak and full of pain to move, much less rise up and get out of bed. Letting my thoughts of escaping the recovery room simmer for a while, I lay there trying to ignore the pain.

"Well," asked the nurse, "what will it be? A big guy lying there all day, or are you going to get out of bed?"

"I don't know how," I growled through clenched teeth.

"All right, let me tell you how. First, like a big worm, scoot your hind end down the bed to the middle. Then, using your thigh and remaining gut muscles, swing your legs over the side of the bed and raise your torso all in the same motion. Now, this will hurt, but the pain is less than childbirth, so let's have a go at it."

Damn, I had to love her graveyard humor. Carefully scooting my tail end down the bed, I became aware of the pulling weight of my arms against the stitches, and brother, that wasn't fun. Finally getting to the middle of the bed, I slowly lowered my legs over the side and, once anchored against the side of the bed by the back of my knees, jacked my torso up so I was sitting on the edge of the bed. No matter how carefully I moved, it hurt like hell! Every movement seemed to be tearing out the stitches, and the bones in my chest were constantly *and noticeably* grating against one another. When that happened, I would take in a searing breath, and the pain would belt me again for expanding my chest against the incision. No matter what I did, the pain was constant and so intense that the tears just ran down my face and across my somewhat bloodied, newly hairless chest. When I finally got it all together and slid my hind end to the edge of the bed, I saw that my feet were still four inches from the floor. "I need a footstool, please," I told the dinky nurse standing at the ready to catch me if I screwed up.

"That wasn't part of the deal," she answered sternly. "You have to get off the bed by yourself and sit in this chair so I can change the sheets. Then you have to crawl back into the bed by yourself. With that, you will be ready to leave for your own room."

Damn, this nurse had to be a retired Marine drill instructor! Realizing I was trapped, I scooted my hind end to the very edge of the bed and, after a lot of thought on the pain that was to follow, dropped the remaining few inches to the floor! *Wrong!* The impact damn near made me pass out. The nurse grabbed my sagging frame and held me up until I recovered enough for the next test. Gritting my teeth and finding that even that hurt my chest, I nodded that I was ready. Damned if I was going to let her beat me at this game. Shuffling over to the chair, I turned around and, using my hands and arms, grabbed the arms and started to lower myself. *Goddamned wrong!* I had forgotten that my arms were attached to my torso, and using them only pulled the stitches in my chest apart. I never forgot that again! I released my grip as the pain knifed through my chest and my lead ass sailed down into the chair, landing with a *whump!* The impact of hitting the seat again almost caused me to pass out. My nurse never said a thing as she changed my sheets and pillowcases. She had seen this many times before, and I guess I was doing all right since I was not dead or heading back to the operating room. But my oh my, what a price I was paying. I even allowed myself the thought that this whole problem could probably have been avoided if I had eaten bark and twigs for my many meals as a conservation officer instead of greasy hamburgers. ... Well, almost but not quite!

Once the sheets were replaced, the nurse happily said, "Let's go. Get up out of the chair and back into bed."

There was no way! My hind end was only inches from the floor in that cheap-ass chair, and there was no way I could get out. Since I couldn't use my arms without tearing my chest apart, how the hell was I to get up? I thought as my eyes got the size of dinner plates. Walking over to me, she said, "Now, this is where we separate the big boys from the also-rans. You have to use your thigh muscles alone and lift yourself up out of the chair. Just your thighs, now."

Knowing she must know what she was talking about and not wanting to make the mistake of using my arms for support again, I put the power to my thighs, and surprisingly, I came up out of the chair. Not without pain, mind you, because any constriction of muscles pulled on the stitches. But what I experienced was manageable. Hurrah for me! I thought. I got this thing whipped! Then I looked at the side of the bed, which was four inches taller than my hind end with my feet on the floor! "Do I get a stepstool now?" I asked hopefully.

"No," came my Marine drill inspector's firm voice. "You have to get into bed by yourself or stay here until you can."

Now she was pissing me off! "How the goddamned hell do I lift my 300-pound ass from the floor into the bed when I have at least forty feet difference between me and the bunk?" I growled.

"Simple," she said. "You get alongside the bunk and, while I hold the opposite side of the bed, roll in."

Yeah, I thought. Just roll in and mash those split chest plates against one another once more. ... Figuring she was right, though, and I wasn't getting it done standing there in that damned open hospital gown five sizes too small to cover my five-sizes-too-large hind end, I dropped my shoulder and rolled. *I would rather have been shot!* Passing out from the pain for a moment, I awakened to her voice congratulating me on escaping the recovery room. Funny, at that moment I would have gladly taken a bullet behind the ear.

I spent the next five days in my hospital room on the road to recovery. That too was an adventure: being poked and prodded by every doctor and every training class, seemingly never being allowed to sleep, not being hungry enough to eat for three days (that didn't hurt my carcass any, causing me to lose thirty-six pounds), not being able to move any which way without instant pain, and having several surreal experiences.

The first I remember was a highly enhanced sense of smell. I had the sensory abilities of a dog! People could walk by in the hallway, and in a few moments I could smell the garlic they had eaten on their pizza the night before! I could identify doctors who came into the room by their body soap, mouthwash, toothpaste, food smells from their last meals, and so on. It was so bad that I could tell the ladies bringing my meals what was under a metal lid before they lifted it to reveal the contents. This went on for five days, and my appetite went to zero, making it difficult for me to eat anything. Finally the nurses fixed me some sugar-free shakes and I was on the road to recovery in the eatery department.

Other experiences were of a more potentially lethal nature. One night a nurse came in and placed a bag of fluid on the holding stand next to the bed. Then she inserted the needle leading from the bag into the shunt on my shoulder. Understanding my rights as a patient and having refused any painkillers except Tylenol after the first day, I asked what she was giving me. The nurse said it was something good for me and had been ordered by my doctor. Persisting, I asked once more what it was. "It is a very strong medicine for your blood infection, Mr. Jones."

"Whoa!" I yelled, wishing I hadn't responded so vigorously because of the ensuing chest pain. "I am not Mr. Jones!"

"This is room 12, isn't it?" she remarked casually as she continued to fiddle with the device to regulate the fluid now flowing into my shoulder.

"Hell no!" I bellowed. "This is room 16!"

"Are you sure?" she asked with a panicky look, immediately stopping what she was doing with the bottle of fluid.

"You're goddamned right I am sure," I answered in a voice designed to wake up my wingmates! With that she speedily unhooked everything and left my room in a flash without another word. I never saw that nurse again. From then on, my two guardian angels were instructed to never doze while I was sleeping.

The following day at about three in the morning, I awoke to the fiddling of another nurse hooking me up to another bag of fluid. I asked what she was giving me, and she said it was medicine to alleviate the pain of my stomach cancer. Having been there once before, I didn't take long to convince her I was not Mr. Panston and she had the wrong room. I never saw that nurse again either! Thank God for a couple of alert guardian angels.

I was honored by my many friends with hundreds of cards and enough flowers to make the Denver Botanic Gardens blush with envy. In fact, I ran out of space in my room and finally had the nurses distribute the overflow of flowers to less fortunate guests in the hospital. I had so much color and greenery in the room that all I needed was a gibbon swinging from some of the plants to be right at home in a jungle. But the smells and colors were great distractions as I passed the time waiting to heal. Nothing helps the healing process quite like one's friends.

Dr. Young, bless his soul, did wire me for sound, and five-and-a-half days after surgery, I was on my way home. I spent my next four days with a still very worried bride, and then she was called back to her classroom because her student teacher was making a mess of it. The next day, after she had left for work and didn't know what I was doing, I did my old walk of two-and-a-half miles up the mountain (slowly, mind you) ending it with a grin. The next day I cleaned up, put on my bullet-proof vest, and went to work without the knowledge of my wife (or my doctor). Why the bullet-proof vest? Just in case I was in a car wreck, I didn't want my still far-from-healed breastbone striking the steering wheel. The vest was designed to whisk away force, and that was why I wore it. It was a bitch, though! I still couldn't carry any kind of weight on my shoulders and a twenty-pound vest sure made it painful, not to mention putting it on with arms that I could hardly lift. But I put up with the shortness of breath and abject pain to be on the safe side.

Back at work, I was moving damn slowly, but mentally I was on the go and it felt great to be back in the saddle. I still remember Neill's look of surprise when I walked in the door just eleven days after my surgery. "What the hell are you doing back?" he bellowed in surprise.

"Well, the last time I looked I was still the boss," I uttered, trying not to piss off my chest.

"Damn, you can't come back to work this soon after heart surgery!" he exclaimed.

"Well, I am, and I plan on staying just as long as the pain allows." With that, I carried on, grinning. *Six weeks' rehabilitation, my last part over the fence!*

Don't get me wrong. Those next few days were something else in terms of pain, especially when I stumbled or someone slapped me on the back in celebration of seeing me around after my successful by-pass surgery. ... Against my wife's wishes and without the doctor's knowledge, I continued working a nine-hour day at the office, surrounded by a very loyal and caring staff.

NEILL HAD DONE his interstate roadblock work well, and October 24 found me on the interstate driving to North Platte, Nebraska. The roadblock and wildlife check station had been set up to run October 25–27 in the brand-new Brady Rest Area just east of North Platte on Interstate 80. Special agents from five Service regions; support staff from the Denver regional office; my law enforcement staff; Refuge officers; Forensic's lab personnel from Ashland and Nebraska; Wildlife enforcement officers from Fort Carson; and Fish and Game officers from the states of Colorado, Louisiana, Montana, Nevada, Utah, Wyoming, Kansas, Idaho, Wisconsin, North and South Dakota, and Nebraska had gathered to conduct the soon-to-be thousands of searches. Rounding out that number of officers were troopers from the Nebraska State Patrol, Immigration and Naturalization Service officers, and the U.S. Marshal's people. In total, 289 law enforcement officers and staff gathered to assist the American hunter to understand the value of our national heritage and the rules of the road.

The evening of October 24 found all team members gathered at the Camino Inn in North Platte for an operational briefing and general get-together. I noticed several sets of eyebrows raised upon discovery of my presence so soon after major surgery. Many old friends were there to greet me, and I found no finer medicine. However, the next few days were to prove rather daunting. In fact, this turned out to be the toughest damn roadblock I ever worked.

Early on the chilly morning of October 25, I got out of my patrol vehicle at the Brady Rest Area. I met Agent Mike Damico and asked him to show me the roadblock preparations. After a few minutes, it became apparent that Mike had done one hell of a job in setting up the on-site infrastructure. The rest stop was brand new and not yet open to the public. It was spacious and one of the best roadblock locations I had seen in my twenty-five years of service. Mike had seen that the ten individual check stations would be well staffed and safely separated from traffic, especially when the hunters or fishermen worked their way out after being processed. There was ample space for any size vehicle to park, and the special areas for interviews, evidence documentation, and administration were close at hand. Every detail had been accounted for, and I failed to find one omission that caused me any heartburn. Neill, Manny, and Mike had done an outstanding job setting up Nebraska's first interstate roadblock. All three officers were later to receive substantial Special Achievement Awards for their outstanding performance, accomplished *in addition* to all their other duties. I felt that the timing was about a week off, at Nebraska's request (the roadblock should have been one week earlier, but the state's pheasant opener had gotten in the way), but other than that, everything appeared to be in top working condition.

There is a method to our madness when setting up an interstate roadblock. Usually we give the hunters five days after the major hunting seasons open, figuring that after five days of living out in the bush and letting your game hang without refrigeration, you have to hit the road to avoid spoilage of the animal's carcass—or your own. By having the roadblock in place at that time, you are able to net most of the major hunting and fishing traffic, sorting out the outlaws in the process.

That day, after an hour in the morning's cold looking over the operation, I was beginning to experience intense chest pains, especially in the area of the incision. Every time I took a step, it was as if someone were inserting and turning a white-hot knife in my chest. It was pretty damn obvious I was not healed enough to play a game of touch football just yet. ... Wanting not to miss the planned event, yet in no position to ignore my surging tides of pain, I excused myself without explanation and shuffled off to my patrol truck. Crawling into the front seat with difficulty, I downed a handful of Tylenol and through wet eyes waited for the burning to subside. In about twenty minutes the pain subsided somewhat, and I realized that the 29-degree cold was raising hell with the incision. Reaching into the back seat of the truck as I always did, and instantly realizing I shouldn't have stretched out my heavy arm like that, I retrieved a heavier winter coat that I always carried for emergencies and crawled into it. For several long moments the new coat did nothing to help the pain, but as it began to warm with my body heat, I began to feel better. Feeling that I had that problem squared away, I stepped out of my truck in time to see the officers arriving for the first of three daily eight-hour shifts. Officers from all walks of life, thrown into unfamiliar inspection teams and led by a basically unknown officer, ambled to their assigned check stations as if nothing were out of the ordinary. Looking through that sea of faces, I recognized over 90 percent as officers with whom I had long-standing associations. Every one of them was an experienced professional, and all knew their jobs thoroughly. Out West, they would be called "good hands." It was like watching Roman legions move into the battle line, and like the Roman legions, this group was bound by proud traditions of heritage, duty, honor, and brotherhood. Pain be damned, I was proud of those officers and their support troops. That feeling gave me the wherewithal to move among them as if everything were all right, even though my chest still advised caution.

Neill had assigned me as a roving supervisor without any immediate responsibility other than to put out fires on the inspection line, so I headed toward the middle of the inspection area. Moments after opening up the inspection stations we had clients, and soon everyone was unloading hunting outfits and checking returning hunters. Piles of deer were tossed limply over each other for closer inspection; freezers were unloaded and their contents examined; piles of pheasants were counted; plastic bags of fish and fish fillets were added up and examined for evidence of species; handfuls of licenses and tags were reviewed for validity and proper ownership; elk were moved with difficulty to check sex and tags; dozens of wet ducks and geese were unloaded for counting and species identification; hindquarters of big game were examined by forensic scientists in an attempt to determine sex from the bone structure of the pelvis; and so it went.

Shuffling slowly up and down the lines of busy officers, I watched for quality of performance, legality of searches, identification and classification of all manner of fish and game being examined, and the handling of the hunters. Several times I was called to assist in the identification of a waterfowl species because of my expertise in that arena, but mostly I remained as a roving trouble shooter. I was very pleased with the officers' professional performance and their handling of the issues that arose. It was beginning to warm up, and the area of my incision was feeling much better. I still couldn't move quickly, lift anything with a weighty payload, or rapidly turn and twist, but my mind was on the alert and being used frequently to sort out difficulties among the hunters and officers, so I was grateful to be in working order.

As a tie-in with our operation, officers from the Nebraska Highway Patrol were running random vehicle safety checks and the INS officers were checking the documents of possible foreigners snared in the roadblock. They too were very professional in their inspections and shortly were seizing quantities of drugs and arresting numerous illegal aliens. I-80 is such a major west-east passage that it made sense that such illegal traffic would be moving along with other commerce, and if the piles of seized drugs and groups of handcuffed individuals were any indication, those groups of officers were paying for their gas and oil on that day's outing.

A few hours into the roadblock, I heard a lot of hell-raising at Station 6. Moving in that direction, I discovered a hunter standing in a large homemade high-walled wooden trailer yelling at the officers below. He was mad at being stopped in another state than the one in which he had hunted, felt the officers in Nebraska had no authority to check the game he had killed in Colorado, and was upset over having to uncover his meat with the possibility of it spoiling in the day's sun. The inspection site team leader (from Nebraska) told the hunter that since he objected to being checked in Nebraska by a Nebraska officer, he would be checked by a Colorado officer. The grouchy lad just looked on in amazement as the Colorado officer began the inspection. It was plain from his expression that he had not anticipated encountering a Colorado officer in Nebraska. I stepped in, identifying myself as a supervisor, and asked the befuddled man how much dry ice he figured he might need to get his meat safely home. He mumbled, "Oh, I guess about five pounds would do it." Calling the dry ice team on my radio, I ordered seven pounds to be sent to

Station 6. Soon the Honda ATV arrived with the dry ice, and the inspection team officers (knowing I couldn't lift anything that high yet) handed the blocks of ice to the hunter. With another look of disbelief his grumbling ceased entirely, the meat was reloaded, dry ice was placed appropriately, and he was on his way, but not before he filled out a customer evaluation sheet on his impressions of the wildlife check station (as everyone was required to do once the inspection was completed). Another congressional letter averted, I thought happily as I walked off to another altercation between a hunter and his inspection team.

That altercation was a jewel! The hunter was in possession of a mule deer without any tags (required by law) that he claimed had been given to him by a farmer friend in Colorado. Knowing he was in Nebraska and figuring the Nebraska lads didn't know up from down about Colorado laws, he folded his arms across his chest as if to say, "Take that and figure it out!" The Nebraska team leader turned the inspection over to the Colorado officer on his team, and when confronted with a Colorado officer knowledgeable in Colorado laws now asking the questions, the hunter began to stammer and change his story. "Well, my farmer friend lives on the Utah-Colorado border, and I think the deer may have been killed in Utah. Yeah, now that I think of it, the deer was killed in Utah." The hunter regained his composure and smugly recrossed his arms as if to say, "Figure that one, you Colorado tule creeper." Faced with that change in story, the team leader quickly and calmly called forward the Utah officer on his team to take over the interview. Now the hunter was really in a pickle, as his body language graphically illustrated. However, he was fast on his feet and said, "I lied, officer; the deer was legally killed in Idaho by a farmer. I don't know why I came up with those stories, but it really came from Idaho. I guess I was being a smartass. I don't suppose there is an Idaho officer here, is there?" he asked.

"Nope. Not on this team," the Nebraska team leader calmly replied. For a moment hope flashed across the man's face and his smugness started to return, but it stopped short when the team leader added, "However, there is an Idaho officer on Team 2, and I will call him." With that, the call was made on the handheld handi-talki and the hunter's illegal deer was finally run to ground after a chase through three states. It was an Idaho deer, taken and possessed illegally and obviously moved across state lines. Little did the illegal shooter realize that once an animal is illegally taken or possessed in one state and moved across state lines or onto the interstate highway system to enable movement across state lines, that is a violation of a federal statute, the Lacey Act. No matter how far or hard that man ran, the law and the dead mule deer would have their day in court because every state officer there was also a deputized federal officer. One thousand dollars later, the smile was removed from the man's face and the arrogance from his walk. And the dead mule deer now seemed to be wearing the trace of a smile. ...

After a while things quieted down other than just mass work efforts to clear the incoming hunter traffic, and I was able to move over to the state trooper section in time to see its drug dogs going over a car as the two worried occupants stood off to one side with long faces. Soon the dog made all kinds of digging motions in the back seat. After the back seat was removed, twelve neatly packed bags of drugs saw the light of day. The two men were quickly arrested, searched, and placed in the back of a waiting patrol car as other officers documented and seized the evidence. This roadblock is having the desired effect, I thought as I responded to a call to meet some dignitaries in the inspection area set up for such administrators to overview the process without interrupting it.

Then and periodically throughout the day, I met many Nebraska public officials and members of the press, all trying to understand the value of what was going on in front of their eyes. For all of them, from concerned local officials to representatives of the governor's office, I explained the history and organization of the operation along with its usefulness in educating the American hunter. As always, a little handholding was good even at the senior levels of government.

Come four in the afternoon, my shift was over. My feet hurt, the weight of my arms was causing me a lot of pain in the top portion of the incision, and beating the pavement for the previous eight hours had taken a toll. However, I had a policy that Neill and I always worked a double shift in such ventures, and today was no different. I went to the truck for several more Tylenol and headed back to the line. On my way back, I noticed a lot of officers from other agencies and divisions arriving for the next shift. Not thinking anything of it since such shift changes were part of the plan, I resumed my place along with several other senior supervisors for my second eight-hour shift. Looking across the sea of faces, I checked for my deputy and was pleased to find Neill on line for the second shift as well. God-damned good officer, I thought. Another quick check showed that all my senior resident agents (first-line supervisors) were also starting their second shifts. That dedication by my tired officers brought a smile to my face and heart. Then I recalled a news report that had been described to me by my agent in Casper. It seemed that Wayne LaPierre, executive vice president for the National Rifle Association (NRA), had found occasion to refer to federal officers as "jack-booted thugs." That epithet angered not only Dominic but many other agents in the squad who canceled their NRA memberships. I thought it was too bad that the NRA had to publicly attack fine officers like Neill and the others. Without them holding the "thin green line," folks like Wayne would never have a critter to pursue in fair chase or a wonder-ful game dinner after the hunt. To my knowledge, Wayne has never retracted that poorly thought-out statement made years ago.

I noticed that the teams at every inspection station seemed to have almost doubled in size. A quick check showed that to be true. Instead of the previous shift's five- or six-person teams, there were now ten to twelve officers for each inspection site. Realizing this overload would soon introduce burnout to the ranks, I hailed Mike Damico, my on-the-ground organizer. "Mike, we have too many men on line. Why did you schedule so many officers for this shift?"

Mike just looked at me for a moment with intense eyes. Mike is a huge man, with a massive full beard that makes him look even more imposing. In fact, I used to call him "Bear" because of his size. But no gentler good Christian man ever lived! Without batting an eye, he said, "Boss, you are still here. The men, knowing you are going to work a second shift with your recent heart surgery and all, feel that if you can continue in the sorry state you are in, so can they!"

For a moment I was shocked. I had never figured on that show of support from a tired bunch of officers who had stood out in the sun and wind on the hard pavement for the previous eight hours, espe-cially in light of the fact that they had been doing all the heavy work digging through hundreds of vehicles and carcasses to conduct their inspections! All I could do was look down that line of officers look-ing back at me and smile a "thank you." The violating sons of bitches, even though they usually have us outmanned and outgunned, had *really* better watch their last parts over the fence if officers as fine as those standing on that line that day are watching them! Jack-booted thugs, my ass!

That first Nebraska interstate roadblock went as many others had gone in other parts of the country in years past. Many people to talk to, lots of vehicles of every shape and size to inspect, officers responding to hundreds of questions, evidence to seize, prisoners to transport, numerous explanations to the hunting and fishing public, interviews of suspects, political hands to hold, and citations to issue. About 2,500 hunters living in forty-two states were checked during that short period. They had been hunting or fishing in nineteen different states. Hundreds of animals, birds, and fish were inspected for compliance with various state Fish and Game requirements and over $28,000 in fines were collected from those accustomed to skating on the dark side. For every citation issued, probably another ten violators got an ass-chewing for minor violations, were allowed to rectify their errors, and were sent on their way without being cited as they could have been. Education was the better part of the equation here rather than a burning reminder in the form of a citation. In addition, 107 non-wildlife violations were detected, from the possession of illegal firearms all the way to the illegal possession of drugs. In fact, over ninety pounds of marijuana were seized, as were twelve vehicles and seventy-five illegal aliens during that three-day operation. It took only thirteen minutes to inspect a returning hunter or fisher if no violations were detected. An inspection can be that efficient when a professional crew of officers can swarm over the vehicle and through the paperwork. That period went to fifty minutes when violations were discovered. As I mentioned earlier, all hunters were requested to fill out a survey regarding the experience and their treatment. Of the 1,035 surveys collected, 1,003 described fair and courteous treatment. Eleven travelers indicated they had been treated unfairly and discourteously, and the balance had no comment.

I have always felt that inspection stations of this nature are not only a valuable enforcement tool but a gentle reminder to the sportsmen and sportswomen of the nation that our natural resources are not only valuable but limited. Unregulated hunting and fishing of those resources will do nothing but drive most species into extinction.

Therefore, the long arm of the law is not only needed but supported by history. Regulated hunting and fishing will strengthen the ethics and awareness of those participating in the sports as well as providing a historical context for those to come. In the meantime, those who think that once they hit the freeways they are immune from the law have a lesson to learn. An interstate roadblock, one of their worst nightmares, can and will appear in the strangest of places. When that happens, the chickens with square faces come home to roost. Even those who abide by the laws of the land have a lesson to learn—the lesson that the men and women of the "thin green line," no matter how far that line is stretched, will always be there for them. Those officers are giving up their todays so others can have their tomorrows with their children and grandchildren.

As it turned out, this was the last roadblock I ever worked. It was like all the rest in that officers from all walks of life were able to work together and learn from each other. They made new friendships and strengthened their belief in what their professional and personal lives stood for. The American hunter also came to understand what the effort was all about and had a chance to meet some of the finest officers in the land. For me, it was one of the toughest damn roadblocks I ever worked because I finally realized that I was mortal and the end of my professional career was nigh. Each painful step I took made reminded me of those facts. But after almost thirty years of hard work, I finally began to see that I was not alone. There were plenty of other officers out there willing to lay everything on the line. Not enough in real numbers to do the job as it needed doing, but enough just as dedicated to the moment and the world of wildlife as I.

Through the pain and passage of time, I came to realize that my moment had come ... and gone. "Summer" was over, and I was now waiting for my next assignment. I only hoped it would be as good as the last.

eight

Dogs

THERE IS SOMETHING beautifully unique and grand about dogs. Unlike cats, who just make good rifle and pistol targets, they are loyal to a fault, understanding, honest, and always eager to share in your life experiences—the good and bad—while never finding fault. They are always ready to go with you at a moment's notice and are crushed if they discover they are not included in your peregrinations. Their desire to please is far superior to that quality in humankind, and in most cases they really *are* your best friends. Sporting dogs eagerly share the lousy weather and your poor shooting, bad temper, and forgetfulness, all of which is forgiven in an instant if you share half a venison sandwich previously dropped in the mud of your duck blind.

God didn't have a plan for this species because He didn't need one. He knew we humans, screwed up as we are, would need just such a critter as a sidekick to lend balance to our lives. Who says God isn't all-knowing? I wonder what kind of dog He has? (Notice I didn't say cat.)

In thirty-two years of wildlife law enforcement, in addition to my one and only dog, a Labrador retriever named Shadow, I have met many other types and characters of dogs. And in many instances, directly or indirectly, I became part of their life stories. Their tales (no pun intended) are humorous, outrageous, unbelievable, or sad. But all of them represent elements of the world of dogs. Their stories are a lot like the others in my series of books—a mix of everything from the best to the worst, all with a flavor of what has been sown and reaped.

Now that I think about it in the quiet of my office, it is almost as if dogs are from another planet. Maybe Pluto, eh? The following dog stories are from my travels trying to keep the world of wildlife intact so your children may enjoy it as much as those who came before us.

Dim Eyes, an Old Dog Named Shadow, and Bright Memories

IN THE SUMMER of 1966 I was working deer spotlighters (an illegal night-hunting practice using a high-intensity light to illuminate the animal) along the boundaries of the Hoopa Indian Reservation in northern California. Working alone as a rookie game warden in that kind of dangerous environment was probably mistake number one. But wildlife law enforcement is historically short-handed and under-funded because of poor leadership and questionable politics at the highest levels. Bottom line, if you did your job the right way, most of the time you were in the outback by your lonesome. Truth be known, if the American people had a proportionate number of penal officers protecting their cities as wildlife officers protecting their natural resources, they would pitch a bitch heard clear to Mars. That's probably one reason why wildlife officers are injured or killed at a significantly higher rate than any other kind of law enforcement officer (based on FBI statistics). Bet you didn't know that, did you? Think of that next time one of your loved ones wants to be a conservation officer, or you are checked by one of those hardworking men or women on the "thin green line." They deserve your praise and understanding, not condemnation. To my way of thinking, protecting the future of your national heritage is just as important as protecting your soul. In both instances, you have only one turn in the barrel. ...

Off my high horse and back to my story. My inexperience had led me to select a location in the bottom of a mountainous area dotted with springs, meadows, and an abundance of fat Columbian black-tailed deer. Unfortunately, what was good for the deer was not so good for me. In order to position myself near large numbers of feeding deer and potential targets, I intended to place my patrol car where the radio couldn't reach any of the state's relay towers in case I needed assistance! Any experienced conservation officers reading these lines will find their hair (what little they have left) going up as they think, "That sure as hell was mistake number two. What a dingbat!" In truth, when I discovered the area was lousy with deer and had a good overlook of the real estate to be shot over, I just quit thinking. Like Custer when he first saw the huge Indian encampment on the Greasy Grass in 1876. ...

Mistakes like that didn't mean a whole lot to me in those early days. I was a young man, larger in size than most, strong as a bull, a crack pistol shot, healthy, and basically immortal—or so I thought. That arrogance quickly led me to mistake number three. What do they say about three strikes and you are out? Well, if it weren't for my two guardian angels working overtime and a Lab pup, I might have been on my way to the dugout, to use a little baseball lingo. Arrogance compounded by stupidity and ignorance can sometimes be a killer!

Loading up my eight-month-old female Labrador pup, Shadow, and supplies for the stakeout after a meaningful kiss for my intensely blue-eyed bride to combat her fears about me working alone, I left the foggy coolness of Eureka for the summer evening heat in the inland mountains of Trinity County. Driving east on state Highway 299 over the coastal range, I soon found myself in the mountainous backcountry above the town of Willow Creek. That area was historically frequented by deer-killing out-of-work lumbermen, Native Americans, hungry college kids, and many other two-legged opportunists.

After driving about twenty miles on dusty mountain logging roads, I finally settled into the area where Willow Creek Warden Hank Marak had told me a lot of deer poaching occurred, based on the gut piles he and other legal backcountry users had discovered. Marak was quite a man and one hell of an outstanding wildlife law enforcement professional. Plain and simply, when Hank got on your trail, he would stay there until you were apprehended for your wrongs. The only way to get this dogged, hardworking officer off your trail was to die a natural death or shoot him—he was that good! Hank was one of the few old-time game wardens who would freely share his experiences with younger officers so they would not make the same mistakes he had in his younger days. And when he gave you his word, no matter the consequences, he would be there by your side when the going got rough. He was a strap-steel-tough but fair man who had been raised in the outback and carried those principles based on living close to the land and its resources throughout his life and profession, a trait not commonly found today in the younger professional ranks. Because of my great respect for him I agreed to spend time in his district providing a hand with some of his law enforcement problems. I had plenty to do in my own neck of the woods but figured Hank wouldn't ask for help unless it was really warranted. That was why I was working in his district that summer evening so long ago.

Parking the patrol vehicle out of sight on an old road overlooking several well-traveled secondary logging roads in an old clear cut, the dog and I settled in for a lonely all-night vigil. Even at that hour it was still about 102 degrees, so sleep was almost out of the question, especially sitting on those old vinyl seat covers the state of California purchased from the lowest bidders for our patrol cars. Just sitting there sweating would have to do, I finally concluded. So I just rested my head on the seat back so my eyes could sweep the country below while accepting my lot on what would likely be a typically boring stakeout. The outlaws know where and when they will be out destroying nature, but all the officer knows is that the illegal killing is going to happen sometime. Hence many stakeouts turn out boring as a result of being in the wrong place at the wrong time. You can only hope to strike it lucky each time.

This was my very first time working spotlighters alone, and I still remember the numerous excited thoughts running through my head like a string of brightly colored beads. I would see the beam of a light striking a deer and, after hearing a shot, would thunder to the scene, apprehending several poachers red-handed over the broken, freshly killed body. Or there would be a chase on the dusty logging roads, but after sliding around several dangerous turns at high speed, my superior driving skills would prevail, producing several arrests for possession of an illegal deer. These thoughts kept my mind busy. Soon the only activity was surprised animal movements outside the darkened patrol car and the occasional faraway hoot of a great horned owl in an old tree left from logging times long past.

After several long hours sweating in the heat, now bored stiff with the quiet and inactivity, I looked into the back seat to see how Shadow was doing. Damn, she was dead to the world. I didn't know how she could sleep in this awful heat, but her snoring, audible for twenty feet around my patrol car, sure testified to that fact. I wished I could sleep as well, for an hour or so anyway. After all, the sound of shooting or a vehicle would wake me up. But the damned heat and sweating precluded any chance of that. Maybe that was why the leadership in Sacramento picked vinyl seats for our patrol cars, I thought sleepily. But I've yet to see a Labrador, especially an eight-month-old pup, be unable to sleep anywhere, anytime.

I smiled at this dog my wife had picked out of a tumble of puppies at the kennel to act as my constant companion. Since she couldn't accompany me herself, I guess she figured a good dog would be an able replacement in my out-of-doors adventures. So before I knew it, she spent some of our hard-earned money and I had a dog. I had always wanted a good dog and had very high expectations for the mutt I would eventually own. However, after paying twenty-five dollars for her, I had to take her to the veterinarian and spend more to have her wormed. It seemed the original owners hadn't taken such good care of the mutt and had allowed her to load up with tapeworms. Now in those days, on a $516 per month salary as a game warden and my bride's teaching salary of less than $4,000 *per year,* extra cash outflows for a dog were not high on my list of priorities. Then all the damn thing, now named Shadow by my wife, did was eat, poop, poop, poop, and sleep. Well, I can't say that was *all* she did. She also managed to chew up everything of value in our apartment and dig up every household flower and shrub, much to the chagrin of our landlords. Then there was that last straw in my expectations for a retriever. When confronted with water, other than that in her drinking bowl, all she did was run from it! Just imagine, a Lab that wouldn't go in water over the top of her toenails! After discovering I had a coward of a Lab who would not swim, I lost all interest and in disgust left her home to be raised by Donna as a lapdog.

I don't remember how Donna managed to get me to take that miserable dog on this particular stakeout. As it turned out, it was damn lucky for me. It was also a turning point in my relationship with Shadow, one that still exists in my soul and memory some thirty-seven years later.

About two o'clock in the morning, as I was finally about to doze off, I heard a booming shot from the canyons below. The sound of the hunt instantly brought me back to the real world! Quickly sitting up and hanging my head out the window to hear better, I carefully listened to the night's sounds. The dog, hearing me stir, opened her eyes and perked up her ears. Finding nothing of interest, she quickly went back to sleep, as evidenced by her deep snores. Ignoring the chainsaw in the back seat, I sat very still, hardly daring to breathe and trying to quiet my now loudly beating heart as I strained my ears.

Soon, off in the distance, I heard the faint sound of an engine laboring hard as it slowly came up out of the canyon below me. *It was coming my way!* It was running slowly in low gear, and after a lifetime of waiting, I finally saw its headlights sweeping back and forth as it maneuvered around the steep, winding logging road below and behind me. On one of its turns, I saw the blue-white, pencil-thin beam of a spotlight searching the draws along the road. Then it dawned on me like the sun on the manure pile behind the barn. *Damn!* My spotlighter appeared to be on the same logging road I was parked on, approaching me from behind, not from the front as I had planned. *That was not good.* Being alone, I needed the element of surprise, along with a car stop in which I made my approach from the rear. Any chance of figuring out how to get turned around and out of my dangerous position into one where I had the element of surprise and control was quickly lost in the onrushing events.

About forty yards below me, the car stopped as its spotlight beam fixed itself on a feeding deer in a small meadow. The deer, a nice four-point buck still in velvet, lowered its head from the light beam as if to run, all to no avail. The light held tightly to the deer's head, blinding it and fixing it to that spot, and even as a rookie I could tell I had a veteran spotlighter. A fireball came out the window from the vehicle's back seat along with the booming report of a heavy rifle. Seconds later the vehicle's lights went out as if to hide the deadly act just performed. Fat chance, I thought as I heard several car doors being opened and then slammed to shut off the dome lights. Like it or not, the law was at hand and soon to be introduced. Listening and watching carefully, I heard several voices as a struggling but dying deer was picked up and hurled still kicking into the back of the vehicle with a soft, hoof-clattering *ka-thump*. My shooters got back into their vehicle, announced by the dome light and the opening and slamming of doors. Watching this drama unfolding below through my binoculars, I identified the vehicle as a Chevrolet station wagon with at least five male occupants. Even at that distance, the rhythm and tone of their voices made me think some of them might be Native Americans.

Killing deer or any game animal at night with the use and aid of a light was a violation of the California State Fish and Game Code, not to mention morally wrong. Since I was at least two miles from the boundaries of the Hoopa Indian Reservation (where taking big game by tribal members with a light in those days was generally condoned), any Native Americans I apprehended with an illegal deer were fair game. On their reservation they were home free, but out in my neck of the bush they were fair game. In short, if they were looking for trouble with a capital T, they were about to find it!

It again occurred to me that my position was bad. There just wasn't any place to hide from the sweep of their headlights or spotlight. I was going to have to turn my vehicle around to make a dangerous head-on car stop because I had stupidly not placed myself for the proper interception of a spotlighter coming from any direction. Being a rookie, I had placed my vehicle for the best view rather than the best position for pursuit, and I was about to pay the price. Head-on car stops, especially if you are alone, outnumbered, and in the outback, are the most dangerous kind for many reasons. First because the folks you are stopping can see your every move through their headlights, just as you can see theirs. Second, if those folks are evil-minded, under the influence, panicky, or emboldened because they outnumber you, events can quickly spin out of control and become lethal.

Knowing it was too late to move without using my back-up lights or leaving a fresh dust trail in the air, I quickly turned my patrol car around on the narrow logging road, hoping I wouldn't go over the edge or hang up on a stump in the dark. Somehow I managed to get it done without a wreck. I was now in position on the logging road, facing the shooters coming my way, who were now just a short distance away. While performing that little maneuver, I kept mechanically reviewing the head-on stopping procedure taught at the academy. It was not a procedure they recommended, but thank heaven the instructors had provided some information in case one got caught with one's pants down. This was not something I had any experience in or wanted to do with the odds I was facing. But sometimes you eat the bear, and sometimes he eats you.

Within moments the suspects' car made the last turn immediately below me on the road. Sitting there with my engine quietly running, I adjusted the red spotlight, waited until the very last moment just before their lights hit my vehicle, then gunned the car out into the center of the road, blocking any chance of their escape! The beam of their headlights flooded my very obvious patrol car, but in their surprise at finding another vehicle on the logging road, they kept coming my way for a few more feet. Then the driver became aware *who the vehicle belonged to!* With that recognition, all hell broke loose! On went his brakes, followed by all kinds of hollering in reaction to the surprise of being faced with a law enforcement vehicle in the outback that early in the morning.

Quickly moving my car to within three feet of his bumper, I effectively blocked any possibility of escape by moving forward, and was also in position to push the other car if they tried to escape backward, providing the opportunity of ramming it into a dirt bank or stump. I turned on my high beams and siren and fixed my red spotlight smack-dab on their windshield, hoping to gain some advantage through the blindness it would cause. That siren's mournful howl rebounding off the mountains sounded unearthly, causing the hair on the back of my neck to rise. There was panic in the other car if flying bodies and moving rifle barrels spoke any truth. People were hurriedly unloading firearms, throwing bottles of whiskey out of windows to avoid being caught with open containers in the vehicle, throwing blankets over the deer in the back, and squeezing shut their hind ends in unison in a frantic microsecond.

Bailing out of my patrol car, I counted five Native American men thrashing around in the light and a multitude of deer legs sticking up in the back of their vehicle. Brother, it appeared I had a hatful of hornets! Using the opened front door of my car as a shield, I bellowed out instructions, identifying myself as a state Fish and Game warden and ordering them to turn off their engine and get out of their vehicle. I made it abundantly clear they were to step out on the driver's side and stand at the edge of the road. That way I could see exactly what they were up to once they regained their composure, and I could control the situation from my vantage point with the protection of my car's engine block if and when the bullets started flying. But no one in the other vehicle moved. They just sat there in stunned silence, looking into my headlights and the glaring red spotlight! Boy, that kind of inaction sure got a rookie's attention. I again ordered the men out of the car on the driver's side, and this time even God heard the command and got out before He realized He didn't have to follow that order.

Instead of coming out the two driver's-side doors, they came out all "seventeen" doors in one giant tumbling belch of humanity! Here I was, a rookie, alone, trying to get this "hoorah" sorted out with men scattered along the edges of the road on both sides of their car. Once out, they just stood there in a gaggle without a wiggle or sound among the lot! The hair on the back of my neck started crawling once again. Those on the passenger side of the car then moved over to the lads on the driver's side of the vehicle as silently as a mouse pissing on a ball of cotton.

That was bad, I thought. Any time a bunch of trapped poachers is quiet or sullen during a situation like that, you may have a giant survival problem in the making. My hair started to rise up even higher than before as my hand drifted toward the comforting butt of my holstered .44 magnum. You may be wondering why my weapon was not out and leveled. Good question. In those days, people for the most part were just different. They still had a healthy respect for law and order and most of the time display of the weapon was not needed. Just the sight of the weapon on the hip and the badge on the shirt was sufficient in most cases. Voice commands worked in most situations and were commonly used without the reinforcement of the business end of a gun. You didn't display a weapon until things got *really* touchy. So in that day and given that way of thinking, even though I was outnumbered, things just were not to the weapons-display stage yet. Close but no cigar. ... Placing my hand firmly on the butt of the pistol and holding a five-cell flashlight in my left hand away from my body with its beam directed head high at the five men, I closed the front door of my patrol car with my knee. Then I walked between the front bumpers of the two closely parked vehicles to get to the side of the road where all my spotlighters were silently standing. I saw that I had five middle-aged Native American men quietly watching my every move. Their silence told me something was very wrong, but for the life of me I just couldn't put my finger on it. I was so nervous over that kind of behavior that I unsnapped the catch on my pistol and loosened it in the holster for fast action if required.

I had seen only five of them get out of the car when they shot the deer, so extra lads hidden somewhere couldn't be the clue to my perceived problem, I thought quickly. Then it crossed my mind that they might rush me in the next moment. I quickly eliminated that idea because of the difference in our sizes. They were all sawed-off half-pint son of a guns, and before them stood a giant. In those days I wore sap gloves (lead-lined across the front knuckles), giving me a hit like an angry mule's kick. I figured I could deck the first three who got in range with my fists and then take my time crushing those still standing. Ah, one can only love that arrogance born of youth. ... Then I thought that one of my lads might be a bad hombre with a weapon, so that was where I placed my undivided attention. My flashlight quickly illuminated all of the men's waists as I looked for the telltale signs of a sheath knife or sidearm. Nothing showed. Thinking along those lines was rookie mistake number four, proving damned near fatal! An officer in such a situation should *never, ever leave out any options!*

The next thing I knew, I heard the unmistakable sound of toenails clicking on metal behind me and to my left. *Damn,* I thought, they had a mean dog in their vehicle and now that problem was heading my way! Quickly turning to defend myself, I discovered it was my Labrador pup leaving her back seat and vaulting out the open driver's-side window of my patrol car into the darkness below. Then I heard a man screaming to the heavens over the sounds of a very upset dog who was letting this unknown someone behind me know who was boss. Now I had five problems ready to bolt to all points of the compass in front of me and a hell of a ruckus going on in the dark to my rear involving an individual I had not yet seen! I'll tell you, that would have been a mental load for a seasoned game warden, let alone a dumb-assed rookie like me! Knowing the dog had her hands, uh, paws full, I quickly bellowed out additional orders, now backed up by the business end of the .44 magnum, to the five men standing in the road. In very clear terms I ordered them to hit the road face down and make themselves look like pancakes. If they intended to try something, it would take a few seconds to get up from that position and join the "party," which would be warning enough for me to swing the hand cannon into action. The poachers hit the dirt as if they were one. Little puffs of dust swirled skyward where they had just stood. They quickly realized their little hunting trip had gone very wrong and to err now would not be good for their constitutions no matter how they looked at it. I don't think they had figured on the dog factor in this little "hoorah."

With that part of the situation under control, I quickly turned to the battle in the rear, which apparently a new Native American acquaintance was losing badly. I found a man on the ground with a very upset black Lab going all over his head like a chainsaw. I got Shadow off the chap, or what was left of him, all the while keeping a wary eye on my five lads on the ground who were all making like soldiers facing an incoming artillery round.

What a mess this sixth lad exhibited in the beam of my flashlight. Most of his face, nose, and one ear had seen better times. Both hands, which he had used to shield his face, looked like they could use a little medical help as well. The blood from his head wounds poured forth in torrents, and that sight didn't help me much in calming down! Lying off to one side was a rather large Bowie knife with about a ten-inch blade!

As near as I could tell in the confusion of the moment, when the men had gotten out of their vehicle, this chap had fallen to the ground, rolling under the car and over to the passenger side. He then waited for me to pass between the cars so he could rise up behind me and see how his Bowie knife worked on my body. Shadow had come out of the car right onto the head of my crouching assailant. Plain and simply, Shadow had saved my life.

Once I had the dog under control (the newest fellow wasn't going anywhere, sitting there on the ground holding what was left of his face and crying like a bear cub without a mother), I seized four illegal deer, two spotlights, several knives, and three rifles from their vehicle. I quickly laid these items on the roadside behind my vehicle (minus their rifle bolts, which I placed in the trunk). During those moments my roadside five still lay face down, hardly daring to breathe. Realizing there was no way I could get that many outlaws to town along with all the evidence in my Mercury Comet, I got on the radio to call Hank for assistance. Every time I keyed the mike, I was rewarded with silence as the radio failed to connect with any local relay towers. I then tried my car-to-car radio (low-frequency, direct line of sight) hoping Hank was out and about close by and would hear my calls for assistance. Again I was rewarded for my earlier rookie folly of locating myself in a deep canyon. Realizing I was stuck, I decided I would load the wounded man in my car and handcuff him. I would get the drivers' licenses from my road-eating five and load their gear and my evidence into the patrol car's trunk and back seat. Then I would start walking the whole damn mess in front of my patrol car toward civilization. I had used this system once before on some sturgeon snaggers (see my first book, *Wildlife Wars*) and figured that was better than sitting way out in the bush waiting for some manner of rescue.

About then I chanced to hear another vehicle approaching the crossroads. I thought, Oh great, that is all I need—another carload of poachers. Thanks to my guardian angels, I was pleasantly surprised to meet a logger and his wife coming home to their backwoods logging show after a late-night shopping spree. Once they saw who I was and recognized the pickle I was in, the logger reached under the seat of his vehicle and, taking out an old Colt .45 single action, said, "Tell me what you want done and it will be so." Boy, was my rookie hind end glad to see those folks! Between the burly logger and the rookie, we managed to get everyone handcuffed or under a belt tie (a form of hand restraint using the belt of the prisoner when one does not have enough handcuffs). We put most of the men in the back of my logger's pickup, and with me following, off we went to the county jail in Hoopa.

Once there I booked my prisoners and gave my logger friend $20 for his troubles. He just grinned through tobacco-stained teeth and remarked, "Happy to oblige." Off they went to his logging camp to prepare breakfast for his woods crew. Then I took "Jim Bowie" to the hospital and got him sewed up to the tune of sixty-one stitches. Boy, was he a mess. I didn't have the heart to file charges against him for attempted assault on a state officer, figuring it would be time better served if I let him act as an advertisement regarding the new game warden and his dog "Chainsaw." ... However, I wasn't totally softheaded, so he did go to jail with his brethren on the illegal deer possession charges as soon as he was sewn up and presentable.

Several weeks later my lads appeared in front of my little grandma hanging judge and received some rather stiff sentences for their deer-shooting activity. After that episode, it was several months before Hank found any more deer gut piles in that area, which told us we had caught the culprits responsible for the earlier illegal deer killing. My mistakes hadn't proved fatal that evening but served to strengthen me in the years that followed. I would continue to make mistakes throughout my career, but luckily I survived and learned from all of them. Anyway, the mistakes I did make were job security for my two guardian angels, who kept most ill winds from coming my way. I must admit, God ran up quite an overtime bill in the protection department, and my angels' feathers got a little frayed in the process. ...

After that incident Shadow was treated just like another person in my family and rarely left my side. When I ate, she ate. When I slept, she slept. When I suffered in the backcountry due to the elements or scope and degree of a particular detail, so did she. When I was successful in my endeavors, you could almost see the happiness in that dog as well. No doubt about it, we were a team.

In the end, Shadow turned out to be one of the best retrievers I ever saw! I routinely watched her making blind retrieves with the use of hand signals up to half a mile away to bring back evidence birds or "sailers" (birds that had been crippled so that they sailed and died hundreds of yards from where they were shot)! Over my hunting career she lost only six birds, and one of those went down a vertical standpipe into an underground culvert. I was offered over $1,000 several times for Shadow by other hunters watching her perform her typical long-range miracle retrieves! However, she was not for sale.

I would often get a motel room after the day's work was done. When I did, I always ordered a room with two beds. That dog would never again sleep on the floor when we were on patrol. I would throw back the sheets, and in she would jump. I would then cover her up, and she would grunt just like a little pig at the special love and attention. In the morning she would still be there under the sheets and loving it. I often chuckled at what the maids must have thought when they found dog hair all over in one of their beds. But it was the very least I could do for a dog that had saved my life.

We worked closely together over the years that followed, sharing many adventures, sandwiches, the great outdoors, sunrises, sunsets, spraying by skunks, and numerous travails involving many flavors of bad guys. As her name implied, she was my shadow.

As the years all too quickly sped by, we both began to dim from a youthful roaring flame to a mature soft light. Years later in North Dakota, Shadow's light dimmed even further and finally went out, but not before she had one last ride in "her" patrol car to the veterinarian. Even after the almost thirty years since the passing of my law enforcement "partner," I get openly misty-eyed and choked up as I remember my wonderful times with that dog and struggle to write these lines. Out of loyalty to Shadow, I never again had a dog as a partner.

When it's my time to have only memories recalled through dim eyes, I pray the good Lord sees to it that when my light finally goes out, I will still cast and see my "Shadow."

Junkyard Dog

NO MATTER WHERE you find yourself, there is always a junkyard dog in the neighborhood. The first thing you notice about this type is that he (it is usually a male) is ill-tempered, larger than most dogs, ugly as a post, and a bully with a set of teeth that makes a great white shark's look like a grin. When working duck hunters around the duck club complex of Lambertville (about thirty buildings clumped together) on the northern end of Colusa County, I always seemed to run into such a mutt at the Duck-Away Duck Club. When checking hunters as they arrived from the field or checking their ducks in the hanging facility (a screened-in area next to the clubhouse used to hang and cool out drawn ducks and geese), it seemed I almost always had to "shoot" my way past this dog to get in and conduct my inspections. This dog was so ill-tempered that I always kept one eye on him and my hand on my sidearm. I figured if he finally overcame his fear and came for me, he was going to experience a 250-grain, .429 Keith Thompson bullet from my .44 magnum traveling at about 1,300 feet per second! Given that dog's size and meanness, I figured I'd have no other choice, because I sure wasn't going to let him use me for his larger-than-life chewbone.

Many hunters I talked with told me that when his master took him into the field on a hunting expedition, he was a holy terror! This mutt jumped and whipped the hell out of any other dog he met. Male or female, if it was a dog, it was in for a big-time ass-whuppin' as far as Junkyard was concerned. More than once, I was checking a hunter in a blind and chanced to see Junkyard steam out of his master's duck blind some yards away, cross several hundred yards of marsh to another blind at a dead run, and attack an unsuspecting dog in that blind, whipping the tar out of him before anyone could do anything. It got so that all the other club members began to raise hell with the owner, but he just ignored the objections regarding the behavior of his beloved junkyard dog, paid the vet bills to repair the ripped-up dogs, and arrogantly went about his business as if nothing had happened. Plain and simply, he had the meanest son of a bitch in the valley and rather enjoyed letting everyone within biting distance know it. This behavior went on for at least two years until the day of a never-to-be-forgotten event in a rice field on the north end of Newhall Farms.

That particular fall day I had been invited by the ranch foreman to bring a friend and hunt pheasants on Newhall Farms just south of the

Lambertville area. A good friend of mine from the Willows area accepted my invitation to be the other half of the twosome. He asked if he could bring along his Brittany spaniel, an excellent little pheasant dog. I told him absolutely, since that little dog had a nose like there was no tomorrow and it was so late in the season that the pheasants would be wilder than March hares. I took a rare half day off from my enforcement duties, and we met on the Newhall Farms land and prepared for a morning of relaxing fun on a stunning fall day. I let out my black Lab Shadow, a big dog weighing about 100 pounds (not overweight, just big) from the back of my pickup, and he let out his little 15-pound Brittany. Our dogs were the best of friends and both females, so they were happy to see each other and did what dogs do when they first get out of the vehicles before a hunt. Jack and I visited while the dogs tended to the important business at hand such as sniffing everything in sight, leaving a "loaf" or two, and scent-posting everything that looked interesting. With that important work done, we headed for a weedy ditch that paralleled a gravel public road leading into the town of Delevan and commenced pheasant hunting.

Shadow, my old brush buster, plowed through the extensive heavy cattail patches in the bottom of the ditch as the Brittany worked the weedy ditch banks. They were such a pro team that Jack and I just let several rooster pheasants scared up by the dogs escape without firing a shot. We watched them fly out of the joy of being in the outdoors, in celebration of being alive and being blessed with a couple of good dogs working the fields like the champions they were.

About that time, down the road from Lambertville to Delevan came a pickup driven by the Duck-Away Duck Club owner, and in the back was the ever-present Junkyard. As that chap passed our two dogs working the weedy ditch along the road, his dog spied them. Without a moment's hesitation, out from the back of the moving pickup came this dog with blood in his eye. Not anticipating the speed of the pickup or his trajectory, Junkyard hit the gravel road face first, lost his footing, and steamrolled right into the ditch. Shadow, surprised at the loud crash in the cattails behind her, lumbered up out of the weeds and onto the near ditch bank to have a look around. Recovering from his rather inglorious entrance, up out of the ditch came Junkyard, heading for the first dog he saw. It just happened to be the tiny Brittany, who immediately rolled over, lay on her back, and urinated all over herself at this unexpected attack by a dog almost ten times her size.

Whomp went Junkyard on top of the Brittany amidst the little dog's terrorized howling, Jack's yelling, and my swearing at this bully of a dog's unexpected attack. About then the Duck-Away Duck Club fellow realized what was happening behind him and slammed on his brakes, stopping his pickup in the middle of the road. Bailing out, he raced back to the scene of his dog mauling the Brittany.

As I raced to the Brittany's aid, Shadow ran to my side as she always did. With a well-placed kick, I boosted the living slats out of the aggressive dog, who literally sailed off the Brittany sideways. The Brittany, realizing she'd better get the hell out of there if she was to live another day, rolled over and scurried up into her master's arms in one inspired leap. A quick once-over revealed that she was somewhat bloodied and wet with slobber but not seriously injured.

Well, Junkyard, recovering from my monster kick in the slats, headed for his next victim, Shadow. Shadow was still at my side looking up at me for instructions and didn't see the Lambertville biter heading her way. I stuck my shotgun barrel down in front of the dog to slow his charge, but his 110-pound flying body just knocked it and me aside as he lunged pell-mell into Shadow. Attacked from out of nowhere and surprised, Shadow set up the worst damn howling I ever heard. It was a combination of abject surprise, pain, terror, and anger all rolled up into one. Quickly recovering but now on the bottom, Shadow turned underneath her assailant and started to fight back. Now we had two very large, capable dogs really going at it. Add to that din one bellowing, really mad game management agent and hollering from Jack, still holding his Brittany, who was barking loud encouragement to Shadow, and Junkyard's owner, who had now crossed the ditch. We now had a rice field riot in the making.

Trying to kick the two dogs apart, I got a two-inch-long tooth slice to my sock-leather boot from Junkyard for my troubles! Looking for a large stick or pipe with which to brain that son of a bitch, I saw his master grabbing him by the collar and getting bitten in short order on his forearm and hand by his fight-crazed dog. That second of interference was all Shadow needed, and though still on the bottom, she reached up, grabbed her assailant by the throat, clamped down with a death grip, and hung on. She had the junkyard dog's head pulled down in a chokehold, leaving his hind end way up in the air as he tried to pull away.

Then the most unexpected thing in the world happened! Out of Jack's arms flew the usually timid, barking little Brittany, who, hitting the ground at a dead run, headed smack-dab for the battle. Without a moment's hesitation, seeing her Lab friend on the ground fighting for her life, she jumped up and grabbed Junkyard's exposed scrotum in her teeth and clamped down, and I do mean *hard! Yaooow* went Junkyard at the top of his very surprised and pained lungs—not to mention pained something else! He was so tall that the Brittany was hanging almost clear off the ground but hanging in there, swaying with the motion of the fight going on at the other end! With Junkyard's attention now riveted elsewhere, Shadow went to work. Up off the ground she came with a vengeance, and I don't think I ever saw more teeth on the front end of my dog.

By now Junkyard was in abject pain! He dared not move his hind end one micron, but he was losing everything not tied down on the other end to a very capable, not to mention pissed and determined, 100-pound black Lab. Junkyard slowly rolled over, lay down, and commenced to howl. I grabbed Shadow off his head before she changed Junkyard to the ugliest dog in the world, and Jack did the same with the Brittany. *Yaooow* went Junkyard in triple forte when Jack grabbed the Brittany, and I couldn't figure out why until I looked a little closer. Junkyard was now "Junkyard the Wonder Dog." The Brittany had exacted her revenge for the hind-end chewing Junkyard had given her, and now she held the keys to Junkyard's family kingdom firmly in her teeth. As neatly removed as any veterinarian could have done, I might add. ... Looking at the Brittany as she lay comfortably in Jack's arms, I could have sworn she was smiling!

Putting Shadow and the Brittany in the back of my truck, Jack and I took my first aid kit and wrapped up the badly torn and bleeding arm of Junkyard's owner. In fact, he was bleeding so much that his face was ashen and I thought for a moment he might lose consciousness because of shock. However, we got him to sit down for a spell, and he finally came around. Then, picking up a loudly groaning Junkyard and his two ears, or what was left of them, he loaded his dog and its parts into the back of his truck. I have no idea where the scrotum went, but I wouldn't be surprised if that little Brittany didn't eat it when she had the chance! With an apology for what had happened, he headed for the vet to see if anything could be done for his softly groaning and for once subdued dog.

Now that things had cooled down, we took the time to look our dogs over for battle damage. Jack's dog had a few puncture wounds on her belly and hind legs but other than that seemed alright. Shadow, on the other hand, had several long gashes in her neck and back, along with numerous puncture wounds in the neck and shoulder area. None were life threatening, just bloody. We took both dogs to the veterinarian in Willows, and after a few stitches and shots, all was well. Both dogs were still pretty chipper, and the vet didn't see any problem in continuing an easy pheasant hunt, so back we went to Newhall Farms and just hunted the interior rice checks and straw spoil piles to avoid any other outside dog problems.

As expected with the two good hunting dogs we had, we killed our limits of two pheasants each in short order. After drawing our birds to prevent spoilage, Jack left for home and I returned to the ever-present wildlife wars, working those hunting over goose decoys in Gunner's Field to see if they had stayed within the prescribed limits. I spent the remainder of the day and into the night watching over vast hordes of ducks leaving Delevan National Wildlife Refuge and flooding into the harvested rice fields between Two and Four Mile Roads to feed. Returning home about midnight, I noticed that Shadow disembarked from the back of my pickup a little tenderly, ate her dinner, and after a big drink of water settled into her bed of clean straw and was soon snoring.

Shadow was a little stiff the next day, but in a few days everything was back in working order. A week or so later, I was back in the Lambertville area checking the lads in that complex after they had had a fine shoot due to heavy rains and strong winds. Checking my way through the clubs, I came to the Duck-Away Duck Club, home of the infamous Junkyard. Today it was different as I approached to check the ducks in the hanging facility. Junkyard got up as usual to let me know who was the boss, then, seeing Shadow in the back of the pickup and remembering that earlier ill-fated meeting, quickly lay back down on the step and behaved himself. I could almost picture what was going on in his mind about the big black dog who had somehow taken him to the cleaners on both ends at the same time (he had never seen the Brittany attack). He looked the worse for wear with the top half of both ears missing and a hind end full of still evident stitches, minus a scrotum. He just lay there, not wanting to move as I went about my business. It was almost as if he had lost heart for being a bully—or was it some other organ?

From then on, no one seemed to have any problem with Junkyard. My, how life can change in the blink of an eye—or in the bite of a Brittany!

Fifi

EVERY YEAR FROM 1971 ON I participated as an instructor at the Service's National Academy in either Washington, D.C., or Glynco, Georgia. My specialty was waterfowl life histories and wing and skin identifications, skills that were used daily by the agents in the field during waterfowl season. I taught those subjects first by myself and later with Agent Pat Bosco, who would travel down from his home in Massachusetts. One day I flew to a training session in Florida, rented a vehicle, and spent some time touring the country along a back-bay waterway in the Florida countryside while I waited for Pat. He was due to arrive by plane in a couple of hours, at which time I was to pick him up. So having nothing better to do, I stopped at a small back-country grocery store, bought some lunch fixings, and prepared to enjoy myself somewhere along a waterway watching the state's unique and storied bird life as I ate my lunch.

After driving about thirty miles looking for just the right place, I found a spot along a swampy area loaded with shorebirds, surrounded by many large oak trees replete with yards of Spanish moss gently swaying in the soft ocean breezes. There were two cement picnic tables at this pull-off, so I took one under the shade of a giant stately oak, laid out my lunch fixings, and commenced to eat and enjoy the quiet of the area with its many species of bird life.

In a matter of about five minutes I had identified eleven avian species and in addition had two blue jays boldly flying down and sharing parts of my lunch. The jays, not paying any attention to me, would land on my table, reach into the open bag of potato chips or package of lunch meat lying within arm's length, and help themselves. It was great having that kind of interaction along with the clean smell of salt air and the quiet breezes cooling me in the hot, humid climate.

Taking another bite of my ham sandwich, I noticed an American egret, not twenty feet away, spear a small fish along the bank, flip it up into the air, and recatch it headfirst, swallowing it straight away. I grinned and looked for more of Nature's interesting world playing out along the marshy shore. Suddenly the egret gracefully leaped from the water with several deep strokes of its great wings, moved about twenty feet up the shore, and resettled. Then it looked intently back toward the area whence it had just come. Doing likewise, I saw the object of its attention. An alligator, about seven feet long, was lazily swimming to shore not thirty feet away from where I continued to share my lunch with the jays. It pulled about two-thirds of its body length out of the water onto the warm, sandy shore and commenced relaxing and sunning itself. Pretty soon the shorebirds returned and began to feed again, all the while keeping a wary eye peeled and a bit of distance between them and the reptilian sunbather. Damn, I thought, if it wasn't so damned hot and humid in this country, it might be a nice place to live, considering the wealth of bird life and the abundance of other forms of wildlife I enjoyed watching so much.

Then from the highway came a large pink Chrysler 300, which pulled up to the vacant picnic table beside mine, spewing dust all over my peaceful lunch. Looking disgustedly at the newcomers, I noticed that the car's license plate read, "New Jersey." Figures, I thought. The driver stepped out and in a typical Northeastern accent groused about the heat and humidity and added something about his wife. He was a rather large, fat fellow, with a nose twice as long as my own Roman-like appendage. Then his wife rolled out of the car, and she was bigger than I! Brother, I thought, no wonder they have a Chrysler 300 sedan. The only thing that would suit them better would be a one-ton truck!

Trying hard to ignore these noisy, bickering newcomers, realizing they had a right to the other picnic table but not to my solitude, I turned away and tried to reclaim a Christian attitude toward my fellow humans (even if they were from New Jersey). Then out of the car tumbled a white ball of barking, urinating, yapping, crapping poodle wanna-be dog! The dog ran every which way, up and down, yapping just as fast as it moved its legs. It almost seemed as if it were keyed to yap every time a leg or tail moved more than a micron, like some damn mechanical toy. Now I had dirt in my food, two noisy people bitching at each other, and a damn yapping dog, and to make matters worse, every shorebird had left for quieter climes. Even the jays who had shared my lunch decided enough was enough and departed for the tops of the giant oaks until things settled down.

Realizing my quiet moment at the shore was gone forever, I stood and was gathering up my luncheon items when I realized that my right foot was suddenly feeling hot and wet! Looking down, I saw that wanna-be dog had hoisted his leg and was urinating right on my tennis shoe. I was so amazed I didn't even think to kick the damn thing into the middle of next week. Finishing its chore about the same moment I realized what was happening, the poodle, knowing what was likely coming next from a flying foot, sprinted off yapping for Mommy—who, by the way, gathered the dog into her arms and without an apology turned her large carcass around and ignored the act she had plainly observed moments before. Man, I was fit to be tied! If I could have gotten my hands on that piss-ant of a dog, it would have gone as far out into the swamp as I could have launched it! Quickly pulling my shoe off, I removed my wet and strong-smelling yellow-stained sock. I used some of my bottled water to rinse off my bare foot as well as the sock. Washing my hands, I put my now bare foot back into my wiped-out but still urine-smelling shoe and tossed the sock into a plastic bag for later washing. No matter what I did to my hands, they still smelled strongly of urine as well.

By now, still bitching at each other, my New Jersey couple had loaded up the other picnic table with food, with wanna-be dog running all over the table top sampling whatever he wanted. The little piss-ant would grab an item of interest and shake the devil out of it until its sharp teeth punctured the food container or the food spilled out onto the table. Then it would help itself, accompanied by the cooing of the woman about how cute the dog was. Yeah, cute, I thought. If that dog was mine ...

Gathering my lunch items, I prepared to leave this battlefield to the loud folks from New Jersey and their yapping "baby," as the female of the pair called the little devil. I hauled half of my lunch fixings back to the car and placed them in the ice chest and upon returning found wanna-be dog on my table, tearing into my loaf of bread. Finally having had a gutful, I said, "Hey, lady, take care of your damn dog, will you?"

"Don't you dare yell at my baby, you *monster,*" was the unexpected response. By now I was starting to harbor bad thoughts about the whole carload and if it hadn't been illegal to do so would have considered ridding the world of the three of them. Picking up what was left of the rest of my lunch I found that my package of cookies had been pissed on by the dog, and I just about lost it! I looked over at the man in disgust at finding my cookies violated, and he looked back at me and said in a shrill, mocking tone, "Don't leave them out if you don't want them to be eaten by baby."

Now, I consider myself a pretty gentle, God-fearing man. However, the devil was rearing up in me that day and, if I hadn't been a credentialed federal officer, I might have tried to knock his head off with a damn good right cross. Jesus, I was hot, not to mention utterly surprised at these folks' ugly manners. I had not been brought up to be that way and had never run into folks of this nature before. I was pretty much at a loss so didn't do anything but fume.

The wanna-be dog was now running all over the place again, yapping at everything in sight, including what was in its head—*nothing.* Then it spotted the gator, which had not yet been spotted by the couple from New Jersey as it lay on the bank minding its own business. *Yip-yip-yip-yip* went the wanna-be dog right up to the right side of the gator, which didn't move. *Yip-yip-yip* went the dog as it ran right over the gator and down the other side, causing the gator to turn to the left just a little—*but not too much!*

"Mister," I said, looking at the gator, only to be interrupted by him saying, "Weren't you just leaving?"

I could not believe what I was hearing! Looking hard at the lad from New Jersey, I slowly sat back down and let the devil take over my soul as I smugly watched the drama unfolding in front of God and everybody. If he wasn't interested in hearing the warning I was about to give, then why waste the time trying to be a good Christian, the devil in me pointed out. That sounded like gospel to me.

Surveying the scene, I thought, In this corner you have Fifi the dingbat dog, and in that corner of the swamp you have "Jaws." I just grinned, now less upset over my wet, stinking foot and the ruined cookies. Then Fifi found the front end of the gator and, standing six inches away from the business end, began to call the gator every name in the book, including a few from New Jersey. *Chomp* went the gator in a blinding flash, and all I saw was Fifi hanging out both sides of the gator's mouth as the gator tastefully rose up on its legs, turned, and slowly ambled back into the water.

"*Eeeeeee,*" the woman screamed, then passed out in a large, greasy heap.

The husband, who had spotted the gator just as Fifi got his come-uppance, was throwing hot dogs at the disappearing gator as if that would change the situation. "Help me, help me," he screamed as he raced to the water's edge in an attempt to dissuade the gator from his selection off the New Jersey lunch menu. I just sat there watching the gator disappear into the swamp with a still wiggling but no longer yip-ping Fifi. I had heard that alligators really loved dogs as a food item and had also heard that they were very fast when they chose to strike. Man, I got to see both in real time, and it was a great lesson in life in the swamp.

"You didn't offer to help, you didn't offer to help," came the man's emotion-stressed voice through my deep interest in the biological spectacle I had just witnessed. Turning, I said, "You were right. Re-member, you asked if I was just leaving. I am leaving now, but out here in the swamps of Florida, don't leave your poodle out or, like my cookies, it might get pissed on." He just looked at me, aghast. I picked up the rest of my food, dropped my cookies in the tableside trash can, and walked to my car.

Turning, I could see that he was trying to revive his large wife, who was showing no signs of coming around. It was probably best because she was going to put a lot of knots on his head for letting Fifi become a blue-plate special. I drove off with a growing grin, thinking my wet shoe and lost cookies had been avenged. That is one lunch I will re-member forever.

Roscoe the Wonder Dog

STEPPING OUT of my patrol truck in the parking lot in Farmington Bay, Utah, I gave my stiff back a long stretch and breathed in the cold predawn, methane-laced swamp air. Utah Conservation Officer Larry Davis got out the passenger side of my vehicle, lit a cigarette, and grinned at me in the false dawn light. Here we were as a team again on a large waterfowl task force composed of agents from my eight-state region and numerous Utah Conservation and Parks officers. This task force operation, which inserted about seventy officers into the Great Salt Lake marshes on the opening weekend of waterfowl hunting season, was somewhat of a trademark of mine and a welcome change from the furious pace of my work as an administrator.

If you take a map of Utah and take a gander at the size of the marsh area around Salt Lake City and then realize that that marsh is surrounded by a zillion people, it won't take but a moment to realize why all of us conservation officers were here. Utah had a ton of waterfowl hunters and with the amount of waterfowl produced by the marshes, not to mention the influx of birds through the annual migration, it was no wonder so many wildlife officers were needed to keep the peace. As I have said in many of my stories, whenever you have a generous mix of people and wildlife, you have many violations of state and federal wildlife laws. The people of Utah, being no different than any other hunting community with the same opportunity, violated the conservation laws with the best of them. Since most of the birds had not been shot at for most of the year, they were especially vulnerable; throw in the young, inexperienced birds who were dumber than posts, and you had a mess in the making.

My partner of several years on these details was carefully examining the mad mix of humanity in the parking lot, and being the amateur historian that I was, I couldn't help but compare him to the quintessential gunfighter of old. Larry was tall, lean, and had a look that spoke of the strength of his Mormon ancestors as they tamed a hard land. I had worked all over the United States and parts of Canada during my enforcement career, and never did I find a finer, more professional conservation officer with a real essence of true human common sense. He was a quiet man, but his eyes never stopped moving as he critically surveyed his domain, and his knowledge of the land and its people was unsurpassed. Yet I found him to be one of the most human-oriented law enforcement officers I ever worked with and always enjoyed watching him interact with people from the very young to the most senior. In our many years of working together, I never saw him lose his temper or make a wrong legal turn when dealing with the many thousands of people we contacted. When that man retires, humanity, wildlife law enforcement, and the resources of this great land of ours will lose a true friend and advocate.

Larry, in his infinite wisdom, had invited along a Fish and Game commissioner who was unschooled in the history of the task force operation and what it was trying to accomplish. This woman, to her credit, had decided to go along with the two of us for the day and learn firsthand about a conservation officer's activities in order to make better decisions as a board member. She arrived shortly after we did, and the three of us, dressed like hunters in order to blend in with the people now streaming out into the field by the hundreds, headed south along a dike running out into the Farmington Bay marsh.

We walked for about three-eighths of a mile along that dike to a point where it branched, with the second dike ambling westward into another portion of the marsh. At that point we were in the middle of a large number of hunters scattered all around, so we decided to stay there and do what we did best once the shooting commenced. It was still dark, with shooting time about fifty minutes away, and the duck hunters were still streaming by us on the dike road. Many of those folks, instead of continuing down the main dike, turned off on the dike heading west. I thought, Terry, you might want to amble off in that direction if the shooting so dictates because of the large number of hunters going that way.

Then it was back to talking with Brenda the commissioner about task force operations, their costs, authorities, previous successes, and what we hoped to accomplish. I was impressed with Brenda, not only for her far-reaching and intelligent questions but her pluck in getting up so early without breakfast and coming into the marsh to learn the ropes. We needed more people like that lady in our business, I thought.

As shooting time approached and then commenced, I noticed heavy shooting coming from the dike that led into the western side of the Farmington Bay Marsh. After about thirty minutes of fast and furious shooting, I told Larry to stay at the T in the dike while I moved to the west on that dike and secreted myself among those hunters, who from the sound of it were having the shoot of their lives. I said if I apprehended anyone, I would record the information and particulars in my diary and send them back to him so he could issue the appropriate citations. If they failed to look Larry up at the T, we would still have the information in my diary and I could file on them later in federal magistrate's court. Larry agreed with a nod, and off I went like a late-arriving duck hunter, scurrying down the westward-running dike. Taking my time and trying to pinpoint where most of the shooting was coming from, I became aware of a group of hunters coming up behind me at a furious pace. Soon they overtook and passed me, but as they came up alongside all I could hear was one man's loud voice talking up his wonder dog, Roscoe. "You guys ain't never seen nothing until you see how this mutt of a dog fetches or retrieves ducks. This dog is a master at not losing any ducks killed, no matter how dense the marsh cover is, and will make a double retrieve [two dead birds at the same time] if necessary." I could hear the other hunters murmuring their approval and wondered myself at the capabilities of this dog, having seen many that were not worth the skin they were wrapped in. Looking Roscoe over as he passed me with the hunters, I just shook my head. He looked like a pot hound of questionable lineage, but nothing like a retriever. Listening to the owner bragging about his dog as they walked farther down the dike, I had to grin. It seemed every dog owner had the world's best dog.

Getting back to the business at hand, I picked a thick patch of bulrushes north of the dike to use for cover as I walked out into the marsh, beginning to watch my duck-hunting compatriots to see if they stayed within the wildlife laws. Looking around at the numerous hunters secreted in the bulrushes and trying to identify the best shooters, I noticed that Roscoe and his group had slipped off the dike and were using it as well as some willows for cover not forty-five yards away. I had about twelve other shooters in the immediate vicinity, so I just settled in and watched. Ducks were flying to and fro in their heretofore quiet marsh, now turned to a madhouse, and as they happened over different groups of hunters and the shooting commenced, there were fewer to fly on, and those that did were wiser.

I hadn't been standing in the knee-deep water of the marsh behind my thick stand of cattails and bulrushes for more than fifteen minutes when all the rich food from the Greek restaurant where Larry had taken me for dinner the evening before began to let me know it was time for that dinner to "see the world of the marsh." The wing-shooting action was so fast and furious that I held off, ignoring the rumblings deep inside so I could do my part of the job and catch those possibly shooting over-limits or restricted waterfowl species.

Peering through my thick stand of rushes, I noticed Roscoe's owner, each time the dog retrieved one of the party's dead ducks, giving the dog hugs and occasionally kissing it right on the end of the nose after an especially difficult retrieve. Anyone who took a parasitology class wouldn't do that to a dog because they are always licking their bottoms—and other parts loaded with parasites such as pinworms—but back to the story. I had to admit the dog was doing really well considering the density of the high grass, bulrushes, and cattails in which the dead and dying ducks fell. I was always glad to see people using a dog in a sport like waterfowl hunting because it reduced the crippling loss rates. I had to grin at the antics of Roscoe and his master as I remembered my days with my dog Shadow, long since gone to the Great Marsh in the Sky. I was happy for the man and his wonder dog.

The rumblings came again from deep within and announced that they were not to be denied, duck shooting or not. Realizing the end was near if I didn't pay attention, I quickly looked around for some high ground out of the water in some deep cover and was dismayed to find nothing but knee-deep water and heavy marsh grass all around me. The marsh was full of people, and hiding was a rather limited prospect. I just didn't want to be seen in such a compromising position before apprehending someone doing something wrong. Call it false pride or whatever, I just didn't want to appear in that kind of a bare-tailed position in front of God and everyone as a law enforcement officer. This time my guts gave me a time frame with their latest rumblings, and it was short! Realizing my thick patch of cattails was my best bet, as long as I hurried, I made my way to the densest section. Carefully removing my sidearm and laying it on some floating but dry rushes, I lowered my pants and hip boots and, carefully crouching until my tail end was just above but not in the knee-deep water, I did what my growling insides had been wanting to do for over an hour. Let me tell you, if size, consistency, and odor are taken into account, I left a masterpiece floating in the marsh. It was a second-hand Greek beauty. I apologize to my readers' sensibilities, but life out there can be hard ... er, soft sometimes ... and there is no way to get around it other than to put it in proper perspective! Carefully stepping to one side so as not to disturb my floating foot-deep, steaming masterpiece or get water in my partially pulled-down hip boots, I took care of the paperwork, then slowly and very carefully, so I wouldn't stumble and fall in the deep water and foot-entangling grass, pulled up my pants and hip boots. Reaching over to the floating bull rushes, I retrieved my Sig Sauer .45 semiautomatic pistol, carefully reholstered it, checked to make sure I still had my badge and wallet, and turned to the sound of now heavy shooting in the vicinity of Roscoe and his friends.

Boom-boom-boom-boom went the rapid sounds of several shotguns almost directly over my patch of cover, in fact, so close overhead I heard the shot hitting the marsh waters around me. It had been some time since I had disappeared into the bulrushes, so Roscoe's friends, not knowing I was still there, were shooting ducks flying directly over me. Looking up, I saw four green-winged teal flaring (climbing high into the sky) and another falling dead as a hammer. It was falling almost directly at me! I quickly sidestepped the fast-falling projectile, and *swish-kerplush* went the teal not three feet from where I stood.

Then I realized what had happened! The falling duck, as if being killed were not indignity enough, had fallen directly into my still steaming Greek "surprise." The pretty green-winged teal male, one of the most beautiful ducks in North America, was now a *brown*, ugly, not to mention horrible-smelling duck! I couldn't believe it! All that was sticking out of my dump were its tail feathers. If that duck had fallen seconds before, I could only imagine what that disaster would have looked like with a ten-ounce bird striking my head at forty-five miles per hour. Plain and simply, it would have knocked me silly, not to mention knocking my Robert Redford–like carcass into the Greek magnificence quietly floating in the swamp!

The odds had to be a zillion to one against a falling duck landing right smack-dab in my Greek delight. I realized God was either playing with me or awfully damned mad at me. Over my thoughts of the moment and what could have been, I could hear Roscoe's owner yelling at him to go get the duck that had just dropped into my little part of the world. Trying hard to keep from laughing, I hurriedly thrashed through the knee-deep water to another thick stand of cattails and bulrushes to get out of the dog's retrieve area. Once hidden, I turned to watch the action.

Splash-splash-splash, I could hear Roscoe coming through the tall stands of vegetation and belly-deep water like a mad rhino. Around and around he went outside my original stand of cattails, trying to locate the fallen duck. Typical retriever, I thought, went short on the retrieve. Then Roscoe smashed straight through my old cattail patch right to the duck. He went to grab the duck and then realized something was just not right. Up flew his head as if he had just stuck his nose in a skunk. Then Roscoe, without a moment's hesitation, began to eat and roll in the offering I had left the god of the swamp. I was in tears watching this minidrama unfold. The dog, still not having winded me (I can't figure out why!), finished what he could of my offering, took a final roll in the remains, then picked up the now brown green-winged teal and headed for his master with toilet paper streaming from both sides of his mouth.

Stepping out of my hiding place just enough to watch Roscoe's return, I saw him make a beeline for his master. The man stood up and said to his admiring buddies, "See, I told you he could make a blind retrieve." Damn, even clear over where I was, I could see that he was really proud of his dog. I could hear the owner calling out encouragement to his dog with outstretched arms to produce an even greater effort in his return. Roscoe didn't disappoint him ... *whump,* straight into his arms Roscoe flew, and I heard the man start to say, "Good dog, good dog, Ros—*ahhhhh,* what did you do? *Ahhhh,* get away, get away, you damn dog! What the hell happened? *Auggghh,* get away." The man started to rise from his kneeling position as he tried to push his horse of a dog away from him. He stumbled and flailed his arms like a windmill trying to catch his balance as he rose from the back edge of the dike, but Roscoe took that for a "come here" and again pushed his nose into the man's face. With that the man fell backward off the rear of the dike, shotgun and all, into about three feet of cold marsh water, duck shit, tule roots, and all.

Confused at his master's momentary disappearance, Roscoe attempted to deliver the duck to another of the party, who jumped off the dike into the marsh only to realize he wasn't wearing any type of protective waterproof boots. "Get away," bellowed the man as he struggled to get out of the water before his leather boots were ruined. The other fellow in the hunting party trotted off down the levee a few yards in hope that Roscoe's master would resurface before he got mobbed by the well-meaning, stinking dog as well. By now I was beside myself with mirth in the cattail patch. Even if someone had shot an over-limit of ducks in front of me at that moment, I doubt I could have written him a ticket because I was laughing so hard! Oh, I just knew God had done this on purpose, I thought.

I knew I couldn't march out of my hiding place at that moment to check Roscoe and his gang of hunters, who were now gathering on the dike trying to figure out what had happened, so I took off through the marsh, pausing to check several other hunters who were doing quite well. So well, in fact, that one had six ducks over the limit. Taking care of that matter and sending that lad on his way to meet my partner at the T in the dike, I continued on and checked another nearby duck hunter, who was legal. Then I worked my way back, a different way, mind you, to Roscoe and the gang. I figured I had better do it that way so they wouldn't figure out who had taken the dump in the marsh that Roscoe had found so delightful. They were still on the dike but a hell of a lot more subdued than before. As I approached the lads to check their ducks, licenses, and weapons, I noticed Roscoe sitting off to one side, all by himself with a long face. He was somewhat brownish tinged, I might add. Talk about a forlorn bunch; they certainly took the marsh award in that department for the day.

Approaching Roscoe, I could tell from about ten feet away that he still carried the essence of what he had happily discovered in the marsh earlier in the day. Trying hard not to laugh over the poor dog's misfortune, I kept walking toward the group. I went up to Roscoe's master, still soaking wet from his cold and untimely immersion in the swamp, identified myself, and asked how he was doing. He grumbled something about not so good, and I about lost it. There was a brown smudge beneath his right eye, about the size of a postage stamp, that was originally not of that marsh. Realizing that must have been where Roscoe nosed him with the duck and knowing what had been on Roscoe's nose, it was all I could do to keep from breaking out in laughter all over again. Checking the man's shotgun, I found it to be unplugged, or capable of carrying more than three shells, and informed him that he would be getting a citation for that violation. The ticket was the last straw on top of the wet hind end and the smell he couldn't seem to get rid of as well as the smell of his dog, and he told his friends he had had enough of the duck-hunting thing and was going home. Checking the other two lads, I found lead shot shells on them (lead shotgun shells are very toxic when ingested by waterfowl as a grit item and therefore illegal for hunting waterfowl in the United

States and Canada) and told them they too would receive citations from Larry, who would be waiting for them at the T in the dike. With that evidence in hand and their personal information in my diary, I sent them down the dike to receive their citations. As they gathered their gear in preparation for leaving, I heard one of them say, "Yeah, we got Roscoe the wonder dog all right. All that SOB did was retrieve a stinking crap duck no one else wanted and a damn game warden all in the same stinking breath. Next time we go hunting, I will bring my wife's damn cat—at least it has more sense than to eat and roll in someone's dump."

As they walked grumbling out of earshot, I heard Roscoe's master say, "Yeah, if I could catch that marsh-crapping bastard, I'd break him in half." With that, I turned and headed back into the marsh to check some more lads, chuckling to myself all the way. I will bet it was a long time before Roscoe got to hunt in a marsh again. And once the wife tried to kiss her returning hunter and discovered what the brown smudge on his cheek was, I'd bet it was even longer before Roscoe the Wonder Dog got a kiss on the nose from his master after a retrieve. ... The hunter probably had the same problem when it came to getting any smooches from his bride.

I told Larry later about the Roscoe incident, and we both had a good laugh as we headed back to the Greek restaurant for another load of very rich food. Look out, Roscoe, here I come!

Big Jake, the Owl, and the Scalped Cook

THERE WAS AN OLD Mexican ranch foreman on the east side of Butte Creek in Butte County not far from Gridley, California, with whom I would occasionally get together in the evenings to shoot feral cats. The feral cat problem in the Sacramento Valley in the mid-1970s was unreal. I did a lot of night work, and seldom did an evening go by in which I did not see fifteen to twenty cats in the headlights of my truck as I ran the back roads and farm roads looking for those violating the laws. They were everywhere, growing and going wild, and there wasn't a ground nester such as rabbits, quail, pheasant, small songbirds, ducklings, or the like that was safe in this cat-rich environment. This was especially true when the Sacramento River overflowed its banks in the winter time (the rainy season for the valley), forcing many a critter, game and nongame alike, to restricted islands or other small patches of dry ground in order to survive. Once these former housecats found one of these land-based "arks," all was over in short order for their prey. Folks, especially cat lovers, need to keep in mind that feral cats are one of the most efficient predators going. They have a knowledge of humankind and how to avoid us, and they return easily to their natural instincts and become deadly superpredators. Hence the deadly way I addressed the issue.

More than once I would see a single cat enter an abandoned culvert trying to hide from my arrival and after I threw in a firecracker to run that cat out to a waiting gun, there would be an explosion of cats, as many as five or ten at a time, trying to escape. So when I had a free evening, I would hook up with Joe Ramon, who was an expert predator caller, and we would spend a few hours calling and shooting cats on the lima-bean farm he managed.

Our method was simple. We would hook up high-powered miners' lamps with elastic straps to our bare heads and then quietly sit back to back in the dark in the middle of one of his many fields, near some tree rows or other favored cat cover. After a few moments of quiet and nonmovement, Joe would start calling with a cottontail-rabbit squeaker. He would do this off and on for about fifteen minutes, and then we would turn on our lamps, which had red lenses that predators couldn't see in the dark but allowed us to see well enough to shoot. It never failed. All around us we would see gleaming cats' eyes in the red light, and we would open up with our shotguns and kill as many as we could. We would repeat the process several times over the next few hours in different places, and some nights we would kill twenty-five to forty cats.

The other member of our cat-killing team was Big Jake. Big Jake was a large, brown Heinz 57–variety dog of immense proportions, including very long legs with the speed of a greyhound and teeth to match those of a tiger shark. Jake would faithfully lie beside Joe on these evening cat shoots and, once the shooting started, would spring to his feet and be off like a shot into the dark after an escaping cat. Soon he would return, seldom without a dead cat in his mouth.

As Joe told it, when Jake was a little puppy, a neighbor had a pair of Siamese cats that were meaner than a one-legged owl standing in a bowl of razor blades and fire ants. It seems one day the puppy was fast asleep on Joe's porch when the two cats happened on the sleeping dog, attacked little Jake, and fairly tore him a new tail end, including blinding him in one eye. I guess Jake never forgot that uninvited beating, and from the day he was big enough to amount to something, he lived to kill cats and did it with relish. Occasionally I would borrow Big Jake and take him along with me when the river flooded, in the process isolating many species of wildlife on little islands of life. I would let Jake out on one end of an island and put Joe on the other and in short order the cats, hunting the wildlife on the island, would be on the move to avoid one hell of a killing machine in the form of Big Jake. They would run to the other end of the island in an attempt to escape, only to find Joe, me, and our shotguns. Either way, it was all over. I'm sure it sounds brutal to cat-loving readers, but due in part to the cat menace, much of the Sacramento Valley lost its quail and cottontail rabbit populations in the 1970s, and I am not sure they ever recovered.

One morning, about three A.M., I met Joe on the east side of his lima-bean fields tending the irrigation water. I stopped to visit, and Joe said he was about done and asked if I would be interested in a cat shoot near one of his big water pumps. On his last two trips to the pump he had seen a flurry of cats in the vicinity and thought maybe a cleanout was in order. The evening had been slow, so I said I was more than ready, and off the two of us and Jake went. We positioned ourselves around a huge concrete standpipe near a pumping station that was silent for the moment, Joe on one side and I on the other. Jake took his customary place beside Joe, and the calling began. Joe hadn't been calling for more than four or five minutes when I heard the most godawful hell-raising on the other side of the pipe. Joe was yelling at the top of his lungs, "Get it off, get it off, help, Terry, get it off."

Jumping up from the ground, I flipped on my headlamp and stepped around the standpipe toward Joe just in time to see Big Jake swing into battle, only to instantly come unglued with the most awful howling I ever heard from a dog. With Joe and Big Jake under unseen attack, and apparently losing at that, my hair stood straight up and was climbing. Flipping the safety off my shotgun, I moved in closer with blood in my eye in order to defend my friend and Jake.

There before me was the godawfulest "hoorah" I had ever witnessed. The dust from the dry lima-bean field had risen six feet into the air and in that dust was an apparition of Joe turning around in crazy circles and Jake, acting if he were directly attached to Joe, going around in the same circles, sometimes with his feet and body clear off the ground! I had never seen a dog levitate, especially one the size of Jake, but he sure as hell was moving through the air in circles with all four feet clear off the ground at least part of the time! Then I saw the center of the "storm." Within this glob of flying forms was a damned long pair of wildly flapping wings and over Jake's *ahoooo*, I could hear what sounded like the clicking of an owl's bill. Once I got closer I could see what had happened, and if it hadn't been so damn serious it would have been a hoot (pun intended).

Joe had been using his cottontail call when apparently a hungry great horned owl, and a big one at that, had been fooled into thinking that Joe's head was a rabbit in distress. In the attack, the owl, one of the biggest I had ever seen, had footed Joe many times in the face and side of the head trying to kill this "rabbit" and was currently hanging on, sideways that is, as Joe flung his body around in fast-turning circles trying to get rid of the agonizing menace. When Jake heard his master all wrapped up in the "hoorah," he joined in, and the owl was all too happy to oblige.

As Jake got closer to see what the hell was the matter with his master, the owl, fearing reinforcements had arrived, went on the offensive and footed Jake on the end of the nose. Jake, innocent as hell one minute and the next grabbed by a winged hornet of some sort on the very soft and sensitive part of his nose, was letting the world know he wanted out. Well, the owl was having none of that and continued the offensive with two tightly closed, taloned feet, one firmly affixed to Joe's right eyebrow and forehead and the other to the top of Jake's soft nose.

Between Jake's piteous *ahoooo* and Joe's screaming, we had a three-ring circus. An owl, like other birds of prey, doesn't let go with his talons unless he wants to, and the harder one pulls away from a bird of prey's taloned feet, the harder it clutches the prey. ... With that in mind, I had a problem. I had a whirling glob of rapidly shifting bodies, two of friend and one of foe. They were changing positions so fast that I knew shooting the owl off Joe's head was not a real option, legal or otherwise. Yet I had to do something or my two friends were going to get injured even further. All I needed was to get involved and have the owl take on a piece of me for good measure as well. Remember, Mr. Owl was still in the driver's seat and still had a knife-sharp clacking bill ready to take on all comers. As I saw it, I didn't have many options.

Quickly emptying the shells out of my shotgun and seeing an opportunity, I swung the gun barrel at the head of the owl on one of Joe's frantic passes. Joe zigged when he should have zagged, and at a fairly high velocity, *bong* went the barrel off Joe's head as I misjudged the angle of attack, knocking him off his feet and hard to the ground in a loud, dusty *whuummp*. Stunned, he lay there for a second, leaving the owl as a semistationary target still attached to his head. Hauling off and swinging the shotgun barrel with even more steam on it this time, I again missed this owl of many charmed lives and smacked Big Jake right on the end of the nose with such force that it tore the taloned foot and the meat it was clutching right off as Jake hurled backward. *Ahooooo* went Jake, this time as if someone had shot him in the hind end! Then Joe staggered up once again and the owl, in order to retain his balance, firmly planted his taloned foot still holding part of Jake's nose right on the bridge of Joe's nose! Now, with this new attack on a very sensitive piece of his real estate, Joe went nuts. Grabbing the owl with both hands, he tried to tear it off his nose and eyebrow. The owl, taking this as bad manners and a new challenge, just hung on tighter and this time used his rapidly clacking bill to good measure on Joe's fingers, gouging out great strips of meat and finger skin. Finally Joe, thoroughly tangled up with his assailant, just stopped and stood there whimpering, not knowing what to do. With that, I had a clear shot and this time carefully smacked the owl in the head with my shotgun barrel, stunning him. He relaxed, let go with his talons and dropped off Joe's head. Jake, seeing his chance in the dim light of my headlamp, thinking it was a cat, I suppose, grabbed the owl. Well, the stunned owl, not to be outdone, grabbed Jake with both sets of talons and the "hoorah" started up all over again. Leaving Jake to his own devices, I got Joe's hands away from his face and head and looked him over. No doubt about it, the first round had gone to the owl! Joe's face and the left side of his head were a bloody mess. It was obvious the owl had footed him numerous times, trying to kill the largest cottontail he had ever seen.

Joe, unmindful of his wounds upon hearing his dog in abject pain, said, "Jake, I got to help Jake." The two of us lurched around the standpipe, and there were Jake and the owl going around and around in the dust. At that point the owl let go, fell off, and lurching to its feet, squared off to meet whatever challenge Jake had to throw his way. Grabbing Jake, I held him back, and then here came Joe with his shotgun. Grabbing Joe's shotgun by the barrel, I pushed it down hard just as it went off and yelled that he couldn't kill the damn bird. "Joe," I said, "it is protected by federal law; you can't kill it."

"The hell you say," said Joe as he jacked another shell into the chamber and tried to raise his shotgun and clean up on the owl that had cleaned up just moments before on him.

"No way, Joe; I'll have to arrest you if you shoot him," I hollered. At that point the owl, no longer hungry for a rabbit of Joe's dimensions, flew off into the nearest row of trees and disappeared, crashing into some tree limbs into the dark of the night. Letting Jake go now that the assailant was gone, I again looked at Joe. "Joe," I said, "You look like crap." By now his face was starting to puff up with loose blood under the skin and we decided to go to his portable cook wagon, used to feed his migrant workers on the ranch, and get some first aid from the sleeping cook.

Needless to say, the great cat-shooting detail turned into an ambulance train as we headed for the cook shack. Man, it seemed like the god of cats had evened up the odds a little on this shindig. ... Upon arrival, Joe got his cook out of bed and began scrounging around inside the trailer for the first aid kit while I tried to clean out the puncture wounds with some hydrogen peroxide. By the time the cook and I got through with Joe's face, with the tincture of iodine and all, he looked worse than when the owl had left him in the last round of the fight. Joe took one look in the mirror and just shook his head. In addition to the wounds on his head and hands, I saw Joe painfully fingering a large goose-egg-sized knot on the side of his head. "Must've hit the standpipe," he said through swollen lips. Knowing it was probably from the shotgun barrel I had swung at the owl at a high rate of speed, I said nothing, not wanting to add fuel to that fire. ...

Then Joe took a look at Jake. He of course had puncture wounds all over his head, but the worst was the three-inch-square patch of skin missing from the top of his nose, just behind the nostril itself. The cook told Joe the best thing to do was to cauterize the area with a piece of hot metal; otherwise it would get infected, Jake being a dog and all. Now, I thought that was not the best thing to do, given the size of Jake and all, but the cook persisted and began to warm up a ten-inch cast-iron skillet on his gas stove to use as a cauterizing iron. Joe finally agreed, and with Joe holding Jake, me standing by the door of my truck (no, I wasn't scared), and the cook approaching with the glowing hot skillet, all hell broke lose. Jake, realizing he was the center of attention, decided he wanted no part of this party and tried to get away from Joe. "Hold him," the cook yelled as he slapped the red-hot skillet not too carefully on the top of Jake's owl-damaged nose and most of the rest of it as well. *Ahooooo* went Jake as he pulled away from Joe and bolted over the surprised and falling-backward cook, biting him square on the top of the head as he passed over and flew into the adjoining ditch full of water to cool off his now burned, not to mention punctured, sore nose. The cook, jumping up without looking, placed his hand square on the business end of the hot skillet and let out a yell heard all the way to China.

Racing over to help the cook, I took a look and about fell over in the dirt. The cook's hair was gone! Jake had scalped him! He looked like Ben Franklin, having gone from a hell of a head of hair to completely bald on top. The cook's hand shot to the top of his head and he let out another yell as Joe just stood there with an open mouth in shock at this latest turn of events. Then I realized the cook had a hairpiece and the dog had lifted it clean off when it bit him on the head.

At that point, I started to laugh totally out of control. Nothing had gone right since Joe and I had met earlier that morning with the owl fight, and now the cook without his hair and with bite marks on his bald head only added to the festivities. Damn, it was funny and I just let it all out. Then, Joe started to laugh through his sore face, and soon we were both laughing uncontrollably. However, the cook wasn't. He was frantically looking for his $200 hairpiece, which he never found, I might add. I don't know if Jake ate it out of revenge or if it got lost in the ditch waters when Jake dove in to soothe his aching cauterized nose. No matter how you looked at it, what a morning's worth of events that turned out to be. Plus, we didn't get any damned cats!

Joe, Jake, and I had several nighttime cat hunts after that, but Joe and I wore hard hats and never had a repeat of that incident with the owl. Jake continued his cat-killing ways, only this time with a vengeance. Every time I saw him after that, he had a dead cat near him announcing a recent kill. It was as if he blamed all the cats in the world for his misfortune with the winged "cat." If only Jake had known that one of the top menu items of a great horned owl is the skunk, followed by the cat!

I never did tell Joe how that large knot got on his forehead, and I sure as hell didn't tell Jake I was responsible for the large patch of skin being removed from his nose. I have found that some things are best left unsaid when dealing with humans and critters alike. I would bet a month's paycheck that owl had a real yarn to spin to his offspring about the night he attacked and vanquished the world's largest cotton-tail rabbit.

A Few More Dogs

SINCE MANY HUNTERS have dogs, it is not surprising that many of the stories that develop in the field of wildlife law enforcement center around their antics and those of their masters. Usually by ten o'clock on the opening day of any hunting season, everybody's dog has the same name: "You son of a bitch."

Once I was working with a deputy chief from a Western state Fish and Game agency, and in checking a shotgun with whose make he was unfamiliar, he accidentally discharged it and blew the tail clean off the hind end of a nearby hunter's dog! It didn't really hurt the dog, just removed his tail, making him rather funny looking. Needless to say, that created quite a ruckus before the smell of gunpowder wafted away.

Another time a violator saw me coming and tried to throw away his over-limit of ducks in the brush, only to have his faithful dog quickly retrieve them, bringing the evidence of the crime right back to the owner. The man and dog repeated the process several times as I approached. I would bet a beer that dog got one hell of a beating after I left and he realized he had received a $450 citation. Then there was the sad day when Brad Davis of Glenn County in California had to put down his very special old dog. The dog was full of cancer and in a lot of pain. The vet had tossed up his hands just days before and told Brad there was no hope and that it was cruel to keep the dog alive any longer. The vet had offered to put the dog down, but Brad just couldn't do it until the two of them could have one more moment together. Brad had taken the dog into the foothills on one of his ranches and after a tearful good-bye shot the dog in the back of the head with his .22-caliber rifle. Brad, full of grief after having had this great partner for eleven years, buried the dog on a knoll so she could "look out" over her old ranch and stomping grounds. Two days later I met Brad in his driveway and tried to console him over his loss, only to see at that very moment his old dog stumbling down the road, back from the grave. That old dog was in so much pain but so happy to see Brad. Even I cried after Brad begged me to take my service revolver and shoot the sick and wounded old dog in his driveway in order to put her out of her misery. I regretfully obliged. That is one dog story I couldn't fully write. I may be tough, but I'm not that tough. ... I can still see Sam (short for Samantha) standing there looking up at her master with a quizzical look in her eyes ... before the lights went out for the final time. I still get tears in my eyes just thinking about that dog's loyalty. Brad has never forgiven himself and, like me, has never had another four-legged partner.

Dogs truly are our best friends, and to think otherwise when one is at your side is criminal. God does not forget the error of your ways like your dog does. Someday you may find yourself living the life of a dog if you are cruel to them during your lifetime. Take heed!

nine

Eating Our Own

THE WELCOME PREDAWN October breezes from the northwest cooled my sun- and windburned face. Borne on those breezes rustling the stand of cattails behind me were the pungent smells of marsh gas, sour water, and rotting vegetation and the sounds of faraway traffic on the interstate. The chew of tobacco was comfortably tucked in my right cheek, and I was right with the world. Standing at my side was my faithful companion, the quintessential Utah conservation officer Larry Davis. The glowing end of his cigarette in the darkness told me he had lit up and was probably mulling over the beginning of another duck season in the Farmington Bay Waterfowl Management Area. I too had been daydreaming about the start of another duck season in the marshes of Utah and the great experiences they always brought. For me, fall in the marshes anywhere in America was always a grand time and place to be. And there were no finer examples than the fall marshes of Utah.

The 500,000-plus acres of marshes surrounding the Great Salt Lake, home to myriad shorebirds, waterfowl, and many other species, would soon experience a disturbance with a magnitude of 5.6 on the Richter Scale: the opening day of waterfowl season. Soon the marshes would be teeming with the American sportsman in his quest to fulfill primal urges associated with hunting during the autumn and winter months as well as filling his game bag with excellent-tasting water-fowl. As if marching to the same drummer, numerous species of ducks and geese unaccustomed to being shot at all year would soon fall prey to high-speed loads of steel shot. This cataclysmic event would include barking dogs, sportsmen falling over their heads into the strong-smelling marsh waters, duck calls resembling everything from a moorhen to an aardvark, shooters scurrying after freshly killed or crippled birds, fistfights over the hapless Canada goose shot twenty-two times as it flew between competing groups of hunters, dogfights, yelling back and forth, more dogfights, and chaos in the air among the feathered community unaccustomed to such mayhem. Ah, fall in the marshes and the opening day of waterfowl hunting season. I can smell, see, and hear it now.

The sport of hunting waterfowl *can* be a living, breathing thing of utmost beauty, grace, and majesty. The seasonal sky is usually cloudless and clear of pollution, the darkest azure blue, and the mornings carry the bite of the winter soon to come. The marsh is dressed up in its fall finery and at that time of the year is home to many species of shorebirds, waterfowl, and tons of other two- and four-legged critters. The sun is still able to lift the midday temperatures into a range where you find yourself wearing more clothing than needed. And the excitement of swarms of low-flying waterfowl directly overhead, along with one's rapid shooting, makes the heart race and the outing complete. As if holding all this fall greatness together, thousands of spiders spin their last skeins of silk, drifting on the gentle breezes among the marsh plants in reckless abandon. For the sportsman constantly cleaning silky strands off his face and shotgun, it is simply another part of this fall rite of passage. Last but not least, the sight of the starkly magnificent mountain ranges adjacent to the Great Salt Lake with their multicolored patches of turning vegetation, coupled with the intense color of the stunning, dark blue water against golden autumn marsh colors, is a memory to those who see and enjoy such special gifts from the hands of God.

SINCE THE FIRST DAYS of my Denver residency as special agent in charge, I annually brought many of my agents from the far-flung corners of the region to mix with the Utah officers during this fall ritual, principally to address the opening day's Oklahoma land rush–like atmosphere in the Great Salt Lake marshes. The Salt Lake Basin has a population of over two million souls, and within that population are thousands of licensed duck and goose hunters. Swirl together those hunters and the adjacent living marshes rich with hundreds of thousands of ducks, geese, and swans and you had the makings of a delightful "game warden's stew." Typically mixed into a "stew" of that magnitude are those with black hearts bent on savaging the resource come hell or high water. Conservation officers find folks of this ilk across the North American continent on a regular basis. Simply put, humankind is predatory and destructive. Some keep those urges under wraps or in control while others let it all hang out. Those chaps walking on the dark side always seemed to forget one very important thing: that there were those of us on the other side carrying a badge who could be just as predatory and relentless when it came to hunting the lawless. And *we* didn't have a bag limit!

The convoluted story told in this chapter was in part the culmination of work that had begun many months if not years earlier. The Service had been working for years on a realistic medical program involving health screening and maintenance for its officer corps. The goal was to set physical standards that were meaningful to the profession, fair, and administered so as to minimize the government's liability in cases of on-the-job injuries or death. The plan was to hire physically fit officer candidates governed by predetermined medical standards and, with regularly administered physicals, to provide health guidance for this cadre of highly trained wildlife law enforcement specialists throughout their careers. Physically and emotionally fit officers would execute the Service's mission in a more professional and efficient manner. Sounds pretty simple, doesn't it?

That was where the wheels came off the wagon! Medical benchmarks that were fair, realistic, and *legal* were rather elusive. No sooner was a benchmark proposed than other federal law enforcement agencies pursuing like goals found themselves legally embroiled in issues relating to that standard! It seemed that for every foot advanced in anyone's medical programs, two would be lost to the courts in legal challenges by aggrieved and negatively impacted officers.

In 1996 the Service proposed a new medical program with standards for the Division of Law Enforcement. Therein begins a convoluted tale in which officers from the Service's Division of Law Enforcement ultimately did the right thing and "ate their own." ... Doesn't make sense, huh? Well, hang on to the willows and read on.

MY REGION always seemed to have an investigative "happening" or two going on, come daylight or dark. Our limited number of officers (twenty-four for three-quarters of a million square miles — approximately thirty-three thousand square miles per officer), coupled with nonexistent budgets, meant we could never do things on a scale that pleased my better "catch dogs." Yet officers like Suazo, Eicher, Kraft, Cooper, Domenici, Hartman, Webb, Young, Klett, Goessman, Prieksat, and others always discovered ways to keep the bad guys off their feed in spite of such Service-generated hindering odds as nonexistent funding. Be it interstate road blocks; covert operations; working the oil, electrical transmission, and mining industries illegally taking migratory birds; cooperative state-federal details; checking the hunting public for compliance; or working along the Canadian border, my lads kept the bad guys hopping from rock to rock. In that process, many a head governed by a black heart rolled like that of Anne Boleyn. Soon a Region 6 reputation of "hustling the bad guys" against many crippling odds became our law enforcement trademark.

Owing to that reputation, I received a phone call from a Mr. J. C. Phillip Spottswood, who was with the U.S. Office of Personnel Management, Medical Policy, and Programs. After introductions, he laid out his most recent assignment and needs. It seemed that he and Dr. Richard Miller, director of Federal Law Enforcement Medical Programs for Federal Occupational Health, U.S. Public Health Service, had been assigned by the Service to observe a law enforcement task force operation in action. They were to participate personally and evaluate the agents' physical activities in the field in relation to the newly proposed Department of the Interior medical program standards. Spottswood said he had heard that I was planning such a task force operation in Utah that fall and asked if that were true. I replied in the affirmative, and he quickly asked if it would be possible for him and Dr. Miller to accompany some of my officers to ascertain how closely their field activities matched the proposed medical standards. I said that would be fine, just as long as they had the blessing of Kevin Adams, chief of Law Enforcement. Spottswood said he would make sure the appropriate arrangements were made with Chief Adams for the required clearances. In the meantime, he would procure ammunition, shotguns, and camouflage hunting clothing at government expense so they would look the part. I found that statement puzzling but let it ride (puzzling in that there was no legitimate need to incur such expenses as an observer). That call was followed by many more over the next several months, making sure Spottswood and Miller could still participate in our "real live" task force operation. Their eagerness, including wanting to look the part with camouflage gear and shotguns, continued to raise my caution flags. However, Spottswood was more or less one of our own, and his program assignment rang true to the Division's needs. So I ignored my basic cautionary law enforcement instincts and accepted that eagerness as a couple of hidebound desk jockeys' excitement over the chance to do something new. That was an oversight destined to have an unusual impact.

IMMEDIATELY PRIOR TO the October 4 waterfowl opener in Utah that year, approximately 100 state and federal conservation officers gathered in Ogden for task force briefings and team assignments. Also present were Phillip Spottswood and Dr. Richard Miller. During that briefing, Senior Resident Agent Robert Standish provided information on waterfowl population numbers, weather forecasts, team assignments, specific geographic assignments, restricted species (swans, canvasbacks) concentration areas, recent changes in federal and state laws, bag and possession limit changes from the year before, license and duck-stamp requirements for all nonresidents in the group desiring to hunt waterfowl during their spare time, and area closures and court dates subsequent to citation issuance. It was a typical Standish briefing: extensively detailed and appropriate to the mission.

As the briefing droned on, a special announcement was made out of the blue. It seemed one special agent from the Service had recently completed his academy training. This officer was reported to be better than the average bear when it came to waterfowl identification. In fact, it was rumored that he was so good, *he was better than God. ...* However, during his final waterfowl examination at the academy, he had missed a five-point duck identification question. Central to that issue was his misidentification of an albino female northern pintail in the collection of test birds to be identified. Agent Rich Grosz was asked to come forward and presented with a framed picture of the duck causing the identification problem that had cost him a perfect score on the examination. Richard's long walk to accept this "trophy" was accompanied by many good-natured but choice "supporting" words from his fellow officers regarding his purported waterfowl identification skills. Larry Davis seemed to be in the middle of the presentation, and I am sure that if anyone had sought out the name of the culprit who had set up Agent Grosz, they might find Davis central to that as well! For some unknown reason, when Agent Rich Grosz returned to his seat holding his cherished "trophy," he had nothing but steely looks for his dad, the special agent in charge who had taught the offending waterfowl identification class some months earlier. What made it funnier was the fact that young Grosz had suspected he might be set up by the older Grosz before that examination. Nonetheless, he still fell into the "slop." Oh well, sometimes you eat the bear, and sometimes he eats you. ...

During a break in the briefing, I visited with several out-of-district agents, clarified points of law, and discussed operational concerns. I also talked to Spottswood and Miller about the officer teams to which they would be assigned. Spottswood was assigned to the special agent team of Pat Bosco and Ellen Kiley, who would be working the marsh on foot—exhausting, hot, and challenging work to say the least. However, those officers were very athletic, and I was sure they would give their examiner the "bird's-eye" view of what was expected in that kind of work detail. Dr. Miller was assigned to the airboat team of Agent Bryce Findley and Utah Conservation Officer Steve Stoinski (now a special agent with the Service, and a damn good one, I might add). There he would get an idea of how a quasi-covert operation was run as well as ordinary boat-patrolling activities in the marshes and open-water areas. The two examiners from Washington, D.C., as a result of their assignments, would now be able to evaluate representative types of work performed by hardworking line officers. I told Spottswood and Miller (both were from out of state) that they would be required to procure nonresident hunting licenses if they chose to hunt ducks anytime during their Utah assignment. This information had been given out during the briefing by Agent Standish, but as a matter of course, I repeated it. Both men acknowledged that they understood the need for a nonresident license and federal duck stamp if they chose to hunt. They also raised several issues regarding overtime pay for work performed the day before the start of the season when the teams were out and about becoming familiar with their assigned areas because long days were the norm. There were also issues of concern regarding trespass. Since they would be working on public lands where trespass would not be an issue, I laid those concerns to rest. The evaluators then left to meet their teammates and get familiar with the plan of attack in the marsh two days hence.

The briefing break over, the "hijinks" continued. As the oldest fed at the briefing, I was cordially assigned to Larry Davis, reportedly the oldest game warden in the *history* of the state of Utah. I guess those assigning the teams felt that since Larry and I were so old (read worthless), we would probably fall asleep in our vehicle somewhere and come skulking in at the end of the operation for the traditional great dinner put on by the state of Utah. The task force organizers surmised that if they assigned the oldest and most "worthless" chaps to work together, there would be little chance that the rest gathered there that evening would be surprised by the number of citations issued by such a decrepit team. The announcement of that assignment was greeted by good-natured hoots, jeers, and hollers at the rather "poor quality" of the Davis-Grosz team. However, Larry and I were used to such ridicule and derision, having been assigned together as a task force team during previous years. Understand that it was a badge of honor to be the number-one ticket-writing team. There were lots of fine officers in that task force, and it was always a challenge to be first in the number of citations issued. However, don't get dismayed about Larry and Terry being out of the running for this great honor, even considering our ages (glacial dirt and us being the same). Keep that "deceit and guile" overcoming youth maxim in mind, in case a miracle were to happen. ...

The day before the opener, Larry and I, like the others, familiarized ourselves with our assigned marsh area, bird flight patterns, and waterfowl concentration areas. Assigning teams of officers to specific areas of the marsh is always good business because most of the marsh will be covered, and officers will not be stumbling over each other, checking and pissing off the same hunters more than once. The area assigned to us was a large portion of the Farmington Bay Waterfowl Management Area, a great section of marsh home to hordes of waterfowl, a ton of hunters, and usually a hatful of shooters walking on the wild side. Larry and I hoped to reintroduce those folks walking on the wild side to the wildlife laws of the land and correct some poor hunter ethics.

STANDING IN THE WATER at the edge of a main levee deep in the marsh, Larry and I remained quietly lost in our thoughts as we waited for daylight. We had arrived several hours before legal shooting hours in order to anchor a good central stakeout location and, in part, to be alone with the marsh, its critters, and our thoughts before being mobbed by the American waterfowl hunting public. The air was cool and full of waterfowl practicing their travels and traditions, announced by the sounds of whistling wings, calls, and droppings occasionally hitting the water around us. The marsh was home to other strange sounds from swimming muskrats, skunks, and mink scurrying around at our feet and the happy croaking of coots picking at the duckweed floating in the water. Occasionally we could hear the calls of great horned owls flying low over the marsh looking for a sleepy duck with its guard down. We could hear peeps and chirps at every point of the compass, our hearts were beating, and life was good.

Then headlights began bouncing and waving on the road leading to the distant parking lots, announcing the coming human invasion. Soon quiet shadows began hurriedly filing by on the levee as these invaders entered the marsh and our daydreaming, announcing the soon-to-start waterfowl season with all its warts in the Great Salt Lake Basin.

Crawling farther into the recesses of my hunting coat for the warmth it afforded, I watched the levee crowd tramping by to see where most went. There was a levee splitting off from ours, leading due west. Troop after troop of these early-morning invaders walked out of sight in the predawn darkness down that westward feeder levee. Soon I could hear the roar of thousands of waterfowl lifting off from their marsh homes in that area as those shadows on the levee aroused the critters from their morning slumbers. Still the quiet shadows from the parking lot came into our area of the marsh, and Larry and I quietly observed the onslaught, all the while formulating a plan on what came next. The morning light to the east was still challenging the night as we continued watching the hordes of hunters now passing by in an almost constant stream. Now I knew how Custer felt, I mused, with just the two of us to enforce the laws in that portion of the marsh amongst all that humanity. The parking lot was swirling with head-lights and barking dogs, portending more ghostly shadows to come. And they did ... and did! Soon our little portion of the marsh was jug-ful of expectant hunters and the air loaded with confused waterfowl flying every which way. What had been a sleepy marsh just hours before was now a living nightmare about to explode like Chicago Central during morning rush hour!

I identified a small group of hunters standing in the cattails at the water's edge some twenty-five yards away as those I would watch at the onset of shooting. Larry, being the veteran he was, quietly identi-fied a group of six hunters lying along the edge of the levee to the north as his intended subjects. With that, we settled in and quietly watched our folks for any signs of illegal activity.

Soon the dark of the morning gave way to the onrushing sun, fol-lowed by skeins of waterfowl dotting the horizon, soft breezes — and the day was on! Single, not-too-sure-of-themselves searching shots were soon replaced by multiple shots until the marsh sounded like what the soldiers of Picket's charge must have experienced in 1863 at Gettysburg. Several hundred shots per minute was the norm as the re-maining waterbound feathered marsh critters fled skyward in panic. Ducks flying over levees laced with gunners hiding in the cattails fell like feathered snowflakes, each leaving a puff of feathers in the air as mute testimony of a living thing now past. Looking over at Larry, I checked my watch. The lads in our part of the marsh had only shot one minute early. That was pretty damn good control, I mouthed to my partner with a smile.

However, a fellow immediately to the south was on his game. As a duck approached, he would shoulder his gun, go into a crouch like he was shooting skeet, rise at the last moment, and powder the duck. Not bad shooting, I thought. But as those killing actions continued un-abated, my own hunting instincts took over. Every time the lad shot, he never even looked to see where the duck fell! He just kept shoot-ing and killing for the pleasure it brought. In fact, he killed everything that came in range! In four minutes and thirty-seven seconds, he killed fifteen ducks with fifteen shots! Since he was more than double over the limit, I had Larry grab him while I continued watching three other shooters farther south on the levee killing what appeared to be exclusively redheads by the sack full (a numerically restricted species that year). Now you can see why learning to identify waterfowl species is so important to a conservation officer *and* to the American hunter, especially when the closed-season species are darting around at forty-five miles per hour in poor light. We ran that group to ground posthaste before all the redheads produced in the marsh that year disappeared into their tote sacks! On our day went as the two of us "captured" those using lead shot in a steel-shot zone, ran to ground those in our little corner of the marsh with over-limits, snapped up those using unplugged shotguns, surprised those killing protected migratory nongame birds, grabbed those killing protected species of waterfowl, intercepted those hunting in the closed areas, and happily stopped those not retrieving their ducks from the marsh once killed (wanton waste). We hustled in this fashion all day, not even stopping for lunch, until the chickens came home to roost in the dark of night. Needless to say, Larry and I paid for the gas and oil that fair day, if the dollar amounts on our citations were any indicator. ...

Arriving back at my motel room that evening with my tail end dragging, looking forward to a good dinner, a long shower, and a little rest, I discovered that my day was only beginning! Pacing the floor outside my room like a cat on a hot tin roof was Special Agent Pat Bosco. Pat is an outstanding agent and migratory bird instructor for the Service. It makes no difference what assignment he is handed. Pat will carry it through with a sureness and focus that many agents can't even come close to duplicating. He has such driven, focused energy that any miscreant whose trail he lands on will soon find himself a goner in a state or federal court of law.

"Pat, what the hell are you doing here?" I asked.

"I have a real problem, and you, being the special agent in charge of this region, are about to get it dumped into your lap. My guy Spottswood the medical examiner *broke the law!* I couldn't believe it! He was told to get a nonresident hunting license and duck stamp if he was going to hunt and *he didn't do it!* He went right ahead and shot a duck and then tried to lie to me about what had happened." Frustration and disbelief really took hold of Pat, and he broke like an egg. "Can you believe that? I watched him shoot a duck and let it lie in the marsh to rot. Then he tried to lie his way out of what he did. He tried to tell me the guy I was watching was the one who shot the duck! Can you believe that? And with Ellen and me watching him! I just can't believe what he did. I told him he was doing the same thing other outlaws were doing and that he was no different than those we were chasing. I just can't believe he did that to me," he uttered again in abrupt disgust! "What is going to happen now? He was sent here by the bigwigs in the Service to observe our physical activities in the field and match them to our new medical program. Now that he has broken the law big time and may be looking at a stint in federal court, what will happen to our medical program? I will just bet it ends up in the toilet. You can also bet the chief of law enforcement will be pissed when he hears what happened, especially if Spottswood ends up in federal court! And, if we don't file on him, that will compound the problem in the eyes of every officer on this task force. There are at least a dozen other guys who already know what happened today, and if we don't file, how is that going to look?"

Poor old Pat, I thought. Wound up tighter than a clock spring and mad enough to eat sawdust and poop out two-by-fours! Not happy about the issue of one of our own breaking the law, I told Pat, "Put together a case report and get it to me fast. If Spottswood's wrong, I will have Standish file on him in federal court."

Pat just looked at me in disbelief. "How are you going to do that?" he asked in a troubled voice. "Washington is going to have a fit if we try to file on one of our own, especially when he was sent here at the behest of the Service to evaluate and write our future medical policy. And more importantly, how is that going to color their views when our officers are injured on duty in the future and can't pass the physical? I can just see that if they are prosecuted by us for this, it may reflect poorly on their judgments about injured officers during subsequent physical examinations in which they are rendering fit-for-duty decisions."

"Pat, do as I say. I need a case report from you and Ellen posthaste. I also need to brief the regional director on the day's events so he doesn't get blindsided by the powers-that-be in Washington. So get cracking! Get that case report to me as fast as you can."

You could see the relief flooding across Pat's face at having that weight lifted from his shoulders. Pat is one honest and ethical officer, and right was right to his way of thinking. If I had taken any other stand or gone political, I would have lost a dear friend and the respect of a fellow officer who is like a brother to me. The American people paid me to fairly enforce the federal conservation laws of the land, and that I would do. However, my turned-to-shit evening did not end with Pat's revelation!

That evening over dinner with other task force officers, I was offhandedly advised by one of them that he had heard that Dr. Miller (with the airboat crew) had done some shooting to put forth the ruse that he was a hunter. In the process, he had shot at some protected migratory nongame birds! I just shook my head at that revelation. ... If that were true, we had both medical officers breaking the laws, just the same as the outlaws we were chasing! After all that had been said and done in the briefing and by me personally regarding their legal obligations, these two lads had stepped into ten thousand years of goose shit and tule roots in the marsh and instantly gone haywire. My thoughts returned to my feelings regarding caution when Spottswood had first told me that he and Dr. Miller would be purchasing hunting gear at government expense to use on the operation. My caution flags had been right, and like a dingbat I had disregarded them. Oh well. I guess that is what I got paid the big bucks for, and that included a helping of "eating my own" if need be. To anyone interested, it tastes a lot like crow. ...

When I met Larry at four the next morning for our trip back into the marsh, he sported a grim look. "I understand our man Spottswood broke the law," he said coolly.

"That is what Pat Bosco relayed to me last night," I replied. There were no further words exchanged until we headed out to the deserted parking lot in the marsh.

"What are you going to do?" he asked as we bumped along the rutted road.

"Wait until I get Pat's case report and then make up my mind," I answered as I chomped down harder on my mouthful of chewing tobacco in frustration over the unexpected dilemma.

"What are you going to do about Dr. Miller?" he slowly asked. Good old Larry, I thought. As good an officer as ever crapped between a pair of boots. Ethical, smart, great with people, and a damned good catch dog. He was also a great friend who was trying in his way to help me think through a situation that had the political properties of black powder next to an open flame.

"Well, when I get the chance to meet up with Agent Findley and Officer Stoinski, I will inquire as to what occurred with them as well. If there appears to be a violation, I will request a posthaste case report. Once read, then and only then will I make a decision as to what the Service's actions will be."

Larry let the subject drop in light of more important things, like our breakfast of salami, Diet Pepsi, and crackers. Walking out on the levee into the marsh, we discussed our routine for the day and reviewed our citations from the day before. We had done quite well in the ticket department, not only in numbers but in quality as well. We had caught an individual with 179 lead shells in his possession (still a task force record in Utah to this day), several with protected species, and six with over-limits. Additionally, there were a hatful of others straying across the line with lesser violations. And we had let an equal number of folks go for screwing up in minor ways. All could have been ticketed, but in some cases we felt a damn good ass-chewing was a better lesson than a fine and proceeded accordingly. Overall, not bad for a long day's work, I thought. Especially for a couple of old farts who creaked and snapped a lot when they walked.

Our second day began at daylight with a roar of shotguns, although not as intense as the previous day. There were fewer ducks because many had been killed the day before and many of those remaining had wised up and were sitting out of gun range in the middle of the marsh's big water areas. However, the shooting was still pretty damn hot and heavy. Soon, we were knee deep in violators, violations, and the ordinary run-of-the-mill dingbats. Our day passed doing what we did best, and *do it well we did!*

That evening Larry and I met Findley and Stoinski at the end of their airboat patrol. After just a couple of questions, it was apparent that I had problems. It seemed that the officers had used Dr. Miller as a decoy shooting from a blind over decoys to convince other nearby suspicious airboat operators that they (the officers) were legitimate sportsmen. While Miller shot, those two officers could sit back and watch other shooters around them breaking the law largely unnoticed. They had done so in the belief that Miller was a knowledgeable and experienced, not to mention licensed, hunter. After all, that was the way it appeared with all his camo gear, new shotgun, and reams of government-supplied shells. However, it soon became apparent Miller didn't know his hat from his hind end when it came to hunting waterfowl. The first gull and avocet that went by, he shot at them! They were protected migratory birds! The two officers, realizing they had a rube in the blind, at once stopped him from shooting unless they were right alongside to coach and guide him as to what to aim at and when to pull the trigger. Later that first day and into the next, Dr. Miller had opportunities to shoot at ducks under the guidance of the officers. He shot at several and knocked down a shoveler, which they were unable to locate. Upon returning to the dock after the second day of the outing, the officers then and only then discovered that Dr. Miller lacked a nonresident hunting license and federal duck stamp! Shocked, they dropped him off at his vehicle after a damn good ass-chewing, then landed and loaded the airboat onto the trailer. They had planned on running me down with that information to see what I wanted done when Larry and I arrived on the scene. After listening to their stories, I asked Agent Findley to initiate a case report with Officer Stoinski's report attached and get it to me posthaste. They agreed, and we parted company.

It was a quiet ride back to the Fish and Game field station for the traditional dinner celebrating the end of the task force. In those days, we hit the marshes with task force numbers of that magnitude only during the opening weekend. That was when most people would be hunting and the greatest numbers of birds would be killed (a lot of the birds were the young of the year and unaccustomed to being shot at—read dumb). Plus, most state and federal agencies had only enough money and personnel to support a two-day operation at that level of intensity because there was pressing work elsewhere with other numerous ongoing big-game and small-game hunting seasons.

As soon as I arrived and parked my vehicle, I was met by a worried Bob Standish. "Did you hear?" he asked with a steely look.

"About Spottswood and Dr. Miller?" I asked.

"Yes," he replied coolly.

"Sure did. I asked Bosco and Findley to get me a written report posthaste. Once Neill and I have a chance to review that, I will make a decision regarding whether we have a good enough case to prosecute them. In the meantime, you keep a lid on the political things over here if the state starts to 'boil' over with noncitation issuance on the spot or special treatment concerns with these two. Let the folks know we will do the right thing regardless of the shooters' unique positions and the political 'hoorah' that will surely follow. Soon as I get those reports, I will be in touch. If they are wrong, and it sure looks that way as of now, I will give you the go-ahead and you can file a Federal Information [formal complaint] on each man for their alleged violations. Any shit that hits the fan will stop at my desk, so once this process is set in motion with my command, you proceed normally. Do we have an understanding, Mr. Standish?"

"Yes, sir," Bob responded. "Now, how about a damned good steak dinner?" he asked with a relieved twinkle in his eyes. Bob was another no-nonsense officer who didn't cotton to politics allowing the guilty to "walk." He had come to me from our Special Operations Branch in Washington, D.C., where he had seen more political pissing backward and lack of sound decisions by some of our people on high than he cared to recall. Not having the stomach anymore for such actions, he changed branches, successfully competing for the Utah supervisory position, and ultimately moved west into my region. I was happy to have him as my first-line supervisor in Utah and a lot got done under his leadership. However, Bob soon saw enough questionable politics, especially in the difficult Utah judicial system and religious arenas (lack of separation between the church and judiciary) that he was sickened. Feeling there would never be the right kind of change between these entities, he retired early and moved to Alaska. The Service, critters, and yours truly lost a very good officer and friend in his early retirement.

Before leaving Utah for Denver the following morning, I had both case reports from the officers to review. After reading them, I grimly concluded that Spottswood and Miller were dead wrong. Our procedure in those days was to send undeveloped leads (remaining questions for the defendants to answer) to officers in the areas where the defendants lived. We did so in this case, and the two men were interviewed regarding their side of the issue. Neither one had any credible explanation of why they had *intentionally* violated the law. The results of those interviews were put into case-report formats and returned to the initiating case agents. Copies were sent to my office as well. There Deputy Hartman and I reviewed the investigations one more time and concluded Spottswood and Miller had indeed criminally violated the

Migratory Bird Treaty Act and the Hunting Stamp Act. Additional charges against Miller for taking migratory birds (gull and avocet) were dropped.

Realizing I had a political problem brewing, I contacted my boss, Regional Director Ralph Morgenweck, and filled him in on the latest circumstances. He listened quietly and then, fixing me with the steely look he tended to manifest during serious conversations, said, "What are you going to do?"

"Both men will be criminally prosecuted for their offenses," I replied.

"Good," he said. Ralph was another of those fairly common-sense fellows working for the government. He was extremely bright, gifted in thinking outside the box and looking down the road, ethical beyond criticism, a great human being, and a dear friend of the resources, not to mention his special agent in charge. After I left his office, I still had to telephone the chief of law enforcement, Kevin Adams, with the latest developments. That discussion might not go as well, I thought, as the one with the regional director.

Kevin Adams had worked his way up through the ranks and was considered by many to be a very bright officer. However, as a senior staff officer (at that time) and principal law enforcement adviser to the Service director, he had an almost impossible task. He had to walk a very fine line between those senior to him within the Service who knew little about the Division of Law Enforcement, those who didn't care if we sank or swam, those truly afraid of what the officers under their authorities could do, those totally opposed to such a function in the first place (as evidenced by our historically underfunded budgets), and enforcing those federal laws mandated to the Service by Congress. On the other side, he had a force of officers used to operating under many kinds of adversity, be it lack of support, nonexistent budgets, lousy equipment, almost impossible challenges, poor supervision, a large portion of the public basically indifferent to the conservation effort, and many dedicated killers who were armed to the teeth and very able to use those arms. Throw into that already seething mix crooked or gutless politicians, and you had a froth better than any that could be drawn on a warm beer! Last but not least, you had a hardened officer core that didn't suffer fools lightly, including their own supervisors ... especially if you broke the law and your supervisors didn't treat you and your violations like everyone else in the same boat. That should make it pretty easy to see the perch on which Kevin sat on the best of days.

I placed a call to the chief regarding my decision on the Spottswood and Miller investigation. When I explained the most recent circumstances of the investigation (I had briefed Kevin earlier when the issue first broke on the scene), I could hear him pausing big time, especially at my decision to prosecute both men in federal court. "What are you going to do?" Kevin slowly asked, making sure he understood my decision.

"I am going to have Standish file an Information on both of them for their violations and process it through federal court in Salt Lake City," I responded.

Suffice it to say, the chief was not pleased, as he showed in the discussion that followed. He was concerned that these legal actions might jeopardize our newest medical program, not to mention the hard feelings the actions would create in future dealings with the two violators. He was also concerned about what the rest of the Service would think in light of sending those folks out to help us and then having them busted for migratory bird violations, which many of the uninformed might think were minor in nature. *(After all, it was just a few dumb birds. ...)* If I put myself in his shoes, I would see that citing the two medical folks for minor violations just wasn't worth the future hassles it would create for him and the division. The chief's strong stand put me in a slight quandary, but after another quick mental review of the facts, I reiterated my point of view. A hundred other state and federal officers were aware of the violations, and sweeping this investigation under the rug would do nothing for the Service's reputation but create an even bigger mess, I concluded. Besides, what's right is right! Disappointed, we hung up, realizing we agreed to strongly disagree.

In those days, unlike today, the chief was only a staff officer to the director. As such, he could not give a direct order to a field-grade officer like me working under the supervision of a regional director. Hence, I was able to disregard his rather strongly worded "request" to find another way around the issue. That cost me his friendship. ... Today, under the new direct-line authority structure from the office of the chief to officers in the field, my refusal would not have held water.

Both Spottswood and Miller were prosecuted federally for taking migratory game birds without valid hunting licenses and for taking migratory waterfowl without valid federal duck stamps. Both men forfeited collateral, choosing not to appear in court to contest the charges. Each paid a $200 fine, and their cases were closed. In essence, we ate our own. And in so doing, we continued in the finest tradition of the Service, a tradition that everyone is treated the same regardless of rank or station. I have often wondered if, as a result of those criminal actions and subsequent prosecutions, the medical program was made any tougher on the agents. ... If so, how ironic!

ten

I Remember

IT IS ONLY FITTING that the last chapter in my series of books begins with the first real chapter in my life. Needless to say, that first chapter was a human adventure that far surpassed any others within the realm of my memory. Those of you who are perceptive and have read my books must realize by now that they represent not only true-life adventures but a love story as well. I will let you conclude which love story my adventures best and most truthfully represent. However, to do so you must be of keen eye and perception. To blink will cost you the key to that "treasure."

I remember her as she came through the door into Miss Billiejean McElroy's eighth grade classroom in 1955. Long, flowing reddish-blond hair, a white blouse, a flowing full-length blue dress, bobby socks, and a faint, nervous smile. Turning to Eugene Miller, my school buddy of many years, I said, "I'm going to marry that girl someday." I didn't have any idea why I even said that! The words just came out of my mouth as if they were not of this world. *And they weren't.* ...

Eugene looked at me in utter amazement and said, "You don't even know who she is. She is a brand-new girl. I have never even seen this one in Quincy before. How can you say that?"

"I don't know," I said with a mischievous grin, "but I am going to marry her someday." He just gave me that look that only a friend who has lots of patience and understanding can give. To all outward appearances, I had just gone off the deep end! At least in the mind of that eighth grader.

The years passed uneventfully after that, with me doing what young kids did who grew up in rural America of yesteryear. I was too shy to ask "that girl" out for a date because I was dirt poor and didn't own a car. A car, of course, was a prerequisite for serious dating in those days. My parents had divorced in the late 1940s and all I had was a very loving mom, who in retrospect was my world. She was a tough lady who worked her tail end off at the local box factory just to make ends meet, doing a man's job for the princely sum of seventy-five cents an hour, if I recall correctly! My sis and I did what we had to do to help Mom so we could survive as a family, but it wasn't easy. In fact, if we had been in that situation today, the welfare folks would have taken us away from my mother. I was born almost a century too late—I really loved the out-of-doors and all it had to offer. After my chores were done, I could always be found at a favorite trout fishing hole, jump-shooting ducks and geese off the nearby beaver ponds during hunting season, stalking the elusive mountain quail, pursuing the ever-alert band-tailed pigeons, or trying to satisfy the ever-present hunger all growing boys have by raiding every black-berry patch, apple orchard, or chokecherry bush in Plumas County. Shotgun shells and .22 shells cost money, so if I had a girlfriend, I wouldn't be able to go hunting or afford my fast-used-up number 6 Eagle Claw hooks (the best for catching trout). You might say I was pretty damn happy without girls ... or so I thought.

I remember seeing that girl, whom I now knew as Donna Larson, dating older high school guys who had cars. She always had a great smile, long, flowing reddish-blond hair, and the most exquisite blue eyes I had ever seen. Seeing her dating all those other guys really both-ered me, but I was just too shy to ask her out, so I had to ignore my feelings, satisfying myself with another covey of mountain quail or a forked-horn buck. I think the closest I ever came to her was when we traded comic books. Boy, does that ever date me. She was a devout Roman Catholic (still is) and I was somewhat of a heathen. OK, I was a certified heathen. In order to be close without her knowing why, I would arrange a comic-book-trading session. She always had those horrible Catholic comic books that were not worth a damn for trad-ing with the other kids because they were nothing but religious stories. As I said, they held little interest for me, or other comic-book readers for that matter. But I would trade her my good Donald Duck, Flash Gordon, or Lash LaRue comic books for those useless Catholic ones. That way I could be near the girl I secretly loved without being dis-covered. If she had been on her toes, she would have discerned why I was there, especially because I always traded two of my good comic books for one of her useless ones. My, how I would like to have those comic books today! I was always drawn to her no matter what, although I never truly understood the force responsible for such feelings. I guess even in those days I had the same sixth sense I do today, or maybe it was my two ever-present guardian angels. … However, as is the case with many other humans when trying to define their world, I never seemed to have the time to try to understand the unique gifts laid before me by the Old Boy upstairs.

I remember one time when a bunch of us East Quincy kids had gathered out at the old gravel pit near where I lived. It had frozen over, and we were out there playing, ice skating (not I; I was too poor to own skates and too clumsy to use them anyway), throwing rocks out across the ice, and other such tomfoolery. All at once there was a commotion at the other end of the gravel pit, and I discovered Donna had fallen through the ice. Racing to her side without a second thought, I pulled her out and assisted her to the fire on the bank to warm up. She politely thanked me and after a few moments by the fire went home for some dry clothes. I went back to my rock throwing amid the friendly ribbing from my buddies for saving a girl. But it sure did feel good to hold her hand, even if only for a brief moment.

As the following years passed, my feelings for Donna grew, but I was still too shy to ask for a date. All my close friends knew I had a crush on her and used to razz me to no end. It would have been easier for me to kill a grizzly bear with a pocket knife than to approach Donna and ask her for a date. Then one day as a high school junior in the locker room after a football practice, I was finally trapped by my friends. Harold Tweedle, my best friend, hunting partner, fishing partner, cocaptain with me of the football team, and president of the junior class, said, "Who are you taking to the prom?"

I said, "Nobody."

He said, "Terry, you have to go."

"Not me," I said. "I don't have a car, I can't dance, and I don't have a date."

"Hell," said Harold, "double-date with Norma and me. You can ask Donna to be your date since you are sweet on her anyway."

I was *almost* trapped, but there was no way I would ever get up enough courage to ask Donna for a date! I would rather face that damn grizzly bear. All my other buddies, overhearing the conversation, gathered around and went to town on me. "You have to be there to represent the team, you can't let us down, you are chicken," and so it went until almost the entire football team was on my tail end trying to get me into the dating game. I was accused of being "chicken," and then I was trapped. In those days, to be called a "chicken" meant you either had to crap or get off the pot, if you get my drift. ... I blurted out, "All right, I will ask Donna for a date," and then realized that I had just sealed my fate. The lads had me. ... Little did I know that this maneuver had been planned by Harold, Norma (Harold's girlfriend at the time and one of Donna's best friends), and the rest of my so-called friends. It was settled in their minds but was far from settled in the pit of my now rolling stomach. I had no idea how to behave around a girl, much less how to approach one or what to do on a date. I had never dated because of being so poor, shy, and interested mainly in the outdoors. Now it was catching up with me like an out-of-control freight train. However, I got through it. Donna, ever gracious, listened to me ramble on about hunting, fishing, and my other avocation, the Second World War, throughout the entire date. You know, that "coming out" was one of the highlights of my life. So was our first kiss, but I won't go there. ...

I remember we were playing Paradise High School, a powerhouse from the Sacramento Valley near Oroville, California, for the first football game of the season. Just before the varsity game I removed my school sweater and handed it to Donna, who was sitting in the stands waiting for the game to start. I said, "Would you keep this for me so it doesn't get stolen out of the men's locker room by kids from Paradise?"

She turned to me, those knowing blue eyes looking clear through me, and said, "I would be glad to. Good luck."

Jesus, did my heart race as I tried to move casually down the bleacher steps without falling clumsily between them in the joy of the moment. I made the first tackle on the kick-off return, and the game went up from there. I didn't have time to get my sweater back before the rooters' bus left for home, so Donna took it home with her. Seems like my guardian angels were doing more than protecting my miserable carcass. However, now that I think about it, maybe they *were* looking out for me.

The next Monday at school, my heart would hardly work as I anticipated our meeting that day. I really wanted her to wear my sweater, a sign to all that we were going steady, but I didn't know if I had the heart to ask her to do so, or worse, if she would even be interested. That damn grizzly bear and pocket knife thing welled up in me again. It was one of those beautiful Plumas County fall days, and the sun shone on Donna's reddish-gold hair as she moved up the steps of the school from where the school bus had let her off to where I stood waiting on the second floor. "You forgot your sweater," she said with her typical warm smile. I couldn't help looking into those beautiful blue eyes, only to notice that they were again almost looking straight through me.

I casually (if that were possible at that moment) said, "Why don't you just keep it?" Again, where those words came from I don't know because at that moment my heart wasn't even working! Yet out they came, with the strength and tone of a Pavarotti.

"OK," she casually replied as she unfolded the sweater lying across her arm and easily slipped into its largeness! God, she was beautiful, and there were those intense blue eyes looking into me again for the answers to the questions she had inside. Man, that was some fine day! Better than ever jump-shooting a pair of mallards off a beaver pond or getting a "double" on mountain quail. However, catching a twenty-plus-inch rainbow trout or killing a four-point (Western count) mule deer was right up there.

I remember that high school life was a beautiful whirlwind after that moment. I now had a partner and friend who, no matter what, was as graceful and beautiful as life could be at its fullest. Her blue-eyed stare always spoke of many more years of wisdom than her young body. It was amazing. I began to see life as it really was meant to be for those fortunate few who had the Builder of the World close at hand and on their side.

I remember Donna teaching me social graces such as how to eat properly, what utensils you used in all situations, and not to eat with my arm on the table (that one didn't take). She introduced me to new foods I still like to this day and taught me to dance (that didn't take too well either). Many an evening we spent with Susan Dragon (another classmate) and Tommy Keith (another nondancer) in Donna's folks' kitchen as the ladies tried to teach us fellows how to dance on our pairs of left feet. My last year in high school and home passed in the love be-tween two kids who really had God's blessing. I finally realized where the strength of that voice had come from that wonderful day at the top of the school steps. It was the voice of a man about to be born.

As summer drew to a close my senior year, I made frantic efforts, with help from Donna, to locate a college near where she was going to school. Donna was very bright and had been accepted at the University of California at Santa Barbara. Even then the university would take only the top 10 percent of the graduating senior class students from California high schools. I was your typical dingbat, or the grass-hopper that fiddled. I had screwed around in school, played sports, and performed at the C-plus level, even to the point of having Donna do some of my chemistry homework so I wouldn't fail. Now the pressure was on. I was in love with Donna and knew I wanted her for my wife. She, without a lot of words, made it plain that her lifelong mate would have to be good to her, good to her children, honest, hard-working, and *educated*. I met part of the formula and could meet the other part given time and marriage, but about that college-educated thing, I wasn't so sure. Being dumber than a box of rocks, and lazy, certainly had its drawbacks. ...

However, I had saved my money since I was about nine for college because my mom didn't have the resources to send me. To be truth-ful, Mom had saved my money since I was nine. If it had been up to me, I would have spent all I earned on gum, soda pop, and candy, so I was glad she was there for me in my moment of need. I would work and bring home any money that I earned from odd jobs such as dig-ging cesspools, slopping hogs, and milking cows. In those days, un-like today, a kid could earn a man's wages if he were a worker. Since I was big for my age, I went after every type of job I could, even dig-ging graves. However, that always scared me. I was always afraid a hand would come out of the dirt from an adjacent grave and grab me. The guys I worked with didn't help those fears either! After I was paid for my toils, Mom would give me a little to spend and put the rest into a bank account under her name. When I was sixteen, I realized I'd need more than just lawn money to go to college, so I went to Cal Cole, the woods boss for Meadow Valley Lumber Company. Keep in mind that a woods boss sat near the right hand of God in those little mountain communities. If you wanted a decent-paying job in those days, that is where you went. Knocking on the door of his home in Meadow Valley, I was met by a tall, strap-steel-tough man who demanded what I wanted in a booming voice. Shaken by his appearance and voice but a man on a mission, I said, "Mr. Cole, my name is Terry Grosz, I am six foot four inches, weigh 200 pounds, and am ready to go to work." I lied about my age (you had to be eighteen in order to work in the woods in those days) and had memorized a false birthdate. Then in abject terror, mostly at the thought of being denied, I stood quietly waiting for his response.

Cal silently looked me over and then demanded, "How old did you say you were, boy?"

"Eighteen, sir," I replied without my eyes leaving his. In those days eye contact and a good handshake went a long way between men.

His pause was excruciating. Then he said, "Be at the landing at eight A.M. Monday."

With that, I had a job that would pay me enough to go to college ($2.25 per hour, to be exact). For the next two summers I worked in the woods doing a man's job, growing by leaps and bounds. As a result of all my hard labor and Mom caring for my money, when I started college I had over $7,000 in the bank! In 1959 that was a pile of money when you consider that a modest house cost about $3,000 in those days! Thank God for moms, especially mine (may God rest her soul).

With Donna's help in the application process, I finally found a small city college in Santa Barbara that would take a "fiddler." I could just imagine what went through the minds of Donna's parents when they discovered that Donna and I would be going to college in the same area. Howard, Donna's dad, was a man of principal and realism mixed with North Dakota prairie wisdom. He understood the very great value of an education, even though life had not blessed him with that opportunity. He was determined that Donna was going to get a college education. Mary Ann, Donna's mom, I'm sure felt the same way but was just a little less vocal about it than Howard. I'm sure neither of them wanted the two of us together during that time of our lives. They would have preferred that we separate and date others to widen our knowledge of the world and gain more life experiences. As the father of a daughter, I can understand that reasoning now. But after finding the one I wanted to marry and share my life with, I was determined not to let her go for any reason, *ever!*

One evening I threw my gear for college into the back of a boat Howard was towing to a friend living in Santa Barbara, hurriedly kissed my mom and sister, and shook my dad's hand (men didn't hug in those days). With that, off Donna and I went to college and a whole new world. For me this was a real adventure because it was my first time away from home. Scary, yes, but a real-life adventure, one of just many that were soon to follow. Driving all night, we arrived in Santa Barbara at daylight the following morning. Howard wasted no time dropping me off at a boardinghouse I had selected on "Cheatum Road," as he called it. Actually it was Chealtingham Road (Howard had a hard time with some words), and I found myself sadly waving good-bye to the love of my life. Without a car, I was like a man on an island. Donna's college in Goleta was at least ten miles away, precluding any kind of close relationship, so off I went to my college and the adventures it held.

When I could I would hitchhike to Goleta and spend the day with Donna, walking the tar-soaked beaches of the Pacific Ocean as we herded the shorebirds in front of us. Since neither of us had any money or means of transportation, this was the only thing we could do unless we were fortunate enough to borrow a friend's car. But our love stood this test of time and distance, and we began planning our engagement during our sophomore year.

During our Christmas break that year we rode the Greyhound bus home and stopped in San Francisco for a six-hour layover. As dawn broke, Donna and I, trying to while away time while we waited for our connecting bus, started walking the streets of San Francisco. I remember some nutcase barking at me as we walked down the streets. Maybe it was the red pants I was wearing; who knows? Every time I turned around, this nut would dart into an alleyway or doorway and hide. Just as soon as we started walking again, out he came, and the barking would recommence. Finally tiring of the game, the barker left, and Donna and I found ourselves magically standing in front of the I. Samuels Jewelry Store on Market Street. Donna, looking in the window of the still-closed store, said, "There it is! Terry, there it is!"

I looked at the jewelry that had been left in the front window overnight (in those days crime wasn't what it is today), and there sat a diamond ring. It was the exact kind of ring Donna wanted, and she was really excited. She was like a little kid, and my love for her during such moments always increased manyfold. When the store opened at seven A.M. (times sure have changed!), in we went. Donna tried on the ring, and the blue eyes I had been in love with since the eighth grade told me I needed to purchase that ring. I remember it was $220 plus tax, and if we wanted the wedding band that went with it, that was an extra $43 (we got the money to buy the band later by picking up pop bottles and saving the $.02 per deposit). That money for the engagement ring was two weeks' damn hard summer work in the woods logging as a choker setter (one who hooks cables around downed logs so the bulldozers can haul them off to the landing, where they can be loaded onto logging trucks). I knew my mom, the keeper of my hard-earned funds for college, would have a fit over such an amount, so a selling job would be needed. But really not such a hard sell because mom and Otis Barnes, my stepdad, really loved Donna. I asked the shopkeeper (I. Samuels himself) to put the ring of Donna's dreams on hold. I had him size it for Donna's finger and told him it had to be delivered to me before Christmas day at my home in Quincy or no deal. A handshake closed the deal, and back we went to the dirty Greyhound depot, I walking and Donna floating. I was to find over the course of our married life that Donna is like a black-billed magpie: she loves anything that glitters, *especially diamonds.*

I remember the thousand years of love that emanated from Donna's intense, beautiful blue eyes when I slipped the ring on her finger that Christmas day so long ago. She easily moved into my arms for a long moment and got the front of my shirt wet where her eyes had rested against my chest. Then, like a pixie, out the bedroom door she bounded to show her mom, dad, and other friends who had gathered at the Larson household. Donna's mom was excited for her. Howard took a quick look and, still not convinced I was the best thing for his little girl, said, "Nice" and went back to fixing Christmas dinner. That didn't slow Donna down. She loved her dad very much and knew she could win him over in short order (she did), so off she went to show others her Christmas gift that was, whether she knew it or not, for life.

I moved from my college in Santa Barbara at the end of two years of study to continue my education at Humboldt State College. Humboldt, at that time the nation's top wildlife management educational institution, was located in Arcata, California. Donna withdrew from her beloved university and followed me to my college of choice, one that was of lesser stature and prestige for her. If I hadn't been so blind, I would have recognized that sacrifice by Donna in support of her fellow would soon become a familiar pattern in our lives.

Our wedding day was February 3, 1963. It had rained for two weeks solid before we came home from college to get married. All the rivers were over their banks, many bridges had washed out, and rock- and mudslides had closed many of the major highways. However, most of our wedding party was able to get through, and on the day of our wedding the clouds abated, the rains stopped, and the sun came forth. It was a good omen, to say the least. But I don't know why I should have been surprised! I remember Donna walking down the aisle, escorted by her dad. God, she was stunning. Typical of Donna, she had found a wedding dress that was a size "teensy" for $25 on sale during the off season. She lost weight down to 125 pounds so she would fit into the dress. Looking at her, I found it hard to breathe. Her eyes were fixed on mine, and their intense blue was scared yet challenging. Howard kissed her gently, looked at me closely one more time, and then handed Donna to me. Her tiny hand slid into mine, and she was now mine forever.

I remember Donna's first teaching job. Times were tough in the Arcata-Eureka logging communities where we lived, and she really had to hustle to find work. She had excellent grades (except in her singing classes—she couldn't carry a tune in a bucket) and strong recommendations from her instructors, but it was still hard. She overcame this adversity by dogged determination, hard work beating the bricks, and outstanding interviews. She finally landed a teaching contract in Eureka for the then wonderful salary of a shade less than $4,000 per annum. But we were "rich," nonetheless. ...

Donna put me through the last year of my master's program because by now I had run out of money from the bank account controlled by my mother. Times were tough, and we lived in a small three-room flat that always smelled strongly of mildew. We ate whatever I could catch or kill, and many times that was asking a lot of Donna. Shark, salmon, oysters, raccoon, ducks, snipe, venison until her blue eyes flashed "enough," and wild hog. Bear meat, elk, trout, skate, boiled pheasant eggs from the school's game pens, and black brant rounded out the table fare. I remember the first time she cooked shark. She cooked it until the urea in the meat broke down and sent us running into the kitchen looking for a bottle of ammonia that had tipped over ... but it was either that or go hungry. Sleeping at night was another matter. The bed in our rented flat was a double bed. I was used to sleeping by myself in a large bed because of my size and spent many nights on the floor with my six-foot-four, 300-pound frame (I had gained fifty pounds the first month we were married—that happens when you marry a great cook). When I finally did learn to sleep with my wife in that little bed, I was in for another surprise. The last occupant of the house had apparently urinated extensively on the mattress while in his drunken stupors, and every time I rolled over with my face to the mattress, that wonderful smell woke me up. But we lived and loved as if every day were the last, and God, what a great woman to have for a mate.

I remember passing the California State Fish and Game Warden's exam and being shipped off to San Bernardino County in Southern California for my law enforcement training. That was just about the time I also needed to be at the college to finish writing my master's thesis. I was 600 miles away, and in order to make the graduation deadline, Donna had to get my thesis drafts to my professors, write out their comments and criticisms, get hold of me after work on the phone, discuss the needed changes, and then type in the alterations I gave her over the phone. Then she would start the rounds with the professors all over again, in addition to her teaching duties! This went on for six weeks, and Donna, very pregnant at the time and doing 95 percent of the work, made the deadline by one day. As a result of her efforts, I graduated on time with my master's degree in wildlife management. As I received my diploma, I looked out at the sea of faces until I located Donna in the crowd. Even at that distance, those intense blue eyes found mine and registered her happiness. Damn, what a woman, I thought. What more was she capable of? It wouldn't be long before I found out. ...

As luck would have it, I was stationed as a game warden in Eureka, California, and we had to move only ten miles to my first duty station (one of the first of many moves). Damn, was I excited! Hunting humans is a heady business, and many times as I excitedly told Donna of the day's events, I noticed a strange but loving look in those intense blue eyes. It didn't take me long to realize that look was of fear and uncertainty for what the future might bring me in the form of danger. More significantly, that look signified the realization that if she let me leap into my vision quest, because of the profession's very demanding nature, she would end up being my second love. Not that I loved her any less, but to do the job right meant the law enforcement profession got all your attention and everything else was relegated to second fiddle. ... Any less than that and you might not come home at the end of the day.

I remember her first pregnancy and the hope Donna had for a son ... for me. Yet even with this burden, she kept close watch on the first fellow in her life. When I came home from the wildlife wars one day, she noticed a broken windshield on my patrol car and a bruise below my right eye. I had gotten into it with six bad guys and arrested the bunch of them, but not before bodily tossing one into the windshield of my car while I knocked another out with my fists. Donna quietly asked if I was going back to that area. I said, "Yes," and she quietly said, "Alone?"

I said, "Yes, there isn't any help, honey. We are really shorthanded, and one officer on the scene in the time of need for the sturgeon is better than none."

She asked, "When?"

I said, "Tomorrow."

She never said another word, just looked at me with those all-knowing eyes and walked off to finish making my dinner. When I prepared for the next day's adventure (I hadn't learned about mortality yet at that stage of my life or career), I was surprised to find her standing on the step of our house, dressed like a man with a hat hiding her long, golden-red hair, holding her .30 M-l carbine with an attached banana clip. I asked, "Where the hell do you think you are going?"

Without a word, she slipped off the porch, heading for my vehicle, and as she got in said, "With you."

"Oh no, you're not!" I said as I headed for her side of the car to let her out, realizing the danger she would be going into. Opening the passenger door, I said, "You get your tail end out and back into the house. This is not a detail in which you can participate!"

Her stone-cold, blue-eyed stare told me that arguing further would be a waste of time. I have seen that look only maybe twenty times since we have been married, and in every instance it was futile to argue. Off we went, sleeping on the rocky ground in sleeping bags, up at four A.M.

and down to the Klamath River to chase sturgeon snaggers. Standing by my car dressed like a man with the carbine at port arms, she stood sentinel while I went about my deadly work on the river. Never did she waver, never did I have any other problems, and she did all that *while eight-and-a-half months pregnant with our firstborn!*

So intense was her nature that as I stood outside the delivery room watching her give birth to our first son, I could only shake my head in wonder. It was almost as if she had willed the first child to be a son for me. When the doctor told her she had a boy, I remember Donna sitting up on the delivery table, fixing me with an intense stare, giving me a thumbs-up, and then promptly passing out.

Several years later I transferred to Colusa, California, in the heart of the Sacramento Valley, forcing Donna to give up her teaching job in Eureka. When she came down to Colusa to look for a place to live, Donna also hustled for another teaching job, which she promptly landed ten miles away in Williams, California. Her excellent reputation as a teacher preceded her, and it was a piece of cake. I hadn't thought for a moment, which is typical of many men, about how my move would impact her career. But Donna went about her new job quietly and professionally, as she had always done, pulling her share of the load in the wagon, so to speak.

When our second son was born, she had a terrible time with the pregnancy and delivery. Chris was almost born dead, but through excellent doctors and the hand of the Lord is today a fortress of a man, strong as a bull (the only man I ever saw who could lift an entire full-grown elk into the back end of a pickup all by himself) yet gentle as a lamb. And, by the way, he is as much in love with his wife, Lisa, as I am with his mother. I told Donna that since her second pregnancy had been so hard on her, it would have to be the last. I could not risk losing her. I saw a fleeting look of pain in those eyes I had come to love so much. Again, I didn't look past my own nose, and my partner paid the price. I didn't stop for a second to think that she had brought us two fine sons, but maybe she would have liked a daughter as well.

When I transferred to Bismarck, North Dakota, Donna gave up her beautiful first-built home, all her friends, and her career. Quiet tears were all that identified the extent of her pain as she headed out with the kids, dogs, and trailer for our next adventure on the North American prairies. What a chapter in our lives that turned out to be. Donna decided to stay at home during that period to raise our two young sons. That was good news because I was on the go almost constantly due to a history of very poor law enforcement in the Dakotas and numerous developing problems with government-owned wetlands being illegally drained by the dirt farmers. I found myself away from home tending to the wildlife wars almost the entire first year we were in North Dakota. With an international border and numerous customs ports of entry and 180-plus National Wildlife Refuges, in overall charge of North and South Dakota and responsible for the protection of over 1.5 million acres of wetlands with the help of only three other special agents, I had my hands full.

One day while I was locked in mortal combat with a bunch of knotheaded attorneys, the people I generally consider the weakest links in the chain of democracy, Donna called. She asked if she could look into adoption of a daughter. She had discovered that the local Catholic church had a program for placing orphaned children from South America and Asia. Beginning to realize just how important my mate was and the sacrifices she had made, I said sure and quickly hung up so I could get back to the battle before I lost the edge.

In April, five months after the adoption process started, Donna had Kimberlee Dawn, a Vietnamese war orphan, age four months, in her arms. It hadn't happened without a battle, though, which ran from saving Kim's life from the onset because of extremely poor health to battling miles of red tape accompanying such an activity as a foreign adoption during wartime. That situation could become even more difficult because many Vietnamese mothers, upon arriving in the United States (having shipped out their babies earlier), wanted their babies back. Donna went after Kim like there was no tomorrow, and today as a result of Donna's efforts and intense love for this little girl, not of our body but of our heart, she is our daughter. There was no Vietnamese mom searching for her, Kim being truly an orphan. Today she is married with three children, and both she and her husband work as correctional officers with wayward kids, trying to improve those children's lot in life.

Our next transfer was to Washington, D.C. Donna broke down and cried like a baby when she heard I had been promoted and was going to more of a desk job than I had previously held. When I asked why the tears, she replied, "Now I will have you back as my husband and father to our children." I hadn't realized the many quiet sacrifices and lonely days she had endured during the two years we were stationed in Bismarck, but as I think back, I realize now that they were considerable. She ran our home, raised our children, and cared for me as I returned exhausted from the everyday battles with those who saw the natural resources of the land as theirs and only theirs. And she did it all on one paltry government income.

The Washington assignment was timely and needed. I spent more time with my family and best friend, with just a little time spent moving through battles in Asia, Arizona, England, Georgia (teaching at the National Academy), and the Klamath River in California for good measure. After two years of Washington, Donna began to see that faraway look in my eyes that must have been observed by other Donnas 150 years earlier as their Terrys looked westward to new lands and adventures. Again, I failed to see the look in her eyes regarding our future peregrinations, and as always she was by my side providing the counsel and support I needed to hurdle any obstacle. A supervisory opportunity arose shortly thereafter in Minnesota, I competed successfully, and off we went.

I remember leaving Virginia and watching my bride of many campaigns crying silently. She really loved Virginia, and again she was having to sacrifice many of the joys of her life for her husband. Minnesota, land of the northern lights, mosquitoes, tornadoes, and long, cold winters did not really appeal to her. Finding a new home she really liked helped, but the arrival of our furniture, which had been destroyed by the movers, marred the moment, to say the least. I watched her adjust to this latest adversity of a $19,000 loss in furniture and the huge chore of fitting our family into the Prior Lake community as I once again went off to the wildlife wars.

Donna adapted to the Minnesota way of life with the energy found only in the very best wildlife law enforcement officers' spouses. Showing her versatility, she got involved in the community, teaching, and church activities, all the while shepherding her children's lives while her man was again off fighting the wildlife wars. Life was good, and I began to realize for the first time in my self-centered universe what a person for all seasons my wife really was. Her love was boundless, her life was totally devoted to her man and children, yet she always found time for others. She grew even stronger in her religion and tolerated several dogs who were forever bringing mud in on the rugs or digging up what precious few flowers she was able to grow. Her reward was ferns. All she asked were a few flowers around her home and some ferns in the back of the house by the porch. They did well ... until a tornado flattened them all to hell.

I remember the blue-eyed look when I told her I was going to try for the Denver special agent in charge position in 1981. She quietly judged her fellow for merit, then put aside her fears and wants and quickly provided the needed support for the bureaucratic battle that was to come. I remember that same intense look in her eyes several weeks after we moved to Denver. Sitting quietly at my feet one evening in the living room of our new home in Evergreen, she said, "This is it. I want the kids to have a home with roots, and this is it." Her eyes searched mine for a response. I had seen that look before, but not often. It was that same "wheels-down" look I had received sixteen years earlier when I told her to get out of my patrol car because she wasn't going with me on a dangerous detail with that damn-fool carbine. We have been in Denver since that date, and the good Lord willing will stay here until He needs another wildlife law enforcement "catch dog" in some faraway place, if you get my drift. ...

Sitting here in the quiet of my study after all those years trying to serve my fellow humans, I now realize that I have served them very well—*that is, except for one person.* For many years I ran as hard as any human could, attempting to put a stop to the great carnage taking place in the natural resource arena of this unique land of ours. There have been times, many of them, when I have fallen short. But with no one have I fallen as short as I have with my wife. I asked her to let me run with my vision quest to the ends of the earth, and she did. I have reached plateaus others could not reach, seen things others will never see, and experienced things others cannot because those things are now gone. I have lived this outstanding life because my bride of over forty years has acceded to my wishes and in essence allowed herself to become my second love. *What a terrible sacrifice to make!* What an effort it had to be to raise our children, be mom and "mister mom," and carry out those duties in the excellent manner that she has, all the while never complaining.

I still remember very clearly that day in eighth grade so long ago; I remember that look when she accepted my letterman's sweater; I remember the look when I slipped the engagement ring on her finger; I remember the look when I graduated with my master's degree; I remember that look accompanying our children's arrival into our family; I remember that look during those times, and there were many, when I sought her counsel; I remember that look as I successfully worked my way up through the U.S. Fish and Wildlife Service; I remember that look when I came out of double bypass surgery; and I will always remember that look I get every time we meet, no matter the length of time apart.

However, I don't know if she noticed *my* look when she walked down that aisle at our wedding; or when she successfully fought so hard for her teaching positions; or when she brought forth my sons and daughter; or when she stood by my side during adversity; or when she worked so hard (while fully employed) and earned her own master's degree; or when she caught her first salmon off the coast of California or halibut off the coast of Alaska; or when she helped me drag out deer and elk in western Colorado; or when she made me some of the world's finest homemade breads, pies, jams, and cakes; or just the last time I held her.

It has been a marriage *truly* made in heaven, accompanied by a very full and complete life. I can only hope that in the remainder of my days as my efforts for the world of wildlife and my fellow human beings begin to dim that Donna realizes my love for her was not of this world either. I will always love her forever, plus one day, for standing by me.

So those of you reading the stories in this and my other books, please realize that the guiding hand of God was not the only one holding me true to my course and calling. Those of you who have husbands or wives in the law enforcement profession, understand that without each other, there is no true course.

So, read between the lines in my series of books. There are tips of the trade galore, along with a love story that burns brightly to this day. A love of all of God's creations, floral, faunal, and human. In that last, most important category, a love that is stronger today than when she walked through that door in junior high school so long ago. A love that is so strong that when I pass, I have every confidence I will be there for her, this time, when it is her turn to cross over that same great divide. My extended arm and hand will be there anxiously waiting. That is the very least I can do for a mate and best friend who devoted her entire worldly life to me.